VEGAN ATHLETE COOKBOOK

500 POWER PACKED, PLANT-BASED RECIPES TO TURN YOU INTO A SUPREME ATHLETE

Kevin Rinaldi

VEGAN COOKBOOK
FOR ATHLETES

THE BEGINNER'S GUIDE WITH RECIPES FOR BODY BUILDING AND MUSCLES. NO MEAT ATHLETE DIET. HIGH PROTEIN MEAL PREP WITH PLANT BASED AND SPORT NUTRITION PRINCIPLES

Kevin Rinaldi

Table of Contents

Introduction

Most people choose to follow a vegan diet for ethical reasons. You can maintain a healthy heart by eating a plant-based diet. Let us look at six additional benefits of the vegan diet.

Nutrient-Rich Diet

If you are someone who consumes a Western diet, you will need to give up animal products and meat when you switch to a vegan diet. This will mean that you will begin to depend on plant-based foods. If you choose to follow a vegan diet where you consume only whole foods, you will replace the meat and animal products with fruit, whole grains, beans, vegetables, peas, pulses, nuts, and seeds. The consumption of these foods leads to an increase in overall nutrients. For example, studies show that a vegan diet increases your intake of fiber, increases the antioxidants in your body, and intake of beneficial plant compounds. The food that you consume on this diet is rich in folate, magnesium, Vitamins A and C and potassium. That being said, you should understand that not every vegan diet provides the same nutrition.

For example, if you do not plan your diet well, you will consume fewer nutrients like calcium, zinc, iodine, Vitamin B2, fatty acids, and iron. It is for this reason that you should always stay away from those vegan food options that are processed and lack nutrients. Try to base your diet around nutrient-rich fortified and whole plant foods. You can also consider some supplements for essential vitamins like Vitamins B12 and D. Make sure to speak to a medical professional before starting any supplements.

Weight Loss

Numerous people have switched to a vegan diet because this diet is low on processed food and far, which in turn leads to weight loss. Numerous observational studies show that a person following a vegan diet has a lower body mass index and is thinner when compared to non-vegans. In addition to these studies, several controlled studies also reported that a vegan diet is more effective for weight loss when compared to other diets. One study showed that a vegan diet helped the subjects lose at least 9.5 lbs within eighteen weeks. A study was also conducted to understand the effects of a low-calorie diet and a vegan diet on weight. The researchers concluded that people following the vegan diet lost more weight when compared to those who followed a low-calorie diet.

Improves Kidney Function and Lowers Blood Sugar

A vegan diet helps to reduce the risk of developing Type II Diabetes and improve the function of the kidneys. A person following a vegan diet has lower blood sugar, thereby reducing the risk of developing Type II Diabetes by . It was noted that the vegan diet had a better impact on the blood sugar levels when compared to the other diets. Another study conducted showed that of the participants who followed a vegan diet were able to reduce their blood sugar levels more than the people who were following an ADA-recommended diet. Other studies show that diabetics who swap their Western diet for a vegan diet reduces the risk of poor kidney function.

Protection against Some Cancers

The World Health Organization claims that you can prevent at least one-third of all cancers by controlling different parts of your lifestyle, especially the diet. For instance, you can reduce the risk of developing colorectal cancer by at least ten percent if you consume legumes. Research suggests that you can reduce the risk of cancer by if you consume at least seven portions of vegetables and fresh fruit each week. Vegans often consume a large quantity of fruit, vegetables, and legumes when compared to non-vegans. 96 different studies concluded that the vegan diet could help to reduce developing or dying from cancer by . A vegan diet is rich in soy products, and this can help to reduce the probability of developing breast cancer. When you avoid certain animal products, you can reduce the risk of developing colon, prostate, and breast cancer. A vegan diet helps to reduce the probability of developing cancer because the diet is devoid of processed meat, smoked meat, meat cooked at high temperature and more. These foods are believed to promote the development of specific types of cancer.

People following the vegan diet also avoid the consumption of dairy products. Some studies show that the consumption of dairy products can slightly increase the risk of developing prostate cancer. On the other hand, there is sufficient evidence to prove that the consumption of dairy products can help to reduce the risk of developing cancers like colorectal cancer. Therefore, one cannot say with certainty that the lack of dairy products helps to reduce the risk of developing cancer. It is difficult to understand why a vegan has a lower risk of developing cancer. Regardless of what the truth may be, it is a good idea to focus on consuming vegetables, fruit and legumes, and reduce your intake of processed, overcooked, and smoked meat.

Lower Risk of Heart Disease

Experts suggest that people should consume legumes, fiber, fruit, and vegetables to decrease the risk of developing heart diseases. When you plan your vegan diet well, you consume these foods in large quantities. Studies that compare the vegan diet and vegetarian diet state that vegans have at least a lower risk of developing hypertension or high blood pressure. A vegan also has a lower risk of dying from heart disease. Numerous controlled studies stated that a vegan diet is more effective at reducing the levels of LDL cholesterol, total cholesterol, and blood sugar when compared to various other diets. This partially helps to improve heart health since any reduction in cholesterol, blood sugar, and blood pressure reduces the risk of developing heart diseases. A vegan, when compared to the general population, consume more nuts and whole grains. These are very good for the heart.

Reduces Pain from Arthritis

Some studies have reported that a vegan diet has a positive effect on people who suffer from arthritis. A study was conducted on 40 people who suffered from arthritis. Some were asked to continue to follow their regular diets while the others were asked to follow the vegan diet. The people on the vegan diet were able to function better and had higher energy levels when compared to those who did not change their diets. A few other studies were conducted to understand the effects of raw, fresh, and probiotic-rich vegan diet on the symptoms of arthritis. These studies reported that people following the vegan diet experienced reduced pain, morning stiffness, and joint swelling.

In simple words, a vegan diet can provide a wide array of health benefits. Researchers and nutritionists are still not sure why these benefits occur. There is, however, no harm in increasing your intake of whole, nutrient-rich, and plant food in your diet.

It is hard for people to switch to a different diet for many reasons. They are used to consuming specific types of food, and if they quit consuming those foods at once, they will begin to have withdrawal symptoms. Your body is used to specific types of food, and it will crave for that food which will make it hard for you to stick to the diet. Instead of going cold turkey, you should try to swap the food you usually consume with the food that you can consume when you follow the vegan diet. Here are a few tips:

Make vegetables the star of your meal. Try to consume a small salad for every meal. Make sure that there are more vegetables on your plate than any other type of food.

When you are hungry, eat a fruit or a bowl of nuts and seeds. This will help you overcome any cravings that you may have.

Keep yourself hydrated.

Most people make the mistake of giving the word 'diet' a negative connotation. It is for this reason that most of them are unable to stick to a diet when they want to switch to a different lifestyle. It is important that you do not do that. Tell yourself that you are switching to a healthier lifestyle that has numerous benefits. Remember that it is okay to give yourself one cheat meal. You can consume this meal on those days when you have cravings. You should remember to never make a habit out of it. Once you begin to lead a vegan lifestyle fully, you will no longer have any meat cravings.

Now that you have learned the benefits of switching to a vegan lifestyle, and understand that there are ample plant-based or nut-based proteins that can help you provide your body with the necessary protein and other nutrients, it is time for you to get started with the recipes.

So read on and make the switch to a vegan lifestyle.

Chapter 1. Veganism in A Nutshell

Veganism began in 1944 when a little group of vegetarians broke away to create the Vegan society. It was their choice not to consume any product that came from any animal. Some choose a vegan lifestyle for ethical reasons, such as the belief that all animal life is valuable, and they work to limit the exploitation of animals as much as possible. Some vegans choose this lifestyle for health reasons and others for environmental reasons.

When eating a vegan diet, these are some foods to avoid:

- Honey

- Fish

- Dairy

- Chicken

- Shellfish

- Meat

On the flip side of that, vegans still enjoy many of the normal fan favorites, such as bean burritos, veggie burgers, pizza, smoothies, and chips just with a twist. Vegans typically swap out those meat-based options with things like the following:

- Seeds

- Nuts

- Tempeh

- Seitan

- Tofu

- Lentils

- Beans

Milk products are also replaced with plant-based milk and honey with plant sweeteners.

If you are living a vegan lifestyle, it is important to ensure that your body is still getting all the vitamins and minerals it needs. There are seven basic supplements I suggest you include when choosing this lifestyle. Always consult your nutritionist or doctor if you have questions.

Vitamin B12 – Yes, you can get b12 from some plant-based options; however, scientists believe that vegans are at a higher risk of b12 deficiency. Too little b12 can lead to anemia. The daily recommended dosage is 2.4 mcg for adults.

Vitamin D – this is the vitamin that helps you to absorb calcium and phosphorus in the gut. Vitamin D also has influence over many other processes, such as muscle recovery, memory, mood, and immune function. Consider taking a vitamin D2 or D3 supplement daily.

Long-Chain Omega-3s – These are your fatty acids; they are important to the structural role for your eyes and brain. The recommended dose is to take a supplement containing EPA and DHA of 200 to 300 mg.

Iodine – This is crucial for the function of your metabolism and the health of your thyroid. The recommended dosage for an adult is 150 mcg of iodine.

Iron – This is essential for helping the body create new red blood cells and DNA, as well as carry oxygen into the blood. Low levels of iron can also result in fatigue. The recommended dosage is 8 milligrams for a male per day and 18 milligrams for a woman per day.

Calcium – This mineral is essential for healthy teeth and bones, as well as the health of the heart. The recommended dosage amount is 1,000 mg per day.

Zinc – This mineral is responsible for the repair of body cells, immune function, and metabolism. Insufficient zinc levels can result in diarrhea, hair loss, and developmental problems. The recommended dosage for zinc is 8 mg per day.

With all this being said, you can achieve many of these vitamins and nutrients through your plant-based diet. However, it is important to consider the use of supplements to offset the gaps between diet and body needs. Always remember to consult your health care professional.

What Is a Vegan Diet

Veganism is one type of a vegetarian diet. Exclusions for those who are vegan include any meat, dairy products, eggs, and any other ingredients that are derived from animals. A growing number of people who follow a vegan diet also do not eat any type of food that has been processed using any kind of animal products, including certain types of wines and white sugar that has been refined. The actual term "vegan" can either refer to the diet itself or a person who has adopted this style of eating.

To those who are not familiar with Veganism, this is the most common question that is asked. Many people have visions of a plate of salad night after night for the rest of their lives. In reality, a vegan diet is quite diverse. It includes fruits, vegetables, legumes, beans, and all grains. Think of the infinite combination of delicious meals that can be made from these ingredients! There are also vegan options for most of the popular dishes people enjoy eating. Some common examples include vegan mayonnaise, vegan cheese, vegan ice cream, vegan hot dogs, vegan pizza, and tons of others.

If you were to ask a vegan if they feel restricted by choosing to follow their diet, their answer would always be a resounding, "No".

Once you have made the decision to become a vegan, it can be difficult to know where to start. Do you shun all animal related products right away? Do you ease into it gently? The simple answer is that it will completely depend on you. While some people may find the switch a simple matter, others may struggle with their decision.

For people who find the commitment difficult in the beginning, one painless way to start is by becoming a vegetarian first. Once you have the basics of vegetarianism down pat, slowly omit dairy and eggs. There is no wrong or right way to go about becoming a vegan so do what feels right for you. In order to keep yourself on the right track, keep the reasons that you chose to become vegan in mind in the first place and the goals that you have set for yourself.

Many people do it; many people talk about it, but there is still a lot of confusion about what a vegan diet actually entails. Because we separate food into their macronutrients: sugars, carbohydrates, and fats, it is most times unclear to most of us. What if we could reassemble these macronutrients to free your mind from doubt and stress? Simplicity is the key here.

Whole foods are unprocessed foods that come from the soil. Today we eat some minimally processed foods such as fresh rice, whole wheat pasta, tofu, nondairy milk, and some nuts and seed butter on a whole food vegan diet. All of this is fine as long as it is done to a minimum. So, here are the different categories:

Legumes (basically lentils and beans) of whole grains.

Fruits and vegetables

Nuts and seeds (including nut butter)

Herbs and spices

All of the above categories constitute a whole vegan diet. How to prepare them is where it is fun; how to season and cook them; and how to mix and match to give them great taste and versatility in your meals. So long as you eat these things daily, you will forget about calories, carbohydrates, and fat forever.

Some of the benefits associated with vegan diets include:

Lower risk of getting heart related disease

Lower cholesterol levels as well as low density lipoprotein

Lower blood pressure

Lower chances of getting type 2 diabetes

Lower risk of cancer

Lower BMI

It is important to note that all these benefits are not acquired just by avoiding animal products like meat. The high consumption of whole foods like whole grains, beans, nuts, seeds, fruits and vegetables which contain beneficial nutrients, vitamins, minerals, antioxidants as well as phytochemicals is what is responsible for all these health gains.

The truth is that most animal products as well as processed foods which consist of of the calories in the average Americans diet do not contain good phytochemicals or antioxidants which are usually found in unrefined plant based foods.

A vegan diet always raises questions regarding it's ability to supply micronutrients to the body. How well these questions are grounded depends a lot on the composition of the diet. Most vegan diets comprising high refined carbohydrate content and little amounts of whole plant foods will easily lack in essential micronutrients. Therefore, vegan athletes need to eat foods that are rich in the following nutrients, fats, and minerals.

Omega 3 essential fats

Minerals like calcium, zinc, iodine, and iron

Vitamins B12 and D

Sources of calcium and iron in the vegan diet

Calcium

Exercise leads to depletion of iron reserves putting athletes at risk of iron deficiency. Professional female athletes are at high risk of iron depletion and anemia according to studies.

In most cases an iron rich diet is important in the needs of a female vegan athlete. However, supplementation might be necessary in special cases such as anemia and iron depletion due to heavy menstruation.

Iron levels in the body should be kept at optimum. High amounts of iron have been linked to cardiovascular conditions and even increase risk of heart attack. For men, the low recommended daily intake of iron can be achieved through eating green leafy vegetables. However, the amount of green leafy vegetables consumed daily should be large enough to ensure that the body gets a good amount of this mineral. If this is not possible, there are other suggestions for great sources of iron which I mention later.

Getting started on a vegan diet

Common misunderstandings among many people–even in the health and fitness industry is that anyone who switches to a vegan diet will automatically become super healthy. There are plenty of vegan junk foods out there, such as frozen veggie pizza and nondairy ice cream, which can really kill your health goals if you eat them all the time. Engaging in healthy foods is the only way you can reap health benefits.

On the other side, certain vegan snacks play a role in keeping you focused. They should be consumed in moderation, sparingly and in small bits.

Decide What a Vegan Diet Means for You

The first step is to make a determination on how to organize your vegan diet to help you move from your present culinary viewpoint. This is really unique, something that ranges from individual to individual. While some people choose not to consume any animal products at all, others make do with tiny bits of dairy or food at times. It really is up to you to decide what and how you want your vegan diet to look like. Perhaps notably, you have to make a large portion of your diet from whole vegan foods.

Understand What You Are Eating

Okay, now that you've made the decision, your next move on your side part requires a lot of study. What do we mean by that? Okay, if this is your first time trying out the vegan diet, the amount of foods containing animal products, particularly packaged foods, will shock you. You will find yourself cultivating the custom of reading tags when shopping. It points out that many pre-packaged foods contain animal products, and you need to keep a close eye on the packaging of the ingredients if you just want to stick to plant products for your new diet. You may have decided to allow a certain number of animal products in your diet; well, you'll just have to look out for foods filled with fats, carbohydrates, salt, preservatives, and other things that may affect your healthy diet.

Find Revamped Versions of Your Favorite Recipes

I'm sure you have plenty of favorite dishes, not necessarily vegan. For most people, leaving everything behind is usually the most difficult part. Nonetheless, there is still a way to meet you halfway. Take some time to think about those things you want that are not based on plants. Think along the lines of taste, shape, consistency, and so on; and search for substitutes throughout the diet based on food plants that can do what you're lacking.

Build a Support Network

Building a new routine is complicated, but it doesn't have to be. Find some friends that are glad to be with you in this lifestyle, or even family members. This will help you stay focused and motivated by having a form of emotional support and openness. You can do fun things like try out and share new recipes with these mates or even hit up restaurants offering a variety of vegan options. You can even go one step further and look up local vegan social media groups to help you expand your knowledge and support network.

Chapter 2. Your Vegan Kitchen

The vegan diet is believed to be amongst the most popular diets these days. Going vegan is not just a diet, but is more of a lifestyle choice that actively eliminates different forms of animal cruelty for the sake of meeting the demands of human beings for clothing, food, or enjoyment. There are various reasons why people embrace veganism. Maybe you want to opt for veganism because it helps improve your overall health, endorses ethical treatment of animals, or merely because it is more environmentally conscious. Regardless of the reasons for opting for a vegan diet, it is amongst the best diets today. You can easily attain your fitness and bodybuilding goals while choosing veganism.

Opting for a vegan diet can help reduce the risk of type II diabetes, along with different heart diseases. A vegan diet is also believed to help improve the health of your kidneys. Apart from this, it increases the presence of high-density lipoprotein (HDL) in your body. This cholesterol molecule is beneficial and helps reduce the risk of different cardiovascular diseases. It also helps tackle and regulate inflammation. There are various health benefits you can reap by following a vegan lifestyle. You can do all this while being environmentally conscious. A vegan diet is rich in fiber and nutrients that your body needs. Therefore, by consuming hearty vegan meals, you improve the energy levels in your body.

Food to eat

A vegan diet is quite nourishing and rich in wholesome foods. Without exceeding your daily calorie intake, you can provide your body with all the nutrients and fiber it needs. So, if you want a lean physique, then the vegan diet works well. However, it doesn't mean you cannot bulk up while following a vegan diet. All that you need to do is be mindful of the proteins you consume.

A vegan bodybuilding diet usually includes the following foods.

- Beans and legumes are a great source of protein, as well as dietary fibers.

- Hemp seeds, sunflower seeds, and Chia seeds, and flaxseeds are not only rich in protein, but also omega-3 fatty acids.

- Soy products like tofu, tempeh, soy milk, soy protein powder, and edamame.

- To meet your daily requirement for vitamin D as well as calcium, start adding calcium-fortified plant-based milk and yogurts.

- Whey isn't the only protein powder you can consume. With the increasing popularity of veganism, there are different vegan protein powders available in the market. According to your exercise and nutritional needs, you can select a protein powder.

- Nutritional yeast, as well as spirulina, are rich in vitamins and minerals.

- Whole grains and cereals, along with oats and other sprouted grain bread, are an excellent source of protein, as well as complex carbs.

- All fruits and vegetables are included.

- Different nuts, as well as nut-based butter, are rich in unhealthy fats as well as proteins.

- Healthy vegan condiments like hummus and tahini are a great way to sneak in healthy fats along with protein.

- Start using healthy oils like olive oil, hemp seed oil, and avocado oil for cooking. These oils are a rich source of healthy Omega-3 fatty acids.

- There are different meat substitutes you can add to your diet that are rich in protein but are made of soy or pea proteins.

- Two superfoods you can start adding to your diet are quinoa and amaranth.

So, there are plenty of protein sources you can easily include in your diet while staying true to veganism. You don't have to depend on animal-based nutrition to meet your body's protein requirements. Apart from this, you can consult with your doctor and start taking any dietary supplements you might require. Taking away the multi-vitamins and along with a vegan protein powder can help ensure that your body gets all the protein it requires while staying well within your calorie limit.

What to avoid

Processed Foods

One of the most popular pieces of advice you will receive about clean eating says that if it's processed, it can't be clean. Basically, if something comes prepackaged and is located within those horrible "middle aisles" of the grocery store, then you should run far and fast away from it. Most clean eating people will slap those boxes right out of your hand.

Processing foods isn't all that bad, and it often improve its safety and bioavailability of some antioxidants and nutrients. It also gives you the chance to quickly fix all of the lovely and delicious dishes on Instagram and Pinterest.

Plus, there are plenty of healthy processed foods out there, such as hummus, whole-grain cereal, tomato sauce. Nutrition is a very complex subject, and sure it might be easier if we could just wipe out complete categories of food, but all this does is hurt your taste buds, wallet, and time.

Unrefined Grains

Unlike the processed food advice, the people who say unrefined grains are better than refined grains are right. Whole grains are a great way to consume fiber, and they have a lot of B vitamins. Refined grains get around 20 various nutrients taken out of them, but then most of them added back in during processing. But there is a caveat; there are a lot of grains that don't add back the important nutrients. If at all possible, go with the unrefined grains to make sure you get all of the nutrients they have to offer.

Sugars

There are some who even include fat and salt into this, but I won't get into how this is such an outdated way of thinking. Foods that have added sugars are pretty much useless, especially for non-athletes. If you are a bodybuilder training for competition, then some added sugars aren't going to hurt you. Sugars, when added to foods in order to make them more palatable, as opposed to the sugars that come natural in some foods, only add calories with no real health benefits.

How to Really Eat Clean

Getting clean shouldn't require a huge overhaul to your diet, especially if you are switching to a plant-based diet. If you go at it that way, then you are probably going about it wrong. Here are some things to keep in mind when getting clean.

Look at the nutrients, and not just the calories.

Don't allow yourself to get caught up in the numbers. When it comes to our bodyweight-conscious world, it's very easy to get caught in the numbers game. While it might work well for a person looking to lose weight, it isn't going to actually make them healthy.

The calorie-counting diet dates back to the 70s and 80s and is a thing of the past. It is much more important that you get all of the nutrients you need to than to focus on your overall calorie balance. Look at it this way; one way will make you feel grumpy and guilty when you do eat. The other gives you energy, stabilizes your blood sugar, and you will discover foods you never knew existed.

Move past refined white flours.

You can cut out the refined white flours you use for baking, and bake some things with unrefined flours and other flour substitutes. It could mean that you have to try out some new recipes and make some mistakes, but it is doable. Besides looking for unrefined wheat flours, you can also try out oat, brown rice, coconut, and almond flour. Using those choices will help to lower your carbohydrate intake, and you can still make delicious dishes with them.

These various flours also come with different nutritional profiles, so you will want to read on them to see which one fits your dietary needs the most.

Balance out your diet.

The two main ideas of clean eating are moderation and balance. You shouldn't avoid dietary fats and carbs completely, or you are going to end up dreading mealtimes. Make sure you eat them, but simply adjust your portion sizes so that it fits into your goals and nutrient needs.

Depending on your system needs, your macro ratio could end up being broken down into several different ways. If you lean more towards unsaturated fats and complex carbohydrates, then you are on the right track. What it all boils down to is to make sure that you are mindful of the foods you eat. You have a problem when you don't know what you are consuming.

Consume more water.

If you can't handle straight water all day long to get in your daily goals, then you can experiment with some other drinks, such as herbal or green tea. You can also flavor your water with lemon, or you can mix in sugar-free electrolytes. You can also have coffee, but if you're serious about being clean, it has to be black and not of that stuff that comes in a fancy cup.

Get plenty of fresh produce.

It doesn't matter what type of diet you're following; the golden rule of clean eating is to include as much fresh produce as you can. Vegetables make any diet healthier and better. They will give you nutrients and vitamins to help you feel as good as you look. It will also ensure that you have enough soluble fiber so that you can absorb all of the nutrition that you can get out of the food you eat.

You can't get all of those benefits from a supplement. That supplement will become an excuse you use so that you can cheat when you do get hungry. So make sure that you figure out your favorite fruits and veggies, and you can use the frozen ones if you need to. Also, don't be afraid to use spices and seasonings.

Look at your meals as if it's a lifestyle.

Eating clean isn't a diet you have to follow. It is simply a lifestyle that you will be able to sustain from here on out. You don't have to go off the deep end and start throwing out all of the food you love. You can enjoy your food, and you will need to do so in order to stick with this new lifestyle. And you may just have to push yourself so that you start cooking things yourself.

With these eight "rules" in mind, I am fully confident that you will be able to eat clean and enjoy the foods that have.

Energy-Boosting Foods

Sweet Potatoes

These tubers are a much better alternative to the white potato. They provide loads of minerals and vitamins, such as beta-carotene, manganese, vitamin C, and disease-preventing dietary fiber. These are a great choice for bodybuilders and athletes because when they are consumed in conjunction with protein after your workout, they act as a catalyst to help the protein move into your muscle tissue and start the repairing process.

Sweet potatoes are considered hypoallergenic and are one of the tops sources for post-workout carbs from most exercises, bodybuilders, and athletes who would like to up their energy but keep body fat down. A baked or steamed small to medium sweet potato can be a great post-workout snack.

Coconut Oil

This is a good fat full of "medium-chained" fats, which make it very easy to digest, as compared to other dietary fats. They are able to provide an easily accessible source of energy. Coconut oil is also a natural way to increase your metabolism, which gives your body the ability to burn more energy and boosts athletic performance. It also helps the function of the thyroid and gets rid of pancreatic stress, which will make you more active. You can easily add a couple of tablespoons into a smoothie.

Bananas

Bananas are a great source of potassium, which is an electrolyte that the body needs but loses when you are exercising. Appalachian State University did a study that found bananas were helpful in fueling cyclist during intense exercise. Bananas are also great at preventing muscle fatigue. Choosing a banana over an energy bar is much better options for some energy. They have a lot less sugar, and they have a lot more nutrients.

Rolled Oats

Oats are full of fiber, and they not only reduce your risk of developing heart disease, but they will also slow your glucose absorption, which will help to keep your energy up and your blood sugar levels steady. Oats also have a lot of B vitamins, which helps your body to change carbohydrates into usable

25

energy.

Walnuts

Since you won't be getting your Omega-3s from fish, walnuts should be your go-to. They are a great way to get those heart-healthy omega-3 fatty acids. Good fats are a very important part of your diet if you are serious about achieving optimal health and fitness. Healthy fats are able to help heal your body from bruises, sprains, and other tissue injuries, as well as aid in energy production. Unhealthy fats, on the other hand, can slow you down. Have a can of walnuts with you at all times just encase you start feeling sluggish, or, if you make your own trail mix, add in some walnuts.

Lentils

Lentils are full of dietary fiber, containing eight grams in a half-cup serving. They are also great at keeping you feeling fuller for longer, and they will keep your energy levels up for your busy day.

Spinach

Spinach is full of folic acid and B vitamins, and both of these will provide you with lots of energy. Spinach can easily be added into different meals, from smoothies to scrambles and casseroles.

Oranges

If you need a quick boost of energy, oranges should be your go-to food. It is full of natural sugars, and they will also give you three grams of fiber, which can help to sustain your energy levels. A single navel orange will help you to meet your daily requirement for vitamin C.

Avocados

This delicious fruit is a great source of healthy fats that can activate your body. Your body can also utilize it for fuel to help you through your day or workout. It is also a great source of B6, folic acid, vitamin K, fiber, and vitamin C. Vitamin C is a great antioxidant that will help to support your adrenal glands, which you can end up overworking during stressful times. While B vitamins help with several functions within the body, they are often seen as the "stress and energy" vitamins. During a workout, your body becomes very stressed, so avocados work like a magic fruit.

Apricots

The last food on this list is apricots. There are some people who believe if they don't eat before a workout, they will end up burning more fat. While this may be true in some instances, it can also cause people to become dizzy, nausea, and lack important energy, which will hinder your ability to get the workout you want. Having a simple snack of an apricot before you workout can help give you the nutrients you need as well as an easily digested fuel to prevent all of those nasty side effects.

If you make sure you consume these energy-producing foods, along with others, you will never be lacking in energy or vitality. And, since you were a bodybuilder first, you should easily be able to slide into a plant-based diet that is full of these healthy energy-inducing foods without having to think about it.

Chapter 3. Impact of Vegan On Athletes and Bodybuilders

Since time immemorial bodybuilders have relied heavily on a high-meat and poultry diet to get the requisite amount of proteins to build muscle mass. However, there is a steady rise in the new wave of bodybuilders who are challenging the traditional norm of getting proteins only from meats and milk and instead are propagating plant-powered food. This new community of bodybuilders believes that with a strict commitment to a plant-based diet and a change in eating habits, one can get enough proteins for bodybuilding. Vegan bodybuilding diet can help in a great way to attain this goal. But before plunging into a full-fledged vegan diet, there are a few tips that can help get started with this regime-Get enough calories-The most important thing for new vegans is to take enough calories on a regular basis so that the body does not consume incoming protein for fueling body growth. This could lead to a deficit.

Have vegetables and fruits in plenty-It is important to take in a good quantity of fruits and vegetables as they keep up the nutrient content in the body and also provide antioxidants to maintain immunity.

Eat legumes and chickpeas-For vegans looking to build muscle, it is important to consume sufficient quantities of legumes and chickpeas. They are a high source of carbohydrates and make for a tasty snack after a rigorous session of workout.

Switch to quinoa instead of rice-Quinoa is a mixture of brown rice and oatmeal and is higher in the overall content of protein than brown rice. Also, it is a complete protein source, which is essential for muscle building.

Soy protein powder-Include soy protein powder with other natural sources of protein to increase the amount of protein in your body. In fact, it should be a must-have for all bodybuilders.

Avoid processed food-In vegan bodybuilding for beginners' diet, the consumption of processed food is limited. Being vegan does not mean that you can have a free hand at eating any amounts of carbohydrates. Eating healthy is of prime importance with a diet containing nuts, fresh fruits, vegetables, and whole grains.

Have a short but intense workout-As a vegan, you should indulge in short, intense workouts. It will not allow the loss of muscle mass and will let your body rely on vegan protein sources through the workout sessions. It has been seen that long workout sessions often lead to fatigue for vegans in the long run.

Have a varied choice in food you consume-As a vegan, you might find yourselves eating the same food repeatedly. Try to avoid this as it can lead to nutritionally deficiencies and not add to muscle building.

Eat frequent meals-Since you can not consume as much protein in each meal as a non-vegetarian, you should add more meals to your day so that there is a steady stream of proteins going into the muscles.

Food rich in muscle-building amino acids-Amino acids are the building blocks of tissues and protein in the body. The body requires 21 amino acids to stay alive, and nine are found in food. These are called essential amino acids, and one of them called cinephile is related to muscle-building and it allows protein synthesis in the body through enzyme activation needed for cell growth. Thus, the leucine content in the meal shows the protein content required for muscle building. So eat foods rich in amino acids and especially leucine.

Making these simple lifestyle changes will go a long way in adjusting to the vegan way of life and will allow the proteins to be absorbed well to create as much muscle mass as a non-vegan diet would.

Planning a proper vegan meal

Meal planning is of the utmost importance when undertaking a vegan diet, especially for bodybuilders and athletes.

There are a few things that you need to keep in mind while planning a proper diet-Calorie Intake-Accurate calorie tracking is the most effective and reliable way to know what is going into the body, how to lose fat, and build muscle. It does not mean starving yourself, but instead, it includes the number of calories you eat and how many you might burn. It is called energy balance.

Work out Macros-There are three macronutrients that the body needs-proteins, fats, and carbohydrates. They make up a major part of our calorie intake and the macronutrient split is essential to build a great looking body for bodybuilders. They dictate how the body will grow and repair tissues, and how much muscle you retain during a weight loss program. The optimal vegan macro split should be-Have a high-protein diet consuming 0.73-1 g per lbs.

Plan meat timing and portions-Once you have figured out how to split the macronutrients in every meal, it is time to plan your meal timing and also the portion size. Since you are getting all the proteins from plants; it is not feasible to get the requisite amounts in just three main meals of the day. Hence, it is pertinent to add more meals at frequent intervals with substantial amounts of protein in each meal. It will help stoke the metabolic fire and burn more fat. In addition to it, the continuous consumption of protein will help in muscle growth at optimal capacity. The timing of the meal is also important. Late night dinners or might-night snacks are a big no. Stay away from food after sunset or reduce it to minimal.

Plan what foods for each meal-It is important to decide on the kind of proteins you want to have in each meal. So planning each meal with care is significant. Include fresh fruits, nuts, and vegetables on a daily basis. Get the macronutrient split right so that there is a proper percentage of each nutrient for adequate muscle repair and growth.

The influence of vegan diet on athletic performance

Evidence has shown that many high performing professional and amateur athletes experience lower immune-competence (weakened immune systems). This is usually accompanied by frequent infection of the upper respiratory tract.

Such symptoms are usually the result of prolonged stress from regular high-intensity training. Similarly, a short period of intense exercise creates a temporary reduction in immune function. Some of the properties of the immune system reduced by high-intensity training include: neutrophil function and the natural cell degeneration number.

Intense workouts have a negative effect on the neutrophil function (white blood cells) and this can lead to poor immune-response and increase in microbial infections. Consequently, it will lead to a disruption in training and affect the athlete's performance. Coaches and trainers, who work with top professional and amateur athletes, usually want training to be continuous without any interruptions due to illness caused by viral infections. That is why it is beneficial for all dedicated athletes who adopt a vegan diet to choose foods that will effectively boost immune-competence. Thus, the athlete will be able to enjoy continuous training without disruptions due to illness.

Plant Based Antioxidants vs Antioxidant Supplements

A diet with relatively high quantity of phytochemicals (chemical compounds that occur naturally in plants) and antioxidants can also reduce oxidative stress caused by intense training. Just one bout of an intense workout can produce a significant amount of oxidative stress in the muscles and blood stream. This may stay on for a couple of days during which the endogenous antioxidant defenses are increased. On the contrary, reactive oxygen species (ROS) created by the intense workout may outweigh the increase in endogenous antioxidants. But regular consumption of high-antioxidant plant based foods keeps ROS at desirable levels and reduces the negative effects of oxidative stress.

31

But it is important to note that antioxidant supplements have not produced predictable results when used to reduce oxidative stress induced by intense training or to curtail inflammatory markers. In some cases, these supplements have actually slowed down recovery. In one study, creatine kinase, which is a major indicator of muscle damage, remained at a high level for a longer period than those who were given a placebo.

In a second study, administering a concentrated antioxidant to the participants raised lipid peroxidation and reduced the level of glutathione peroxidase – an antioxidant enzyme. Other reports and some studies of chronic diseases show that high micronutrient whole foods, which contain complex mixtures of phyto-nutrients and antioxidants, are more potent than supplements containing high doses of isolated antioxidants. There is also strong evidence showing that vegetables protect the body against coronary heart failure which also involves oxidative damage. But the benefit of using antioxidant vitamin supplements to prevent this disease is not clear.

Broccoli, collards, kale, bok choy and other green vegetables, provide a significantly higher quantity of micronutrients per kilocalorie than other foods. They also contain protein. Virtually all colorful vegetables are rich in antioxidants. In addition, fruits like kiwi, oranges, sour cherries, pomegranates, berries and black currants, have high quantities of antioxidants. Seeds like black unhulled sesame seed and pistachio nuts also have high amounts of antioxidants including vitamin E.

The Positive Effect of Vegan Diets on Athletic Success

In the American Journal of Clinical Nutrition, many reviews of successful athletes who ate vegan diets are documented. As far back the 1890s, vegan long distance walkers and cyclists in Britain and the U.S. performed better than those who ate meat. A vegan became one of the first athletes to finish the marathon race under two and a half hours, in 191In 1970, research conducted to compare pulmonary function and muscle width in athletes revealed that there was no difference between athletes on vegan and non-vegan diets.

In the same vein, a 1986 study conducted on groups of vegan and non-vegan peers showed that there is no difference between their endurance, pulmonary function, limb circumferences and total serum protein. In athletic events that required endurance due to their long duration, the performance of vegans and non-vegans was at par. In 1989, when they consumed the same amount of carbohydrate, there was no difference in the time taken to complete a 10 km race in West Germany. Even though these results show that there is no reduction in performance among vegan athletes, some people still express reservations about vegan diets for athletes.

Calorie and protein requirements

A diet for the vegan athletes should take into account extra energy requirements above that of moderate level activity. The low calorie density in many of the plant foods makes energy requirements become a major consideration.

During exercises, there is an increased protein breakdown and oxidation which is then followed by heightened muscle protein synthesis and further breakdown of proteins during recovery. The rise in the levels of circulating amino acids after one takes a protein-containing meal normally stimulates intramuscular protein synthesis in addition to slightly suppressing muscle breakdown of proteins.

Ingesting just carbohydrates into the body does not induce such increases in protein synthesis by the muscles. Furthermore, protein-containing meals have significant benefits to the immunity, muscle soreness as well as overall health as compared to carbohydrate-only meals.

Because of this, timing of protein content in meals is an important factor in recovery, muscle mass gain and maintenance.

The branched chain amino acids (BCAA) supplements; isoleucine, valine and leucine in a ratio of 1:1:2 have been specifically studied for their effects on muscle protein synthesis, performance and recovery. The oxidation of leucine supplements is significantly regulated during endurance exercises thus showing the necessity for increased intake of protein by athletes.

Research has suggested that the BCAA supplements do not affect performance significantly but they attenuate exercise-induced muscle damages and also promote muscle protein synthesis. Plant proteins like sesame seeds, tofu, pumpkin seeds and sunflower seeds are great sources of BCAA supplements.

Protein Requirements for Vegan Athletes

Every athlete (both vegan and non vegan) require a greater protein quantity than sedentary individuals. Nevertheless, the amount of protein that is required has been a point of disagreement and confusion between the scientific community and the athletes. Proteins might comprise of 5 percent of the energy that is burned during exercises thus resulting in the need of positive nitrogen balance as raw material for the anabolic processes. This is to replace the losses and build any additional muscle mass. Insufficient ingestion of proteins leads to insufficient recovery and negative nitrogen balance.

Potential Dangers of Excess Proteins

There are no confirmed benefits for any athlete to consume over 200g protein. In fact, excess proteins usually have negative effects on the calcium stores, bone health, cardiovascular health and kidney function.

It is highly encouraged to use whole food protein sources like tofu, seeds, nuts and hemp seed meals which have been blended into smoothies and shakes.

It is important to note that isolated proteins powders are micronutrient-poor as compared to whole foods. Furthermore, their usage might pose health risks to individuals since excess animal proteins usually promotes cancers as a result of the increases in insulin growth factor 1-commonly referred to as IGF-

Animal proteins are not the only proteins which elevate IGF-1 levels but the isolated proteins from plant different plant sources also have a similar effect. The main factor which defines excess proteins for athletes is yet to be clearly defined due to the scarce studies on protein safety amongst athletes.

Muscle growth

There is a big difference between maximizing health, and maximizing muscle growth and body size. It is clear that a well-designed vegan diet will meet the nutritional demands of an agility and speed athlete like tennis, basketball, skiing, track and soccer. It used to be believed that is was not ideal maximizing muscle growth in larger athletes such as football linebackers or body builders. But there are modern techniques and vegan friendly supplements which can help.

Plant protein concentrates like maca, rice, hemp protein powders and pea are options whenever the athlete wishes to remain vegan or significantly reduce their dependency on the animal products while still supporting a high body mass.

In addition to promoting excellent health, an intelligently and carefully designed supplemented vegan diet will meet the caloric needs and supply enough protein to the body.

Chapter 4. Meal Plan, Recipes and Advice

When it comes to athletes there are some basic rules that still apply even after you choose to make a transition to the vegan diet. An athlete's body is like a machine that has to deal with the stress of hard and long workouts, everyday stress, as well as stress caused by sleep deprivation due to the long workouts before a big game. For these reasons, nutrition is essential to achieve higher performance and provide it with ways to deal with the stress caused by the different factors we mentioned. The necessary nutrients will not change even if you alter the way you eat and whether you follow an omnivorous or vegan diet you must make sure your sports, nutrition, as well as your habits, are helping you achieve your dreams.

The first thing you should keep in mind is that you should not work out when your stomach is empty. If you were not able to eat within two hours before your training, you could grab a fruit such as one banana or something else that is recommended by your sports dietitian in order for you to keep your blood sugar on a steady level. If your workout is short, for instance it lasts 45 minutes, generally, a piece of fruit will be enough.

You will just have to make sure that your stomach is familiar with this fruit so as to digest it easily. When you have longer workouts, that last for 60 to 90 minutes, you will need to be hydrated appropriately and add more carbs so as to ensure their constant flow. If your workout lasts for over 90 or 120 minutes, you will need a combination of solid food and liquid hydration. For instance, you could eat a bar, boiled potato, or rice.

A rule that applies to everyone, and especially athletes, is that you should not skip your breakfast. This rule exists for a reason. Breakfast will set the pace for your body to use nutrients throughout the rest of the whole day. It is an often occurrence to hear people say that they are not hungry when they wake up and prepare for the day. This is perfectly acceptable, but you shouldn't be on an empty stomach since fueling your body is essential to have energy. Even little things could be added to your breakfast, so as to start building an appetite that could later turn into a full and fitting breakfast. For example, you could have a fruit or prepare a smoothie. You should start small and be consistent on your breakfast for about a week to let your body get used to obtaining nutrients during the morning. From then on you will be able to indulge in a delicious breakfast that will fuel your body with energy.

You should plan out all the meals of 2 to 3 days before your game, so as to ensure that your body will have all the necessary nutrients it needs for your big event by topping its energy and to be certain that you will be at your optimal performance. We see many athletes overlooking this fact and later they feel dizzy or lethargic on such an important day.

To make this planning step easier, you could consult with your sports dietician and include foods that you like and will not cause any distress to your stomach. Keep in mind, that you should not include foods that are high in fiber and saturated fat. You could make a combination of carbs and proteins with a carb to protein ratio of 2:1 or else 3:1 to ensure that your blood sugar levels and proteins stay in check. Another way that you could enforce this is by cooking your meals ahead of time.

Another thing you should keep in mind is that you should never skip your recovery nutrition, in other words meal. If you do this, you will fail in producing results that you strove so hard to achieve throughout your training program. By either consulting with a sports dietician or by yourself, you should figure out which recovery process works best for your training and make it happen within 30 to 45 minutes after your training is over.

You should also eat 90 minutes after that meal and your performance will be at its peak. But why you should eat after 30 to 45 minutes after training? According to experts, that recovery time will expire after 45 to 60 minutes and you will feel more tired and depleted of energy if you skip this. Recovery nutrition in its liquid form appears to be easier for the stomach and it is digested more easily. It also comes in handy when you are not at home to prepare any solid food. You could prepare a drink that is full of proteins or with some amino acids to consume after your training. When you return home, you could prepare a meal with equally distributed amounts of proteins, omega fats, complex carbs, and vegetables. This will stabilize again your blood sugar and keep your body energized.

Last but not least, before you go to sleep, you should consume a snack dense with nutrients and that includes some berries, healthy fats, nuts, and proteins. Generally, foods that will not elevate your blood sugar levels but at the same time protect it from dropping throughout the night. There is a belief that you should not eat before going to bed and it mostly satisfies phycological needs that have to do with self-control and believing that we are not overeating.

However, when it comes to sports nutrition there is little psychological benefit from fasting before going to sleep. It is a fact the level of blood sugar will fall rapidly during sleep to maintain the processes of the body. If we do not fuel it with nutrients, the body will have nothing to rebuild from. You shouldn't ask yourself if you should eat or not, but rather what type of food would be best for you during a particular time of the day. The body of athletes is moving constantly and thus it will constantly need refueling to rebuilt itself. One of the worst things athletes of any kind could do is to restrict their intake f nutrients and hope to get an improved performance through that.

You shouldn't be stressed when it comes to eating right in order to attain the nutrients you need. For instance, you can build a framework with seven foods that feel most important to you or your sports dietician and try to include them in your diet for each day throughout the week. An example of such a framework can be:

Cruciferous Vegetables and Leafy Greens: An amazing addition to your vegan diet that is very beneficial for your health.

Berries and Other Fruit: They present us with the most vibrant colors and have anti-inflammatory, anti-cancer, and antioxidant properties.

Flaxseeds and Other Seeds and Nuts: Walnuts and flaxseeds are rich in Omega-3 and also flaxseeds are antiangiogenic.

Beans: According to a 2007 American Institute for Cancer Research study we should consume beans every day for their many health benefits.

White or Green Tea: Tea is rich in antioxidants and also includes beneficial phytochemicals such as ECGC that are exclusive to the tea bush.

Garlic and Onions: According to research half a cup of onions each day is able to reduce the risk of certain cancers by 50-. Garlic would be an added plus.

Tumeric: It is able to help us against cancer and heart disease due to its curcumin and pigment.

The above is an example of a framework for you to work with and add foods that benefit you and you would love to eat each day. However, it can be difficult for most people to think of ways to incorporate those foods into their meals. Admittedly it is a hard part, especially for extremely busy athletes. To solve this problem, you could at first try to add those foods into your three basic meals. As an example, we will take the foods mentioned above and try to include them into the three basic meals, breakfast, lunch, and dinner:

Breakfast:

You can make a morning smoothie or oatmeal that will include some of the foods of your framework before you start your day. For example, you can have:

Other Fruit and Berries

Other nuts and Flaxseeds

White or green Tea Leaves

Beans

Tumeric

Lunch:

For lunch, you can have a big bowl of salad with a number of vegetables, beans, greens, and create a dressing based with nuts such as tahini with garlic or cashew ranch. In this salad you can include:

Seeds and Nuts

Onions

Greens

Beans

Cruciferous Vegetables

Fruit

Tumeric

Whole Grain

Dinner:

You will have many choices for dinner when you base it around greens, grain, and beans. For example, you can have tacos and burritos, curries, pasta, and combine them with garlic or onions. The foods you could include in dinner are:

Greens

Mushrooms

Cruciferous or other Vegetables

Turmeric

Beans

Whole Grain

Seeds and nuts as dressing or topping

Garlic and Onion

When we place all the foods together we can create a sample meal plan for a day which will include all the foods of your framework along with other foods such as mushrooms, and whole grains. Keep in mind that your ideal meal plan would be better if you included the seven foods of your choice at the proportions your sports dietician should indicate. A sample meal plan includes:

Breakfast: A smoothie with additionally tea, water, or coffee

Morning Snack: Tea, fruit with an optional addition of nut butter.

Lunch: A big salad with beans and a dressing based on nuts. Optionally you could use at the side whole grain such as whole-wheat bread, quinoa, or rice.

Afternoon Snack: Whole grain, such as bread or crackers, or veggies with hummus and tea.

Dinner: Foods that contain beans, grain, and green with garlic and onion.

If required, you may need supplements of vitamin D3, B12, and DHA/EPA. Diets that are based on plants and whole-food, even though they are high in various micronutrients, they do not offer enough vitamin D3, B12, and DHA/EPA. You can get these three nutrients from a single source if it is recommended and also keep in mind that there are people who follow omnivorous diets that lack those vitamins too. It is just that vegans may be at a higher risk of developing a deficiency in them due to the complete lack of animal food. Let us see in more detail a few recipes that will help you in preparing your three basic meals.

Recipes for Breakfast:

Banana and Berry Smoothie:

Smoothies are an easy way, through which you will be able to obtain the nutrients you need for breakfast. You can make smoothies with blueberries, strawberries, and blackberries or any other fruit you like. It could also help you experimenting with different fruit so as to not get bored with the taste.

Ingredients:

- 2 medium-sized and ripe bananas
- 2 spoonful of walnuts or Brazil nuts
- 2 spoonful of flaxseeds
- 2 ½ cups of water

- 2 ½ cups of frozen berry

- 2 baby spinach or any other greens soft in taste

Optional:

- Green tea leaves

- Fresh turmeric

- Tofu

Directions::

Pour all the ingredients in a blender and blend until they get smooth.

Oatmeal:

- 1 cup of oats

- ¼ spoonful of cinnamon

- 2 cups of water

- 1 spoonful of grounded flaxseeds

- ½ cup of frozen berries

- 1 spoonful of chia seeds

- ¼ cup of grounded almonds

- 3 spoonful of pumpkin seeds

- Maple syrup for taste - optional

Directions::

Place the oats, cinnamon, and water together in a saucepan that is in medium heat.

Heat the ingredients until they are simmering, and stir often until the water is absorbed which takes approximately five minutes.

Pour in and stir the flaxseeds and berries until they are heated enough and then, take them off the heat.

Pour the end result in a bowl and top it with pumpkin seeds, maple syrup, chia seeds, and almonds.

Recipes for Lunch:

For lunch you can create a rich salad with various dressings that is full of cruciferous veggies, greens, grain, seeds, and beans. The dressing you can top it with could be free of oil and based on nuts for added taste. Let us see in more detail how to create an amazing salad:

Directions::

Cut one large lettuce and add a handful of the following:

Arugula

Dandelion greens

Baby kale

Mustard Greens

Add at least one of the cruciferous vegetables such as:

Cabbage

Radishes

Broccoli

Add also green onions as well as any other of the vegetables you like such as

Tomatoes

Carrots

Celery

Finish the salad with a cup of beans as well as a dressing that is based on nuts. You will be able to serve this salad with brown rice or with whole-grain sides to fill you more. Let us see how you will be able to make two dressings that are delicious with a salad.

Tahini and Garlic Dressing:

Ingredients:

- ½ cup of tahini
- 2 cloves of garlic or more for your taste
- ¼ cup of water and if needed more for thinner results
- 2 spoonfuls of lemon juice
- 2 spoonfuls of tamari reduced in sodium

Directions::

Toss the garlic cloves after you peel them over medium heat in a dry skillet for 5 to 10 minutes up until they have taken a light brown color. This will help take down the intensity of the garlic a bit and retain its flavor.

Add the garlic to your food processor blender and mince them.

Then, add the other ingredients to the blender and mince them until they are smooth. Add the water until you achieve a thin texture, but not so thin that it will not stick to the salad leaves.

Keep in mind that it will thicken in the fridge too, so you could always add more water before you actually use it.

If you feel that the flavor is too strong, you could add extra Tahini or water.

Cashew Ranch Dressing:

Ingredients:

- 1 and ¼ cups of cashews - you can soak them if you want a creamier dressing
- 1 cup of water to blend
- 1 and 1/2 spoonful of lemon juice
- 1 spoonful of apple cider vinegar
- ½ spoonful of garlic powder
- 1.5 spoonful of onion powder
- 1 spoonful of dried dill
- 1 spoonful of sea salt
- ½ spoonful of dried basil
- ¼ spoonful of freshly grounded black pepper

Directions:

You should blend all the ingredients in a high-speed blender up until they are smooth and creamy to suit your taste.

Keep in mind that you should not blend them for too long since the dressing will get hot. If it is too thick for your taste, you could add more water.

Another thing to keep in mind is that it will thicken more in the fridge; if this happens, add more water to it.

Recipes for Dinner:

An appropriate dinner could be rice, pasta, tacos or stews, and many more foods of your choice that include:

Garlic and Onions

Whole Grain

Beans

Greens

Seeds and Nuts

Turmeric

Vegetables

Mushrooms

Let us see in more detail an amazing recipe that will make you full and that tastes great:

Tempeh Tacos:

Keep in mind that if you don't like soy, you will be able to replace it with any other bean.

Ingredients:

- 54 grams of crumbled tempeh
- 2 corn tortillas
- oy sauce or tamari low in sodium
- 40 grams of BBQ sauce - preferably without oil
- cup of shredded green or red cabbage
- ½ bunch of chopped and fresh cilantro
- cup of chopped pineapple
- pickled onions for garnish
- errano pepper or Jalapeño

Directions:

Use a medium pan and preheat it over medium to high heat.

Once it is warm enough, heat each corn tortilla for one minute on one side and then flip it to heat the other side for approximately 10 seconds.

After you heat each tortilla, place it on a plate that is covered by an almost damp kitchen towel in order to maintain its warmth.

Use a pan to heat over medium heat the crumbled tempeh and stir it often to prevent it from sticking.

Once it is heated, sprinkle the tempeh with soy sauce or tamari sauce and stir it often up until the tempeh is heated thoroughly.

Then, add the barbecue sauce and mix them well until they are heated thoroughly.

To complete this recipe, take a spoonful of the tempeh blend and place it onto a warm tortilla.

Then add the pineapple, red cabbage, jalapeño, pickled onions, and cilantro. Repeat this process for the rest of the tortillas

The above are only a few recipes out of the many others you can find in order to have the best and extremely tasty food on your plate. Many people think that vegan recipes lack many things that would make food delicious and the fact of the matter is that they are completely wrong. Vegan food lacks nothing when compared to food that contains meat and meat by-products. Athletes will be able to taste amazing foods while at the same time maintain all the nutrients they need to be at their peak performance. Vegan foods do not restrict your creativity, on the contrary, they will allow you to unleash your imagination and make foods that will be mouth-dropping, healthy, and environmentally friendly.

Chapter 5.
Morning Meals to Power Your Day

Chocolate, Avocado, and Banana Smoothie

Preparation:
5 Minutes

Cooking:
0 Minutes

Serves:
1

Directions

1. Place all the ingredients in the order in a food processor or blender and then pulse for 2 to 3 minutes at high speed until smooth.
2. Pour the smoothie into a glass and then serve.

Ingredients

- 1 medium frozen banana
- 2 small dates, pitted
- 1/2 cup steamed and frozen cauliflower florets
- 1/4 of a medium avocado
- 1 teaspoon cinnamon
- 1 tablespoon cacao powder
- 1/2 teaspoon sea salt
- 1 teaspoon maca
- 1/2 scoop of vanilla protein powder
- 2 tablespoon cacao nibs
- 1 tablespoon almond butter
- 1 cup almond milk

Nutritions: *Calories: 100 Cal, Fat: 100 g, Carbs: 100 g, Protein: 100 g, Fiber: 100 g*

Breakfast Sandwich

 Preparation:
5 Minutes

 Cooking:
6 Minutes

 Serves:
4

Ingredients

- ¼ of a medium avocado, sliced
- 1 vegan sausage patty
- 2 teaspoon olive oil
- 1 cup kale
- 1/8 teaspoon salt
- 1/8 teaspoon black pepper
- 1 Tablespoon pepitas
- 1 English muffin, halved, toasted

For the Sauce:
- 1 teaspoon jalapeno, chopped
- 1/8 teaspoon smoky paprika
- 1 tablespoon mayonnaise, vegan

Directions

1. Take a saute pan, place it over medium heat, add oil and when hot, add the patty and cook for 2 minutes.
2. Then slip the patty, push it to one side of the pan, add kale and pepitas to the other side, season with black pepper and salt, and cook for 2 to 3 minutes until kale has softened.
3. When done, remove the pan from heat and prepare the sauce by whisking its ingredients until combined.
4. Assemble the sandwich and for this, spread mayonnaise on the inside of muffin, top with avocado slices and patty, and then top with kale and pepitas.
5. Serve straight away

Nutritions: *Calories: 207.3 Cal, Fat: 4.5 g, Carbs: 26.2 g, Protein: 15.5 g, Fiber: 8 g*

Broccoli and Quinoa Breakfast Patties

Preparation:
5 Minutes

Cooking:
6 Minutes

Serves:
4

Ingredients

- 1 cup cooked quinoa, cooked
- 1/2 cup shredded broccoli florets
- 1/2 cup shredded carrots
- 2 cloves of garlic, minced
- 2 teaspoon parsley
- 1 1/2 teaspoon onion powder
- 1 1/2 teaspoon garlic powder
- 1/3 teaspoon salt
- 1/4 teaspoon black pepper
- 1/2 cup bread crumbs, gluten-free
- 2 tablespoon coconut oil
- 2 flax eggs

Directions

1. Prepare patties and for this, place all the ingredients in a large bowl, except for oil and stir until well combined and then shape the mixture into patties.
2. Take a skillet pan, place it over medium heat, add oil and when hot, add prepared patties in it and cook for 3 minutes per side until golden brown and crispy.
3. Serve patties with vegan sour creams.

Nutritions: *Calories: 229.6Cal, Fat: 11.1 g, Carbs: 27.7g, Protein: 9.3g, Fiber: 6.6 g*

Potato Skillet Breakfast

 Preparation:
5 Minutes

 Cooking:
15 Minutes

 Serves:
5

Ingredients

- 1 ½ cup cooked black beans
- 1 1/4 pounds potatoes, diced
- 12 ounces spinach, destemmed
- 1 1/4 pounds red potatoes, diced
- 2 small avocados, sliced, for topping
- 1 medium green bell pepper, diced
- 1 jalapeno, minced
- 1 large white onion, diced
- 1 medium red bell pepper, diced
- 3 cloves of garlic, minced
- 1/2 teaspoon red chili powder
- 1/4 teaspoon salt
- 1 teaspoon cumin
- 1 tablespoon canola oil

Directions

1. Switch on the oven, then set it to 425 degrees F and let it preheat.
2. Meanwhile, take a skillet pan, place it over medium heat, add oil and when hot, add potatoes, season with salt, chili powder, and cumin, stir until mixed and cook for 2 minutes.
3. Transfer pan into the oven and roast potatoes for 20 minutes until cooked, stirring halfway through.
4. Then add remaining onion, bell peppers, garlic, and jalapeno, continue roasting for another 15 minutes, stirring halfway, and remove the pan from heat.
5. Transfer pan over medium heat, cook for 5 to 10 minutes until potatoes are thoroughly cooked, then stir spinach and beans and cook for 3 minutes until spinach leaves have wilted.
6. When done, top the skillet with cilantro and avocado and then serve.

Nutritions: *Calories: 198.6 Cal, Fat: 7 g, Carbs: 32 g, Protein: 3.8 g, Fiber: 4.4 g*

Scrambled Tofu Breakfast Tacos

Preparation:
5 Minutes

Cooking:
10 Minutes

Serves:
4

Ingredients

- 12 ounces tofu, pressed, drained
- 1/2 cup grape tomatoes, quartered
- 1 medium red pepper, diced
- 1 medium avocado, sliced
- 1 clove of garlic, minced
- 1/4 teaspoon ground turmeric
- 1/4 teaspoon ground black pepper
- 1/4 teaspoon salt
- 1/4 teaspoon cumin
- 1 teaspoon olive oil
- 8 corn tortillas

Directions

1. Take a skillet pan, place it over medium heat, add oil and when hot, add pepper and garlic and cook for 2 minutes.
2. Then add tofu, crumble it, sprinkle with black pepper, salt, and all the spices, stir and cook for 5 minutes.
3. When done, distribute tofu between tortilla, top with tomato and avocado, and serve.

Nutritions: *Calories: 240 Cal, Fat: 8 g, Carbs: 26 g, Protein: 12 g, Fiber: 4 g*

Peanut Butter and Banana Bread Granola

Preparation:
10 Minutes

Cooking:
32 Minutes

Serves:
6

Ingredients

- 1/2 cup Quinoa
- 1/2 cup mashed banana
- 3 cup rolled oats, old-fashioned
- 1 cup banana chips, crushed
- 1 cup peanuts, salted
- 1 teaspoon. salt
- 1 teaspoon. cinnamon
- 1/4 cup brown sugar
- 1/4 cup honey
- 2 teaspoon. vanilla extract, unsweetened
- 1/3 cup peanut butter
- 6 tablespoon. unsalted butter

Directions

1. Switch on the oven, then set it to 325 degrees F and let it preheat.
2. Meanwhile, take two rimmed baking sheets, line them with parchment sheets, and set aside until required.
3. Place oats in a bowl, add quinoa, banana chips, cinnamon, salt, and sugar and stir until combined.
4. Take a small saucepan, place it over medium-low heat, add butter and honey and cook for 4 minutes until melted, stirring frequently.
5. Then remove the pan from heat, add banana and vanilla, stir until mixed, then spoon the mixture into the oat mixture and stir until incorporated.
6. Distribute granola evenly between two baking sheets, spread evenly, and then bake for 25 minutes until golden brown, rotating the sheets halfway.
7. When done, transfer baking sheets on wire racks, cool the granola, then break it into pieces and serve.
8. Serve straight away.

Nutritions: *Calories: 655 Cal, Fat: 36 g, Carbs: 70 g, Protein: 18 g, Fiber: 12 g*

Sweet Potato Breakfast Hash

Preparation:
5 Minutes

Cooking:
28 Minutes

Serves:
4

Ingredients

- 4 cups cubed sweet potatoes, peeled
- 1/2 teaspoon sea salt
- 1/2 teaspoon turmeric
- 1/2 teaspoon cumin
- 1 teaspoon smoked paprika
- 2 cups diced white onion
- 2 cloves of garlic, peeled, minced
- 1/4 cup chopped cilantro
- 1 tablespoon coconut oil
- ½ cup vegan guacamole, for serving
- 1 ½ cup pica de Gallo

Directions

1. Take a skillet pan, place it over medium heat, add oil and when it melts, add onion, potatoes, and garlic, season with salt, paprika, turmeric, and cumin, stir and cook for 25 minutes until potatoes are slightly caramelized.
2. Then remove the pan from heat, add cilantro and distribute evenly between serving plates.
3. Top the sweet potato hash with guacamole and pico de gallo and then serve.

Nutritions: *Calories: 211.3 Cal, Fat: 8 g, Carbs: 22.2 g, Protein: 12.5 g, Fiber: 3.5 g*

Chickpea Flour Omelet

Preparation:
5 Minutes

Cooking:
12 Minutes

Serves:
1

Ingredients

- 1/4 cup chickpea flour
- 1/2 teaspoon chopped chives
- ½ cup spinach, chopped
- 1/4 teaspoon turmeric
- 1/4 teaspoon garlic powder
- 1/8 teaspoon ground black pepper
- 1/2 teaspoon baking power
- 1 tablespoon nutritional yeast
- 1/2 teaspoon vegan egg
- 1/4 cup and 1 tablespoon water

Directions

1. Take a bowl, place all the ingredients in it, except for spinach, whisk until combined and let it stand for 5 minutes.
2. Then take a skillet pan, place it over low heat, grease it with oil and when hot, pour in prepared and cook for 3 minutes until edges are dry.
3. Then top half of the omelet with spinach, fold with the other half and continue cooking for 2 minutes.
4. Slide omelet to a plate and serve with ketchup.

Nutritions: *Calories: 150 Cal, Fat: 2 g, Carbs: 24.4 g, Protein: 10.2 g, Fiber: 5.8 g*

Preparation:
10 Minutes

Cooking:
25 Minutes

Serves:
6

Ingredients

- 6 tablespoons chocolate chips, semi-sweet
- ½ cup chopped strawberries
- Powdered sugar as needed for topping

Dry Ingredients:
- 1/4 cup oats
- 1 1/2 tablespoon ground flaxseeds
- 1 1/2 cup whole wheat pastry flour
- 2 1/2 tablespoon cocoa powder
- 1/4 teaspoon salt
- 2 teaspoons baking powder

Wet Ingredients:
- 1/3 cup mashed bananas
- 2 tablespoon maple syrup
- 2 tablespoon coconut oil
- 1/2 teaspoon vanilla extract, unsweetened
- 1/4 cup applesauce, unsweetened
- 1 3/4 cup almond milk, unsweetened

Directions

1. Take a medium bowl, place all the dry ingredients in it, and whisk until mixed.
2. Take a large bowl, place all the wet ingredients in it, whisk until combined, and then whisk in dry ingredients mixture in four batches until incorporated, don't overmix.
3. Let the batter stand at room temperature for 5 minutes and in the meantime, switch on the waffle iron and let it preheat until hot.
4. Then ladle one-sixth of the batter in it and cook until golden brown and firm.
5. Cook remaining waffles in the same manner and when done, top them with chocolate chips and berries, sprinkle with sugar and then serve.

Nutritions: *Calories: 261 Cal, Fat: 10 g, Carbs: 41 g, Protein: 6 g, Fiber: 6 g*

Vegetarian Breakfast Casserole

Preparation:
10 Minutes

Cooking:
35 Minutes

Serves:
4

Ingredients

- 5 medium potatoes, about 22 ounces, boiled
- 10 ounces silken tofu
- 5 ounces tempeh, cubed
- 1 tablespoon chives, cut into rings
- 1 medium white onion, peeled chopped
- ¾ teaspoon ground black pepper
- 1 ½ teaspoon salt
- 1 teaspoon turmeric
- 2 1/2 teaspoons paprika powder
- 1 1/2 tablespoons olive oil
- 1 tablespoon corn starch
- 1 teaspoon soy sauce
- 1 tablespoon barbecue sauce
- 1/2 teaspoon liquid smoke
- 1/2 cup vegan cheese

Directions

1. Switch on the oven, then set it to 350 degrees F and let it preheat.
2. Meanwhile, peel the boiled potatoes, then cut them into cubes and set aside until required.
3. Prepare tempeh and for this, take a skillet pan, place it over medium heat, add half of the oil, and when hot, add half of the onion and cook for 1 minute.
4. Then add tempeh pieces, season with 1 teaspoon paprika, add soy sauce, liquid smoke and BBQ sauce, season with salt and black pepper and cook tempeh for 5 minutes, set aside until required.
5. Take a large skillet pan, place it over medium heat, add remaining oil and onion and cook for 2 minutes until beginning to soften.
6. Then add potatoes, season with ½ teaspoon paprika, salt, and black pepper to taste and cook for 5 minutes until crispy, set aside until required.
7. Take a medium bowl, place tofu in it, then add remaining ingredients and whisk until smooth.
8. Take a casserole dish, place potatoes and tempeh in it, top with tofu mixture, sprinkle some more cheese, and bake for 20 minutes until done.
9. Serve straight away.

Nutritions: *Calories: 212 Cal, Fat: 7 g, Carbs: 28 g, Protein: 11 g, Fiber: 5 g*

Scrambled Eggs with Aquafaba

Preparation:
5 Minutes

Cooking:
15 Minutes

Serves:
2

Ingredients

- 6 ounces tofu, firm, pressed, drained
- 1/2 cup aquafaba
- 1 1/2 tablespoons olive oil
- 1 tablespoon nutritional yeast
- 1/4 teaspoon black salt
- 1/8 teaspoon ground turmeric
- 1/4 teaspoon ground black pepper

Directions

1. Take a food processor, add tofu, yeast, black pepper, salt, and turmeric, then pour in aquafaba and olive oil and pulse for 1 minute until smooth.
2. Take a skillet pan, place it over medium heat, and when hot, add tofu mixture and cook for 1 minute.
3. Cover the pan, continue cooking for 3 minutes, then uncover the pan and pull the mixture across the pan with a wooden spoon until soft forms.
4. Continue cooking for 10 minutes until resembles soft scrambled eggs, folding tofu mixture gently and heat over medium heat, then remove the pan from heat and season with salt and black pepper to taste.
5. Serve straight away

Nutritions: *Calories: 208 Cal, Fat: 5.1 g, Carbs: 31.3 g, Protein: 8.3 g, Fiber: 10.4 g*

Chickpea and Zucchini Scramble

 Preparation:
5 Minutes

 Cooking:
20 Minutes

 Serves:
2

Ingredients

- 1/2 cup diced zucchini
- 1/4 cup chopped onions
- ¼ teaspoon ground black pepper
- 1 tablespoon thyme, chopped
- ½ teaspoon salt
- 1/2 cup chickpea flour
- 1 teaspoon olive oil
- 1/2 cup vegetable broth

Directions

1. Take a medium bowl, add chickpea flour and then whisk in broth until smooth.
2. Take a medium skillet pan, place it over medium-high heat, add oil and when hot, add onion and cook for 5 minutes.
3. Add zucchini, continue cooking for 5 minutes until vegetables begin to brown, and then season vegetables with black pepper, salt, and thyme and stir until mixed.
4. Then stir in chickpea flour mixture and cook for 5 to 10 minutes until cooked and mixture is no longer wet
5. Serve straight away

Nutritions: *Calories: 231 Cal, Fat: 4 g, Carbs: 40 g, Protein: 12 g, Fiber: 11 g*

Sweet Potato and Apple Latkes

Preparation:
5 Minutes

Cooking:
15 Minutes

Serves:
4

Ingredients

- 1 large sweet potato, peeled, grated
- 1/2 of medium white onion, diced
- 1 apple, peeled, cored, grated
- 2 tablespoons spelt flour
- 1 tablespoon arrowroot powder
- ½ teaspoon cracked black pepper
- 1 teaspoon salt
- 1 teaspoon turmeric
- 1 tablespoon olive oil and more for frying
- Tahini lemon drizzle, for serving

Directions

1. Wrap grated potato and apple in a cheesecloth, then squeeze moisture as much as possible and then place in a bowl.
2. Add remaining ingredients and then stir until combined.
3. Take a skillet pan, place it over medium-high heat, add oil and when hot, drop in prepared batter, shape them into a round patty and cook for 4 minutes per side until crispy and brown.
4. Serve latkes with Tahini lemon drizzle.

Nutritions: *Calories: 174.4 Cal, Fat: 9.5 g, Carbs: 18.5 g, Protein: 4.5 g, Fiber: 2.6 g*

Breakfast Tacos

 Preparation:
15 Minutes

 Cooking:
0 Minutes

 Serves:
4

Ingredients

For The Filling:
► 12 ounces of cooked black bean and tofu scramble
► For the Mango Pineapple Salsa:
► 1/3 cup diced tomatoes
► 1 medium shallot, peeled, diced
► ½ cup diced mango
► 1 jalapeno, deseeded, diced
► 2 teaspoon minced garlic
► ½ cup diced pineapple
► 1 tablespoon cilantro
► ¼ teaspoon cracked black pepper
► ¼ teaspoon salt
► 2 tablespoons lime juice

For The Tacos:
► 1 avocado, pitted, diced
► 4 small tortillas, warmed
► Chopped cilantro for garnish

Directions

1. Prepare salsa and for this, place all its ingredients in a bowl and stir until mixed.
2. Then prepare tofu scramble, distribute it evenly between tortillas and top evenly with prepared salsa and avocado.
3. Garnish with cilantro and serve.

Nutritions: *Calories: 283.6 Cal, Fat: 3.3 g, Carbs: 50.7 g, Protein: 13 g*

Enchilada Breakfast Casserole

Preparation:
10 Minutes

Cooking:
25 Minutes

Serves:
8

Ingredients

- 15 ounces cooked corn
- 1 batch of vegan breakfast eggs
- 15 ounces cooked pinto beans
- 3 medium zucchini, sliced into rounds
- 10 ounces of vegan cheddar cheese, shredded
- 24 ounces red enchilada sauce
- 12 corn tortillas, cut into wedges
- Shredded lettuce for serving
- Vegan sour cream for serving

Directions

1. Take a skillet pan, grease it with oil and press the vegan breakfast eggs into the bottom of the pan in an even layer.
2. Spread with 1/3 of enchilada sauce, then sprinkle with half of the cheese and cover with half of the tortilla wedges.
3. Cover the wedges with 1/3 of the sauce, then layer with beans, corn, and zucchini, cover with remaining tortilla wedges, and spread the remaining sauce on top.
4. Cover the pan with lid, place it over medium heat and cook for 25 minutes until cheese had melted, zucchini is tender, and sauce is bubbling.
5. When done, let the casserole stand for 10 minutes, top with lettuce and sour cream, then cut the casserole into wedges, and serve.

Nutritions: *Calories: 197.8 Cal, Fat: 8.9 g, Carbs: 15 g, Protein: 12 g, Fiber: 1.5 g*

Leeks Spread

Preparation:
5 Minutes

Cooking:
10 Minutes

Serves:
4

Ingredients

- 3 leeks, sliced
- 2 scallions, chopped
- 1 tablespoon avocado oil
- ¼ cup coconut cream
- Salt and black pepper to the taste
- ¼ teaspoon garlic powder
- ½ teaspoon thyme, dried
- 1 tablespoon cilantro, chopped

Directions

1. Heat up a pan with the oil over medium heat, add the scallions and the leeks and sauté for 5 minutes.
2. Add the rest of the ingredients, cook everything for 5 minutes more, blend using an immersion blender, divide into bowls and serve for breakfast.

Nutritions: *Calories 83, Fat 4.2, Fiber 2, Carbs 11.3, Protein 1.6*

Eggplant Spread

Preparation:
10 Minutes

Cooking:
25 Minutes

Serves:
4

Ingredients

- 1 pound eggplants
- 2 tablespoons olive oil
- 4 spring onions, chopped
- ½ teaspoon chili powder
- 1 tablespoon lime juice
- Salt and black pepper to the taste

Directions

1. Arrange the eggplants in a roasting pan and bake them at 400 degrees F for 25 minutes.
2. Peel the eggplants, put them in a blender, add the rest of the ingredients, pulse well, divide into bowls and serve for breakfast.

Nutritions: *Calories 97, Fat 7.3, Fiber 4.6, Carbs 8.9, Protein 1.5*

Eggplant and Broccoli Casserole

Preparation:
10 Minutes

Cooking:
35 Minutes

Serves:
4

Ingredients

- 1 pound eggplants, roughly cubed
- 1 cup broccoli florets
- 1 cup cashew cheese, shredded
- ¼ cup almond milk
- 2 scallions, chopped
- 1 tablespoon olive oil
- 2 tablespoons flaxseed mixed with 2 tablespoons water
- 1 tablespoon cilantro, chopped
- Salt and black pepper to the taste

Directions

1. In a roasting pan, combine the eggplants with the broccoli and the other ingredients except the cashew cheese and the almond milk and toss.
2. In a bowl, combine the milk with the cashew cheese, stir, pour over the eggplant mix, spread, introduce the pan in the oven and bake at 380 degrees F for 35 minutes.
3. Cool the casserole down, slice and serve.

Nutritions: *Calories 161, Fat 11.4, Fiber 6.6, Carbs 12.8, Protein 4.2*

Creamy Avocado and Nuts Bowls

 Preparation:
5 Minutes

 Cooking:
0 Minutes

 Serves:
4

Ingredients

- 1 tablespoon walnuts, chopped
- 1 tablespoon pine nuts, toasted
- 2 avocados, peeled, pitted and roughly cubed
- 1 tablespoon lime juice
- 1 tablespoon avocado oil
- Salt and black pepper to the taste
- ¼ cup coconut cream

Directions

1. In a bowl, combine the avocados with the nuts and the other ingredients, toss, divide into smaller bowls and serve for breakfast.

Nutritions: *Calories 273, Fat 26.3, Fiber 7.5, Carbs 11.1, Protein 3.1*

Avocado and Watermelon Salad

 Preparation:
5 Minutes

 Cooking:
0 Minutes

 Serves:
4

Ingredients

- 2 cups watermelon, peeled and roughly cubed
- 2 avocados, peeled, pitted and roughly cubed
- 1 tablespoon lime juice
- 1 tablespoon avocado oil
- ¼ cup almonds, chopped

Directions

1. In a bowl, combine the watermelon with the avocados and the other ingredients, toss and serve for breakfast.

Nutritions: *Calories 270, Fat 23.1, Fiber 3, Carbs 16.7, Protein 3.7*

Chia and Coconut Pudding

Preparation:
10 Minutes

Cooking:
0 Minutes

Serves:
4

Ingredients

- ¼ cup walnuts, chopped
- 2 cups coconut milk
- ¼ cup coconut flakes
- 3 tablespoons chia seeds
- 1 tablespoon stevia
- 1 teaspoon almond extract

Directions

1. In a bowl, combine the milk with the coconut flakes and the other ingredients, toss, leave aside for 10 minutes and serve for breakfast.

Nutritions: *Calories 414, Fat 39.2, Fiber 8.5, Carbs 14.3, Protein 7.1*

Chapter 6.
Dinner Meals to Fuel and Recover

Instant Savory Gigante Beans

Preparation:
55 Minutes

Serves:
6

Ingredients

- 1 lb Gigante Beans soaked overnight
- 1/2 cup olive oil
- 1 onion sliced
- 2 cloves garlic crushed or minced
- 1 red bell pepper (cut into 1/2-inch pieces)
- 2 carrots, sliced
- 1/2 tsp salt and ground black pepper
- 2 tomatoes peeled, grated
- 1 Tbsp celery (chopped)
- 1 Tbsp tomato paste (or ketchup)
- 3/4 tsp sweet paprika
- 1 tsp oregano
- 1 cup vegetable broth

Directions

1. Soak Gigante beans overnight.
2. Press SAUTÉ button on your Instant Pot and heat the oil.
3. Sauté onion, garlic, sweet pepper, carrots with a pinch of salt for 3 - 4 minutes; stir occasionally.
4. Add rinsed Gigante beans into your Instant Pot along with all remaining ingredients and stir well.
5. Lock lid into place and set on the MANUAL setting for 25 minutes.
6. When the beep sounds, quick release the pressure by pressing Cancel, and twisting the steam handle to the Venting position.
7. Taste and adjust seasonings to taste.
8. Serve warm or cold.
9. Keep refrigerated.

Nutritions: *Calories 502.45, Calories From Fat 173.16, Total Fat 19.63g , Saturated Fat 2.86g*

Instant Turmeric Risotto

Preparation:
40 Minutes

Serves:
4

Ingredients

- 4 Tbsp olive oil
- 1 cup onion
- 1 tsp minced garlic
- 2 cups long-grain rice
- 3 cups vegetable broth
- 1/2 tsp paprika (smoked)
- 1/2 tsp turmeric
- 1/2 tsp nutmeg
- 2 Tbsp fresh basil leaves chopped
- Salt and ground black pepper to taste

Directions

1. Press the SAUTÉ button on your Instant Pot and heat oil.
2. Sauté the onion and garlic with a pinch of salt until softened.
3. Add the rice and all remaining ingredients and stir well.
4. Lock lid into place and set on and select the "RICE" button for 10 minutes.
5. Press "Cancel" when the timer beeps and carefully flip the Quick Release valve to let the pressure out.
6. Taste and adjust seasonings to taste.
7. Serve.

Nutritions: *Calories 559.81, Calories From Fat 162.48, Total Fat 18.57g , Saturated Fat 2.4g*

Nettle Soup with Rice

Preparation:
40 Minutes

Serves:
5

Ingredients

- 3 Tbsp of olive oil
- 2 onions finely chopped
- 2 cloves garlic finely chopped
- Salt and freshly ground black pepper
- 4 medium potatoes cut into cubes
- 1 cup of rice
- 1 Tbsp arrowroot
- 2 cups vegetable broth
- 2 cups of water
- 1 bunch of young nettle leaves packed
- 1/2 cup fresh parsley finely chopped
- 1 tsp cumin

Directions

1. Heat olive oil in a large pot.
2. Sauté onion and garlic with a pinch of salt until softened.
3. Add potato, rice, and arrowroot; sauté for 2 to 3 minutes.
4. Pour broth and water, stir well, cover and cook over medium heat for about 20 minutes.
5. Cook over medium heat for about 20 minutes.
6. Add young nettle leaves, parsley, and cumin; stir and cook for 5 to 7 minutes.
7. Transfer the soup in a blender and blend until combined well.
8. Taste and adjust salt and pepper.
9. Serve hot.

Nutritions: *Calories 421.76, Calories From Fat 88.32, Total Fat 9.8g , Saturated Fat 1.54g*

Okra with Grated Tomatoes (Slow Cooker)Cooker)

Preparation:
3 h 10 minutes

Serves:
4

Directions

1. Add okra in your Crock-Pot: sprinkle with a pinch of salt and pepper.
2. Add in chopped onion, garlic, carrots, and grated tomatoes; stir well.
3. Pour water and oil, season with the salt, pepper, and give a good stir.
4. Cover and cook on LOW for 2-3 hours or until tender.
5. Open the lid and add fresh parsley; stir.
6. Taste and adjust salt and pepper.
7. Serve hot.

Ingredients

- ▶ 2 lbs fresh okra cleaned
- ▶ 2 onions finely chopped
- ▶ 2 cloves garlic finely sliced
- ▶ 2 carrots sliced
- ▶ 2 ripe tomatoes grated
- ▶ 1 cup of water
- ▶ 4 Tbsp olive oil
- ▶ Salt and ground black pepper
- ▶ 1 Tbsp fresh parsley finely chopped

Nutritions: *Calories 223.47, Calories From Fat 123.5, Total Fat 14g, Saturated Fat 1.96g*

Oven-baked Smoked Lentil 'Burgers'

Preparation:
1 h 20 min

Serves:
6

Directions

1. Cook lentils in salted water until tender or for about 30-35 minutes; rinse, drain, and set aside.
2. Heat oil in a frying skillet and sauté onion, garlic and mushrooms for 4 to 5 minutes; stir occasionally.
3. Stir in the tomato paste, salt, basil, salt, and black pepper; cook for 2 to 3 minutes.
4. Stir in almonds, vinegar, coconut aminos, liquid smoke, and lentils.
5. Remove from heat and stir in blended tofu and corn starch.
6. Keep stirring until all ingredients combined well.
7. Form mixture into patties and refrigerate for an hour.
8. Preheat oven to 350 F.
9. Line a baking dish with parchment paper and arrange patties on the pan.
10. Bake for 20 to 25 minutes.
11. Serve hot with buns, green salad, tomato sauce...etc.

Ingredients

- 1 1/2 cups dried lentils
- 3 cups of water
- Salt and ground black pepper to taste
- 2 Tbsp olive oil
- 1 onion finely diced
- 2 cloves minced garlic
- 1 cup button mushrooms sliced
- 2 Tbsp tomato paste
- 1/2 tsp fresh basil finely chopped
- 1 cup chopped almonds
- 3 tsp balsamic vinegar
- 3 Tbsp coconut aminos
- 1 tsp liquid smoke
- 3/4 cup silken tofu soft
- 3/4 cup corn starch

Nutritions: *Calories 439.12, Calories From Fat 148.97, Total Fat 17.48g, Saturated Fat 1.71g*

Powerful Spinach and Mustard Leaves Puree

 Preparation:
50 Minutes

 Serves:
4

Ingredients

- 2 Tbsp almond butter
- 1 onion finely diced
- 2 Tbsp minced garlic
- 1 tsp salt and black pepper (or to taste)
- 1 lb mustard leaves, cleaned rinsed
- 1 lb frozen spinach thawed
- 1 tsp coriander
- 1 tsp ground cumin
- 1/2 cup almond milk

Directions

1. Press the SAUTÉ button on your Instant Pot and heat the almond butter.
2. Sauté onion, garlic, and a pinch of salt for 2-3 minutes; stir occasionally.
3. Add spinach and the mustard greens and stir for a minute or two.
4. Season with the salt and pepper, coriander, and cumin; give a good stir.
5. Lock lid into place and set on the MANUAL setting for 15 minutes.
6. Use Quick Release - turn the valve from sealing to venting to release the pressure.
7. Transfer mixture to a blender, add almond milk and blend until smooth.
8. Taste and adjust seasonings.
9. Serve.

Nutritions: *Calories 180.53, Calories From Fat 82.69, Total Fat 10g, Saturated Fat 0.65g*

Quinoa and Rice Stuffed Peppers (oven-baked)

Preparation:
35 Minutes

Serves:
8

Ingredients

- 3/4 cup long-grain rice
- 8 bell peppers (any color)
- 2 Tbsp olive oil
- 1 onion finely diced
- 2 cloves chopped garlic
- 1 can (11 oz) crushed tomatoes
- 1 tsp cumin
- 1 tsp coriander
- 4 Tbsp ground walnuts
- 2 cups cooked quinoa
- 4 Tbsp chopped parsley
- Salt and ground black pepper to taste

Directions

1. Preheat oven to 400 F/200 C.
2. Boil rice and drain in a colander.
3. Cut the top stem section of the pepper off, remove the remaining pith and seeds, rinse peppers.
4. Heat oil in a large frying skillet, and sauté onion and garlic until soft.
5. Add tomatoes, cumin, ground almonds, salt, pepper, and coriander; stir well and simmer for 2 minutes stirring constantly.
6. Remove from the heat and add the rice, quinoa, and parsley; stir well.
7. Taste and adjust salt and pepper.
8. Fill the peppers with a mixture, and place peppers cut side-up in a baking dish; drizzle with little oil.
9. Bake for 15 minutes.
10. Serve warm.

Nutritions: *Calories 335.69, Calories From Fat 83.63, Total Fat 9.58g, Saturated Fat 1.2g*

VEGAN COOKBOOK FOR ATHLETES

Quinoa and Lentils with Crushed Tomato

Preparation:
35 Minutes

Serves:
4

Ingredients

- 4 Tbsp olive oil
- 1 medium onion, diced
- 2 garlic clove, minced
- Salt and ground black pepper to taste
- 1 can (15 oz) tomatoes crushed
- 1 cup vegetable broth
- 1/2 cup quinoa, washed and drained
- 1 cup cooked lentils
- 1 tsp chili powder
- 1 tsp cumin

Directions

1. Heat oil in a pot and sauté the onion and garlic with the pinch of salt until soft.
2. Pour reserved tomatoes and vegetable broth, bring to boil, and stir well.
3. Stir in the quinoa, cover and cook for 15 minutes; stir occasionally.
4. Add in lentils, chili powder, and cumin; cook for further 5 minutes.
5. Taste and adjust seasonings.
6. Serve immediately.
7. Keep refrigerated in a covered container for 4 - 5 days.

Nutritions: *Calories 397.45, Calories From Fat 138.18, Total Fat 15.61g, Saturated Fat 2.14g*

Silk Tofu Penne with Spinach

Preparation:
25 Minutes

Serves:
4

Ingredients

- 1 lb penne, uncooked
- 12 oz of frozen spinach, thawed
- 1 cup silken tofu mashed
- 1/2 cup soy milk (unsweetened)
- 1/2 cup vegetable broth
- 1 Tbsp white wine vinegar
- 1/2 tsp Italian seasoning
- Salt and ground pepper to taste

Directions

1. Cook penne pasta; rinse and drain in a colander.
2. Drain spinach well.
3. Place spinach with all remaining ingredients in a blender and beat until smooth.
4. Pour the spinach mixture over pasta.
5. Taste and adjust the salt and pepper.
6. Store pasta in an airtight container in the refrigerator for 3 to 5 days.

Nutritions: *Calories 492.8, Calories From Fat 27.06, Total Fat 3.07g, Saturated Fat 0.38g*

Slow-Cooked Butter Beans, Okra and Potatoes Stew

 Preparation:
6 h 5 min

 Serves:
6

Directions

1. Combine all ingredients in your Slow Cooker; give a good stir.
2. Cover and cook on HIGH for 6 hours.
3. Taste, adjust seasonings, and serve hot.

Ingredients

- 2 cups frozen butter (lima) beans, thawed
- 1 cup frozen okra, thawed
- 2 large Russet potatoes cut into cubes
- 1 can (6 oz) whole-kernel corn, drained
- 1 large carrot sliced
- 1 green bell pepper finely chopped
- 1 cup green peas
- 1/2 cup chopped celery
- 1 medium onion finely chopped
- 2 cups vegetable broth
- 2 cans (6 oz) tomato sauce
- 1 cup of water
- 1/2 tsp salt and freshly ground black pepper

Nutritions: *Calories 241.71, Calories From Fat 11.22, Total Fat 1.28g, Saturated Fat 0.27g*

Soya Minced Stuffed Eggplants

Preparation:
1 h

Serves:
4

Ingredients

- 2 eggplants
- 1/3 cup sesame oil
- 1 onion finely chopped
- 2 garlic cloves minced
- 1 lb soya mince* see note
- Salt and ground black pepper
- 1/3 cup almond milk
- 2 Tbsp fresh parsley, chopped
- 1/3 cup fresh basil chopped
- 1 tsp fennel powder
- 1 cup of water
- 4 Tbsp tomato paste (fresh or canned)

Directions

1. Rinse and slice the eggplant in half lengthwise.
2. Submerge sliced eggplant into a container with salted water.
3. Soak soya mince in water for 10 to 15 minutes.
4. Preheat oven to 400 F.
5. Rinse eggplant and dry with a clean towel.
6. Heat oil in large frying skillet, and sauté onion and garlic with a pinch of salt until softened.
7. Add drained soya mince, and cook over medium heat until cooked through.
8. Add all remaining ingredients (except water and tomato paste) and cook for a further 5 minutes; remove from heat.
9. Scoop out the seed part of each eggplant.
10. Spoon in the filling and arrange stuffed eggplants onto the large baking dish.
11. Dissolve tomato paste into the water and pour evenly over eggplants.
12. Bake for 20 to 25 minutes.
13. Serve warm.

Nutritions: *Calories 287.32, Calories From Fat 141.77, Total Fat 16.42g, Saturated Fat 2.02g*

Triple Beans and Corn Salad

Preparation:
15 Minutes

Serves:
8

Directions

1. In a large bowl, combine beans, corn, pepper, onion, and garlic.
2. Season salad with the salt and pepper; stir to combine well.
3. In a separate bowl, whisk together olive oil, red wine vinegar, lemon juice, cilantro, and cumin.
4. Pour olive oil dressing over salad, and toss to combine well.
5. Refrigerate for one hour and serve.

Ingredients

- 1 can (15 oz) kidney beans, drained and rinsed
- 1 can (15 oz) white beans, drained and rinsed
- 1 can (15 oz) black beans, rinsed and drained
- 1 can (11 oz) frozen corn kernels thawed
- 1 green bell pepper, chopped
- 1 red onion, chopped
- 1 clove crushed garlic
- 1 Tbsp salt and ground black pepper to taste
- 1/2 cup olive oil
- 3 Tbsp red wine vinegar
- 3 Tbsp lemon juice
- 1/4 cup chopped fresh cilantro
- 1/2 Tbsp ground cumin

Nutritions: *Calories 696, Calories From Fat 155.25, Total Fat 17.62g, Saturated Fat 3g*

Vegan Raw Pistachio Flaxseed 'Burgers'

Preparation:
15 Minutes

Serves:
4

Directions

1. Add all ingredients into a food processor or high-speed blender; process until combined well.
2. Form mixture into patties.
3. Refrigerate for one hour.
4. Serve with your favorite vegetable dip.

Ingredients

- 1 cup ground flaxseed
- 1 cup pistachio finely sliced
- 2 cups cooked spinach drained
- 2 Tbsp sesame oil
- 4 cloves garlic finely sliced
- 2 Tbsp lemon juice, freshly squeezed
- Sea salt to taste

Nutritions: *Calories 273, Calories From Fat 184.41, Total Fat 21.6g, Saturated Fat 2.72g*

Vegan Red Bean 'Fricassee'

Preparation:
40 Minutes

Serves:
4

Ingredients

- 4 Tbsp olive oil
- 1 onion finely sliced
- 2 cloves garlic finely chopped
- Salt and freshly ground black pepper to taste
- 1 can (15 oz) red beans
- 1 large carrot grated
- 1 1/2 cup vegetable broth
- 1 cup of water
- 1 can (6 oz) tomato paste
- 1 tsp ground paprika
- 1 tsp parsley

Directions

1. Heat oil in a large pot and sauté onion and garlic with a pinch of salt until soft.
2. Add red beans together with all remaining ingredients and stir well.
3. In a separate pan, sauté onion and garlic in the olive oil.
4. Reduce heat to medium, and simmer for 25 to 30 minutes.
5. Taste and adjust salt and pepper if needed.
6. Serve hot.

Nutritions: *Calories 318.72, Calories From Fat 136.25, Total Fat 15.44g, Saturated Fat 2.31g*

Chapter 7. Get Your Green with Salads and Dressings

Strawberry-Pistacho Salad

There are essentials to a strawberry plate of mixed greens, yet like a serving of mixed greens, nearly anything goes. Here is a rundown of the nuts and bolts, with a couple of tips to make your pistachio plate of mixed greens the best one on the table!

Lettuce: Use lettuce, green or red leaf.

Berries: Strawberries can be swapped with any sort of berry.

Pistachios: Use almonds, pecans or walnuts instead of pistachios.

A Perfect Strawberry Salad

For an extremely beautiful strawberry plate of mixed greens, keep the lettuce equally hacked or torn, cut the berries and green onions.

To include additional flavor, broil the pistachios (and all nuts) in a little dish until they are scarcely carmelized and fragrant. Enable them to cool totally before adding to this serving of mixed greens. Cooking nuts makes them crunchier and truly improves their flavor!

A bowl of pistachio strawberry plate of mixed greens loaded up with crisp fixings like feta, cranberries, quinoa, and lettuce.

To Make Strawberry Salad:

Cook quinoa and put in a safe spot, ensure it is completely cooled before adding to the plate of mixed greens.

Consolidate dressing fixings and refrigerate.

Include cooled quinoa, cut strawberries, cranberries, cut green onions, and cleaved, simmered pistachios and disintegrated feta cheddar.

Sprinkle dressing over the plate of mixed greens, hurl delicately and serve right away.

A hand pouring the vinaigrette over the pistachio strawberry serving of mixed greens.

What Goes Best With This Salad?

Bread garnishes go extraordinary on this serving of mixed greens to give it some additional crunch. Be that as it may, a side of meagerly cut garlic bread or wafers likewise functions admirably!

This is unquestionably a plate of mixed greens that can remain without anyone else as an entrée, yet if it's filled in as a side, it goes extraordinary with pork cleaves or flame broiled chicken bosoms new off the barbecue!

Progressively Delicious Side Salad Recipes

(In the event that you can't choose)

Caesar Salad – constantly an incredible alternative

Dark Bean Quinoa Salad – sound!

Chickpea Salad – overly invigorating

Cobb Salad – a work of art

Tomato Avocado Salad – incredible in the late spring!

Pistachio Strawberry Salad

Planning TIME 20 minutes

Complete TIME 20 minutes

SERVINGS 6 servings

Creator Holly Nilsson

COURSE Salad, Side Dish

Cooking American

This pistachio strawberry plate of mixed greens is such a tasty summer dish!

Fixings

1 lb strawberries

6 cups leaf lettuce washed

3/4 cup cooked quinoa

1/4 cup dried cranberries

3 green onions

1/3 cup cooked pistachios

1/3 cup feta cheddar disintegrated

Dressing

1/4 cup juice vinegar

3 tablespoons maple syrup

2 tablespoons dijon mustard

1/2 teaspoon crisp basil slashed

1/4 teaspoon garlic powder

1/2 teaspoon each salt and pepper

1/2 cup vegetable oil

Guidelines

Join all dressing fixings in a container with a tight fitting top. Shake well and refrigerate.

Add all fixings to an enormous bowl, sprinkle with dressing and hurl well.

Strawberries have a place in plates of mixed greens. Would i be able to get a so be it?!

They additionally have a place with pistachios. It's a match made in foodie paradise. Blend it in with some avocado and you will start to feel as if life is great. Totally flawless simply the manner in which it is. Presently finish everything off with some feta and your mind will be completely blown. You could likewise go the course of goat cheddar if you want. What's more, I'm somewhat believing that if you love goat cheddar then you totally need to do it.

Strawberry Avocado and Pistachio Salad with a Creamy Poppyseed Dressing. All the best flavors join in this serving of mixed greens. Child spinach stacked up with delicious new strawberries, salty pistachios and smooth avocado. Sprinkle everything with a simple to make and lighter poppyseed dressing.

I sense that I've been in my very own reality recently. Cut off from web based life and blog life. Despite the fact that it's just been a couple of days that I've been marginally MIA. I have a feeling that I'm totally unware of present circumstances and off track. 38 weeks pregnant, and think about what was the deal? A channel burst in the mass of our home. Where? Directly by the little children room and where the infant will be dozing in the blink of an eye. Obviously right?

So it's been a hurricane of individuals coming over and giving appraisals, fixing things, tearing up ground surface, setting up around 10 fans. I can't recollect what life resembles without the consistent murmuring (noisy murmuring) of fans as they dry the dividers and the planks of flooring.

Homeownership right? Welcome to it. The centers and I just purchased this house around 3 months prior. It's our first large issue we've needed to manage. I'd state other than me simply being lacking in persistence because of pregnancy we've dealt with it well. What's more, the little children have done well with being migrated since their room is as of now destroyed.

Strawberry Avocado and Pistachio Salad with a Creamy Poppyseed Dressing. All the best flavors join in this plate of mixed greens. Child spinach stacked up with succulent crisp strawberries, salty pistachios and velvety avocado. Shower everything with a simple to make and lighter poppyseed dressing.

Despite everything i've been cooking, swollen lower legs what not. A young lady needs to eat right?

Additionally cutting foods grown from the ground into clumsily thin cuts is strangely quieting to me at the present time. Taking as much time as is needed to layer my avocado just so gives me a feeling of achievement and euphoria.

Also simply taking a gander at the strawberries fulfills me to be alive.

Strawberry Avocado and Pistachio Salad with a Creamy Poppyseed Dressing. All the best flavors join in this plate of mixed greens. Infant spinach stacked up with delicious crisp strawberries, salty pistachios and rich avocado. Sprinkle everything with a simple to make and lighter poppyseed dressing.

The rich poppyseed dressing on this plate of mixed greens is like the poppyseed dressing that I utilized on my other Strawberry Salad with Poppyseed Dressing. (what is it with me and strawberries in my serving of mixed greens?)

However, this dressing is made lighter by utilizing yogurt to make it velvety, and I cut out the sugar and utilized Agave. You could likewise utilize nectar, however you will see a slight nectar taste. Which is fine by me and I'm certain you would concur that nectar is essentially unadulterated bliss in a jug.

The salty pistachios matched with the delicious strawberries and velvety avocado sprinkled with the sweet and tart poppyseed dressing is sufficient to cause me to disregard the way that my home is truly destroyed and that I have an infant coming in about fourteen days or less.

Classic Kale Salad

My work of art, go-to, made-it-a-million-times Every day Kale Salad. ♡

This plate of mixed greens is made with five straightforward fixings — super-delicate crisp kale (see tips underneath), naturally crushed lemon juice, lotsa Parm, a shower of olive oil, and a sprinkling of your preferred nuts. What's more, I'm letting you know, it is delightful.

I've been making some rendition of this kale plate of mixed greens for about 10 years now, and even the most hesitant kale eaters in my life have constantly adored this one. It's anything but difficult to prepare in no time flat. It's anything but difficult to gussy up with some other most loved plate of mixed greens include ins you may have as a top priority. (<–Just sayin', a cut avocado in there will never be a poorly conceived notion.) And the best part is that this kale plate of mixed greens formula truly goes with pretty much everything!

So if you're searching for a super-basic and solid side serving of mixed greens to go with supper today around evening time, get some crisp kale and check out it!

Kale Salad Ingredients

Ordinary KALE SALAD INGREDIENTS:

To make this simple kale plate of mixed greens formula, you will require:

New kale: Any sort will work here, for example, wavy kale or dinosaur (lacinato) kale.

Parmesan: Freshly-ground, it would be ideal if you Don't hesitate to utilize the coarse side of your grater (like what I have captured underneath) or the super fine side of the grater — or both! ♡

Lemon juice: Freshly-pressed, if you don't mind If you don't have a great juicer as of now, I'm fixated on this one.

Olive oil: Good-quality additional virgin.

Nuts: I like including some toasted cut or fragmented almonds to this serving of mixed greens for a touch of additional crunch and protein. Be that as it may, don't hesitate to include whatever different nuts or seeds you love best, or skip them completely.

Salt and Pepper: A great sprinkling of each to season and complete this serving of mixed greens.

The most effective method to Make Kale Salad

You know the drill! To make those extreme kale leaves pleasant and delicate, they need a speedy back rub before we include different fixings. So once you have evacuated and disposed of those extreme kale stems (you can either cut them off with a knife, or expel them by running your fingers down the stems), proceed and generally cleave the kale as finely as you might want. Then add it to an enormous blending bowl, sprinkle with a couple glugs of olive oil, and afterward get your hands in there and rub the kale simply like you would massage mixture. I commonly knead my kale for 1-2 minutes, so it doesn't get excessively soft. In any case, simply continue rubbing until the kale arrives at your ideal degree of freshness.

Simple Kale Salad Recipe

The most effective method to MAKE KALE SALAD:

To make this kale plate of mixed greens formula, essentially...

Back rub the kale. With olive oil, as coordinated above, in an enormous blending bowl.

Include the rest of the fixings. Lemon juice, Parmesan and nuts. Hurl until equitably consolidated.

Season. Give the serving of mixed greens a taste and season

with ocean salt and newly split pepper, to taste. (I suggest loads of dark pepper, particularly.)

Serve. Then serve it up immediately while it's pleasant and new!

Kale Salad Recipe with Parmesan and Almonds

Potential VARIATIONS:

While this base kale plate of mixed greens formula is too straightforward, there are a wide range of heavenly fixings that you can include or sub in too. For instance, don't hesitate to...

Include a protein: Cooked chicken, steak, or tofu would all be incredible added to this serving of mixed greens.

Include new veggies: Such as cucumber, carrots, as well as red onion.

Include new or dried organic product: Such as new apples, berries, grapefruit, grapes. Or then again dried cranberries or apricots.

Include jostled veggies: Such as sun-dried tomato, broiled red peppers, or artichoke hearts.

Include beans: Such as chickpeas or white beans.

Include bread garnishes: Homemade or locally acquired.

Utilize a different cheddar: In lieu of Parmesan, don't hesitate to include disintegrated blue cheddar, feta cheddar or goat cheddar.

Utilize different nuts/seeds: Such as pepitas, pine nuts, pecans, walnuts or sunflower seeds.

This simple kale plate of mixed greens formula just takes 5 minutes to make with 5 simple fixings, and tastes extraordinary with pretty much everything! Don't hesitate to alter the extents of any of the fixings beneath, to taste, and see notes above for discretionary fixing include ins as well.

Fixings

1 bundle (around 5 ounces) kale, generally cleaved with extreme stems disposed of

2 tablespoons olive oil

2 tablespoons crisply pressed lemon juice

1/2 cup destroyed Parmesan cheddar

1/3 cup cut almonds, toasted

ocean salt and crisply crushed dark pepper

Directions

Add the kale to a huge blending bowl and sprinkle equitably with the olive oil. Utilizing your fingers, rub the oil into the kale for 1-2 minutes until the kale has softened.

Include the lemon juice, Parmesan and almonds. Hurl until uniformly consolidated.

Taste and season with anyway a lot of salt and dark pepper that you'd like, then hurl again until consolidated.

Serve promptly and appreciate!

Confetti Quinoa Salad

Fixings

1 cup uncooked quinoa

1 little to medium-sized head radicchio, cored and finely hacked (to yield around 2 cups)

6-ounce sack infant spinach, finely cleaved

3/4 cup sun-dried tomatoes, finely hacked

1/2 - 3/4 cup ground parmesan cheddar (see note)

1/2 cup finely hacked crisp basil

1/2 cup decreased fat feta cheddar

1/4 cup pine nuts, toasted

2 cloves garlic, minced

1/4 cup finely hacked kalamata olives, discretionary

1/4 cup balsamic vinegar (or white balsamic – see note)

2 tablespoons extra-virgin olive oil

1 teaspoon legitimate salt

1/2 teaspoon ground dark pepper

Bearings

Get ready quinoa as indicated by bundle bearings. In the wake of cooking, permit to cool totally and lighten with a fork.

In an enormous bowl, join cooled quinoa, radicchio, spinach, tomatoes, parmesan, basil, feta, pine nuts, garlic, and olives (if utilizing). Mix to join.

In a little bowl, whisk together vinegar, olive oil, salt and pepper. Pour over quinoa blend and mix completely to join.

Chill until serving.

Formula Notes

Parmesan: The flavor profile and decisiveness of parmesan can fluctuate strikingly relying upon the brand and quality, and that can truly affect the last kind of this plate of mixed greens. Contingent upon the kind of your parmesan and whether you're including the olives, you will probably require just ½ cup of parmesan. In any case, if your parmesan isn't exactly as delightful, you may require the additional piece of salty-tang from the full ¾ cup of cheddar. We suggest that you start with the more unassuming ½ cup and perceive how you like the taste – you can generally include more if you pick.

Balsamic Vinegar: For the motivations behind introduction, white (or brilliant) balsamic yields a prettier and all the more dynamically shaded serving of mixed greens because it doesn't tinge different fixings with the darker shade of common balsamic vinegar. If customary balsamic is all you have close by, however, unquestionably simply utilize that – the serving of mixed greens will in any case be exquisite and will taste similarly as awesome.

Make-Ahead Option: This plate of mixed greens can without much of a stretch be made a day or two ahead and refrigerated until serving.

Winter Sunshine Salad

Fixings

2 little fennel bulbs, cored and meagerly cut

2 ruby red grapefruits, suprêmed and juice held (see Tip)

2 cups (140 g) destroyed red cabbage

1 red or orange chime pepper, daintily cut

1 tablespoon

new lime juice Salt and dark pepper

½ cup (30 g) slashed cilantro

1 avocado, diced or cut

¼ cup (30 g) pecan pieces

Directions

Consolidate the fennel, grapefruit portions and squeeze, cabbage, ringer pepper, and lime squeeze in a huge bowl. Season with salt and pepper to taste, then hurl to consolidate. (Now, you can refrigerate the plate of mixed greens medium-term.)

When prepared to serve, add the cilantro and hurl to com-bine. Partition into bowls, then separation avocado and pecans uniformly between plates of mixed greens.

NOTES

TIP: The key to strip free citrus portions is a procedure called suprêming. To suprême citrus, cut off the two finishes just until the substance is uncovered. Beginning at the top, utilize a paring knife to cut the skin and white substance off, expelling as meager tissue as could be allowed. Hold the organic product in your nondominant hand and make shallow vertical cuts between each section, along the characteristic divisions. Do this over a bowl to get any juices. Dispose of any seeds just as the center part and the layer that isolates the portions

This food is light and reviving with a collection of winter greens, crunchy veggies and regular organic product. It's topped with a sweet and tart dressing made with clementines and nectar, and makes the ideal side plate of mixed greens for cold winter nighttimes!

This post was initially distributed in January 201It has been refreshed with new photographs and content, including supportive tips for perusers. The formula has likewise been changed in accordance with utilize all the more regularly proper fixings. A photograph of the past rendition of this plate of mixed greens is incorporated toward the finish of this post.

Overhead perspective on Winter Salad in a huge dark bowl and bested with Citrus Honey Dressing.

It's the second seven day stretch of January and the brief days, cold breeze and persistent snow are as of now finding a workable pace. That is to say, I love the periodic virus evening where I can twist up by the fire in a comfortable cover and taste on a sweltering cup of tea, yet can we simply have somewhat more sunlight and daylight?

Without sun, this winter citrus plate of mixed greens has been my little beam of daylight. When citrus season hits, this straightforward plate of mixed greens is a staple in our home, and the orange nectar dressing goes on pretty much every serving of mixed greens.

WHY YOU'LL LOVE THIS SUNSHINE SALAD FOR WINTER TOO:

It's very easy to make. Simply mix up the dressing, collect the fixings and hurl.

You need only a bunch of elements for both the serving of mixed greens and dressing.

It's absolutely adjustable. Utilize the winter foods grown from the ground you have close by.

Fixings to make Winter Salad masterminded on a wooden surface.

Fixings TO MAKE THIS WINTER SALAD WITH CITRUS:

For the serving of mixed greens:

Spinach

Red cabbage

Carrot

Clementines

Blood orange

Kiwi organic product

Goat cheddar

For the dressing:

Clementines

Nectar

Red wine vinegar

Additional virgin olive oil

Parsley

Destroyed carrot and red cabbage on a plate alongside a container of dressing.

Directions: to MAKE THIS WINTER FRUIT AND VEGGIE SALAD:

To begin with, make your dressing. Simply include the entirety of the fixings, aside from the parsley, to your blender and mix on high until all around consolidated. Fill a container or glass dish, mix in the parsley, and cover and refrigerate until prepared to utilize.

Next, include the entirety of the serving of mixed greens fixings to a huge bowl. Shower on the ideal measure of dressing and hurl to join. Serve right away

Every now and again ASKED QUESTIONS:

How would you store citrus nectar dressing? Since the dressing contains puréed clementines, it ought to be put away in the fridge. The dressing will solidify a little, so simply let it sit at room temperature for a couple of moments and afterward shake or mix it before utilizing.

To what extent will the dressing last? If put away appropriately, this dressing should keep going for 2-3 days.

Would you be able to make this plate of mixed greens ahead of time? As referenced, the dressing can be made ahead of time and put away in the cooler. You can likewise set up your foods grown from the ground ahead of time and store in the cooler. In any case, to maintain a strategic distance from a shriveled plate of mixed greens, you should stand by to join the fixings and hurl with the goat cheddar and dressing until just before serving.

Extra TIPS AND SUGGESTIONS FOR MAKING CITRUS SALAD WITH HONEY DRESSING:

If you don't have spinach, kale is another healthy winter green that functions admirably in this serving of mixed greens.

I included kiwi natural product, yet you can utilize other winter organic product, for example, persimmons or pomegranate arils.

You can switch up the citrus component by utilizing grapefruit or different assortments of oranges, for example, cara.

While I utilized clementines in the dressing, you can likewise utilize oranges or tangerines. Simply ensure whatever you utilize is seedless.

To make it an all the more filling plate of mixed greens, include some chicken or sprinkle a few nuts, for example, pecans, almonds or pistachios.

When causing the dressing, to make certain to include the parsley after the dressing is mixed. If you mix it in, your dressing will be tinted green.

To make this plate of mixed greens sans dairy, simply forget about the goat cheddar.

Fixings to make Winter Salad organized in an enormous bowl beside a container of dressing and goat cheddar..

WHAT DO YOU EAT WITH A WINTER SALAD:

Pair it with a generous quiche or egg heat for early lunch.

Add it to supper nearby these turkey burgers or this salmon quinoa prepare.

Appreciate it all alone for lunch. Simply include some protein, for example, chicken, shrimp or salmon to make it a full supper.

OTHER CITRUSY SALADS YOU MIGHT ENJOY:

Grapefruit Salad with Cilantro and Goat Cheese is tart and reviving with blended greens, herbs and velvety goat cheddar, all beat with a citrus cilantro dressing.

Citrus Crunch Salad is a more advantageous adaptation of coleslaw with crunchy veggies and pecans, disintegrated blue cheddar and a tart citrus vinaigrette.

For the dressing:

2 clementines, stripped and isolated into pieces (around 1 cup)

1/4 cup nectar

2 tablespoons red wine vinegar

2 tablespoons additional virgin olive oil

2 teaspoons dried parsley

For the serving of mixed greens:

6 cups infant spinach, stuffed

1 cup destroyed carrot

1 cup destroyed red cabbage

2 clementines, stripped and isolated into pieces

2 kiwi organic product, stripped and cut

1 blood orange, cut

1/4 cup disintegrated goat cheddar

Guidelines

Make the dressing: Add all the dressing fixings to a blender, aside from the parsley, and mix on high until all around consolidated. The dressing will be thick. Mix in the parsley. Fill a dish or container with a top and store in the cooler.

Collect the serving of mixed greens: In a huge bowl, include the entirety of the plate of mixed greens fixings, sprinkle on the ideal measure of dressing and hurl to join. Serve right away.

Chapter 8.
Food Before, During and After Workouts

Crunchy Granola

Preparation:
10 Minutes

Cooking:
20 Minutes

Serves:
1

Skill:
Beginner

Ingredients

► ½ cup Oats
► Dash of Salt
► 2 tbsp. Vegetable Oil
► 3 tbsp. Maple Syrup
► 1/3 cup Apple Cider Vinegar
► ½ cup Almonds
► 1 tsp. Cardamom, grounded

Directions

1. Preheat the oven to 375 ˚F.
2. After that, mix oats, pistachios, salt, and cardamom in a large bowl.
3. Next, spoon in the vegetable oil and maple syrup to the mixture.
4. Then, transfer the mixture to a parchment-paper-lined baking sheet.
5. Bake them for 13 minutes or until the mixture is toasted. Tip: Check on them now and then. Spread it out well.
6. Return the sheet to the oven for further ten minutes.
7. Remove the sheet from the oven and allow it to cool completely.
8. Serve and enjoy.

Tip: If you desire, you can even add seeds to it like chia seeds or flax seeds, etc.

Nutritions: *Calories: 763Kcal, Proteins: 12.9g, Carbohydrates: 64.8g, Fat: 52.4g*

Chocolate Almond Bars

Preparation:
10 Minutes

Cooking:
20 Minutes

Serves:
12 bars

Skill:
Beginner

Ingredients

- 1 cup Almonds
- 1 ½ cup Rolled Oats
- 1/3 cup Maple Syrup
- ¼ tsp. Sea Salt
- 5 oz. Protein Powder
- 1 tsp. Cinnamon

Directions

1. For making these delicious vegan bars, you first need to place ¾ cup of the almonds and salt in the food processor.
2. Process them for a minute or until you get them in the form of almond butter.
3. Now, stir in the rest of the ingredients to the processor and process them again until smooth.
4. Next, transfer the mixture to a greased parchment paper-lined baking sheet and spread it across evenly.
5. Press them slightly down with the back of the spoon.
6. Chop down the remaining ¼ cup of the almonds and top it across the mixture.
7. Finally, place them in the refrigerator for 20 minutes or until set.

Tip: You can add chocolate chips to it if desired. If adding, melt them in the microwave until melted and then pour it above the bars before placing it in the refrigerator.

Nutritions: *Calories: 166cal, Proteins: 12.8g, Carbohydrates: 17.6g, Fat: 6g*

Flax Crackers

 Preparation:
5 Minutes

 Cooking:
60 Minutes

 Serves:
4-6

 Skill:
Beginner

Ingredients

- 1 cup Flaxseeds, whole
- 2 cups Water
- ¾ cup Flaxseeds, grounded
- 1 tsp. Sea Salt
- ½ cup Chia Seeds
- 1 tsp. Black Pepper
- ½ cup Sunflower Seeds

Directions

1. First, place all the ingredients in a large mixing bowl and mix them well. Soak them for 10 to 15 minutes.
2. After that, transfer the mixture to a parchment paper-lined baking sheet and spread it evenly. Tip: Make sure the paper lines the edges as well.
3. Next, bake it for 60 minutes at 350 °F.
4. Once the time is up, flip the entire bar and take off the parchment paper.
5. Bake for half an hour or until it becomes crispy and browned.
6. Allow it to cool completely and then break it down.

Tip: You can pair it with hummus or with dips.

Nutritions: *Calories: 251cal, Proteins: 9.2g, Carbohydrates: 14.9g, Fat: 16g*

Chocolate Protein Bites

Preparation:
10 Minutes

Cooking:
20 Minutes

Serves:
12 bites

Skill:
Beginner

Ingredients

- ½ cup Chocolate Protein Powder
- 1 Avocado, medium
- 1 tbsp. Chocolate Chips
- 1 tbsp. Almond Butter
- 1 tbsp. Cocoa Powder
- 1 tsp. Vanilla Extract
- Dash of Salt

Directions

1. Begin by blending avocado, almond butter, vanilla extract, and salt in a high-speed blender until you get a smooth mixture.
2. Next, spoon in the protein powder, cocoa powder, and chocolate chips to the blender.
3. Blend again until you get a smooth dough-like consistency mixture.
4. Now, check for seasoning and add more sweetness if needed.
5. Finally, with the help of a scooper, scoop out dough to make small balls.

Tip: If desired, you can coat the balls in extra cocoa powder.

Nutritions: *Calories: 46cal, Proteins: 2g, Carbohydrates: 2g, Fat: 2g*

Spicy Roasted Chickpeas

 Preparation:
10 Minutes

 Cooking:
25 Minutes

 Serves:
6

 Skill:
Begginer

Ingredients

- ½ tsp. Cumin
- 2 × 15 oz. Chickpeas
- ¼ tsp. Cayenne Pepper
- ¼ cup Olive Oil
- ½ tsp. Onion Powder
- 1 tsp. Sea Salt
- ¾ tsp. Garlic Powder
- ½ tsp. Chili Powder
- ¾ tsp. Paprika
- Sea Salt, as needed

Directions

1. Preheat the oven to 425 ° F.
2. After that, put the chickpeas in a strainer lined with a paper towel and allow to dry for 10 to 15 minutes.
3. Then, transfer the chickpeas onto a baking paper-lined baking sheet and then spoon some olive oil over it.
4. Coat the chickpeas with the oil. Sprinkle a dash of salt over it.
5. Now, put the baking sheet in the oven and bake for 23 to 25 minutes tossing them every 5 minutes or until they are golden brown.
6. Once they have become crispy, remove the sheet from the oven.
7. Next, mix all the remaining seasoning ingredients in another bowl until combined well.
8. Finally, stir the chickpeas into this mixture and toss well.
9. Serve immediately.

Tip: You can decrease and increase the quantity of the spices based on your spice level preference.

Nutritions: *Calories: 212 Kcal, Protein: 9.3g, Carbohydrates: 28.9g, Fat: 7.4g*

Preparation:
10 Minutes

Cooking:
10 Minutes

Serves:
2

Skill:
Beginner

Ingredients

- 1 cup Walnuts, raw
- 2 cups Tart Cherries, dried
- 1 cup Pumpkin Seeds, raw
- 1 cup Almonds, raw
- ½ cup Vegan Dark Chocolate
- 1 cup Cashew

Directions

1. First, mix all the ingredients needed to make the trail mix in a large mixing bowl until combined well.
2. Store in an air-tight container.

Tip: If desired, you can add the chocolate of your choice.

Nutritions: *Calories: 596 Kcal, Protein: 17.5g, Carbohydrates: 46.1g, Fat: 39.5g*

Chapter 9.
Small Plates and Sides

Black Bean Balls

Preparation:
20 Minutes

Serves:
12 balls

Ingredients

- 420g can black beans, rinsed
- 80g raw cacao powder
- 30g almond butter
- 15ml maple syrup

Directions

1. In a food processor, combine 420g black beans, 60g cacao powder, almond butter, and maple syrup.
2. Process until the mixture is well combined.
3. Shape the mixture into 12 balls.
4. Roll the balls through remaining cacao powder.
5. Place the balls in a refrigerator for 10 minutes.
6. Serve.

Nutritions: *Calories 245, Total Fat 3g, Total Carbohydrate 41.4g, Dietary Fiber 17.1g, Total Sugars 3.1g, Protein 13.1g*

Chia Soy Pudding

Preparation:

5 Minutes + inactive time

Serves:

2

Ingredients

- 45g almond butter
- 15ml maple syrup
- ¼ teaspoon vanilla paste
- 235ml soy milk
- 45g chia seeds
- 1 small banana, sliced
- 10g crushed almonds

Directions

1. Combine almond butter, maple syrup, vanilla, and soy milk in a jar.
2. Stir in chia seeds.
3. Cover and refrigerate 3 hours.
4. After 3 hours, open the jar.
5. Top the chia pudding with banana and crushed almonds.
6. Serve.

Nutritions: *Calories 298, Total Fat 13.8g, Total Carbohydrate 37.2g, Dietary Fiber 10.8g, Total Sugars 17.4g, Protein 10.1g*

Blueberry Ice Cream

Preparation:
10 Minutes + inactive time

Serves:
4

Ingredients

- 140g raw cashews, soaked overnight
- 125g silken tofu
- 230g fresh blueberries
- 5g lemon zest
- 100ml maple syrup
- 100ml coconut oil
- 15g almond butter

Directions

1. Rinse and drain cashews.
2. Place the cashews, blueberries, pale syrup, coconut oil, and almond butter in a food processor.
3. Process until smooth.
4. Transfer the mixture into the freezer-friendly container.
5. Cover with a plastic foil and freeze for 4 hours.
6. Remove the ice cream from the fridge 15 minutes before serving.
7. Scoop the ice creams and transfer into a bowl.
8. Serve.

Nutritions: *Calories 544, Total Fat 40.7g, Total Carbohydrate 43.4g, Dietary Fiber 2.6g, Total Sugars 28g, Protein 8.1g*

Chickpea Choco Slices

Preparation:
10 Minutes

Cooking:
50 Minutes

Serves:
12 slices

Ingredients

- 400g can chickpeas, rinsed, drained
- 250g almond butter
- 70ml maple syrup
- 15ml vanilla paste
- 1 pinch salt
- 2g baking powder
- 2g baking soda
- 40g vegan chocolate chips

Directions

1. Preheat oven to 180C/350F.
2. Grease large baking pan with coconut oil.
3. Combine chickpeas, almond butter, maple syrup, vanilla, salt, baking powder, and baking soda in a food blender.
4. Blend until smooth. Stir in half the chocolate chips-
5. Spread the batter into the prepared baking pan.
6. Sprinkle with reserved chocolate chips.
7. Bake for 45-50 minutes or until an inserted toothpick comes out clean.
8. Cool on a wire rack for 20 minutes. slice and serve.

Nutritions: *Calories 426, Total Fat 27.2g, Total Carbohydrate 39.2g, Dietary Fiber 4.9g, Total Sugars 15.7g, Protein 10g*

Sweet Green Cookies

Preparation:
10 Minutes

Cooking:
30 Minutes

Serves:
12 cookies

Ingredients

- 165g green peas
- 80g chopped Medjool dates
- 60g silken tofu, mashed
- 100g almond flour
- 1 teaspoon baking powder
- 12 almonds

Directions

1. Preheat oven to 180C/350F.
2. Combine peas and dates in a food processor.
3. Process until the thick paste is formed.
4. Transfer the pea mixture into a bowl. Stir in tofu, almond flour, and baking powder.
5. Shape the mixture into 12 balls.
6. Arrange balls onto baking sheet, lined with parchment paper. Flatten each ball with oiled palm.
7. Insert an almond into each cookie. Bake the cookies for 25-30 minutes or until gently golden.
8. Cool on a wire rack before serving.

Nutritions: *Calories 221, Total Fat 10.3g, Total Carbohydrate 26.2g, Dietary Fiber 6g, Total Sugars 15.1g, Protein 8.2g*

Chocolate Orange Mousse

Preparation:
10 Minutes + inactive time

Serves:
4

Ingredients

- 450g can black beans, rinsed, drained
- 55g dates, pitted, soaked in water for 15 minutes
- 30ml coconut oil
- 110ml maple syrup
- 60ml soy milk
- 1 orange, zested

Directions

1. Place the black bean in a food processor.
2. Add drained dates and process until smooth.
3. Add coconut oil, maple syrup, and soy milk. Process for 1 minute.
4. Finally, stir in lemon zest.
5. Spoon the mixture into four dessert bowls.
6. Chill for 1 hour before serving.

Nutritions: *Calories 375, Total Fat 8g, Total Carbohydrate 68.5g, Dietary Fiber 12.1g, Total Sugars 35.9g, Protein 11.3g*

Easy Mango Tofu Custard

Preparation:
5 Minutes +
inactive time

Serves:
2

Directions

1. Combine all ingredients in a food blender.
2. Blend until creamy.
3. Divide among two serving bowls.
4. Refrigerate 30 minutes.
5. Serve.

Ingredients

▸ 100g mango puree
▸ 300g soft tofu
▸ 15ml lime juice
▸ 15ml maple syrup

Nutritions: *Calories 148, Total Fat 5.8g, Total Carbohydrate 17g, Dietary Fiber 1.1g, Total Sugars 13.9g, Protein 10.2g*

Chickpea Cookie Dough

Preparation:
10 Minutes

Serves:
4

Directions

1. Drain chickpeas in a colander.
2. Remove the skin from the chickpeas.
3. Place chickpeas, peanut butter, vanilla, cinnamon, and chia in a food blender.
4. Blend until smooth.
5. Stir in chocolate chips and divide among four serving bowls.
6. Serve.

Ingredients

- 400g can chickpeas, rinsed, drained
- 130g smooth peanut butter
- 10ml vanilla extract
- ½ teaspoon cinnamon
- 10g chia seeds
- 40g quality dark Vegan chocolate chips

Nutritions: *Calories 376, Total Fat 20.9g, Total Carbohydrate 37.2g, Dietary Fiber 7.3g, Total Sugars 3.3g, Protein 14.2g*

Cacao Thin Mints with Protein Powder

Preparation:
10 Minutes +
inactive time

Serves:
10 cookies

Directions

1. Combine protein powder and cacao powder in a bowl.
2. In a separate bowl, combine vanilla, peppermint extract, stevia, and coconut oil.
3. Fold the liquid ingredients into the dry ones. Stir until smooth.
4. Line small cookie sheet with parchment paper.
5. Drop 10 mounds of prepared batter onto the cookie sheet.
6. Sprinkle the cookies with ground almonds.
7. Place in a freezer for 20 minutes or until firm.
8. Serve.

Ingredients

- 60g rice protein powder, chocolate flavor
- 35g cacao powder
- 5ml vanilla extract
- 5ml peppermint extract
- ½ teaspoon liquid stevia
- 90ml melted and cooled coconut oil
- 40g ground almonds

Nutritions: *Calories 251, Total Fat 22g, Total Carbohydrate 7.1g, Dietary Fiber 4.3g, Total Sugars 0.5g, Protein 12.1g*

Banana Bars

Preparation:
10 Minutes

Cooking:
30 Minutes

Serves:
8

Ingredients

- 130g smooth peanut butter
- 60ml maple syrup
- 1 banana, mashed
- 45ml water
- 15g ground flax seeds
- 95g cooked quinoa
- 25g chia seeds
- 5ml vanilla
- 90g quick cooking oats
- 55g whole-wheat flour
- 5g baking powder
- 5g cinnamon
- 1 pinch salt

Topping:
- 5ml melted coconut oil
- 30g vegan chocolate, chopped

Directions

1. Preheat oven to 180C/350F.
2. Line 16cm baking dish with parchment paper.
3. Combine flax seeds and water in a small bowl. Place aside 10 minutes.
4. In a separate bowl, combine peanut butter, maple syrup, and banana. Fold in the flax seeds mixture.
5. Once you have a smooth mixture, stir in quinoa, chia seeds, vanilla extract, oat, whole-wheat flour, baking powder, cinnamon, and salt.
6. Pour the batter into prepared baking dish. Cut into 8 bars.
7. Bake the bars for 30 minutes.
8. In the meantime, make the topping; combine chocolate and coconut oil in a heat-proof bowl. Set over simmering water, until melted.
9. Remove the bars from the oven. Place on a wire rack for 15 minutes to cool.
10. Remove the bars from the baking dish, and drizzle with chocolate topping.
11. Serve.

Nutritions: *Calories 278, Total Fat 11.9g, Total Carbohydrate 35.5g, Dietary Fiber 5.8g, Total Sugars 10.8g, Protein 9.4g*

Preparation:
5 Minutes +
inactive time

Serves:
10 balls

Ingredients

- 1 ripe banana
- 40g cashew nuts
- 30g chopped dried apricots
- 2 Medjool dates, chopped
- 15g ground flax seeds
- 55g vanilla flavored brown rice protein powder
- 2 tablespoons oatmeal
- ¼ teaspoon vanilla paste

Directions

1. Slice the banana into ¾-inch thick slices and microwave on medium for 7 minutes. This step will remove unnecessary liquid.
2. Place the cashews into a food blender. Blend on high until coarsely ground. Add the oatmeal and flax seeds and blend until you have almost fine powder.
3. Add the banana, dates, apricots, and vanilla paste. Blend until you have a sticky dough.
4. Shape the mixture into 10 balls and arrange onto a plate.
5. Refrigerate for 15 minutes before serving.

Nutritions: *Calories 133, Total Fat 4.9g, Total Carbohydrate 12.6g, Dietary Fiber 3.1g, Total Sugars 3.9g, Protein 10.8g*

Pumpkin Pudding

Preparation:

5 Minutes +
inactive time

Serves:

4

Directions

1. In a bowl, combine all ingredients, until smooth.
2. Divide between four dessert glasses and chill for 30 minutes before serving.
3. Enjoy.

Ingredients

- 470ml soy milk
- 245g organic pumpkin puree
- 30ml maple syrup
- ½ teaspoon cinnamon
- ¼ teaspoon ground ginger
- ¼ teaspoon ground nutmeg
- 55g vanilla flavored brown rice protein powder

Nutritions: *Calories 163, Total Fat 2.4g, Total Carbohydrate 21.8g, Dietary Fiber 4.1g, Total Sugars 13g, Protein 15g*

Fast mug Cake

Preparation:
5 Minutes

Cooking:
4 Minutes

Serves:
2

Ingredients

- 25g blanched almond flour
- 30g vanilla flavored brown rice protein powder
- 10g maple sugar
- ½ teaspoon baking soda
- ¼ teaspoon baking powder
- 60ml almond milk
- 10ml melted coconut oil
- ½ teaspoon lemon juice
- 30g fresh blueberries

Directions

1. In a large bowl, combine the flour, protein powder, maple sugar, baking soda, and baking powder.
2. Stir in the almond milk, melted coconut, and lemon juice.
3. Fold in the fresh blueberries, without squeezing or crushing.
4. Divide the mixture between two microwave-safe mugs.
5. Microwave the cake for 2 minutes. Remove from the microwave and continue in 30-second intervals, up to 4 minutes, or until the dough is spongy.
6. Serve.

Nutritions: *Calories 239, Total Fat 15.8g, Total Carbohydrate 12.8g, Dietary Fiber 3.4g, Total Sugars 6.8g, Protein 13.9g*

Rich Mango Pudding

Preparation:
5 Minutes + inactive time

Serves:
6

Directions

1. Combine all ingredients in a food blender.
2. Blend on high until smooth. Adjust flavor as desired.
3. Divide the mixture between six dessert cups and refrigerate for 30 minutes.
4. Serve after.

Ingredients

- 450g fresh mango
- 115ml full-fat coconut milk
- 110g vanilla flavored vegan protein powder
- 45g chia seeds
- 30ml maple syrup
- 290ml water
- 10ml fresh lime juice

Nutritions: *Calories 209, Total Fat 7g, Total Carbohydrate 22.1g, Dietary Fiber 3.8g, Total Sugars 14.6g, Protein 14.6g*

Preparation:
5 Minutes

Cooking:
20 Minutes

Serves:
10 donuts

Ingredients

- 85g coconut flour
- 110g vanilla flavored germinated brown rice protein powder
- 25g almond flour
- 50g maple sugar
- 30ml melted coconut oil
- 8g baking powder
- 115ml soy milk
- ½ teaspoon apple cider vinegar
- ½ teaspoon vanilla paste
- ½ teaspoon cinnamon
- 30ml organic applesauce

Additional:
- 30g powdered coconut sugar
- 10g cinnamon

Directions

1. In a bowl, combine all the dry ingredients.
2. In a separate bowl, whisk the milk with applesauce, coconut oil, and cider vinegar.
3. Fold the wet ingredients into dry and stir until blended thoroughly.
4. Heat oven to 180C/350F and grease 10-hole donut pan.
5. Spoon the prepared batter into greased donut pan.
6. Bake the donuts for 15-20 minutes.
7. While the donuts are still warm, sprinkle with coconut sugar and cinnamon.
8. Serve warm.

Nutritions: *Calories 270, Total Fat 9.3g, Total Carbohydrate 28.4g, Dietary Fiber 10.2g, Total Sugars 10.1g, Protein 20.5g*

Sweet Hummus

Preparation:
10 Minutes

Serves:
4

Directions

1. Combine soy milk, maple syrup, chickpeas, pumpkin puree, vanilla, and carrots in a food processor.
2. Process until smooth.
3. Serve, topped with fresh blueberries.

Ingredients

- 60ml vanilla soy milk
- 30ml maple syrup
- 400g can chickpeas, rinsed, drained
- 125g pumpkin puree, organic
- 5ml vanilla extract
- 200g fresh blueberries
- 2 carrots, finely grated

Nutritions: *Calories 252, Total Fat 3.1g, Total Carbohydrate 48g, Dietary Fiber 10.5g, Total Sugars 19.2g, Protein 10.3g*

Soft Cacao Ice Cream

Preparation:

10 Minutes

Serves:

2

Directions

1. Combine banana, soy milk, cocoa powder, peanut butter, maple syrup, and protein powder in a food processor.
2. Process until smooth.
3. Divide the ice cream between two serving bowls.
4. Sprinkle with cocoa nibs and crushed almonds
5. Serve.

Ingredients

- 2 bananas, frozen (slice before freezing)
- 15ml soy milk
- 15g raw cacao powder
- 15g peanut butter
- 5ml maple syrup
- 30g chocolate brown rice protein powder
- 10g cocoa nibs, to garnish
- 20g crushed almonds

Nutritions: *Calories 297, Total Fat 11.3g, Total Carbohydrate 40.6g, Dietary Fiber 9.3g, Total Sugars 17.9g, Protein 18.8g*

Lentil Balls

Preparation:
10 Minutes + inactive time

Serves:
16 balls

Directions

1. Combine all ingredients in a large bowl, as listed.
2. Shape the mixture into 16 balls.
3. Arrange the balls onto a plate, lined with parchment paper.
4. Refrigerate 30 minutes.
5. Serve.

Ingredients

- 150g cooked green lentils
- 10ml coconut oil
- 5g coconut sugar
- 180g quick cooking oats
- 40g unsweetened coconut, shredded
- 40g raw pumpkin seeds
- 110g peanut butter
- 40ml maple syrup

Nutritions: *Calories 305, Total Fat 13.7g1, Total Carbohydrate 35.4g, Dietary Fiber 9.5g, Total Sugars 6.3g, Protein 12.6g*

Homemade granola

Preparation:
10 Minutes

Cooking:
24 Minutes

Serves:
8

Ingredients

- 270g rolled oats
- 100g coconut flakes
- 40g pumpkin seeds
- 80g hemp seeds
- 30ml coconut oil
- 70ml maple syrup
- 50g Goji berries

Directions

1. Combine all ingredients on a large baking sheet.
2. Preheat oven to 180C/350F.
3. Bake the granola for 12 minutes. Remove from the oven and stir.
4. Bake an additional 12 minutes.
5. Serve at room temperature.

Nutritions: *Calories 344, Total Fat 17.4g, Total Carbohydrate 39.7g, Dietary Fiber 5.8g, Total Sugars 12.9g, Protein 9.9g*

Peanut Butter Quinoa Cups

Preparation:
10 Minutes

Serves:
6

Directions

1. Combine peanut butter, coconut butter, and coconut oil in a microwave-safe bowl.
2. Microwave on high until melted, in 40-second intervals.
3. Stir in the puffed quinoa. Stir gently to combine.
4. Divide the mixture among 12 paper cases.
5. Place in a freezer for 1 hour.
6. Serve.

Ingredients

- 120g puffed quinoa
- 60g smooth peanut butter
- 40g coconut butter
- 30ml coconut oil
- 25ml maple syrup
- 5ml vanilla extract

Nutritions: *Calories 231, Total Fat 14.7g, Total Carbohydrate 21.2g, Dietary Fiber 3g, Total Sugars 4.7g, Protein 6.3g*

Cookie Almond Balls

Preparation:

15 Minutes

Serves:

16 balls

Directions

1. Combine almond meal and protein powder in a large bowl.
2. Fold in almond butter, Stevia, coconut oil, and coconut cream.
3. If the mixture is too crumbly, add some water. Fold in chopped chocolate and stir until combined.
4. Shape the mixture into 16 balls.
5. You can additional roll the balls into almond flour.
6. Serve.

Ingredients

- 100g almond meal
- 60g vanilla flavored rice protein powder
- 80g almond butter or any nut butter
- 10 drops Stevia
- 15ml coconut oil
- 15g coconut cream
- 40g vegan chocolate chips

Nutritions: *Calories 132, Total Fat 8.4g, Total Carbohydrate 6.7g, Dietary Fiber 2.2g, Total Sugars 3.1g, Protein 8.1g*

Spiced Dutch Cookies

Preparation:
20 Minutes

Cooking:
8 Minutes

Serves:
6

Ingredients

- 180g almond flour
- 55ml coconut oil, melted
- 60g rice protein powder, vanilla flavor
- 1 banana, mashed
- 40g Chia seeds

Spice mix:
- 15g allspice
- 1 pinch white pepper
- 1 pinch ground coriander seeds
- 1 pinch ground mace

Directions

1. Preheat oven to 190C/375F.
2. Soak chia seeds in ½ cup water. Place aside 10 minutes.
3. Mash banana in a large bowl.
4. Fold in almond flour, coconut oil, protein powder, and spice mix.
5. Add soaked chia seeds and stir to combine.
6. Stir until the dough is combined and soft. If needed add 1-2 tablespoons water.
7. Roll the dough to 1cm thick. Cut out cookies.
8. Arrange the cookies onto baking sheet, lined with parchment paper.
9. Bake 7-8 minutes.
10. Serve at room temperature.

Nutritions: *Calories 278, Total Fat 20g, Total Carbohydrate 13.1g, Dietary Fiber 5.9g, Total Sugars 2.4g, Protein 13.1g*

Avocado pudding with Chia

Preparation:

10 Minutes +
inactive time

Serves:

4

Directions

1. In a food blender, combine avocados, cacao, coconut cream, coconut oil, Vanilla WPI, and Stevia.
2. Blend until smooth.
3. Divide among four serving bowls.
4. Refrigerate 10 minutes.
5. Sprinkle with chia seeds and serve.

Ingredients

- 2 large avocados, peeled, pitted
- 40ml unsweetened cacao
- 45g coconut cream
- 15ml coconut oil, melted
- 30g vanilla flavored rice protein powder
- 4 drops Stevia
- 15g Chia seeds

Nutritions: *Calories 278, Total Fat 22.6g, Total Carbohydrate 16.2g, Dietary Fiber 11.4g, Total Sugars 0.6g, Protein 12.1g*

Chapter 10.
Desserts to Make Your Day Sweet

Banana-Nut Bread Bars

Preparation:
5 Minutes

Cooking:
30 Minutes

Serves:
9 bars

Ingredients

- Nonstick cooking spray (optional)
- 2 large ripe bananas
- 1 tablespoon maple syrup
- ½ Teaspoon vanilla extract
- 2 cups old-fashioned rolled oats
- ½ Teaspoons salt
- ¼ Cup chopped walnuts

Directions

1. Preheat the oven to 350°f. Lightly coat a 9-by-9-inch baking pan with nonstick cooking spray (if using) or line with parchment paper for oil-free baking.
2. In a medium bowl, mash the bananas with a fork. Add the maple syrup and vanilla extract and mix well. Add the oats, salt, and walnuts, mixing well.
3. Transfer the batter to the baking pan and bake for 25 to 30 minutes, until the top is crispy. Cool completely before slicing into 9 bars. Transfer to an airtight storage container or a large plastic bag.

Nutritions: *Calories: 73; Fat: 1g; Protein: 2g; Carbohydrates: 15g; Fiber: 2g; Sugar: 5g; Sodium: 129mg*

Lemon Coconut Cilantro Rolls

Preparation:
10 Minutes +
30 min chill

Serves:
16 pieces

Ingredients

- ½ Cup fresh cilantro, chopped
- 1 cup sprouts (clover, alfalfa)
- 1 garlic clove, pressed
- 2 tablespoons ground brazil nuts or almonds
- 2 tablespoons flaked coconut
- 1 tablespoon coconut oil
- Pinch cayenne pepper
- Pinch sea salt
- Pinch freshly ground black pepper
- Zest and juice of 1 lemon
- 2 tablespoons ground flaxseed
- 1 to 2 tablespoons water
- 2 whole-wheat wraps, or corn wraps

Directions

1. Put everything but the wraps in a food processor and pulse to combine. Or combine the Ingredients in a large bowl. Add the water, if needed, to help the mix come together.
2. Spread the mixture out over each wrap, roll it up, and place it in the fridge for 30 minutes to set.
3. Remove the rolls from the fridge and slice each into 8 pieces to serve as appetizers or sides with a soup or stew.
4. Get the best flavor by buying whole raw brazil nuts or almonds, toasting them lightly in a dry skillet or toaster oven, and then grinding them in a coffee grinder.

Nutritions: *Calories: 66; Total Fat: 4g; Carbs: 6g; Fiber: 1g; Protein: 2g*

Tamari Almonds

Preparation:
5 Minutes

Cooking:
15 Minutes

Serves:
8

Ingredients

- 1 pound raw almonds
- 3 tablespoons tamari or soy sauce
- 2 tablespoons extra-virgin olive oil
- 1 tablespoon Nutritional yeast
- 1 to 2 teaspoons chili powder, to taste

Directions

1. Preheat the oven to 400°f.
2. Line a baking sheet with parchment paper.
3. In a medium bowl, combine the almonds, tamari, and olive oil until well coated.
4. Spread the almonds on the prepared baking sheet and roast for 10 to 15 minutes, until browned.
5. Cool for 10 minutes, then season with the Nutritional yeast and chili powder.
6. Transfer to a glass jar and close tightly with a lid.

Nutritions: *Calories: 364; Fat: 32g; Protein: 13g; Carbohydrates: 13g; Fiber: 7g; Sugar: 3g; Sodium: 381mg*

Tempeh Taco Bites

Preparation:
5 Minutes

Cooking:
45 Minutes

Serves:
3 dozen

Ingredients

- 8 ounces tempeh
- 3 tablespoons soy sauce
- 2 teaspoons ground cumin
- 1 teaspoon chili powder
- 1 teaspoon dried oregano
- 1 tablespoon olive oil
- 1/2 cup finely minced onion
- 2 garlic cloves, minced
- Salt and freshly ground black pepper
- 2 tablespoons tomato paste
- 1 chipotle chile in adobo, finely minced
- 1/4 cup hot water or vegetable broth, homemade or store-bought, plus more if needed
- 36 phyllo pastry cups, thawed
- 1/2 cup basic guacamole, homemade or store-bought
- 18 ripe cherry tomatoes, halved

Directions

1. In a medium saucepan of simmering water, cook the tempeh for 30 minutes. Drain well, then finely mince and place it in a bowl. Add the soy sauce, cumin, chili powder, and oregano. Mix well and set aside.
2. In a medium skillet, heat the oil over medium heat. Add the onion, cover, and cook for 5 minutes. Stir in the garlic, then add the tempeh mixture and cook, stirring, for 2 to 3 minutes. Season with salt and pepper to taste. Set aside.
3. In a small bowl, combine the tomato paste, chipotle, and the hot water or broth. Return tempeh mixture to heat and in stir tomato-chile mixture and cook for 10 to 15 minutes, stirring occasionally, until the liquid is absorbed.
4. The mixture should be fairly dry, but if it begins to stick to the pan, add a little more hot water, 1 tablespoon at a time. Taste, adjusting seasonings if necessary. Remove from the heat.
5. To assemble, fill the phyllo cups to the top with the tempeh filling, using about 2 teaspoons of filling in each. Top with a dollop of guacamole and a cherry tomato half and serve.

Mushroom Croustades

Preparation:
10 Minutes

Cooking:
10 Minutes

Serves:
12 croustades

Ingredients

- 12 thin slices whole-grain bread
- 1 tablespoon olive oil, plus more for brushing bread
- 2 medium shallots, chopped
- 2 garlic cloves, minced
- 12 ounces white mushrooms, chopped
- 1/4 cup chopped fresh parsley
- 1 teaspoon dried thyme
- 1 tablespoon soy sauce

Directions

1. Preheat the oven to 400°f. Using a 3-inch round pastry cutter or a drinking glass, cut a circle from each bread slice. Brush the bread circles with oil. Bake until the bread is toasted, about 10 minutes.
2. Meanwhile, in a large skillet, heat the 1 tablespoon oil over medium heat. Add the shallots, garlic, and mushrooms and sauté for 5 minutes to soften the vegetables. Stir in the parsley, thyme, and soy sauce and cook until the liquid is absorbed, about 5 minutes longer. Spoon the mushroom mixture into the croustade cups and return to the oven for 3 to 5 minutes to heat through. Serve warm.

Stuffed Cherry Tomatoes

 Preparation:
15 Minutes

 Cooking:
0 Minutes

 Serves:
6

Directions

1. Place the cherry tomatoes open-side up on a platter.
2. In a small bowl, ¬combine the avocado, lemon juice, bell pepper, scallions, tarragon, and salt.
3. Stir until well ¬combined. Scoop into the cherry tomatoes and serve immediately.

Ingredients

- 2 pints cherry tomatoes, tops removed and centers scooped out
- 2 avocados, mashed
- Juice of 1 lemon
- ½ Red bell pepper, minced
- 4 green onions (white and green parts), finely minced
- 1 tablespoon minced fresh tarragon
- Pinch of sea salt

Spicy Black Bean Dip

Preparation:
10 Minutes

Cooking:
0 Minutes

Serves:
2 cups

Ingredients

- 1 (14-ounce) can black beans, drained and rinsed, or 1½ cups cooked
- Zest and juice of 1 lime
- 1 tablespoon tamari, or soy sauce
- ¼ Cup water
- ¼ Cup fresh cilantro, chopped
- 1 teaspoon ground cumin
- Pinch cayenne pepper

Directions

1. Put the beans in a food processor (best choice) or blender, along with the lime zest and juice, tamari, and about ¼ cup of water.
2. Blend until smooth, then blend in the cilantro, cumin, and cayenne.
3. If you don't have a blender or prefer a different consistency, simply transfer it to a bowl once the beans have been puréed and stir in the spices, instead of forcing the blender.

Nutritions: *Calories: 190; Total Fat: 1g; Carbs: 35g; Fiber: 12g; Protein: 13g*

French Onion Pastry Puffs

Preparation:
10 Minutes

Cooking:
35 Minutes

Serves:
24 puffs

Ingredients

- 2 tablespoons olive oil
- Salt and freshly ground black pepper
- 18 pitted black olives, quartered
- 1 garlic clove, minced
- 1 teaspoon chopped fresh rosemary
- 1 tablespoon capers
- 1 sheet frozen vegan puff pastry, thawed
- 2 medium sweet yellow onions, thinly sliced

Directions

1. In a medium skillet, heat the oil over medium heat. Add the onions and garlic, season with rosemary and salt and pepper to taste. Cover and cook until very soft, stirring occasionally, about 20 minutes. Stir in the capers and set aside.
2. Preheat the oven to 400°f. Roll out the puff pastry and cut into 2- to 3-inch circles using a lightly floured pastry cutter or drinking glass. You should get about 2 dozen circles.
3. Arrange the pastry circles on baking sheets and top each with a heaping teaspoon of onion mixture, patting down to smooth the top.
4. Top with 3 olive quarters, arranged decoratively—either like flower petals emanating from the center or parallel to each other like 3 bars.
5. Bake until pastry is puffed and golden brown, about 15 minutes. Serve hot.

Cheezy Cashew–Roasted Red Pepper Toasts

Preparation:
15 Minutes

Cooking:
0 Minutes

Serves:
16-24 toast

Ingredients

- 2 jarred roasted red peppers
- 1 cup unsalted cashews
- 1⁄4 cup water
- 1 tablespoon soy sauce
- 2 tablespoons chopped green onions
- 1⁄4 cup Nutritional yeast
- 2 tablespoons balsamic vinegar
- 2 tablespoons olive oil

Directions

1. Use canapé or cookie cutters to cut the bread into desired shapes about 2 inches wide. If you don't have a cutter, use a knife to cut the bread into squares, triangles, or rectangles. You should get 2 to 4 pieces out of each slice of bread. Toast the bread and set aside to cool.
2. Coarsely chop 1 red pepper and set aside. Cut the remaining pepper into thin strips or decorative shapes and set aside for garnish.
3. In a blender or food processor, grind the cashews to a fine powder. Add the water and soy sauce and process until smooth. Add the chopped red pepper and puree. Add the green onions, Nutritional yeast, vinegar, and oil and process until smooth and well blended.
4. Spread a spoonful of the pepper mixture onto each of the toasted bread pieces and top decoratively with the reserved pepper strips. Arrange on a platter or tray and serve.

Baked Potato Chips

 Preparation:
10 Minutes

 Cooking:
30 Minutes

 Serves:
4

Ingredients

- 1 large russet potato
- 1 teaspoon paprika
- ½ Teaspoon garlic salt
- ¼ Teaspoon vegan sugar
- ¼ Teaspoon onion powder
- ¼ Teaspoon chipotle powder or chili powder
- ⅛ Teaspoon salt
- ⅛ Teaspoon ground mustard
- ⅛ Teaspoon ground cayenne pepper
- 1 teaspoon canola oil
- ⅛ Teaspoon liquid smoke

Directions

1. Wash and peel the potato. Cut into thin, 1/10-inch slices (a mandoline slicer or the slicer blade in a food processor is helpful for consistently sized slices).
2. Fill a large bowl with enough very cold water to cover the potato. Transfer the potato slices to the bowl and soak for 20 minutes.
3. Preheat the oven to 400°f. Line a baking sheet with parchment paper.
4. In a small bowl, combine the paprika, garlic salt, sugar, onion powder, chipotle powder, salt, mustard, and cayenne.
5. Drain and rinse the potato slices and pat dry with a paper towel.
6. Transfer to a large bowl.
7. Add the canola oil, liquid smoke, and spice mixture to the bowl. Toss to coat.
8. Transfer the potatoes to the prepared baking sheet.
9. Bake for 15 minutes. Flip the chips over and bake for 15 minutes longer, until browned. Transfer the chips to 4 storage containers or large glass jars.
10. Let cool before closing the lids tightly.

Nutritions: *Calories: 89; Fat: 1g; Protein: 2g; Carbohydrates: 18g; Fiber: 2g; Sugar: 1g; Sodium: 65mg*

Mushrooms Stuffed With Spinach And Walnuts

 Preparation:
10 Minutes

 Cooking:
6 Minutes

 Serves:
4-6

Ingredients

- 2 tablespoons olive oil
- 8 ounces white mushroom, lightly rinsed, patted dry, and stems reserved
- 1 garlic clove, minced
- 1 cup cooked spinach
- 1 cup finely chopped walnuts
- 1/2 cup unseasoned dry bread crumbs
- Salt and freshly ground black pepper

Directions

1. Preheat the oven to 400°f. Lightly oil a large baking pan and set aside. In a large skillet, heat the oil over medium heat. Add the mushroom caps and cook for 2 minutes to soften slightly. Remove from the skillet and set aside.
2. Chop the mushroom stems and add to the same skillet. Add the garlic and cook over medium heat until softened, about 2 minutes. Stir in the spinach, walnuts, bread crumbs, and salt and pepper to taste. Cook for 2 minutes, stirring well to combine.
3. Fill the reserved mushroom caps with the stuffing mixture and arrange in the baking pan. Bake until the mushrooms are tender and the filling is hot, about 10 minutes. Serve hot.

Salsa Fresca

Preparation:
15 Minutes

Cooking:
0 Minutes

Serves:
4

Ingredients

- 3 large heirloom tomatoes or other fresh tomatoes, chopped
- ½ Red onion, finely chopped
- ½ Bunch cilantro, chopped
- 2 garlic cloves, minced
- 1 jalapeño, minced
- Juice of 1 lime, or 1 tablespoon prepared lime juice
- ¼ Cup olive oil
- Sea salt
- Whole-grain tortilla chips, for serving

Directions

1. In a small bowl, combine the tomatoes, onion, cilantro, garlic, jalapeño, lime juice, and olive oil and mix well. Allow to sit at room temperature for 15 minutes. Season with salt.
2. Serve with tortilla chips.
3. The salsa can be stored in an airtight container in the refrigerator for up to 1 week.

Veggie Hummus Pinwheels

Preparation:
10 Minutes

Cooking:
0 Minutes

Serves:
3 cups

Ingredients

► 3 whole-grain, spinach, flour, or gluten-free tortillas
► 3 large swiss chard leaves
► ¾ Cup edamame hummus or prepared hummus
► ¾ Cup shredded carrots

Directions

1. Lay 1 tortilla flat on a cutting board.
2. Place 1 swiss chard leaf over the tortilla. Spread ¼ cup of hummus over the swiss chard. Spread ¼ cup of carrots over the hummus. Starting at one end of the tortilla, roll tightly toward the opposite side.
3. Slice each roll up into 6 pieces. Place in a single-serving storage container.
4. Repeat with the remaining tortillas and filling and seal the lids.

Nutritions: *Calories: 254; Fat: 8g; Protein: 10g; Carbohydrates: 39g; Fiber: 8g; Sugar: 4g; Sodium: 488mg*

Asian Lettuce Rolls

Preparation:
15 Minutes

Cooking:
5 Minutes

Serves:
4

Ingredients

- 2 ounces rice noodles
- 2 tablespoons chopped thai basil
- 2 tablespoons chopped cilantro
- 1 garlic clove, minced
- 1 tablespoon minced fresh ginger
- Juice of ½ lime, or 2 teaspoons prepared lime juice
- 2 tablespoons soy sauce
- 1 cucumber, julienned
- 2 carrots, peeled and julienned
- 8 leaves butter lettuce

Directions

1. Cook the rice noodles according to package Directions.
2. In a small bowl, whisk together the basil, cilantro, garlic, ginger, lime juice, and soy sauce. Toss with the cooked noodles, cucumber, and carrots.
3. Divide the mixture evenly among lettuce leaves and roll.
4. Secure with a toothpick and serve immediately.

Pinto-Pecan Fireballs

Preparation:
5 Minutes

Cooking:
30 Minutes

Serves:
20 pieces

Ingredients

- 1-1⁄2 cups cooked or 1 (15.5-ounce) can pinto beans, drained and rinsed
- 1⁄2 cup chopped pecans
- 1⁄4 cup minced green onions
- 1 garlic clove, minced
- 3 tablespoons wheat gluten flour (vital wheat gluten)
- 3 tablespoons unseasoned dry bread crumbs
- 4 tablespoons tabasco or other hot sauce
- 1⁄4 teaspoon salt
- 1⁄8 teaspoon ground cayenne
- 1⁄4 cup vegan margarine

Directions

1. Preheat the oven to 350°f. Lightly oil a 9 x 13-inch baking pan and set aside. Blot the drained beans well with a paper towel, pressing out any excess liquid. In a food processor, combine the pinto beans, pecans, green onions, garlic, flour, bread crumbs, 2 tablespoons of the tabasco, salt, and cayenne. Pulse until well combined, leaving some texture. Use your hands to roll the mixture firmly into 1-inch balls.
2. Place the balls in the prepared baking pan and bake until nicely browned, about 25 to 30 minutes, turning halfway through.
3. Meanwhile, in small saucepan, combine the remaining 2 tablespoons tabasco and the margarine and melt over low heat. Pour the sauce over the fireballs and bake 10 minutes longer. Serve immediately.

Sweet Potato Biscuits

Preparation:
60 Minutes

Cooking:
10 Minutes

Serves:
12 biscuits

Ingredients

- 2 pints cherry tomatoes, tops removed and centers scooped out
- 2 avocados, mashed
- Juice of 1 lemon
- ½ Red bell pepper, minced
- 4 green onions (white and green parts), finely minced
- 1 tablespoon minced fresh tarragon
- Pinch of sea salt

Directions

1. Bake the sweet potato at 350°F for about 45 minutes, until tender.
2. Allow it to cool, then remove the flesh and mash.
3. Turn the oven up to 375°F and line a baking sheet with parchment paper or lightly grease it. Measure out 1 cup potato flesh.
4. In a medium bowl, combine the mashed sweet potato with 1½ tablespoons of the coconut oil and the maple syrup. Mix together the flour and baking powder in a separate medium bowl, then add the flour mixture to the potato mixture and blend well with a fork.
5. On a floured board, pat the mixture out into a ½-inch-thick circle and cut out 1-inch rounds, or simply drop spoonfuls of dough and pat them into rounds.
6. Put the rounds onto the prepared baking sheet. Brush the top of each with some of the remaining 1½ tablespoons melted coconut oil. Bake 10 minutes, or until lightly golden on top. Serve hot.

Nutritions: *Calories: 116; Total Fat: 4g; Carbs: 19g; Fiber: 3g; Protein: 3g*

Lemon And Garlic Marinated Mushrooms

Preparation:
15 Minutes

Cooking:
0 Minutes

Serves:
4

Directions

1. In a medium bowl, whisk together the oil, lemon juice, garlic, marjoram, fennel seed, salt, and pepper. Add the mushrooms and parsley and stir gently until coated.
2. Cover and refrigerate for at least 2 hours or overnight. Stir well before serving.

Ingredients

- 3 tablespoons olive oil
- 2 tablespoons fresh lemon juice
- 2 garlic cloves, crushed
- 1 teaspoon dried marjoram
- 1/2 teaspoon coarsely ground fennel seed
- 1/2 teaspoon salt
- 1/4 teaspoon freshly ground black pepper
- 8 ounces small white mushrooms, lightly rinsed, patted dry, and stemmed
- 1 tablespoon minced fresh parsley

Garlic Toast

 Preparation:
5 Minutes

 Cooking:
5 Minutes

 Serves:
1 slice

Ingredients

- 1 teaspoon coconut oil, or olive oil
- Pinch sea salt
- 1 to 2 teaspoons Nutritional yeast
- 1 small garlic clove, pressed, or ¼ teaspoon garlic powder
- 1 slice whole-grain bread

Directions

1. In a small bowl, mix together the oil, salt, Nutritional yeast, and garlic.
2. You can either toast the bread and then spread it with the seasoned oil, or brush the oil on the bread and put it in a toaster oven to bake for 5 minutes.
3. If you're using fresh garlic, it's best to spread it onto the bread and then bake it.

Nutritions: *Calories: 138; Total Fat: 6g; Carbs: 16g; Fiber: 4g; Protein: 7g*

Vietnamese-Style Lettuce Rolls

 Preparation:
15 Minutes

 Cooking:
0 Minutes

 Serves:
4

Ingredients

- 2 green onions
- 2 tablespoons soy sauce
- 2 tablespoons rice vinegar
- 1 teaspoon sugar
- 1/8 teaspoon crushed red pepper
- 3 tablespoons water
- 3 ounces rice vermicelli
- 4 to 6 soft green leaf lettuce leaves
- 1 medium carrot, shredded
- 1/2 medium english cucumber, peeled, seeded, and cut lengthwise into 1/4-inch strips
- 1/2 medium red bell pepper, cut into 1/4-inch strips
- 1 cup loosely packed fresh cilantro or basil leaves

Directions

1. Cut the green part off the green onions and cut them lengthwise into thin slices and set aside. Mince the white part of the green onions and transfer to a small bowl. Add the soy sauce, rice vinegar, sugar, crushed red pepper, and water. Stir to blend and set aside.
2. Soak the vermicelli in medium bowl of hot water until softened, about 1 minute. Drain the noodles well and cut them into 3-inch lengths. Set aside.
3. Place a lettuce leaf on a work surface and arrange a row of noodles in the center of the leaf, followed by a few strips of scallion greens, carrot, cucumber, bell pepper, and cilantro. Bring the bottom edge of the leaf over the filling and fold in the two short sides. Roll up gently but tightly. Place the roll seam side down on a serving platter. Repeat with
4. Remaining Ingredients. Serve with the dipping sauce.

Guacamole

Preparation:
10 Minutes

Cooking:
0 Minutes

Serves:
2

Ingredients

- 2 ripe avocados
- 2 garlic cloves, pressed
- Zest and juice of 1 lime
- 1 teaspoon ground cumin
- Pinch sea salt
- Pinch freshly ground black pepper
- Pinch cayenne pepper (optional)

Directions

1. Mash the avocados in a large bowl. Add the rest of the Ingredients and stir to combine.
2. Try adding diced tomatoes (cherry are divine), chopped scallions or chives, chopped fresh cilantro or basil, lemon rather than lime, paprika, or whatever you think would taste good!

Nutritions: *calories: 258; Total Fat: 22g; Carbs: 18g; Fiber: 11g; Protein: 4g*

Conclusion

As an athlete, it may sound like the vegan diet may not provide you the right nutrition. But I am sure after reading these recipes; you can very well debunk that myth.

Over the course of the book, I've given you a bunch of tasty and easy to cook recipes which will make sure that you get your share of protein and carbs. Remember that while being a meat free athlete isn't easy, this is hardly a reason to quit!

One of the greatest benefits of going vegan is the increased level of health you will experience and this manifests well beyond just your physique. Add to this the potent combination of healthy plant based protein and you have a winner! You can also choose to supplement with vegan protein powder.

Remember to prep your meals ahead of time for maximum convenience. I hope you've enjoyed the recipes in this book. Let me know what you think!

HIGH PROTEIN VEGAN COOKBOOK

MEAL PREP RECIPES FOR BEGINNERS. SPORT NUTRITION PLANT BASED DIET. EASY GUIDE FOR ATHLETES AND BUILDING MUSCLES. LOW CARB FOR HEALTHY EATING, BEING SMART AND LOVE YOUR BODY

Kevin Rinaldi

Table of Contents

Introduction

A vegan diet is a stricter form of the vegetarian diet that mandates eating only non-animal products. While vegetarians may afford themselves some wiggle room to eat something non-vegetarian once in a while, vegans typically don't use any products that contain any ingredients originating from or tested on animals.

A vegan will typically choose this diet because of health, ethical, or environmental reasons. If the person had health problems because of a diet rich in animal foodstuffs or opposes the unethical treatment of animals in the food industry or considers human exploitation of the environment over the top, then the vegan diet is the most appropriate solution.

A vegan diet is most often accompanied by but doesn't necessarily include the idea of toning down on consumerism. In other words, a vegan is an animal lover who rebels against the consumer culture and strikes his own path through the world. In other words, vegan is a hardcore vegetarian.

Pop quiz! Which (vegans or vegetarian) cannot have a fur coat? Answer—vegans! Vegans tend to be a lot more strict about their choices. And now you know. Both nutritionally speaking, often are low in saturated fat and cholesterol while being high in minerals, vitamins, and fibers. Both of the diets required careful meal planning or supplementation to duck the potential deficiencies.

Chapter 1. Vegan as A Lifestyle

Before we even start here, I want to point out that this will never be a complete guide to everything dieting and nutritional. There's just too much stuff out there to fit into a book like this. However, what we are going to do here is give you the most critical factors that will actually affect your health, starting with the most significant thing to focus on and working our way to progressively less important, so pay particular attention at the start.

I also want to point out that none of this is my opinion. I didn't throw open the laptop and get to typing my thoughts. This is a fact, solid, proven fact through various studies and analyses. People much smarter than me have looked at these studies and compiled the five factors that affect the outcome more than the others, the ones that I will share... now.

Calorie balance. The biggest thing that you absolutely need to focus on is this little fella, which is basically how many calories are coming into your body through eating and drinking versus how much energy (measured in calories) is leaving on a regular basis.

Food composition. Aka, what your foods are made of and where your fats, carbs, and proteins come from.

Macronutrient amounts. A big word that just means how much fat, carbs, and protein that you consume on a daily basis.

Nutrient timing. When you eat your meals and (obviously) how you space them out during the day.

Supplements. Notice that this is down here, at number five, despite all the buzz you get around them. These are still important, but here's the basic definition: all those powders, pills, extracts, etc., that you can take to improve your diet.

And that's it! Really. See how relatively simple that is? When you get down to it, it isn't as challenging to wrap your mind around as some of the naysayers like to claim. This should be pretty obvious, but they all affect each other. Changing any of them, or multiple of them can change a lot of stuff. The no-brainer example is that if you eat less, you lose weight. If you happen to be overweight, that means a lot of health benefits.

Look, I want to point out something here. As much as we'd all like a magical pill that could solve all our problems, it doesn't exist. Veganism and eating right might be the right answer and something that makes your life better, but it's baby steps. You don't eat some legumes, and the next day everything's 100% better. If you choose to adopt a vegan diet, I want you to be fully aware that, like with everything else in life, it will take some time. Focus on the most significant things first, like calorie balance, and once things start making sense and you're comfortable, move to the other ones.

Benefits of a Vegan Diet

Animal products carry with them a whole array of health risks, all of which are avoided on a vegan diet, which boasts the following benefits:

lowered cancer risk

improved kidney function

lowered risk of Alzheimer's disease

reduced arthritis symptoms

weight loss

Keep in mind that a lot of studies showing these benefits typically have a small sample size. There isn't enough interest in the scientific community to fund large-scale studies of a vegan diet. However, weight loss is the best confirmed and comes about as a result of avoiding saturated fats and animal protein that is responsible for weight gain, especially when combined.

Calories

I'm going to say something here that might make you gasp and turn away in horror. Ready? Physics. Yes, physics. If you don't like it, I'm sorry, but it's crucial for your understanding of calories, the enigmatic little fellas themselves. But don't worry, I'll try and keep this understandable and readable.

The First Law of Thermodynamics, for those of us who paid attention to science class, states that your body weight is dependent only on the difference between the amount of calories than you consume versus the amount of calories that you burn (aka, your calorie balance). In other words, your weight is determined by how much you eat versus how many calories you expel doing stuff per day. You can eat a lot, if you do a ton of stuff during the day, and not gain weight. The flip is also true.

But what is a calorie? A calorie is the amount of energy required to raise the temperature of one liter of water by one degree Celsius. Gah. Science words again. Here's what you need to know: it's a unit of energy. When you eat, you consume the energy stored within your food. You then have more energy to do things like a frolic in the meadow, workout, or read a book on veganism. Now, in a perfect world, you'd use exactly the amount of energy that you ate each day, but it doesn't always work that way. Most of the time, we eat more calories than we expel, so you have a leftover bunch of calories hanging around after the day is done with nothing to do. Some will go into the muscles and liver as glycogen, but then, when that fills up... it gets stored as fat. The dreaded fat.

Here are the three states of calorie balances. You will only be able to be in one of these states at a time.

Negative calorie balance. Basically, you are not giving yourself enough calories, so you're losing weight. You might have a very high activity rate or something like that, but if you are expelling more calories than you are gaining, this will make you drop some pounds. This might sound great, but be careful: the necessary energy you absolutely need won't just appear: it'll come from the breakdown of body tissue.

Neutral calorie balance. You did it. You nailed it right on the head. You have eaten exactly the amount of calories that you need each day, which means you will not gain or lose weight. If you haven't changed weight in a few months, congratulations, you're in neutral calorie balance!

Positive calorie balance. This is where most of us get into trouble: we're eating too many calories and not doing enough to get rid of them, so we start stacking on the weight. The calories that we don't end up using are stored as fat or glycogen in the liver and muscles.

Calories can be confusing to a lot of people because if you aren't eating enough, you won't gain muscles... but eat incorrectly, and you'll be gaining fat, not muscle. If you just aren't eating enough, you will not be able to put on any muscle even though you have very low body fat. It's a tightrope, but fortunately for everyone, it isn't that hard of a tightrope to walk down once you get the hang of it.

How Do I Track Calories Correctly?

Did you notice that I put the word "correctly" on there? Yeah, that's there for a reason. There are a billion ways to track calories, but none of them will help you if you aren't doing it right. If this seems confusing to you, you aren't alone. Many people find this hard to do, and most of the apps and programs are incredibly unintuitive, complicated, or full of ads that make it a nightmare. It can actually be pretty simple. Here, I'll be sharing with you a suite of strategies and tools that you can use and, just as importantly, which foods actually need to be tracked and which you can safely ignore.

Get out your checklist, because you're going to need three, count 'em, three things for this. The first is the food. Duh. Second is a calorie tracker app (try out Fitatu, which is free in the app store), and your basic kitchen scale, which doesn't have to be terribly expensive. Think less than $40 range. Some people try and do this without a scale, but that's just not realistic for beginners. I'm sure that some scientists don't need a calculator, but for the vast majority of us, you might as well make it easy instead of instantly making it difficult. Eyeballing, it takes skill and practice, and getting off can screw up the whole plan.

Here's how it works. First, throw your food (not literally) on the scale and get the right amount in terms of grams, so you know how many calories you'll be getting from it. This is actually important, so you need to make sure to do two things:

First, you're going to make sure that your macro and calorie counter is accurate. Second, you're going to need to be smart about it and not bog yourself down all the time. Streamline! Here's the five-point system for getting your scale to do these two things. Okay? Let's do it!

First, you really don't need to sweat the small stuff. Consider anything under 50 calories to not be worth counting, in general. Some coffee might fall into this category or some cream. Minor things. This isn't meant to be horrible, but it will be if you of every single thing down to that level. The important thing is to keep it reasonable. Adding up a bunch of these tiny items can make a big difference.

Second, just weigh the food once. For example, if you eat oatmeal frequently, just measure what you need in a day for the oatmeal in a bowl. The next day, you don't have to carefully measure out everything unless you want to, because you should be able to accurately eyeball what you need for oatmeal. Sure, knock yourself out and weigh everything every day, but I'm telling you—it isn't going to make as much difference as you might be worried.

Third, you need to know if your food is raw or cooked because it makes a difference for calories. If you weigh rice before and after the water goes into it, it's going to be enormously different. Anything that might affect the weight should be considered, like a banana peel throwing off the scale.

Fourth, check the macro and calorie values in your tracker app. Just because it's in the app does not mean it is accurate. If you think a value might be off, just check with something like Web M.D. to make sure. Yes, it really does happen. You don't want to mess up your diet because your values are wrong.

Fifth, you only really need the food scale for one-off occasions. Meal plans are the best way to do things since they are more reliable and easier, and since they are recurring, you will find yourself not needing your food scale all the time after a while. This means that you will eventually need the food scale for stuff you are not too familiar with.

How to Calculate Your Daily Calorie Needs

Well, we're past the definitions! It's actually not that difficult, right? The calorie balance is the thing that will make or break your diet, and you can either be in positive, negative, or neutral calorie states. Which state are you in right now? You might not know. The only way to truly know which state that you are in is to know how many calories your body spends every day. Since you can't just ask your body this question, you're going to need to use formulas. And, like all formulas, some are easier than others, and some are more accurate than others.

The easiest way is to calculate your TDEE, which is a fancy way of describing your total daily energy expenditure (how many calories you burn in a day). The way you calculate is by estimating the number of calories you burn while resting, which is known as the basal Metabolic Rate, aka BMR. Then, once you know that number, you throw on an estimated number of calories that you burn through how often you exercise.

Unless you happen to be a genius, you won't know what your TDEE is off-hand. Never to fear! You can follow this here link, and it will do all the work for you.

It's gonna ask you for various stats, like height, weight, age, and activity. It's not going to be 100% accurate, seeing as nobody is exactly alike, but you just need an estimate, and it should be close. Do you think the TDEE calculator is off? No worries. Here's how to test it. Use the estimated TDEE value and eat how many calories it

167

recommends per day. Weigh yourself twice a week, and if something changes, it's off. If you start gaining weight, decrease the TDEE by 100 calories. If you keep gaining weight, do it again. The same goes for the opposite. Losing weight? Add 100 calories a day. You want to find that perfect TDEE where you are not gaining or losing weight.

High-Protein Vegan Food Sources

Without getting all technical on you, it's crucial to eat the right food. How many calories you eat is first and foremost, but this is a close second. There are four factors of food sources that you're going to need to consider, which are protein sources, carbohydrate sources, fat sources, and micronutrients. I'll be going over each. Now, I want to point out that your diet must work for you. If you absolutely despise a certain kind of food, don't have it in your diet. Find another alternative, or your diet will probably not last all that long. However, if I had to give you four bullet points to live by as a vegan, it's this.

Get most of your protein from foods high in essential amino acids

Get most of your carbs from whole grains, fruits, and veggies

Get most of your fats from sources of unsaturated fat

Eat foods mostly high in vitamins and minerals

Without further ado, let's get into the science of it all!

Proteins

Proteins are crucial. I literally could not go over all the scientific reasons you need protein, but I'll say it this way: if you don't have the right protein, you basically fall apart. Things go real bad, real fast. That's why it's so important to nail it.

For the workout enthusiasts, you'll need to know this: protein is responsible for building new muscles, and it's what prevents your current muscles from going away. Most (90%) of the protein you eat gets turned into amino acids, which becomes part of the amino acid pool that your body will use to build or repair muscle or other tissues. Carbs and fat can be stored for later use, but amino acids cannot, so you need to have protein every day.

How to find quality vegan protein sources

The title gives it away, but you need quality vegan protein sources. There are several ways that you can measure the quality of a vegan protein source, including the concept of bioavailability, which is a complicated word that literally just means how much of the protein you consume actually ends up getting absorbed into your bloodstream. You could also judge protein quality based on how much of the protein is composed of those essential amino acids (and how much is non-essential amino acids, which your body can make and doesn't need to get from food). Tragically for veganism, animal protein sources are usually regarded as better because they are better digested and have a higher percentage of essential amino acids than plant-based proteins. Fortunately for veganism, this is not generally a problem. There are a few exceptions, including a fruit-only diet, which probably is a poor decision, and people trying to build up muscle.

If you're a run of the mill vegan that does not fall into those subcategories, you should be fine from pumpkin seeds, chia seeds, oats, lentils, kidney beans, black beans, mung beans, and peanuts. A lot of beans. There are others, of course, but these are some great ones to consider.

If you are a person trying to build muscle, fret not! I'll explain that in more detail later.

Carbohydrates

Carbs are the last of the three main macronutrients. There's quite a bit of argument over carbs, but first, let's figure out what they actually are. They're found in foods including vegetables, whole grains, pastries, candy, potatoes, and fruits. They're often considered the body's preferred energy source. It's extremely important for all parts of your life and, like protein, has a variety of reasons as to why. One vital thing is that carbs supply the nervous system with its fuel, for lack of a better term. That means more fatigue resistance, more workout motivation, and better muscle recruitment. A lot of the fatigue-related to long-duration training is linked to this, so you have to give your nervous system enough of a source of blood glucose to keep things up and running smoothly.

Carbs refuel glycogen stores. Glycogen is a provider of energy for high-intensity workouts, but it also stores in the muscle and plays a hand in muscle growth. If you want to get more muscle, you need to give yourself enough carbs.

Carbs secrete insulin. Eat more carbs, secrete more insulin. That's great, seeing as insulin has a profound effect on muscle growth. I could give you a long and complicated explanation as to why, but I'll keep it short: insulin helps muscle tissue grow.

How to find quality vegan carbohydrate sources

Look for unprocessed whole foods, like legumes, whole grains, many veggies, and fruit, oh wonderful fruit. They contain vitamins, minerals, antioxidants, and fiber. Avoid foods made with refined grains, as they have less of these nutrients, and duck anything with sugar thanks to unnecessary calories. For high carb whole grain sources, look for whole-grain pasta, whole-grain cereal, whole grain bread, and more—but avoid the sugar. For high carb fruits, look for apples, oranges, pears, mangos, and bananas. For high carb legumes, look for peas, beans, and lentils. Some other good options that I haven't gone over are sweet or long-duration potatoes, normal and brown rice, canola or meal, and tortillas.

Dietary Fats

I'd be willing to bet that you hear more rumors about this one than any other, largely because it has the word "fat" in it, which is often associated with something unhealthy. Well, I'll tell you right now that you shouldn't read into that too much because you need some dietary fats. Without going into the science of it, they're crucial. They fit in a lot of important things, from helping you absorb vitamins to regulate hormone production, make your hair and skin look good, and more. It's important, and not "bad like was previously believed.

Now, there is some credence to avoiding foods with a lot of saturated fats. Think cheese, whole milk, ice cream, fatty meats, butter, that kind of thing. There's a debate about it and what it does with your risk of heart problems, but as of now, from me to you, I'd just try and keep a limit on foods high with saturated fats. Unsaturated fats? They can actually lower your LDL cholesterol (something you want). Within this, there are monounsaturated fats, which include canola oil and olive oil, and then there are polyunsaturated fats, which include soy oil and sunflower corn. Trans fatty acids (formed by infusing vegetable oil with hydrogen) helps keep food fresh for a more extended time. Sound great? Well, not exactly, as studies have shown that a pretty small amount of them can increase your risks of various problems, like heart disease and depression, and obviously, you don't want that. What's the solution? Avoid (or limit) food with partially hydrogenated oils and hydrogenated oils (margarine and hard butter, for example).

Basically, you've got three categories of fat: unsaturated, saturated, and trans fats. I'll be explaining each, briefly.

Unsaturated fats can actually be broken down into monounsaturated fats and polyunsaturated fats—which are healthy fats and should be included in your diet because they have excellent health benefits. You need fat, okay? It all boils down to that. No matter what your neighbor says, a healthy person needs to have some fun to function. Think 15 to 25 percent of all daily calories. Of this, you should get most of that from your unsaturated fats. Turn to your old pals—avocados, olives, olive oil, nuts and butter (but not highly processed kinds), flaxseed oil, flax seeds, and many other types of seeds. Good? Good.

Then, we have saturated fats. They're easily found in animal products like butter, cheese, dairy, fatty steaks, etc. They often play the villain in media, but in reality, they're not as bad as they're supposed to be. Now, you should absolutely limit your consumption of saturated fats, but vegans don't consume any of the things I just mentioned, so a vegan already does that.

Trans fats. Like transformers, but less interesting. They're the Frankenstein of fats, as they're made by adding hydrogen to liquid vegetable oils, which makes them more solid and less... liquidy. The point is that this will increase the shelf life of many processed foods. Now, the other ones are kind of grey, but trans fats are actually bad for your health, so avoid these. Want to know where you find these most often? Fast food, fried food, and more. Yeah. That's why you should avoid them.

Macronutrients

The first thing that you need to focus on is your calorie balance, but number two is macronutrients. They are, simply put, the three main ingredients that you need to survive. The three macronutrients are carbs, dietary fat, and proteins. We just went over these, so I won't spend too much time here. Instead, I'll jump straight into what you really need to know.

How Much Protein Should You Consume as a Vegan?

Remember the thing about protein deficiencies with a vegan diet? Well, that can absolutely be a thing, but here's the fun part: it's only a problem if you let it be a problem. You need protein to gain muscle, period. How much? Well, high protein diets work the best, with .08 to 1 gram/lb of body weight. Let's say that you're just an average, active person who would like to see some muscle gains, but that's not your entire priority. In that case, you're looking at less protein. Your bare minimum would be 0.3 grams/lb per day, but for most folks, this translates to about 40 grams of protein a day—something very attainable.

I want to point out that that is the minimum, and it won't hurt to go over that. Shoot for a higher value, like 0.4 to 0.5. That's particularly important if you're a vegan or vegetarian, seeing as plant-based protein sources are generally digested less efficiently. So, eat more protein than your meat-eating friends to make up for this little fact.

But... can you eat too much protein? Well, yes and no. It's not likely. You'd have to try hard to eat too much of it, especially if you stick to unprocessed or minimally processed, quality sources, and if your higher protein intake doesn't end up lowering your carb and fat intakes to a critical level. Keep it balanced, in other words. There are studies showing kidney and various health problems from high protein diets, that's usually because the participant had preexisting problems or if they were also eating a lot of processed foods and saturated fats. Don't read too much into that, as fears around protein shakes are pretty unfounded generally speaking. Do keep in mind that if you do have a lot of protein in your diet, make sure to drink plenty of water.

Chapter 2. Benefits of The Vegan Diet

Lowers Blood Pressure

The plant-based diet is known to lower blood pressure. This is due to the fact that the plant-based diet has very little amounts of sugars, which aid in raising the blood pressure. If you have a condition of high blood pressure, a plant-based diet is the right remedy for you.

Lowers Cholesterol Level

Let me start by asking you a question; how much do you think one egg affects your cholesterol? One egg a day could increase your dietary cholesterol from 97 to 418 mg in a single day! There was a study done on seventeen lacto-vegetarian college students. During this study, the students were asked to consume 400kcal in test foods along with one large egg for three weeks. During this time, their dietary cholesterol raised to these numbers. To put it in perspective, 200 to 239 mg/dL is considered borderline high.

Maintains Healthy Skin

We all know people who try every skin product imaginable just to get clear, smooth skin. What these people fail to understand is that how we look is more or less dictated by our food choices. Consequently, plant-based diets have a higher chance of providing your skin with the nutrients it needs to stay healthy. For instance, tomatoes provide the body with lycopene. This component safeguards the skin from sun damage. Sweet potatoes are known to provide us with vitamin C. The production of collagen will help your skin glow and encourage fast healing.

Boosts Your Energy

Minerals and vitamins are good sources of energy for the body. Plants are not only rich in them, but also contain phytonutrients, antioxidants, proteins, and healthy fats. All of these are essential nutrients for your brain. In addition, they are easy to digest, which makes it easy for the body to obtain energy from them.

Lowers Blood Sugar Levels

The plant-based diet has little or no sugars at all. Most non-plant diets are known to contain high levels of sugars. This, in turn, causes diabetes. A plant-based diet lowers the level of blood sugar thereby making it healthy for your body.

Enhances Your Digestion

Good digestion calls for plenty of fiber. The good news is that plants offer sufficient fiber to facilitate good digestion. It is vital to understand that you cannot just start eating tons of vegetables and fruits without a plan. If you are starting this diet, you should start slow. Your body needs ample time to adjust. Therefore, you should introduce your new diet slowly to prevent constipation, since most of it is composed of fiber.

Prevents Chronic Diseases

Besides aiding in weight loss, a whole-food plant-based diet has also been proven to help lower the risks of various chronic health conditions.

Cardiac Conditions

This is the most widely-known benefit of whole-food plant-based diets as they have higher probabilities of keeping your cardiac health sound. But, the strength of this benefit is dependent on the types and quality of the food in your diet plan. Major research done on over 200,000 people concluded that the risk of having heart disease was lower in those people whose diet plan was plant-based and was rich in whole grains, veggies, nuts, legumes, and fruits than those who were following non-plant-based diets.

But, plant-based diet plans that are unhealthy because of the inclusion of fruit juices, refined grains, and sugary drinks showed an increased risk of cardiac complications. This is why it is very important to stick to the right foods and follow a healthy plant-based diet plan.

Cancer

According to various research studies, a plant-based diet plan can lower the risks of various forms of cancer. A study of over 69,000 people found that the risk of gastrointestinal cancer was very low for vegetarian diet followers, especially for Lacto-ovo vegetarian diet followers (the ones who consume both dairy and eggs).

In another study of over 77,000 people, it was proven that there was a 22 percent reduced risk of having colorectal cancer in those who followed a vegetarian diet plan than those who didn't. The safest was pescatarians (those vegetarians who consume fish) as they had a significant 43 percent lower risk of colorectal cancer than non-vegetarian diet plan followers.

Cognitive Decline

Various studies found that diet plans high in fruit and veggie content can prevent or slow Alzheimer's disease and cognitive decline in adults. The reason is that many foods in plant-based diet plans are high in antioxidants and plant compounds that act as protective agents against the development of Alzheimer's disease and reversing cognitive damage.

A review of nine research studies of around 31,000 people found that those who consumed more veggies and fruits had a significant 20 percent lower risk of having dementia or cognitive impairment.

Diabetes

A whole-food plant-based diet plan can play a significant role in lowering the risk of contracting diabetes or managing the illness. In a study involving over 200,000 people, it was proven that there was a 34 percent reduced risk of having diabetes if you followed a healthy, plant-based diet in comparison to an unhealthy, non-plant-based plan.

In another research study, it was proven that both Lacto-ovo vegetarian and vegan diet plans could lower the risk of type 2 diabetes by a whopping 50 percent in comparison to non-plant-based diet plans. Plant-based diet plans are also known to cause improvements in blood sugar level control in people with diabetes as compared to non-plant-based diets.

Saves Time and Money

A plant-based diet is generally known to be cheaper compared to a non-plant diet such as meat. When it also comes to cooking, a plant-based diet takes less time to be ready thereby saving you some valuable time which you can use to do other things.

Faster Recovery After Workouts

Athletes, runners, and bodybuilders on plant-based diets report that they recover faster after workouts, meaning they can fit in more training than their omnivorous counterparts. This may be due to increased antioxidants, vitamins, potassium, or a decrease in the inflammatory compounds found in meat and dairy.

More Eco-Friendly Diet

The whole-food plant-based diet plan is not only beneficial in terms of health but also proven to be better for the ecosystem. Plant-based diet plan followers tend to have a smaller effect on the environment in comparison to other diet plan followers.

Sustainable eating approaches can help lower greenhouse gas effects as well as land and water consumption required for factory farming. These factors are known to be the major cause of harm to the ecosystem and global warming.

Chapter 3. Why Athletes Should Go Vegan

Getting your body in shape requires figuring out the kind of diet you can hold indefinitely. This would most commonly be a diet that's affordable, light on your digestion, and in line with your personal beliefs and lifestyle.

When you add the requirement of achieving athletic results on a vegan diet, you've entered a whole new paradigm of eating that comes down to having a scientifically based and competitive diet that lets you achieve your inner potential to the fullest.

Veganism. You see it all over the place, and lots and lots of people like to talk about it, which, of course, leads to a completely reliable source of information... ha! Wouldn't that be great? But, as humanity kicks in, you start to realize that a lot of these sources are completely untrustworthy.

Now, as more and more people talk about it and more and more opinions get thrown around, mixed in with some fallacies and judgments, combined with some paranoia, and you get yourself a nice, tasty Stew of Ignorance with just a dabble of truth at the bottom, but you can't even see it because of all the stuff floating around on top of it. Don't drink the Stew of Ignorance! Instead, look for real sources who are on the side of the facts (that's me).

The first "ingredient" that mucks up the Stew of Ignorance is myths. Myths, myths, myths. There's about a bazillion of them associated with veganism, but let's knock off each one, one at a time, good and bad, and give you a real picture of what veganism is actually about. Pour out that Stew of Ignorance!

Chapter 4. Improve Athletic Performance and Muscle Growth

When you start any diet, you usually do so with an end goal in mind. This goal serves as motivation to keep you on track. Unlike with most diets, a whole foods plant-based diet is not something you commit to with the mindset that you will only stick with it until that goal is met. This type of diet is more of a lifestyle change that will benefit you for years. Having an end goal of losing weight can help you get started but you need to dive deeper into what will keep you motivated and committed to this type of lifestyle.

The health benefits alone can be motivating enough, though for most this isn't enough incentive to stick with the diet for the long haul. This is especially important since your family and friends may not be on the same path as you. Finding a deeper 'why' in terms of what specifically you want to get from this diet will help remind you that you aren't just eating healthy to fit into your skinny jeans but are doing it to have more energy, less medical issues, and a better quality of life. Before you begin your journey with a whole food plant-based diet you need to clearly state why you are doing it and then commit to sticking with your 'why' for the long term.

Stock up on healthy food and eliminate unhealthy processed foods One of the first things to do when starting out on a whole foods diet is the go through your pantry and cupboards and get rid of everything that is not of nutritional value. This can be difficult for many because the thought of just throwing out food seems like such a waste. To make it easier, you can try to give these items away to friends or family or even donate them to a food shelter. Replace these unhealthy items with fruits, vegetables and beans and whole grains. If you do end up keeping the unhealthy options because you just can't bring yourself to throw it out, keep it out of sight. Keep fruits, nuts, and seeds easily accessible on the counter so you are more likely to reach for these healthier food options.

Snack healthy and make your meals at home

Fruits, vegetables, nuts, and seeds are ideal snacks that are quick to prepare or grab and go. Unhealthy snacking tends to be the number one reason why individuals are unable to lose weight or fully commit to a healthier plant-based diet. This is often because there are many triggers or habits you have grown accustomed to that make it easier to choose unhealthy options. For instance, buying breakfast or lunch instead of cooking your meals at home can hinder your results. Prepping your breakfast and lunches for the week might take a little extra work on the weekend, but it is crucial when you want to truly reap the benefits from a whole food plant-based diet.

Do one thing at a time

Making a lifestyle change is often challenging. Very few people can switch to a whole foods plant-based diet successfully. Hence, making all these changes all at once can become overwhelming or seem impossible. Instead of trying to dive right into this type of diet, give yourself time to adjust to the different foods. Begin by simply adding more fruits and veggies to your diet. Eat these items first when it comes to mealtime. Then replace your animal meats, processed flours or sugars with whole grains and natural sweeteners. Commit to eating one fully plant-based meal for the first week. Simply switching from animal products to plant-based options and swapping out processed and sugary foods with healthier options can have the biggest impact on your health.

Start your day right

One of the first meals you should try switching to plant-based is breakfast. Not only is breakfast one of the most important meals of your day, it sets the tone for the day. If you eat an unhealthy breakfast first thing in the morning, you are more likely to have an unhealthy lunch and dinner. Breakfast can also be one of the unhealthiest meals of the day as people tend to opt for quick and convenient solutions without realizing fresh fruits and veggie wraps can be just as quick and easy.

Breakfast can be the easiest meal to transition over to a whole foods plant-based diet. To make the transition easier, you can start by simply adding veggies or fruit to your breakfast. Mix in some spinach, mushrooms, peppers, and other veggies to your eggs. You can also blend a fruit smoothie or just grab a banana on your way out. These foods are filling and can make the switch to a plant-based diet easier.

Be aware of harmful chemicals and ingredients.

Not all fresh produce is treated equally. Much of the offseason items you find at the grocery store can be harmful to your health as they are treated with pesticides or other chemicals. Genetically modified organisms (GMOs) are also of great concern given their genetically engineered DNA. A GMO refers to any organism whose genetics have been altered or modified with the DNA of another organism through genetic engineering. Through this process, most crops and products have grown to be pesticide-resistant, weather resistant, and modified to grow in greater quantities. When this occurs, it can be incredibly harmful as these plants are often treated with toxic chemicals. These chemicals should kill the plant, however, because of the modifications made to the plant's genetic makeup, the chemicals are instead absorbed. These chemicals are then transferred to your own body when you consume any GMO foods.

In addition to the health risks posed by GMOs, they are incredibly harmful to the environment as they cause original nutrient-dense plants to become extinct, resulting in only the GMO versions of these plants to be available. This has become a widespread concern in many countries around the world which have already taken measures to limit or ban the production of GMO foods.

When shopping, always buy organic whenever possible. This is an important aspect of the whole foods plant-based diet as it brings awareness to the quality of foods and influences how the crops and produce are grown and how livestock are reared. Organic foods are untreated and are of the most natural state possible.

Join an online community

Joining groups with other individuals who already living a whole food plant-based lifestyle can help make the transition easier. It is a good idea to join different communities to learn more about the diet itself. Online social groups are also a great place to turn to when you need ideas for recipes, meal plans, or how to get the rest of your family on the same page as you. You can find groups that are about whole foods and

181

plant-based diets by doing a quick search on Facebook or Instagram. Some social media groups to check out:

- Eat to live Daily

- My Vegan Dreams

- Plant Based Nutrition Support Group

Get the proper tools for your kitchen

You probably already have most of the tools and essentials necessary for a plant-based diet in your kitchen. This includes things like knives, cutting boards, and strainers. There are additional tools that can make prepping and cooking whole foods more enjoyable. Rice cookers, steamer basket, blender, Instapots, and other kitchen appliances can make cooking easier. Stocking up on storage containers will help your meal prep like a pro (we will go over meal prepping more in detail later on). A whole foods plant-based diet doesn't have to be a lot of work and stocking your kitchen with the right tools will lessen the workload.

Plan ahead when eating out

A lot of people get stuck on how they can enjoy dining out when dedicated to a whole foods plant-based diet, but this shouldn't be a concern. Many local restaurants already use locally sourced foods which means they use quality products. However, this isn't always the case with chain restaurants which is something you want to keep in mind. If you are planning on enjoying an evening out, do your research first.

Look for places that specialize in vegan or organic foods. Feel free to call the restaurant ahead of time to see how your dietary needs can be accommodated. Another thing you want to do is read through reviews as this will allow you to see what others are saying about the location and if they are willing to make menu changes to accommodate customers. Places to read reviews can include: • The restaurants social media page such as Facebook or Instagram.

- Yelp

- Zagat

- OpenTable

- Trip Advisor

Eating a whole foods plant-based diet doesn't mean your nights out need to end, it simply means finding new, interesting spots that you may have overlooked before.

Experiment, a lot!

A plant-based diet offers a variety of dishes that can be enjoyed. Many find eating most of their meals in raw form or uncooked, to be the best. Others like to steam their food, spice up their veggies, and include a variety of textures and flavors. Have an open mind and embrace a new way of cooking. Experiment with various ingredients, profiles, and styles of cooking until you find one you enjoy and can stick with for a majority of your meals. Find a few stable meals and recipes that you can use regularly, but also continue to try new things. It is also a good idea to continue experimenting, even if you have found a preference, to keep things interesting.

Keep things simple

When you are eating a diet that focuses on consuming more plants and whole foods, counting calories is of little importance. Many people at first struggle with how much food they find themselves consuming throughout the day. Rest assured, that since most of the foods you are eating are nutrient-dense as opposed to calorically dense, it is normal to eat more. Do not worry about how many calories you consume, instead, listen to your body and avoid depriving it of food when you feel hungry. However, just be sure the foods you eat are providing value.

A plant-based diet doesn't just involve changing what you eat, it also involves changing the way you think about food. When you feel apprehensive about snacking on another fruit bowl or nuts, remind yourself that you are supplying your body with vital nutrients and vitamins that it needs, so you don't want to deprive it. Learn to enjoy the foods you are eating and let go of the idea that you have to count calories or fear how much you are eating.

Mindful eating can help you build a better relationship with the food you eat and let go of the anxiety that comes with counting calories or perfect portions. With mindful eating, you engage all your senses, you savor every bite and focus on the taste and textures as you chew. By practicing this type of mindfulness while you eat, you learn to enjoy food more as well as honor your body and health at the same time.

How to grocery shop?

When shopping you want to first buy as much of your produce from local farmer's markets. When at the grocery store, always have a list prepared so you are less likely to deviate and choose unhealthy options. Stick to the perimeter of the store. It is the perimeter of the grocery store where you will find most of the fresh produce. This is where you want to do a majority of your shopping.

Cutting back on meat

In the Western world, meat has taken over the center stage for meals. This is why many individuals struggle with eliminating meat from their diets. When you are first starting out on a plant-based diet, you want to begin by limiting the meat products you consume and replace them with more veggies. Begin experimenting with alternative protein sources like legumes and beans. To give you a visual, picture this, instead of making meat a centerpiece on your place, use it as an accessory or decorative component.

Transitioning to a whole food plant-based diet can be fun, simple, and one of the best things you can do for your health and well-being, but you may still have some questions in the back of your mind. You have probably heard a number of misconceptions or concerns about plant-based diets.

Chapter 5.
Breakfast Recipes

Berry and Ginger Smoothie

 Preparation:
5 Minutes

 Cooking:
1 Minutes

 Serves:
2

Ingredients

- 1 cup cauliflower florets
- 1 cup frozen raspberries
- 2 1-inch piece of ginger, peeled
- 1 cup strawberries
- 2 cups almond milk, unsweetened

Directions

1. Add all the ingredients in the order into a food processor and blender and then pulse for 1 to 2 minutes until blended.
2. Distribute the smoothie among glasses and then serve.

Nutritions: *351 Cal; 8.3 g Fat; 2 g Saturated Fat; 58.4 g Carbohydrates; 15 g Fiber; 30 g Sugars; 15.4 g Protein*

Spinach and Chia Seeds Smoothie

 Preparation:
5 Minutes

 Cooking:
1 Minutes

 Serves:
2

Ingredients

- 2 teaspoons chia seeds
- 1 cup spinach leaves
- 1 frozen banana
- 1/2 of a medium avocado, peeled, pitted
- 2 tablespoons hemp hearts
- 2 cups almond milk, unsweetened

Directions

1. Add all the ingredients in the order into a food processor and blender and then pulse for 1 to 2 minutes until blended.
2. Distribute the smoothie among glasses and then serve.

Nutritions: *288 Cal; 2.8 g Fat; 1.2 g Saturated Fat; 27 g Carbohydrates; 2.6 g Fiber; 12 g Sugars; 9.2 g Protein*

Zucchini and Banana Smoothie

Preparation:
5 Minutes

Cooking:
1 Minutes

Serves:
2

Ingredients

- 1 cup chopped zucchini
- 1 teaspoon cinnamon
- 2 frozen bananas
- 4 tablespoons almond butter
- 2 cups almond milk, unsweetened

Directions

1. Add all the ingredients in the order into a food processor and blender and then pulse for 1 to 2 minutes until blended.
2. Distribute the smoothie among glasses and then serve.

Nutritions: *300 Cal; 8 g Fat; 2 g Saturated Fat; 30 g Carbohydrates; 9 g Fiber; 18 g Sugars; 8 g Protein*

Berries and Hemp Seeds Smoothie

Preparation:
5 Minutes

Cooking:
1 Minutes

Serves:
2

Ingredients

- 1/4 cup hemp seeds
- 1 banana
- 2 tablespoons chia seeds
- 1 cup mixed frozen fruits
- 2 cups of water

Directions

1. Add all the ingredients in the order into a food processor and blender and then pulse for 1 to 2 minutes until blended.
2. Distribute the smoothie among glasses and then serve.

Nutritions: *189.6 Cal; 1 g Fat; 0.4 g Saturated Fat; 34.8 g Carbohydrates; 4.4 g Fiber; 10.5 g Sugars; 12 g Protein*

Banana Oats Smoothie

Preparation:
5 Minutes

Cooking:
1 Minutes

Serves:
2

Directions

1. Add all the ingredients in the order into a food processor and blender and then pulse for 1 to 2 minutes until blended.
2. Distribute the smoothie among glasses and then serve.

Ingredients

- 2 teaspoons chia seeds
- 1/2 cup ground rolled oats
- 2 frozen bananas
- 2 cups almond milk, unsweetened
- 1 cup crushed ice

Nutritions: *148 Cal; 2.6 g Fat; 0.8 g Saturated Fat; 25.3 g Carbohydrates; 4.3 g Fiber; 11.5 g Sugars; 6 g Protein*

Preparation:
5 Minutes

Cooking:
1 Minutes

Serves:
2

Ingredients

- 2 cups frozen mango cubes
- 2 frozen bananas
- 2 oranges, peeled
- 1/4 teaspoon ground black pepper
- 1/2 teaspoon turmeric powder
- 2 cups almond milk, unsweetened

Directions

1. Add all the ingredients in the order into a food processor and blender and then pulse for 1 to 2 minutes until blended.
2. Distribute the smoothie among glasses and then serve.

Nutritions: *185 Cal; 4 g Fat; 1.8 g Saturated Fat; 34 g Carbohydrates; 3.3 g Fiber; 28 g Sugars; 5 g Protein*

191

Cranberry Green Smoothie

 Preparation:
5 Minutes

 Cooking:
1 Minutes

Serves:
4

Ingredients

- 1/2 cup frozen cranberries
- 2 cups spinach
- 1/2 cup frozen chopped banana
- 1 tablespoon hemp seeds
- 3/4 cup almond milk, unsweetened
- 1/4 teaspoon cinnamon powder
- 3/4 cup water, cold

Directions

1. Add all the ingredients in the order into a food processor and blender and then pulse for 1 to 2 minutes until blended.
2. Distribute the smoothie among glasses and then serve.

Nutritions: *176 Cal; 8 g Fat; 6 g Saturated Fat; 26 g Carbohydrates; 6 g Fiber; 10 g Sugars; 2 g Protein*

Strawberry and White Bean Smoothie

 Preparation:
5 Minutes

 Cooking:
1 Minutes

 Serves:
2

Directions

1. Add all the ingredients in the order into a food processor and blender and then pulse for 1 to 2 minutes until blended.
2. Distribute the smoothie among glasses and then serve.

Ingredients

- 1 cup cooked white beans
- 2 frozen bananas, chopped
- 1 cup strawberries, halved
- 1 tablespoon hemp seeds
- 1/2 teaspoon vanilla extract, unsweetened
- 3/4 cup of water

Nutritions: *226 Cal; 3 g Fat; 0 g Saturated Fat; 45 g Carbohydrates; 8 g Fiber; 19 g Sugars; 8 g Protein*

Peanut Butter Protein Smoothie

Preparation:
5 Minutes

Cooking:
1 Minutes

Serves:
4

Ingredients

- 2 cups kale
- 2 tablespoons hemp seeds
- 1 frozen banana
- 2 tablespoons cacao powder, unsweetened
- 1 tablespoon peanut butter
- 1 scoop vanilla protein powder
- 1 cup almond milk, unsweetened
- 2/3 cup water
- 2 cups of ice cubes

Directions

1. Add all the ingredients in the order into a food processor and blender and then pulse for 1 to 2 minutes until blended.
2. Distribute the smoothie among glasses and then serve.

Nutritions: *286 Cal; 11.6 g Fat; 1 g Saturated Fat; 28 g Carbohydrates; 6 g Fiber; 11 g Sugars; 16.8 g Protein*

Cherry and Banana Smoothie

 Preparation:
5 Minutes

 Cooking:
1 Minutes

 Serves:
4

Ingredients

- 1 cup cauliflower rice, frozen
- 2 tablespoons flesh of aloe vera
- 1 cup frozen sweet cherries
- 2 frozen bananas
- 1/2 cup almond milk, unsweetened

Directions

1. Add all the ingredients in the order into a food processor and blender and then pulse for 1 to 2 minutes until blended.
2. Distribute the smoothie among glasses and then serve.

Nutritions: *150 Cal; 2.2 g Fat; 1.5 g Saturated Fat; 26 g Carbohydrates; 2 g Fiber; 13 g Sugars; 7.3 g Protein*

Turmeric Green Smoothie

Preparation:
5 Minutes

Cooking:
1 Minutes

Serves:
4

Ingredients

- 2 cups baby spinach leaves
- 1 frozen banana
- 2 oranges, peeled
- 2 tablespoon ginger, peeled, chopped
- 1/4 teaspoon ground black pepper
- 1 teaspoon ground turmeric
- 1/2 cup coconut milk, unsweetened
- 2 cups of water

Directions

1. Add all the ingredients in the order into a food processor and blender and then pulse for 1 to 2 minutes until blended.
2. Distribute the smoothie among glasses and then serve.

Nutritions: *180 Cal; 3.6 g Fat; 1 g Saturated Fat; 37.1 g Carbohydrates; 2.5 g Fiber; 25.7 g Sugars; 4.1 g Protein*

Preparation:
10 Minutes

Cooking:
15 Minutes

Serves:
2

Ingredients

- ▶ 2 slices of whole-wheat bread
- ▶ 1/4 of avocado, sliced
- ▶ 1 cup mixed salad greens
- ▶ 1/4 cup alfalfa sprouts
- ▶ 1/4 teaspoon ground black pepper
- ▶ 1/4 teaspoon salt
- ▶ 2 teaspoons sunflower seeds, unsalted
- ▶ 1 teaspoon apple cider vinegar
- ▶ 1 teaspoon olive oil
- ▶ 1/4 cup hummus

Directions

1. Take a skillet pan, place it over medium heat and when hot, add bread slices and cook for 4 minutes until toasted on both sides.
2. Then take a medium bowl, add greens in it, season with black pepper and salt, add oil and vinegar and toss until mixed.
3. Spread hummus on one side of each toast, then top evenly with prepared green mixture, avocado, and sprouts and then sprinkle with sunflower seeds.
4. Serve straight away.

Nutritions: *429 Cal; 22 g Fat; 3 g Saturated Fat; 46.4 g Carbohydrates; 15.1 g Fiber; 1 g Sugars; 16.2 g Protein*

Chocolate and Banana Oatmeal

 Preparation:
5 Minutes

 Cooking:
15 Minutes

 Serves:
2

Ingredients

- 1 small banana, sliced
- 1 cup rolled oats, old-fashioned
- 1/4 teaspoon salt
- 2 tablespoons chocolate-hazelnut spread
- 2 cups of water

Directions

1. Take a small saucepan, place it over medium-high heat, pour in water, stir in salt, and bring it to a boil.
2. Then add oats, stir until mixed, switch heat to medium level, and cook for 5 minutes or more until all the cooking liquid has been absorbed by the oats.
3. When done, remove the pan from heat, let oat stand for 3 minutes and then fluff with a fork.
4. Top oats with banana and chocolate-hazelnut spread and then serve.

Nutritions: *295 Cal; 8.7 g Fat; 5.8 g Saturated Fat; 50 g Carbohydrates; 6.3 g Fiber; 17 g Sugars; 6.6 g Protein*

VEGAN COOKBOOK FOR ATHLETES

French Toast with Berry Compote

Preparation:
10 Minutes

Cooking:
30 Minutes

Serves:
4

Ingredients

For French Toast:
- 4 bread slices, whole-grain, each about 3/4-inch thick
- 1/2 cup chickpea liquid or aquafaba
- 1/4 cup almond flour
- 1/4 teaspoon salt
- 1/8 teaspoon ground cinnamon
- 1/4 tablespoon orange zest
- 1 tablespoon maple syrup
- 3/4 cup almond milk, unsweetened

For Berry Compote:
- 1/2 teaspoon maple syrup
- 1/2 cup frozen blueberries, thawed
- 1/4 cup applesauce

Directions

1. Switch on the oven, then set it to 400 degrees F and let it preheat.
2. Meanwhile, take a medium bowl, add flour in it along with cinnamon, salt, maple syrup, and aquafaba and whisk until smooth.
3. Transfer this mixture to a shallow dish, then add orange zest and stir until mixed.
4. Take a skillet pan, place it over medium-low heat, and wait until it gets hot.
5. Then dip each slice of bread into the prepared mixture, let soak for a few seconds, then turn the slice and continue soaking for some more seconds.
6. Transfer bread slice into the heated skillet pan and then cook for 3 minutes per side until golden brown.
7. Transfer toast to a plate and repeat with the remaining bread slices.
8. Take a baking sheet, place a wire rack on it, then arrange prepared toast on it and bake for 10 minutes until crispy.
9. Meanwhile, prepare the berry compote and for this, place berries in a food processor, add maple syrup and apple sauce, and then pulse for 2 minutes until smooth.
10. When done, top the French toast with berry compote and then serve.

Nutritions: *178 Cal; 3.5 g Fat; 0.5 g Saturated Fat; 27.7 g Carbohydrates; 5 g Fiber; 8 g Sugars; 9 g Protein*

Chocolate Chip and Coconut Pancakes

 Preparation:
10 Minutes

 Cooking:
20 Minutes

 Serves:
4

Ingredients

- 2 bananas, sliced
- ¾ cup buckwheat flour
- 1 tablespoon coconut flakes, unsweetened
- 2 tablespoons rolled oats, old-fashioned
- 1/8 teaspoon sea salt
- 1/2 tablespoon baking powder
- 1/3 cup mini chocolate chips, grain-sweetened
- 1/4 cup maple syrup
- 1 teaspoon vanilla extract, unsweetened
- 1/2 tablespoon flaxseeds
- 1/4 cup of water
- 1/2 cup applesauce, unsweetened
- 1 cup almond milk, unsweetened

Directions

1. Take a small saucepan, place it over medium heat, add flaxseeds, pour in water, stir until mixed and cook for 3 minutes or until sticky mixture comes together.
2. Then immediately strain the flaxseed mixture into a cup, discard the seeds, and set aside until required.
3. Take a large bowl, add oats and flour in it, stir in salt, baking powder, and coconut flakes and then whisk until combined.
4. Take another bowl, add flax seed reserve along with maple syrup, vanilla, applesauce, and milk and then whisk until combined.
5. Transfer this mixture into the oat-flour mixture, stir until combined, and then fold in chocolate chips until mixed.
6. Take a skillet pan, place it over medium-low heat, spray it with oil and when hot, pour in one-fourth of the batter, spread gently into a pancake shape, and cook for 5 minutes per side until golden brown on both sides.
7. Transfer pancake to a plate and repeat with the remaining batter.
8. Serve pancakes with sliced banana.

Nutritions: *205.5 Cal; 5 g Fat; 2 g Saturated Fat; 37.7 g Carbohydrates; 5.2 g Fiber; 4 g Sugars; 6 g Protein*

Chocolate Pancake

Preparation:
15 Minutes

Cooking:
15 Minutes

Serves:
6

Ingredients

- 3/4 cup whole-grain flour
- 1 tablespoon ground flaxseed
- 2 tablespoons cocoa powder, unsweetened
- 1 tablespoon baking powder
- 1 tablespoon maple syrup
- 1/4 teaspoon of sea salt
- 1 tablespoon mini chocolate chips
- 1 teaspoon vanilla extract, unsweetened
- 1/4 cup applesauce, unsweetened
- 1 tablespoon apple cider vinegar
- 1 cup almond milk, unsweetened

Directions

1. Take a medium bowl, add flour and flaxseed in it, and then whisk in baking powder, cocoa powder, salt, and chocolate chips until well combined.
2. Take another bowl, add vanilla, maple syrup, vinegar and milk in it, whisk until mixed and then add this mixture into the flour.
3. Add apple sauce, whisk until smooth batter comes together, and let it stand for 10 minutes at room temperature until thickened.
4. Then take a skillet pan, take a skillet pan, place it over medium heat, spray it with oil and when hot, pour in some of the prepared batter, spread gently into a pancake shape, and cook for 3 minutes per side until golden brown on both sides.
5. Transfer pancake to a plate and repeat with the remaining batter.
6. Serve straight away.

Nutritions: *251 Cal; 1 g Fat; 0.3 g Saturated Fat; 58.7 g Carbohydrates; 3 g Fiber; 5.7 g Sugars; 7 g Protein*

Chickpea Omelet

 Preparation:
10 Minutes

 Cooking:
12 Minutes

 Serves:
2

Ingredients

- 1 cup chickpea flour
- 4 ounces sautéed mushrooms
- 3 green onions, chopped
- 1/2 teaspoon garlic powder
- 1/2 teaspoon onion powder
- 1/2 teaspoon baking soda
- 1/3 cup nutritional yeast
- 1/4 teaspoon ground white pepper
- 1/4 teaspoon ground black pepper
- 1 cup of water

Directions

1. Take a medium bowl, add chickpea flour in it, then add remaining ingredients except for onion and mushrooms and whisk until smooth batter comes together.
2. Take a frying pan, place it over medium heat, spray it with oil, and when hot, pour in half of the batter and spread it gently.
3. Top with half of mushroom and onion, cook for 3 to 4 minutes until the bottom has turned nicely golden brown, then flip it and continue cooking for 2 minutes until cooked.
4. Transfer omelet to a plate and then repeat with the remaining batter.
5. Serve straight away.

Nutritions: *150 Cal; 2 g Fat; 0.1 g Saturated Fat; 24.4 g Carbohydrates; 5.8 g Fiber; 5.1 g Sugars; 10.2 g Protein*

VEGAN COOKBOOK FOR ATHLETES

Polenta with Pears and Cranberries

Preparation:
10 Minutes

Cooking:
12 Minutes

Serves:
4

Ingredients

- 1 cup dried cranberries
- 1 teaspoon ground cinnamon
- 2 pears, peeled, cored, diced
- 1/4 cup brown rice syrup
- 2 cups of Polenta, warm

Directions

1. Take a medium saucepan, place it over medium heat, add rice syrup, and cook for 2 minutes until hot.
2. Then add berries and pears, sprinkle with cinnamon, stir until mixed and cook for 10 minutes until tender.
3. Distribute polenta among bowls, top with cooked berries mixture, and then serve.

Nutritions: *227 Cal; 1.5 g Fat; 0.2 g Saturated Fat; 49 g Carbohydrates; 5 g Fiber; 4 g Sugars; 9 g Protein*

Fruit and Nut Oatmeal

 Preparation:
5 Minutes

 Cooking:
10 Minutes

 Serves:
3

Ingredients

- 2 tablespoons chopped apples
- 1/4 cup fresh berries
- 3/4 cup rolled oats
- 1/2 of banana, sliced
- 2 tablespoons apricot
- 2 tablespoons cranberries
- 1/4 teaspoon ground cinnamon
- 1/4 teaspoon of sea salt
- 2 tablespoons chopped walnuts
- 2 tablespoons raisins
- 2 tablespoons maple syrup
- 1 1/2 cup water

Directions

1. Take a small saucepan, place it over high heat, add oats, pour in water, and bring it to a boil.
2. Switch heat to medium-low level, simmer for 5 minutes until oats have cooked, then remove the pan from heat and stir in salt and cinnamon.
3. Distribute oats evenly among bowls, top with remaining ingredients, drizzling with maple syrup in the end, and then serve.

Nutritions: *152.5 Cal; 3.4 g Fat; 0.5 g Saturated Fat; 30 g Carbohydrates; 3 g Fiber; 10 g Sugars; 3.5 g Protein*

Brown Rice Breakfast Pudding with Dates

Preparation:
10 Minutes

Cooking:
12 Minutes

Serves:
4

Ingredients

- 1 cup dates, pitted, chopped
- 3 cups cooked brown rice
- 1 apple, cored, chopped
- 1/4 teaspoon salt
- 1 cinnamon stick
- 1/4 cup raisins
- 1/4 teaspoon ground cloves
- 1/4 cup slivered almonds, toasted
- 2 cups almond milk, unsweetened

Directions

1. Take a medium saucepan, place it over medium-low heat, add rice, stir in dates, cinnamon, and cloves, pour in milk, stir until mixed, and then cook for 12 minutes until thickened.
2. Then remove cinnamon stick from the pudding and remove the pan from heat.
3. Add apple and raisins into the pudding, season with salt, and stir until mixed.
4. Garnish pudding with almonds and then serve.

Nutritions: *196.4 Cal; 3.1 g Fat; 0.6 g Saturated Fat; 34.1 g Carbohydrates; 2.5 g Fiber; 6.5 g Sugars; 7.9 g Protein*

Overnight Oats with Chia

 Preparation:
8 h 5 minutes

 Cooking:
1 Minutes

 Serves:
2

Ingredients

- 2 bananas, peeled, sliced
- 1/2 cup mixed berries
- 1 1/2 cup rolled oats
- 2 tablespoons chia seeds
- 1/2 teaspoon cinnamon
- 2 tablespoons maple syrup
- 1 teaspoon vanilla extract, unsweetened
- 1/2 cup almond milk, unsweetened
- 1 cup of water

Directions

1. Take two 16 ounces mason jars, add all the liquid ingredients in them evenly except for banana and berries, then shut the jars with lid and place them in the refrigerator overnight.
2. When ready to eat, mix the oats, top with banana and berries and then serve.

Nutritions: *263 Cal; 9 g Fat; 2 g Saturated Fat; 33 g Carbohydrates; 6 g Fiber; 9 g Sugars; 19 g Protein*

Chapter 6.
Lunch Recipes

Avocado, Spinach and Kale Soup

Preparation:
10 Minutes

Cooking:
0 Minutes

Serves:
4

Ingredients

- 2 avocados, pitted, peeled and cut in halves
- 4 cups vegetable stock
- 2 tablespoons cilantro, chopped
- Juice of 1 lime
- 1 teaspoon rosemary, dried
- ½ cup spinach leaves
- ½ cup kale, torn
- Salt and black pepper to the taste

Directions

1. In a blender, combine the avocados with the stock and the other ingredients, pulse well, divide into bowls and serve for lunch.

Nutritions: *Calories 300, Fat 23, Fiber 5, Carbs 6, Protein 7*

Curry spinach soup

Preparation:
10 Minutes

Cooking:
0 Minutes

Serves:
4

Ingredients

► 1 cup almond milk
► 1 tablespoon green curry paste
► 1 pound spinach leaves
► 1 tablespoon cilantro, chopped
► Salt and black pepper to the taste
► 4 cups veggie stock
► 1 tablespoon cilantro, chopped

Directions

1. In your blender, combine the almond milk with the curry paste and the other ingredients, pulse well, divide into bowls and serve for lunch.

Nutritions: *Calories 240, Fat 4, Fiber 2, Carbs 6, Protein 2*

Arugula and Artichokes Bowls

Preparation:
5 Minutes

Cooking:
0 Minutes

Serves:
4

Ingredients

- 2 cups baby arugula
- ¼ cup walnuts, chopped
- 1 cup canned artichoke hearts, drained and quartered
- 1 tablespoon balsamic vinegar
- 2 tablespoons cilantro, chopped
- 2 tablespoons olive oil
- Salt and black pepper to the taste
- 1 tablespoon lemon juice

Directions

1. In a bowl, combine the artichokes with the arugula, walnuts and the other ingredients, toss, divide into smaller bowls and serve for lunch.

Nutritions: *Calories 200, Fat 2, Fiber 1, Carbs 5, Protein 7*

Minty arugula soup

Preparation:
5 Minutes

Cooking:
10 Minutes

Serves:
4

Ingredients

- 3 scallions, chopped
- 1 tablespoon olive oil
- ½ Cup coconut milk
- 2 cups baby arugula
- 2 tablespoons mint, chopped
- 6 cups vegetable stock
- 2 tablespoons chives, chopped
- Salt and black pepper to the taste

Directions

1. Heat up a pot with the oil over medium high heat, add the scallions and sauté for 2 minutes.
2. Add the rest of the ingredients, toss, bring to a simmer and cook over medium heat for 8 minutes more.
3. Divide the soup into bowls and serve.

Nutritions: *Calories 200, Fat 4, Fiber 2, Carbs 6, Protein 10*

Spinach and Broccoli Soup

Preparation:
10 Minutes

Cooking:
20 Minutes

Serves:
4

Ingredients

- 3 shallots, chopped
- 1 tablespoon olive oil
- 2 garlic cloves, minced
- ½ pound broccoli florets
- ½ pound baby spinach
- Salt and black pepper to the taste
- 4 cups veggie stock
- 1 teaspoon turmeric powder
- 1 tablespoon lime juice

Directions

1. Heat up a pot with the oil over medium high heat, add the shallots and the garlic and sauté for 5 minutes.
2. Add the broccoli, spinach and the other ingredients, toss, bring to a simmer and cook over medium heat for 15 minutes.
3. Ladle into soup bowls and serve.

Nutritions: *Calories 150, Fat 3, Fiber 1, Carbs 3, Protein 7*

Coconut zucchini cream

Preparation:
10 Minutes

Cooking:
25 Minutes

Serves:
4

Ingredients

- 1 pound zucchinis, roughly chopped
- 2 tablespoons avocado oil
- 4 scallions, chopped
- Salt and black pepper to the taste
- 6 cups veggie stock
- 1 teaspoon basil, dried
- 1 teaspoon cumin, ground
- 3 garlic cloves, minced
- ¾ cup coconut cream
- 1 tablespoon dill, chopped

Directions

1. Heat up a pot with the oil over medium high heat, add the scallions and the garlic and sauté for 5 minutes.
2. Add the rest of the ingredients, stir, bring to a simmer and cook over medium heat for 20 minutes more.
3. Blend the soup using an immersion blender, ladle into bowls and serve.

Nutritions: *Calories 160, Fat 4, Fiber 2, Carbs 4, Protein 8*

Zucchini and Cauliflower Soup

Preparation:
10 Minutes

Cooking:
25 Minutes

Serves:
4

Ingredients

- 4 scallions, chopped
- 1 teaspoon ginger, grated
- 2 tablespoons olive oil
- 1 pound zucchinis, sliced
- 2 cups cauliflower florets
- Salt and black pepper to the taste
- 6 cups veggie stock
- 1 garlic clove, minced
- 1 tablespoon lemon juice
- 1 cup coconut cream

Directions

1. Heat up a pot with the oil over medium heat, add the scallions, ginger and the garlic and sauté for 5 minutes.
2. Add the rest of the ingredients, bring to a simmer and cook over medium heat for 20 minutes.
3. Blend everything using an immersion blender, ladle into soup bowls and serve.

Nutritions: *Calories 154, Fat 12, Fiber 3, Carbs 5, Protein 4*

Preparation:
10 Minutes

Cooking:
25 Minutes

Serves:
4

Ingredients

- 1 pound Swiss chard, chopped
- ½ cup shallots, chopped
- 1 tablespoon avocado oil
- 1 teaspoon cumin, ground
- 1 teaspoon rosemary, dried
- 1 teaspoon basil, dried
- 2 garlic cloves, minced
- Salt and black pepper to the taste
- 6 cups vegetable stock
- 1 tablespoon tomato passata
- 1 tablespoon cilantro, chopped

Directions

1. Heat up a pan with the oil over medium heat, add the shallots and the garlic and sauté for 5 minutes.
2. Add the swiss chard and the other ingredients, toss, bring to a simmer and cook over medium heat for 20 minutes more.
3. Divide the soup into bowls and serve.

Nutritions: *Calories 232, Fat 23, Fiber 3, Carbs 4, Protein 3*

Avocado, Pine Nuts and Chard Salad

Preparation:
5 Minutes

Cooking:
15 Minutes

Serves:
4

Ingredients

- 1 pound swiss chard, roughly chopped
- 2 tablespoons olive oil
- 1 avocado, peeled, pitted and roughly cubed
- 2 spring onions, chopped
- ¼ Cup pine nuts, toasted
- 1 tablespoon balsamic vinegar
- Salt and black pepper to the taste

Directions

1. Heat up a pan with the oil over medium heat, add the spring onions, pine nuts and the chard, stir and sauté for 5 minutes.
2. Add the vinegar and the other ingredients, toss, cook over medium heat for 10 minutes more, divide into bowls and serve for lunch.

Nutritions: *Calories 120, Fat 2, Fiber 1, Carbs 4, Protein 8*

Grapes, Avocado and Spinach Salad

Preparation:
10 Minutes

Cooking:
0 Minutes

Serves:
4

Ingredients

- 1 cup green grapes, halved
- 2 cups baby spinach
- 1 avocado, pitted, peeled and cubed
- Salt and black pepper to the taste
- 2 tablespoons olive oil
- 1 tablespoon thyme, chopped
- 1 tablespoon rosemary, chopped
- 1 tablespoon lime juice
- 1 garlic clove, minced

Directions

1. In a salad bowl, combine the grapes with the spinach and the other ingredients, toss, and serve for lunch.

Nutritions: *Calories 190, Fat 17.1, Fiber 4.6, Carbs 10.9, Protein 1.7*

Greens and Olives Pan

Preparation:
10 Minutes

Cooking:
15 Minutes

Serves:
4

Ingredients

- 4 spring onions, chopped
- 2 tablespoons olive oil
- ½ cup green olives, pitted and halved
- ¼ cup pine nuts, toasted
- 1 tablespoon balsamic vinegar
- 2 cups baby spinach
- 1 cup baby arugula
- 1 cup asparagus, trimmed, blanched and halved
- Salt and black pepper to the taste

Directions

1. Heat up a pan with the oil over medium high heat, add the spring onions and the asparagus and sauté for 5 minutes.
2. Add the olives, spinach and the other ingredients, toss, cook over medium heat for 10 minutes, divide between plates and serve for lunch.

Nutritions: *Calories 136, Fat 13.1, Fiber 1.9, Carbs 4.4, Protein 2.8*

Preparation:
10 Minutes

Cooking:
30 Minutes

Serves:
4

Ingredients

- 3 cups Swiss chard, chopped
- 6 cups vegetable stock
- 1 cup mushrooms, sliced
- 2 garlic cloves, minced
- 1 tablespoon olive oil
- 2 scallions, chopped
- 2 tablespoons balsamic vinegar
- ¼ cup basil, chopped
- Salt and black pepper to the taste
- 1 tablespoon cilantro, chopped

Directions

1. Heat up a pot with the oil over medium high heat, add the scallions and the garlic and sauté for 5 minutes.
2. Add the mushrooms and sauté for another 5 minutes.
3. Add the rest of the ingredients, toss, bring to a simmer and cook over medium heat for 20 minutes more.
4. Ladle the soup into bowls and serve.

Nutritions: *Calories 140, Fat 4, Fiber 2, Carbs 4, Protein 8*

Tomato, Green Beans and Chard Soup

Preparation:
10 Minutes

Cooking:
35 Minutes

Serves:
4

Ingredients

- 2 scallions, chopped
- 1 cup swiss chard, chopped
- 1 tablespoon olive oil
- 1 red bell pepper, chopped
- Salt and black pepper to the taste
- 1 cup tomatoes, cubed
- 1 cup green beans, chopped
- 6 cups vegetable stock
- 2 tablespoons tomato passata
- 2 garlic cloves, minced
- 2 teaspoons thyme, chopped
- ½ Teaspoon red pepper flakes

Directions

1. Heat up a pot with the oil over medium heat, add the scallions, garlic and the pepper flakes and sauté for 5 minutes.
2. Add the chard and the other ingredients, toss, bring to a simmer and cook over medium heat for 30 minutes more.
3. Ladle the soup into bowls and serve for lunch.

Nutritions: *Calories 150, Fat 8, Fiber 2, Carbs 4, Protein 9*

Hot roasted peppers cream

Preparation:
10 Minutes

Cooking:
30 Minutes

Serves:
4

Ingredients

- 1 red chili pepper, minced
- 4 garlic cloves, minced
- 2 pounds mixed bell peppers, roasted, peeled and chopped
- 4 scallions, chopped
- 1 cup coconut cream
- Salt and black pepper to the taste
- 2 tablespoons olive oil
- ½ tablespoon basil, chopped
- 4 cups vegetable stock
- ¼ cup chives, chopped

Directions

1. Heat up a pot with the oil over medium heat, add the garlic and the chili pepper and sauté for 5 minutes.
2. Add the peppers and the other ingredients, toss, bring to a simmer and cook over medium heat for 25 minutes.
3. Blend the soup using an immersion blender, divide into bowls and serve.

Nutritions: *Calories 140, Fat 2, Fiber 2, Carbs 5, Protein 8*

Eggplant and Peppers Soup

Preparation:
10 Minutes

Cooking:
40 Minutes

Serves:
4

Ingredients

- 2 red bell peppers, chopped
- 3 scallions, chopped
- 3 garlic cloves, minced
- 2 tablespoon olive oil
- Salt and black pepper to the taste
- 5 cups vegetable stock
- 1 bay leaf
- ½ cup coconut cream
- 1 pound eggplants, roughly cubed
- 2 tablespoons basil, chopped

Directions

1. Heat up a pot with the oil over medium heat, add the scallions and the garlic and sauté for 5 minutes.
2. Add the peppers and the eggplants and sauté for 5 minutes more.
3. Add the remaining ingredients, toss, bring to a simmer, cook for 30 minutes, ladle into bowls and serve for lunch.

Nutritions: *Calories 180, Fat 2, Fiber 3, Carbs 5, Protein 10*

Eggplant and Olives Stew

 Preparation:
10 Minutes

 Cooking:
30 Minutes

 Serves:
4

Ingredients

- 2 scallions, chopped
- 2 tablespoons avocado oil
- 2 garlic cloves, chopped
- 1 bunch parsley, chopped
- Salt and black pepper to the taste
- 1 teaspoon basil, dried
- 1 teaspoon cumin, dried
- 2 eggplants, roughly cubed
- 1 cup green olives, pitted and sliced
- 3 tablespoons balsamic vinegar
- ½ Cup tomato passata

Directions

1. Heat up a pot with the oil over medium heat, add the scallions, garlic, basil and cumin and sauté for 5 minutes.
2. Add the eggplants and the other ingredients, toss, cook over medium heat for 25 minutes more, divide into bowls and serve.

Nutritions: *Calories 93, Fat 1.8, Fiber 10.6, Carbs 18.6, Protein 3.4*

Cauliflower and Artichokes Soup

Preparation:
10 Minutes

Cooking:
25 Minutes

Serves:
4

Ingredients

- 1 pound cauliflower florets
- 1 cup canned artichoke hearts, drained and chopped
- 2 scallions, chopped
- 2 tablespoons olive oil
- 2 garlic cloves, minced
- 6 cups vegetable stock
- Salt and black pepper to the taste
- 2/3 cup coconut cream
- 2 tablespoons cilantro, chopped

Directions

1. Heat up a pot with the oil over medium heat, add the scallions and the garlic and sauté for 5 minutes.
2. Add the cauliflower and the other ingredients, toss, bring to a simmer and cook over medium heat for 20 minutes more.
3. Blend the soup using an immersion blender, divide it into bowls and serve.

Nutritions: *Calories 207, Fat 17.2, Fiber 6.2, Carbs 14.1, Protein 4.7*

Hot cabbage soup

Preparation:
10 Minutes

Cooking:
30 Minutes

Serves:
4

Ingredients

- 3 spring onions, chopped
- 1 green cabbage head, shredded
- 2 tablespoons olive oil
- 1 tablespoon ginger, grated
- 1 teaspoon cumin, ground
- 6 cups vegetable stock
- Salt and black pepper to the taste
- 1 teaspoon hot paprika
- 1 teaspoon chili powder
- 1 tablespoon cilantro, chopped

Directions

1. Heat up a pot with the oil over medium heat, add the spring onions, ginger and the cumin and sauté for 5 minutes.
2. Add the cabbage and the other ingredients, stir, bring to a simmer and cook over medium heat for 25 minutes more.
3. Ladle the soup into bowls and serve for lunch.

Nutritions: *Calories 117, Fat 7.5, Fiber 5.2, Carbs 12.7, Protein 2.8*

Zucchini muffins

Preparation:
5 Minutes

Cooking:
30 Minutes

Serves:
6

Ingredients

- 4 scallions, chopped
- 1 tablespoon olive oil
- 2 zucchinis, chopped
- 1 yellow bell pepper, chopped
- Salt and black pepper to the taste
- 2 tablespoons flaxseed mixed with 3 tablespoons water
- 1 cup almond flour
- 1 cup almond milk
- 1 teaspoon baking powder
- 2 tablespoons chives, chopped

Directions

1. Heat up a pan with the oil over medium heat, add the scallions, zucchini is and the bell pepper and sauté for 5 minutes.
2. In a bowl, combine the scallions mix with the rest of the ingredients, stir well, divide into a muffin tray and bake at 390 degrees f for 25 minutes.
3. Divide the muffins between plates and serve them for breakfast.

Nutritions: *Calories 258, Fat 21.8, Fiber 4.9, Carbs 11.9, Protein 6.6*

Preparation:
5 Minutes

Cooking:
0 Minutes

Serves:
2

Ingredients

- ½ cup coconut flesh, unsweetened and shredded
- 1 cup coconut milk
- ¼ cup dates, chopped
- 1 teaspoon vanilla extract
- 1 tablespoon stevia
- 1 cup berries, mashed

Directions

1. In a bowl, combine the coconut flesh with the coconut milk, the dates and the other ingredients, whisk well, divide into 2 bowls and serve.

Nutritions: *Calories 572, Fat 47.2, Fiber 11.5, Carbs 38.8, Protein 5.8*

Tomato oatmeal

Preparation:
5 Minutes

Cooking:
20 Minutes

Serves:
4

Ingredients

- 3 cups water
- 1 cup coconut milk
- 1 tablespoon avocado oil
- 1 cup coconut flesh, unsweetened and shredded
- ¼ cup cherry tomatoes, chopped
- A pinch of red pepper flakes
- 1 teaspoon chili powder

Directions

1. Meanwhile, heat up a pan with the oil over medium-high heat, add the tomatoes, chili powder and pepper flakes and sauté for 5 minutes
2. Add the coconut and sauté for 5 minutes more.
3. Add the remaining ingredients, toss, bring to a simmer, cook over medium heat fro 10 minutes more, divide into bowls and serve for breakfast.

Nutritions: *Calories 170, Fat 17.8, Fiber 1.5, Carbs 3.8, Protein 1.5*

Mushroom muffins

 Preparation:
10 Minutes

 Cooking:
30 Minutes

 Serves:
8

Ingredients

- 1 cup cauliflower rice
- 2 tablespoons flaxseed mixed with 3 tablespoons water
- Salt and black pepper to the taste
- 1 cup cashew cheese, grated
- 4 scallions, chopped
- 1 red bell pepper chopped
- 1 cup white mushrooms, sliced
- Cooking spray

Directions

1. In a bowl, combine the cauliflower rice with the flaxseed mix, scallions and the other ingredients, and whisk well.
2. Grease a muffin pan with the cooking spray, divide the mushrooms mix, bake at 350 degrees f for 30 minutes and serve for breakfast.

Nutritions: *Calories 123, Fat 5.6, Fiber 1.3, Carbs 10.8, Protein 7.5*

Classic black beans chili

 Preparation:
10 Minutes

 Cooking:
3 h

 Serves:
4

Ingredients

- ½ cup quinoa
- 2 and ½ cups veggie stock
- 14 ounces canned tomatoes, chopped
- 15 ounces canned black beans, drained
- ¼ cup green bell pepper, chopped
- ¼ cup red bell pepper, chopped
- A pinch of salt and black pepper
- 2 garlic cloves, minced
- 1 carrots, shredded
- 1 small chili pepper, chopped
- 2 teaspoons chili powder
- 1 teaspoon cumin, ground
- A pinch of cayenne pepper
- ½ cup corn
- 1 teaspoon oregano, dried

For the vegan sour cream:
- A drizzle of apple cider vinegar
- 4 tablespoons water
- ½ cup cashews, soaked overnight and drained
- 1 teaspoon lime juice

Directions

1. Put the stock in your slow cooker.
2. Add quinoa, tomatoes, beans, red and green bell pepper, garlic, carrot, salt, pepper, corn, cumin, cayenne, chili powder, chili pepper and oregano, stir, cover and cook on High for 3 hours.
3. Meanwhile, put the cashews in your blender.
4. Add water, vinegar and lime juice and pulse really well.
5. Divide beans chili into bowls, top with vegan sour cream and serve.
6. Enjoy!

Nutritions: *Calories 300, Fat 4, Fiber 4, Carbs 10, Protein 7*

Amazing potato dish

Preparation:
10 Minutes

Cooking:
3 h

Serves:
4

Ingredients

- 1 and ½ pounds potatoes, peeled and roughly chopped
- 1 tablespoon olive oil
- 3 tablespoons water
- 1 small yellow onion, chopped
- ½ cup veggie stock cube, crumbled
- ½ teaspoon coriander, ground
- ½ teaspoon cumin, ground
- ½ teaspoon garam masala
- ½ teaspoon chili powder
- Black pepper to the taste
- ½ pound spinach, roughly torn

Directions

1. Put the potatoes in your slow cooker.
2. Add oil, water, onion, stock cube, coriander, cumin, garam masala, chili powder, black pepper and spinach.
3. Stir, cover and cook on High for 3 hours.
4. Divide into bowls and serve.
5. Enjoy!

Nutritions: *Calories 270, Fat 4, Fiber 6, Carbs 8, Protein 12*

Textured Sweet Potatoes and Lentils Delight

Preparation:
10 Minutes

Cooking:
4 h 30 minutes

Serves:
6

Ingredients

- 6 cups sweet potatoes, peeled and cubed
- 2 teaspoons coriander, ground
- 2 teaspoons chili powder
- 1 yellow onion, chopped
- 3 cups veggie stock
- 4 garlic cloves, minced
- A pinch of sea salt and black pepper
- 10 ounces canned coconut milk
- 1 cup water
- 1 and ½ cups red lentils

Directions

1. Put sweet potatoes in your slow cooker.
2. Add coriander, chili powder, onion, stock, garlic, salt and pepper, stir, cover and cook on high for 3 hours.
3. Add lentils, stir, cover and cook for 1 hour and 30 minutes.
4. Add water and coconut milk, stir well, divide into bowls and serve right away.
5. Enjoy!

Nutritions: *Calories 300, Fat 10, Fiber 8, Carbs 16, Protein 10*

Incredibly tasty pizza

Preparation:
1 h 10 minutes

Cooking:
1 h 45 minutes

Serves:
3

Ingredients

For the dough:
- ½ teaspoon Italian seasoning
- 1 and ½ cups whole wheat flour
- 1 and ½ teaspoons instant yeast
- 1 tablespoon olive oil
- A pinch of salt
- ½ cup warm water
- Cooking spray

For the sauce:
- ¼ cup green olives, pitted and sliced
- ¼ cup kalamata olives, pitted and sliced
- ½ cup tomatoes, crushed
- 1 tablespoon parsley, chopped
- 1 tablespoon capers, rinsed
- ¼ teaspoon garlic powder
- ¼ teaspoon basil, dried
- ¼ teaspoon oregano, dried
- ¼ teaspoon palm sugar
- ¼ teaspoon red pepper flakes
- A pinch of salt and black pepper
- ½ cup cashew mozzarella, shredded

Directions

1. In your food processor, mix yeast with italian seasoning, a pinch of salt and flour.
2. Add oil and the water and blend well until you obtain a dough.
3. Transfer dough to a floured working surface, knead well, transfer to a greased bowl, cover and leave aside for 1 hour.
4. Meanwhile, in a bowl, mix green olives with kalamata olives, tomatoes, parsley, capers, garlic powder, oregano, sugar, salt, pepper and pepper flakes and stir well.
5. Transfer pizza dough to a working surface again and flatten it.
6. Shape so it will fit your slow cooker.
7. Grease your slow cooker with cooking spray and add dough.
8. Press well on the bottom.
9. Spread the sauce mix all over, cover and cook on high for 1 hour and 15 minutes.
10. Spread vegan mozzarella all over, cover again and cook on high for 30 minutes more.
11. Leave your pizza to cool down before slicing and serving it.

Nutritions: *Calories 340, Fat 5, Fiber 7, Carbs 13, Protein 15*

Rich beans soup

Preparation:
10 Minutes

Cooking:
7 h

Serves:
4

Ingredients

- 1 pound navy beans
- 1 yellow onion, chopped
- 4 garlic cloves, crushed
- 2 quarts veggie stock
- A pinch of sea salt
- Black pepper to the taste
- 2 potatoes, peeled and cubed
- 2 teaspoons dill, dried
- 1 cup sun-dried tomatoes, chopped
- 1 pound carrots, sliced
- 4 tablespoons parsley, minced

Directions

1. Put the stock in your slow cooker.
2. Add beans, onion, garlic, potatoes, tomatoes, carrots, dill, salt and pepper, stir, cover and cook on low for 7 hours.
3. Stir your soup, add parsley, divide into bowls and serve.
4. Enjoy!

Nutritions: *Calories 250, Fat 4, Fiber 3, Carbs 9, Protein 10*

Chapter 7. Dinner

Smoky tempeh burrito bowls

Preparation:
1 h 45 minutes

Serves:
3

Ingredients

- 15 oz. Can black beans
- ½ teaspoon cumin powder
- 1 cup uncooked brown rice
- Water
- 10 oz. Tempeh
- 1 tablespoon avocado oil
- ½ white onion, diced
- 1 tablespoon olive oil
- 2 garlic cloves, minced
- 15 oz. Tomato sauce
- 1 whole chipotle in adobo sauce
- 1 tablespoon adobo sauce
- Red cabbage, sliced

Directions

1. Add 1" water to a saucepan and bring to a simmer. Add the steamer basket on top and add tempeh to the basket. Steam for 15 minutes. Cube and set aside.
2. Heat a skillet over medium heat. Add oil and onion. Cook for 3 minutes add garlic and cook for 2 minutes.
3. Add chipotle pepper, adobo sauce, and tomato sauce and mix. Heat until starts to bubble, reduce the heat and simmer for 4 minutes.
4. Transfer the sauce to a blender and blend on high until smooth. Transfer the sauce back to the skillet and heat over low heat.
5. Add the black beans to a pan and heat over medium heat. Once boils, reduce the heat, add cumin, and add salt.
6. Heat a skillet over medium heat. Add oil and cubed steamed tempeh and cook for 8 minutes until crisp. Add to the red sauce and mix well. Cover with the lid for 3 minutes, remove and simmer over low heat.
7. Divide everything among 4 serving bowls. Add red cabbage.
8. Serve and enjoy.

Sweet and sour tempeh

Preparation:
20 Minutes

Serves:
2

Ingredients

- 1 brown onion
- 1 packet tempeh, gluten-free
- 1 teaspoon sesame oil
- 1 tablespoon sunflower oil
- ½ bell pepper
- 1/3 cup rice vinegar
- 1 tablespoon ketchup
- 4 tablespoons coconut sugar
- 1 teaspoon tamari
- 2 teaspoons cornstarch
- 4 teaspoons water
- Handful of snow peas

Directions

1. Dissolve cornstarch in water.
2. Mix rice vinegar, ketchup, coconut sugar and tamari in a pan placed over medium heat. Bring to a boil. Remove from heat, add cornstarch mixture, and set aside.
3. Cut tempeh into squares. Cut bell peppers into slices and prepare the snow peas. Add sesame and sunflower oil into a pan. Fry tempeh until brown.
4. Dice onion and add to the tempeh and cook until browned. Add prepped veggies and cook for about 3 minutes. Add the sauce, mix well to coat well, and cook for 2 minutes.
5. Serve and enjoy.

Korean braised tofu

Preparation:
10 Minutes

Serves:
4

Ingredients

- 14 oz. Block firm tofu, cut into 16 squares
- 1 tablespoon sugar
- 1 scallion, thinly cut
- 1 onion, thinly cut
- 3 tablespoons soy sauce
- 1 tablespoon korean chili powder
- 4 tablespoons sake
- Sesame seeds, toasted

Directions

1. Add onion slices in a pan and add tofu on top. Mix soy sauce, korean chili powder, sake, and sugar in a bowl and add over tofu slices.
2. Cover pan. Increase heat to high and cook until it boils. Turn heat to medium-high and cook for 5 minutes, baste with sauce.
3. Remove lid, increase heat to high and cook until sauce reduces.
4. Transfer to a plate, garnish with sesame seeds and serve.

Red lentil tikka masala

Preparation:
30 Minutes

Serves:
5

Ingredients

- 1 onion, diced
- 2 tablespoons olive oil
- 3 garlic cloves, minced
- 1 jalapeno pepper, minced
- 1 tablespoon ginger, grated
- 1 ½ tablespoons garam masala
- 1 tablespoon tomato paste
- 1 tablespoon coconut sugar
- 28 oz can tomatoes, crushed
- 1 cup red lentils
- 1 ½ cups vegetable broth
- ½ cup of coconut milk
- ¼ cup cilantro, chopped
- Salt and pepper, to taste

Directions

1. Cook onions and jalapeno pepper in hot olive oil in a pan until soft. Add garam masala, garlic, ginger, and tomato paste and stir for 1 minute.
2. Add coconut sugar, tomatoes, and vegetable broth. Mix well and add red lentils.
3. Bring to a simmer, turn the heat down and cook for about 30 minutes.
4. Add cilantro and coconut milk and mix. Serve and enjoy.

Easy thai red tofu curry

Preparation:
30 Minutes

Serves:
4

Ingredients

- 16 oz. Tofu, pressed and cut into ½" cubes
- 4 garlic clove, minced
- 2 tablespoons sesame oil
- 4 tablespoons soy sauce
- 3 tablespoons rice vinegar
- 1 tablespoon brown sugar
- 1 teaspoon red pepper flakes
- 3 tablespoons corn starch
- 1 yellow onion, minced
- 1 teaspoon ginger, grated
- 1 red bell pepper, sliced
- 1 cup cremini mushrooms, sliced
- 3 tablespoons red curry paste
- 13 oz. Coconut milk
- 1 tablespoon sambal oelek
- 1 lime, zest and juice
- 8 thai basil leaves, ribboned
- Cooked rice

Directions

1. Drain and press the tofu for 30 minutes. Mix 1 garlic clove, 3 tablespoons soy sauce, 2 tablespoons sesame oil, 1 tablespoon brown sugar, rice vinegar, red pepper flakes and corn starch in a bowl.
2. Cut tofu into cubes and add to the freezer bag, add the marinade and refrigerate for 30 minutes. Transfer tofu to a bowl and add cornstarch. Mix well.
3. Heat coconut oil in a pan over medium heat. Fry tofu cubes for 2 minutes on each side. Transfer to a bowl.
4. Add ¼ cup water to the pan and bring to a simmer. Add garlic, ginger and minced onion and turn the heat to medium. Cook for 5 minutes. Add mushrooms and red bell pepper. Add 3 tablespoons red curry paste and mix well.
5. Add coconut milk, lime juice and zest and soy sauce. Mix well and cook for 15 minutes.
6. Serve with rice.

240

Barbecue baked seitan strips

Preparation:
1 h

Serves:
4

Ingredients

- ½ cup nutritional yeast
- 3 cups vital wheat gluten
- 1 ½ teaspoon smoked paprika
- 1 ½ tablespoon garlic powder
- 1 teaspoon onion powder
- ½ teaspoon dried oregano
- ½ teaspoon dried basil
- 3 ½ cups vegetable broth
- 2 cups vegan barbecue sauce
- 5 tablespoons olive oil
- 5 tablespoons maple syrup
- 3 tablespoons soy sauce
- 1 teaspoon liquid smoke
- 1 teaspoon garlic powder
- 1 ½ teaspoons black pepper

Directions

1. Preheat the oven to 390f.
2. Mix gluten, yeast, 1 ½ tablespoon garlic powder, 1 teaspoon smoked paprika, 1 teaspoon onion powder, ½ teaspoon black pepper, ½ teaspoon oregano and ½ teaspoon basil in a bowl.
3. Mix 1 cup bbq sauce, 2 tablespoons maple syrup, 1 ½ cups vegetable broth, 2 tablespoons olive oil and 1 tablespoon soy sauce in a bowl. Add liquid to dry ingredients and mix well. Knead the mixture until the dough is formed. Let rest.
4. Mix the remaining broth, bbq sauce, maple syrup, olive oil, soy sauce, liquid smoke, black pepper, garlic powder, and smoked paprika in a bowl and mix well to make a marinade.
5. Place dough on a flat surface and flatten. Add a little oil and roll out to 1" thick and rectangle shape. Add 1 cup marinade to a tray and place dough on top. Cover with the remaining marinade. Bake for 1 hour adds 1 cup broth if it dries in between.
6. Serve and enjoy.

Teriyaki glazed tofu steaks

Preparation:
15 Minutes

Serves:
3

Ingredients

- 14 oz. Block tofu
- 1 teaspoon garlic, minced
- 1/2 teaspoon ginger, grated
- 1 tablespoon lemon juice
- 4 tablespoons soy sauce
- 2 tablespoons maple syrup
- 1 tablespoon rice vinegar
- 1/4 teaspoon corn starch
- 1/4 teaspoon dijon mustard
- Oil

Directions

1. Mix all ingredients except oil and tofu in a bowl to make the sauce. Cut tofu into 1/2" thick slices.
2. Coat a pan with oil and heat over medium-high. Add the tofu steaks. Flip and cook until crust is brown from all sides. Leave last batch in pan and add half of teriyaki sauce.
3. Coat the tofu steaks thoroughly with the sauce and cook for 2 minutes. Repeat with the remaining tofu steaks and sauce. Serve and enjoy.

Easy vegan chilli sin carne

Preparation:
40 Minutes

Serves:
6

Ingredients

- 3 garlic cloves, minced
- 2 tablespoon olive oil
- 2 celery stalks, chopped
- 1 red onion, sliced
- 2 red peppers, chopped
- 2 carrots, peeled and chopped
- 1 teaspoon chili powder
- 1 teaspoon ground cumin
- 1 lb canned tomatoes, chopped
- 14 oz can red kidney beans, drained and rinsed
- 3 1/2 oz split red lentils
- 14 oz frozen soy mince
- 1 cup vegetable stock
- Salt and pepper, to taste
- Basmati rice, cooked

Directions

1. Heat olive oil in a pan. Cook carrots, onion, celery, garlic and peppers over medium heat until softened. Add chili powder, cumin and salt and pepper and mix well to combine.
2. Add kidney beans. Lentils, chopped tomatoes, vegetable stock and soy mince. Cook for about 25 minutes, stirring often.
3. Serve with basmati rice.

243

Teriyaki tofu stir fry over quinoa

Preparation:
30 Minutes

Serves:
4

Ingredients

- 1 lb. Asparagus
- 14 oz. Firm tofu
- 2 tablespoon green onions, chopped
- 4 tablespoon tamari
- 2 teaspoon cooking oil
- 1 tablespoon sesame oil
- 5 garlic cloves, minced
- 1 1/2 tablespoon rice vinegar
- 1/2 tablespoon ginger, grated
- 1/4 cup coconut sugar
- 1/2 cup water
- 2 teaspoon cornstarch
- 4 cups quinoa, cooked

Directions

1. Cut tofu block in half. Squeeze to remove excess liquid. Cut into 1/2" thick cubes and fry in 1 teaspoon cooking oil on medium-high heat until lightly brown on all sides. Add 1 tablespoon tamari and toss. Set aside.
2. Mix 3 tablespoon tamari, sesame oil, rice vinegar, garlic cloves, ginger, coconut sugar, corn starch and water in a bowl for sauce. Cut asparagus into 2" long pieces and dice other veggies.
3. Heat 1 teaspoon cooking oil in a pan over medium-high heat. Cook diced veggies until crispy. Add in the tofu. Add in the sauce. Lower heat and cook until sauce thickens.
4. Turn off heat and add over the cooked quinoa. Serve and enjoy.

Vegan fall farro protein bowl

Preparation:
45 Minutes

Serves:
2

Ingredients

- 1 cup carrots, diced
- 1 cup sweet potatoes, diced
- 15 oz. Can chickpeas, drained and rinsed
- 1 1/2 cups water
- 2 teaspoons cooking oil
- 4 oz. Smoky tempeh strips
- 1/2 cup farro, uncooked
- 2 cups mixed greens
- 2 tablespoon almonds, roasted
- 1/4 cup hummus
- 4 lemon wedges
- Salt and pepper, to taste

Directions

1. Preheat the oven to 375f and prepare a baking sheet.
2. Mix carrots and sweet potatoes with 1 teaspoon cooking oil and salt and pepper in a bowl. Spread on one half of the baking sheet.
3. Mix chickpeas, remaining oil, 1/8 teaspoon black pepper and pinch salt in a bowl. Spread on the second half of the baking sheet.
4. Add tempeh strips on the baking sheet and roast all for 30 minutes. Flip and shuffle everything at half point.
5. Add farro grains, water, and pinch of salt to a pot and place over medium heat. Cover, bring to a boil and reduce the heat and cook for 25 minutes.
6. Divide farro, greens, and roasted tempeh, chickpeas, and potatoes among 4 bowls. Top with wedges, almonds, and hummus. Serve and enjoy.

Black bean and quinoa balls and spiralized zucchini

Preparation:
55 Minutes

Serves:
4

Ingredients

- 4 zucchinis
- 1/4 cup sesame seeds
- 1 can black beans
- 1/2 cup quinoa
- 2 tablespoon tomato paste
- 1/4 cup oat flour
- 1/2 tablespoon sriracha
- 2 tablespoon nutritional yeast
- 1 teaspoon garlic powder
- 1 1/2 tablespoon herbs, chopped
- 1 tablespoon apple cider vinegar
- 1 cup cherry tomatoes, halved
- 1/2 cup sun-dried tomatoes
- 1 garlic clove
- 2 tablespoon pine nuts, toasted
- 2 tablespoon nutritional yeast
- 1 teaspoon oregano
- A handful basil
- Salt and pepper, to taste

Directions

1. Add 1 cup water and quinoa to a pot and cook for about 15 minutes. Drain water and let cool. Add black beans to a bowl and mash with a fork.
2. Add sesame seeds, quinoa, oat flour, sriracha, yeast, tomato paste and spices and mix well. Shape the mixture into balls. Place on a lined baking sheet.
3. Bake at 400 f for 40 minutes.
4. Add 1/2 cup cherry tomatoes, sun-dried tomatoes, apple cider vinegar, garlic clove, pine nuts, yeast, basil, oregano and salt and pepper to a blender and blend until creamy to make the sauce.
5. Spiralize zucchinis and add to a bowl. Add tomato sauce and 1/2 cup cherry tomatoes to the bowl and add 5 quinoa balls per serving. Serve and enjoy!

246

Mongolian seitan (vegan mongolian beef)

Preparation:
30 Minutes

Serves:
6

Ingredients

- 2 tablespoon + 2 teaspoon vegetable oil
- 3 garlic cloves, minced
- 1/2 teaspoon ginger, minced
- 1/3 teaspoon red pepper flakes
- 1/2 cup soy sauce
- 2 teaspoons corn starch
- 2 tablespoons cold water
- 1/2 cup + 2 tablespoons coconut sugar
- 1 lb homemade seitan
- Rice, cooked, for serving

Directions

1. Heat 2 teaspoons vegetable oil in a pan over medium heat. Add garlic and ginger and mix well. Add red pepper flakes after 30 seconds and cook for 1 minute.
2. Add coconut sugar and soy sauce and mix well. Reduce the heat to medium-low and cook for 7 minutes. Mix cornstarch and water and add to the pan and mix well to combine. Cook for 3 minutes reduce the heat to lowest and simmer.
3. Heat the remaining oil in a skillet over medium-high heat. Add the seitan and cook for 5 minutes.
4. Reduce the heat and add the sauce to the pan. Mix well to coat every seitan piece and cook until all sauce adheres. Remove from heat.
5. Serve with rice.

Broccoli & black beans stir fry

Preparation:
60 Minutes

Serves:
6

Ingredients

- 4 cups broccoli florets
- 2 cups cooked black beans
- 1 tablespoon sesame oil
- 4 teaspoons sesame seeds
- 2 cloves garlic, finely minced
- 2 teaspoons ginger, finely chopped
- A large pinch red chili flakes
- A pinch turmeric powder
- Salt to taste
- Lime juice to taste (optional)

Directions

1. Steam broccoli for 6 minutes. Drain and set aside.
2. Warm the sesame oil in a large frying pan over medium heat. Add sesame seeds, chili flakes, ginger, garlic, turmeric powder, and salt. Sauté for a couple of minutes.
3. Add broccoli and black beans and sauté until thoroughly heated.
4. Sprinkle lime juice and serve hot.

Stuffed peppers

Preparation:
40 Minutes

Serves:
8

Ingredients

- 2 cans (15 ounces each) black beans, drained, rinsed
- 2 cups tofu, pressed, crumbled
- 3/4 cup green onion s, thinly sliced
- 1/2 cup fresh cilantro, chopped
- 1/4 cup vegetable oil
- 1/4 cup lime juice
- 3 cloves garlic, finely chopped
- 1/2 teaspoon salt
- 1/2 teaspoon chili powder
- 8 large bell peppers, halved lengthwise, deseeded
- 3 roma tomatoes, diced

Directions

1. Mix together in a bowl all the ingredients except the bell peppers to make the filling.
2. Fill the peppers with this mixture.
3. Cut 8 aluminum foils of size 18 x 12 inches. Place 2 halves on each aluminum foil. Seal the peppers such that there is a gap on the sides.
4. Grill under direct heat for about 15 minutes.
5. Sprinkle with some cilantro and serve.

Sweet 'n spicy tofu

Preparation:
45 Minutes

Serves:
8

Ingredients

▶ 14 ounces extra firm tofu; press the excess liquid and chop into cubes.
▶ 3 tablespoons olive oil
▶ 2 2-3 cloves garlic, minced
▶ 4 tablespoons sriracha sauce or any other hot sauce
▶ 2 tablespoons soy sauce
▶ 1/4 cup sweet chili sauce
▶ 5-6 cups mixed vegetables of your choice (like carrots, cauliflower, broccoli, potato, etc.)
▶ Salt to taste (optional)

Directions

1. Place a nonstick pan over medium-high heat. Add 1 tablespoon oil. When oil is hot, add garlic and mixed vegetables and stir-fry until crisp and tender. Remove and keep aside.
2. Place the pan back on heat. Add 2 tablespoons oil. When oil is hot, add tofu and sauté until golden brown. Add the sautéed vegetables. Mix well and remove from heat.
3. Make a mixture of sauces by mixing together all the sauces in a small bowl.
4. Serve the stir fried vegetables and tofu with sauce.

Eggplant & mushrooms in peanut sauce

Preparation:
32 Minutes

Serves:
6

Ingredients

- 4 Japanese eggplants cut into 1-inch thick round slices
- 3/4 pounds of shiitake mu shrooms, stems discarded, halved
- 3 tablespoons smooth peanut butter
- 2 1/2 tablespoons rice vinegar
- 1 1/2 tablespoons soy sauce
- 1 1/2 tablespoons, peeled, fresh ginger, finely grated
- 1 1/2 tablespoons light brown sugar
- Coarse salt to taste
- 3 scallions, cut into 2-inch lengths, thinly sliced lengthwise

Directions

1. Place the eggplants and mushroom in a steamer. Steam the eggplant and mushrooms until tender. Transfer to a bowl.
2. To a small bowl, add peanut butter and vinegar and whisk.
3. Add rest of the ingredients and whisk well. Add this to the bowl of eggplant slices. Add scallions and mix well.
4. Serve hot.

Green beans stir fry

 Preparation:
30 Minutes

 Serves:
6-8

Ingredients

- 1 1/2 pounds of green beans, stringed, chopped into 1 ½-inch pieces
- 1 large onion, thinly sliced
- 4 star anise (optional)
- 3 tablespoons avocado oil
- 1 1/2 tablespoons tamari sauce or soy sauce
- Salt to taste
- 3/4 cup water

Directions

1. Place a wok over medium heat. Add oil. When oil is heated, add onions and sauté until onions are translucent.
2. Add beans, water, tamari sauce, and star anise and stir. Cover and cook until the beans are tender.
3. Uncover, add salt and raise the heat to high. Cook until the water dries up in the wok. Stir a couple of times while cooking.

Collard greens 'n tofu

Preparation:
15 Minutes

Serves:
4

Directions

1. Place a large skillet over medium-high heat. Add oil. When the oil is heated, add tofu and cook until brown.
2. Add rest of the ingredients and mix well.
3. cook until greens wilts and almost dry.

Ingredients

- 2 pounds of collard greens, rinsed, chopped
- 1 cup water
- 1/2 pound of tofu, chopped
- Salt to taste
- Pepper powder to taste
- Crushed red chili to taste

Cassoulet

Preparation:
35 Minutes

Serves:
4

Ingredients

- ¼ cup (60 ml) olive oil, divided
- 4 ounces (113 g) quit-the-cluck seitan, chopped
- 1/3 of a smoky sausage, chopped
- 1½ cups (240 g) chopped onion
- 2 ounces (57 g) minced shiitake mushrooms
- 2 large carrots, peeled, sliced into ¼-inch (6 mm) rounds
- 2 stalks celery, chopped
- 1½ cups (355 ml) vegetable broth, divided
- 1 teaspoon liquid smoke
- 3 cans (each 15 ounces, or 425 g) white beans of choice, drained and rinsed
- 1 can (14.5 ounces, or 410 g) diced tomatoes, undrained
- 2 tablespoons (32 g) tomato paste 1 tablespoon (15 ml) tamari
- 1 tablespoon (18 g) no chicken bouillon paste, or 2 bouillon cubes, crumbled
- 2 tablespoons (8 g) minced fresh parsley
- 2 teaspoons dried thyme
- ½ teaspoon dried rosemary salt and pepper
- 2 cups (200 g) fresh bread crumbs
- ½ cup (40 g) panko crumbs

Directions

1. Preheat the oven to 375°f (190°c, or gas mark 5).
2. Heat 1 tablespoon (15 ml) of olive oil in a large skillet over medium heat.
3. Add the seitan and sausage. Cook for 4 to 6 minutes, occasionally stirring, until browned. Transfer to a plate and set aside.
4. Add the onion and a pinch of salt to the same skillet. Cook for 5 to 7 minutes until translucent. Transfer to the same plate. Add the shiitakes, carrots, and celery to the skillet and cook for 2 minutes. Add 1 tablespoon (15 ml) vegetable broth and the liquid smoke. Cook for 2 to 3 minutes, stirring until the liquid is absorbed or evaporated.
5. Return the seitan and onions to the skillet and add the beans, tomatoes, tomato paste, tamari, bouillon, parsley, thyme, rosemary, and remaining broth. Cook for 3 to 4 minutes, stirring to combine. Season with salt and pepper to taste and transfer to a large casserole pan.
6. Toss together the fresh bread crumbs, panko crumbs, and the remaining 3 tablespoons (45 ml) olive oil in a small bowl. Spread evenly over the bean mixture. Bake for 30 to 35 minutes until the crumbs are browned.

Nutritions: *Protein content per serving: 22 g*

Double-garlic bean and vegetable soup

Preparation:
25 Minutes

Serves:
4

Ingredients

- 1 tablespoon (15 ml) olive oil
- 1 teaspoon fine sea salt
- 1 (240 g) minced onion 5 cloves garlic, minced
- 2 cups (220 g) chopped red potatoes
- ⅔ cup (96 g) sliced carrots
- Protein content per serving cup (60 g) chopped celery
- 1 teaspoon italian seasoning blend
- Protein content per serving teaspoon red pepper flakes, or to taste
- Protein content per serving teaspoon celery seed
- 4 cups water (940 ml), divided
- 1 can (14.5 ounces, or 410 g) crushed tomatoes or tomato puree
- 1 head roasted garlic
- 2 tablespoons (30 g) prepared vegan pesto, plus more for garnish
- 2 cans (each 15 ounces, or 425 g) different kinds of white beans, drained and rinsed
- Protein content per serving cup (50 g)
- 1-inch (2.5 cm) pieces green beans
- Salt and pepper

Directions

1. Heat the oil and salt in a large soup pot over medium heat. Add the onion, garlic, potatoes, carrots, and celery. Cook for 4 to 6 minutes, occasionally stirring, until the onions are translucent. Add the seasoning blend, red pepper flakes, and celery seed and stir for 2 minutes. Add 3 cups (705 ml) of the water and the crushed tomatoes.

2. Combine the remaining 1 cup (235 ml) water and the roasted garlic in a blender. Process until smooth. Add to the soup mixture and bring to a boil. Reduce the heat to simmer and cook for 30 minutes.

3. Stir in the pesto, beans, and green beans. Simmer for 15 minutes. Taste and adjust the seasonings. Serve each bowl with a dollop of pesto, if desired.

Nutritions: *Protein content per serving: 21 g*

Mean bean minestrone

Preparation:
45 Minutes

Serves:
6

Ingredients

- 1 tablespoon (15 ml) olive oil
- 1/3 cup (80 g) chopped red onion
- 4 cloves garlic, grated or pressed
- 1 leek, white and light green parts, trimmed and chopped (about 4 ounces, or 113 g)
- 2 carrots, peeled and minced (about 4 ounces, or 113 g)
- 2 ribs of celery, minced (about 2 ounces, or 57 g)
- 2 yellow squashes, trimmed and chopped (about 8 ounces, or 227 g)
- 1 green bell pepper, trimmed and chopped (about 8 ounces, or 227 g)
- 1 tablespoon (16 g) tomato paste
- 1 teaspoon dried oregano
- 1 teaspoon dried basil
- ⅓ teaspoon smoked paprika
- '¼ To ¼ teaspoon cayenne pepper, or to taste
- 2 cans (each 15 ounces, or 425 g) diced fire-roasted tomatoes
- 4 cups (940 ml) vegetable broth, more if needed
- 3 cups (532 g) cannellini beans, or other white beans
- 2 cups (330 g) cooked farro, or other whole grain or pasta
- Salt, to taste
- Nut and seed sprinkles, for garnish, optional and to taste

Directions

1. In a large pot, add the oil, onion, garlic, leek, carrots, celery, yellow squash, bell pepper, tomato paste, oregano, basil, paprika, and cayenne pepper. Cook on medium-high heat, stirring often until the vegetables start to get tender, about 6 minutes.
2. Add the tomatoes and broth. Bring to a boil, lower the heat, cover with a lid, and simmer 15 minutes.
3. Add the beans and simmer another 10 minutes. Add the farro and simmer 5 more minutes to heat the farro.
4. Note that this is a thick minestrone. If there are leftovers (which taste even better, by the way), the soup will thicken more once chilled.
5. Add extra broth if you prefer a thinner soup and adjust seasoning if needed. Add nut and seed sprinkles on each portion upon serving, if desired.
6. Store leftovers in an airtight container in the refrigerator for up to 5 days. The minestrone can also be frozen for up to 3 months.

Nutritions: *Protein content per serving: 9g*

Sushi rice and bean stew

Preparation:
45 Minutes

Serves:
6

Ingredients

For the sushi rice:
- 1 cup (208 g) dry sushi rice, thoroughly rinsed until water runs clear and drained
- 1¾ cups (295 ml) water
- 1 tablespoon (15 ml) fresh lemon juice
- 1 teaspoon toasted sesame oil
- 1 teaspoon sriracha
- 1 teaspoon tamari
- 1 teaspoon agave nectar or brown rice syrup

For the stew:
- 1 tablespoon (15 ml) toasted sesame oil
- 9 ounces (255 g) minced carrot (about 4 medium carrots)
- 1/3 cup (80 g) chopped red onion or ¼ cup (40 g) minced shallot
- 2 teaspoons grated fresh ginger or ⅓ teaspoon ginger powder 4 cloves garlic, grated or pressed
- 1½ cups (246 g) cooked chickpeas
- 1 cup (155 g) frozen, shelled edamame
- 3 tablespoons (45 ml) seasoned rice vinegar
- 2 tablespoons (30 ml) tamari
- 2 teaspoons sriracha, or to taste
- 1 cup (235 ml) mushroom-soaking broth
- 2 cups (470 ml) vegetable broth
- 2 tablespoons (36 g) white miso
- 2 tablespoons (16 g) toasted white sesame seeds

Directions

1. To make the sushi rice: combine the rice and water in a rice cooker, cover with the lid, and cook until the water is absorbed without lifting the lid. (alternatively, cook the rice on the stove top, following the directions on the package.) While the rice is cooking, combine the remaining sushi rice ingredients in a large bowl.
2. Let the rice steam for 10 minutes in the rice cooker with the lid still on. Gently fold the cooked rice into the dressing. Set aside.
3. To make the stew: heat the oil in a large pot on medium-high heat. Add the carrots, onion, ginger, and garlic. Lower the temperature to medium and cook until the vegetables start to get tender, stirring often about 4 minutes.
4. Add the chickpeas, edamame, vinegar, tamari, and sriracha. Stir and cook for another 4 minutes. Add the broths, and bring back to a slow boil. Cover with a lid, lower the heat, and simmer for 10 minutes.

257

5. Place the miso in a small bowl and remove 3 tablespoons (45 ml) of the broth from the pot. Stir into the miso to thoroughly combine. Stir the miso mixture back into the pan, and remove from the heat.

6. Divide the rice among 4 to 6 bowls, depending on your appetite. Add approximately 1 cup (235 ml) of the stew on top of each portion of rice. Add 1 teaspoon of sesame seeds on top of each serving, and serve immediately.

7. If you do not plan on eating this dish in one shot, keep the rice and stew separated and store in the refrigerator for up to 4 days.

8. When reheating the stew, do not bring to a boil. Slowly warm the rice with the stew on medium heat in a small saucepan until heated through.

Giardiniera chili

Preparation:
35 Minutes

Serves:
6

Ingredients

- 1 tablespoon (15 ml) neutral-flavored oil
- 1 medium red onion, chopped
- 4 carrots, peeled and minced (9 ounces, or 250 g)
- 2 zucchini, trimmed and minced (11 ounces, or 320 g)
- 4 roma tomatoes, diced (14 ounces, or 400 g)
- 4 cloves garlic, grated or pressed
- 1 tablespoon (8 g) mild to medium chili powder
- 1 teaspoon ground cumin
- ½ teaspoon smoked paprika
- ½ teaspoon liquid smoke
- ¼ teaspoon fine sea salt, or to taste
- ¼ teaspoon cayenne pepper, or to taste
- 2 tablespoons (32 g) tomato paste
- 1 can (15 ounces, or 425 g) diced fire-roasted tomatoes
- ½ cup (120 ml) vegetable broth
- ½ cup (120 ml) mushroom-soaking broth or extra vegetable broth
- 1 can (15 ounces, or 425 g) pinto beans, drained and rinsed
- 1 can (15 ounces, or 425 g) black beans, drained and rinsed
- ½ cup (60 g) nutritional yeast

Directions

1. Heat the oil on medium-high in a large pot and add the onion, carrots, zucchini, tomatoes, and garlic. Cook for 6 minutes, stirring occasionally until the carrots start to get tender. Add the chili powder, cumin, paprika, liquid smoke, salt, cayenne pepper, and tomato paste, stirring to combine. Cook another 2 minutes. Add the diced tomatoes, broths, beans, and nutritional yeast. Bring to a low boil. Lower the heat, cover with a lid, and simmer 15 minutes, stirring occasionally. Remove the lid and simmer for another 5 minutes.
2. Serve on top of a cooked whole grain of choice or with your favorite chili accompaniments.
3. Leftovers can be stored in an airtight container in the refrigerator for up to 4 days or frozen for up to 3 months.

Nutritions: *Protein content per serving: 28 g*

Shorba (lentil soup)

 Preparation:
30 minutes

 Serves:
6

Ingredients

- 1 tablespoon (15 ml) olive oil
- 1 medium onion, minced
- 1 large carrot, peeled and chopped
- 1 fist-size russet potato, cut into small cubes (about 7 ounces, or 198 g)
- 4 large cloves garlic, minced
- 2 teaspoons grated fresh ginger root
- 1 to 2 teaspoons berbere, to taste
- 1/3 teaspoon turmeric
- 1 cup (192 g) brown lentils, picked over and rinsed
- 6 cups (1.4 l) water, more if desired
- 1 tablespoon (16 g) tomato paste
- 1 tablespoon (18 g) vegetable bouillon paste, or 2 bouillon cubes
- Salt and pepper

Directions

1. Heat the oil in a large soup pot over medium heat. Add the onion, carrot, and potato. Cook for 5 to 7 minutes, stirring occasionally until the onions are translucent. Stir in the garlic, ginger, berbere, turmeric, and lentils and cook and stir for 1 minute until fragrant. Add the water, tomato paste, and bouillon. Bring to a boil, and then reduce the heat to a simmer. Cook for 30 minutes, stirring occasionally until the lentils are tender. Taste and adjust the seasonings.

Nutritions: *Protein content per serving: 10g*

The whole enchilada

Preparation:
20 Minutes

Serves:
6

Ingredients

For the sauce:
- ► 2 tablespoons (30 ml) olive oil 1/3 cup (80 g) chopped red onion 4 ounces (113 g) tomato paste
- ► 1 tablespoon (15 ml) adobo sauce
- ► 1 tablespoon (8 g) mild to medium chili powder
- ► 1 teaspoon ground cumin
- ► 3 cloves garlic, grated or pressed
- ► 1/3 teaspoon fine sea salt, or to taste
- ► 2 tablespoons (15 g) whole wheat pastry flour or (16 g) all-purpose flour
- ► 2 cups (470 ml) water

For the filling:
- ► 1 protein content per serving teaspoons olive oil
- ► 1/3 cup (53 g) chopped red onion
- ► 1 sweet potato, trimmed and peeled, chopped (about 8.8 ounces, or 250 g)
- ► 1 yellow squash, trimmed and chopped (about 5.3 ounces, or 150 g)
- ► 2 cloves garlic, grated or pressed
- ► 1 tablespoon (8 g) nutritional yeast
- ► 1 smoked paprika
- ► 1/4 teaspoon liquid smoke
- ► Pinch of fine sea salt, or to taste
- ► 1 (258 g) cooked black beans
- ► 3 tablespoons (45 ml) enchilada sauce
- ► 12 to 14 corn tortillas
- ► 1 recipe creamy cashew sauce
- ► Chopped fresh cilantro, to taste hot sauce, to taste

Directions

1. To make the sauce: heat the oil on medium heat in a large skillet. Add the onion and cook until fragrant while occasionally stirring, about 2 minutes. Add the tomato paste, adobo sauce, chili powder, cumin, garlic, and salt. Saute for 2 minutes, stirring frequently. Sprinkle the flour on top and cook 2 minutes, stirring frequently. Slowly whisk in the water and cook until slightly thickened, about 6 minutes, frequently whisking to prevent clumps. Remove from the heat and set aside.

2. To make the filling: heat the oil in a large skillet on medium heat. Add the onion and sweet potato and cook 6 minutes or until the potato starts to get tender, stirring occasionally. Add the squash and garlic and cook for 4 minutes,

stirring occasionally. Add the nutritional yeast, paprika, liquid smoke, and salt, stir to combine, and cook for another minute. Add the beans and enchilada sauce and stir to combine. Cover the pan and simmer until the vegetables are completely tender about 4 minutes. Add a little water if the plants stick to the skillet. Adjust the seasonings if needed.

3. Preheat the oven to 350°f (180°c, or gas mark 4).

4. Place the sauce in a large shallow bowl. If you aren't using pre-shaped, uncooked tortillas, follow the direction in the recipe notes to soften the tortillas so that they are easier to work with. Ladle about 1/3 cup (80 ml) of enchilada sauce on the bottom of a 9 x 13-inch (23 x 33 cm) baking dish. Dip each tortilla in the sauce to coat only lightly. Don't be too generous and gently scrape off the excess sauce with a spatula; otherwise, you will run out of sauce. Add a scant ¼ cup (about 45 g) of the filling in each tortilla. Fold the tortilla over the filling, rolling like a cigar. Place the enchiladas in the pan, seam side down. Make sure to squeeze them in tight so that there's room in the dish for all of them. Top evenly with the remaining enchilada sauce. Add the creamy cashew sauce consistently on top.

5. Bake for 20 to 25 minutes or until the top is set, and the enchiladas are heated through. Garnish with cilantro and serve with hot sauce.

Nutritions: *Protein content per serving:6g*

Black bean and avocado salad

Preparation:
45 Minutes

Serves:
6

Ingredients

- 1 cup (172 g) cooked black beans
- ⅓ cup (82 g) frozen corn (run under hot water, drained)
- 3 tablespoons (15 g) minced scallion
- 6 cherry tomatoes, cut into quarters
- 2 cloves garlic, minced
- 1 teaspoon minced fresh cilantro, or to taste
- Pinch of dried oregano 1 chipotle in adobo
- 1 tablespoon (15 ml) fresh lemon juice
- 1 tablespoon (15 ml) apple cider vinegar 1 tablespoon (15 ml) vegetable broth
- 1 teaspoon nutritional yeast
- 2 tablespoons (15 g) roasted salted pepitas (hulled pumpkin seeds)
- 2 avocados, pitted, peeled, and chopped
- Salt and pepper

Directions

1. Combine the beans, corn, scallion, cherry tomatoes, garlic, cilantro, and oregano in a medium-size bowl. Using a small blender or a mortar and pestle, thoroughly combine the chipotle, lemon juice, vinegar, broth, and nutritional yeast to form a dressing. Pour over the bean mixture and stir in the pepitas. Gently stir in the avocados. Season to taste with salt and pepper. Serve promptly so that the avocado doesn't discolor.

Nutritions: *Protein content per serving: 8 g*

Mediterranean quinoa and bean salad

Preparation:
35 Minutes

Serves:
6

Ingredients

▸ 1¾ cups (213 g) dry ivory quinoa, rinsed
▸ 2 (590 ml) vegetable broth
▸ 2 tablespoons (30 ml) apple cider vinegar
▸ 2 tablespoons (30 ml) fresh lemon juice
▸ 3 tablespoons (45 ml) extra-virgin olive oil
▸ ⅔ cup (40 g) finely chopped red onion
▸ 2 to 3 cloves garlic, minced, or to taste
▸ Protein content per serving teaspoon red pepper flakes, or to taste
▸ Salt and pepper
▸ 1 (266 g) cooked cannellini beans
▸ 24 jumbo pitted kalamata olives, minced
▸ Half of red bell pepper, cored and diced
▸ Half of yellow bell pepper, cored and diced
▸ 8 ounces (227 g) mini heirloom tomatoes, halved or quartered depending on size
▸ 6 tablespoons (24 g) minced fresh parsley
▸ 15 leaves fresh basil, cut in chiffonade

Directions

1. Combine the quinoa with the broth in a medium saucepan. Bring to a boil and then reduce the heat to a simmer. Cover and cook until all liquid is absorbed, 12 to 15 minutes. The quinoa should be tender and translucent, and the germ ring should be visible along the outside edge of the grain. Set aside to cool completely.

2. In a large bowl, combine the vinegar, lemon juice, oil, onion, garlic, red pepper flakes, salt, and pepper. Stir the beans into the dressing. Add the cooled quinoa, olives, bell peppers, tomatoes, and parsley into the bowl with the beans. Fold with a rubber spatula to thoroughly yet gently combine.

3. Cover and chill for an hour to let the flavors meld. Garnish with basil upon serving. Leftovers can be stored in an airtight container in the refrigerator for up to 4 days.

Nutritions: *Protein content per serving:6g*

Tabbouleh verde

Preparation:
40 Minutes

Serves:
6

Ingredients

- 1 cup (186 g) dry whole-wheat couscous
- ⅓ cup (120 ml) vegetable broth, brought to a boil
- 3 tablespoons (45 ml) extra-virgin olive oil
- 2 tablespoons (30 ml) fresh lemon juice
- 2 tablespoons (30 ml) fresh lime juice
- 1½ cups (258 g) cooked black beans
- 1½ cups (225 g) diced heirloom green tomato (any other color will do.)
- 1 cup (150 g) diced green bell pepper (any different color will do.)
- ⅓ cup (5 g) loosely packed fresh cilantro leaves, minced
- ⅓ cup (20 g) minced scallion
- 1 small jalapeno, seeded and minced
- ⅓ teaspoon toasted cumin seeds
- Salt and pepper, optional
- Roasted pepitas (hulled pumpkin seeds), for garnish
- 1 lemon, cut into 4 to 6 wedges
- 1 lime, cut into 4 to 6 wedges

Directions

1. Mix the couscous with the broth in a large glass bowl. Add the oil, lemon juice, and lime juice. Stir well. Cover and let stand 5 minutes until the liquids are absorbed. Fluff with a fork.
2. Add the beans, tomato, bell pepper, cilantro, scallion, and jalapeno on top. Rub the cumin seeds between your fingers while adding them to release the flavor. Fold to combine with a rubber spatula. Adjust the seasonings to taste. Refrigerate for at least 30 minutes to chill and to let the flavors meld.
3. Serve and garnish each portion with a small handful of pepitas and a wedge of lemon and lime to drizzle before eating.
4. Leftovers can be stored in an airtight container in the refrigerator for up to 4 days.

Nutritions: *Protein content per serving: 9 g*

265

Curried bean and corn salad

Preparation:
15 Minutes

Serves:
6

Ingredients

- Protein content per servi ng cup (90 g) whole freekeh
- 3 cups (705 ml) salted water
- 1 can (15 ounces, or 425 g) chickpeas, drained and rinsed
- 1 cup (164 g) fresh or frozen corn (run under hot water, drained)
- ¼ cup (40 g) minced red onion
- ¼ cup (32 g) minced celery
- ¼ cup (38 g) minced bell pepper (any color)
- 3 tablespoons (12 g) minced fresh parsley
- 1 tablespoon (6 g) curry powder (mild or hot)
- 1 teaspoon ground cumin
- 1 teaspoon garam masala
- 1teaspoon ginger powder
- 1teaspoon fine sea salt
- 1 clove garlic
- 2 tablespoons (30 ml) seasoned rice vinegar
- 3 tablespoons (45 ml) olive oil

Directions

1. Bring the freekeh and salted water to a boil in a medium-size saucepan. Reduce to simmer and cook for 45 minutes, occasionally stirring, until tender. Drain and run under cold water, draining again. Transfer to a medium-size bowl. Add the chickpeas, corn, onion, celery, bell pepper, and parsley.

2. Heat the curry powder, cumin, and garam masala in a small skillet over medium heat. Stir and cook for 3 to 4 minutes until fragrant. Do not burn. Transfer to a small blender and add the ginger powder, salt, garlic, and vinegar. Blend until smooth. Add the olive oil and blend again to emulsify. Pour the dressing (to taste) over the bean mixture. Stir to coat and let sit for 15 minutes for the flavors to meld. The salad can also be covered and refrigerated for up to 3 days.

Nutritions: *Protein content per serving:27g*

Preparation:
45 Minutes

Serves:
6

Ingredients

For the marinated eggplant:

- 1 tablespoon (16 g) tahini
- 1 tablespoon (15 ml) olive oil
- 1 tablespoon (15 ml) fresh lemon juice
- 1 tablespoon (15 ml) white balsamic vinegar
- 1protein content per serving teaspoons nutritional yeast protein content per serving teaspoon onion powder protein content per serving teaspoon harissa paste, or to taste 1 clove garlic, grated or pressed protein content per serving teaspoon ground cumin salt, to taste 1 small eggplant (a little over 10 ounces, or 280 g), trimmed, cut in two widthwise and then length¬wise in protein content per serving-inch (1.3 cm) slices

For the balela:

- 1 tablespoon (15 ml) extra-virgin olive oil
- 2 tablespoons (30 ml) fresh lemon juice
- 2 tablespoons (30 ml) white balsamic vinegar
- ⅓ cup (53 g) minced red onion
- 2 cloves garlic, grated or pressed
- 1 (246 g) cooked chickpeas
- 1 (258 g) cooked black beans
- 1 of a roasted red or yellow bell pepper, chopped
- 1 small tomato, seeded if desired, minced
- 3 tablespoons (18 g) minced fresh mint leaves
- 3 tablespoons (11 g) minced fresh parsley
- Salt and pepper
- Red pepper flakes, to taste

Directions

1. To make the marinated eggplant: combine the tahini, oil, lemon juice, vinegar, nutritional yeast, onion powder, harissa paste, garlic, cumin, and salt in a shallow pan. Brush a generous amount of this mixture on both sides and edges of each piece of eggplant and place in the shallow pan. Place the container in the refrigerator for 1 hour to marinate.

2. Preheat the oven to 450°f (230°c, or gas mark 8). Place the slices of eggplant on a large rimmed baking sheet.

3. Bake for 8 minutes, flip the slices, and bake for another 6 to 8 minutes until tender and golden brown. Remove from the oven and set aside. Once cool enough to handle, cut the eggplant slices into ^-inch (8 mm) cubes.

4. To make the balela: in a large bowl, combine the oil, lemon juice, vinegar, onion, and garlic. Add the chick¬peas, black beans, roasted bell pepper, tomato, mint, parsley, cubed eggplant, salt, ground pepper, and red pepper flakes to taste. Chill overnight and serve cold or brought back to room temperature. Leftovers can be stored in an airtight container for up to 4 days, and they get even better with each passing day.

Carrot and radish slaw with sesame dressing

 Preparation:
10 Minutes

 Serves:
4

Directions

1. Mix the oil, vinegar, sugar and tamari in a bowl.
2. Add the carrots, radishes and cilantro.
3. Toss to coat evenly.
4. Let sit for 10 minutes.
5. Transfer to a food container.

Ingredients

- 2 tablespoons sesame oil, toasted
- 3 tablespoons rice vinegar
- ½ teaspoon sugar
- 2 tablespoons low sodium tamari
- 1 cup carrots, sliced into strips
- 2 cups radishes, sliced
- 2 tablespoons fresh cilantro, chopped
- 2 teaspoons sesame seeds, toasted

Roasted veggies in lemon sauce

Preparation:
15 Minutes

Cooking:
20 Minutes

Serves:
5

Ingredients

- 2 cloves garlic, sliced
- 1 ½ cups broccoli florets
- 1 ½ cups cauliflower florets
- 1 tablespoon olive oil
- Salt to taste
- 1 teaspoon dried oregano, crushed
- ¾ cup zucchini, diced
- ¾ cup red bell pepper, diced
- 2 teaspoons lemon zest

Directions

1. Preheat your oven to 425 degrees f.
2. In a baking pan, add the garlic, broccoli and cauliflower.
3. Toss in oil and season with salt and oregano.
4. Roast in the oven for 10 minutes.
5. Add the zucchini and bell pepper to the pan.
6. Stir well.
7. Roast for another 10 minutes.
8. Sprinkle lemon zest on top before serving.
9. Transfer to a food container and reheat before serving.

Spinach with walnuts & avocado

 Preparation:
5 Minutes

 Serves:
1

Directions

1. Put the spinach, strawberries and onion in a glass jar with lid.
2. Drizzle dressing on top.
3. Top with avocado and walnuts.
4. Seal the lid and refrigerate until ready to serve.

Ingredients

- 3 cups baby spinach
- ½ cup strawberries, sliced
- 1 tablespoon white onion, chopped
- 2 tablespoons vinaigrette
- ¼ medium avocado, diced
- 2 tablespoons walnut, toasted

Nutritions: *296 calories; 18 g fat(2 g sat); 10 g fiber; 27 g carbohydrates; 8 g protein; 63 mcg folate; 0 mg cholesterol; 11 g sugars; 0 g added sugars; 11,084 iu vitamin a; 103 mg, Vitamin c; 192 mg calcium; 7 mg iron; 195 mg sodium; 385 mg*

Chapter 8.
Desserts and Snacks Recipes

Cheesy popcorn

Preparation:
45 Minutes

Serves:
6

Ingredients

- Popcorn kernels (two tablespoons)
- Grapeseed oil (one tablespoon)
- Coconut oil (one tablespoon)
- Pink or sea salt (to taste)
- Nutritional yeast (one tablespoon)
- Black pepper (to taste)

Directions

1. Heat coconut oil in a saucepan over medium heat. Put in the popcorn, apply the lid and shake the pot side to side to coat the kernels in the oil. Leave pot still until you hear the popcorn start to pop. Shake the pot periodically to ensure no popcorn sticks to the bottom and the un-popped kernels find their way to the bottom.
2. When the popping begins to slow, get your bowl ready and tip the popcorn into it when the popping has practically stopped.
3. Drizzle the popcorn with the grapeseed oil and toss through, then generously apply salt to your liking, top with the nutritional yeast. Give it a good shake again so the yeast has a chance to stick to the oil, then sprinkle a little black pepper over top. Enjoy!

Veggie chips

Preparation:
15 Minutes

Serves:
6

Ingredients

▸ Paprika (quarter teaspoon)
▸ Salt and pepper (to taste)
▸ Olive oil (two teaspoons)
▸ Sweet potato (one medium)

Directions

1. Cut the sweet potato into thin slices by using a vegetable peeler. This produces even, thin, uniform slices that cook very quickly.
2. Put the slices into a bowl and drizzle a little oil on and toss. Repeat until every slice is coated but it shouldn't be drenched in oil.
3. Lay them out in a single layer with no overlapping on baking trays with baking paper.
4. Sprinkle with salt, pepper, and paprika to your liking.
5. Bake for twenty minutes at 350f, switching the trays halfway through. Be sure to keep checking them to ensure they don't overcook.
6. They are ready when crispy and smell amazing. Enjoy!

Thai vegan rice rolls

 Preparation:
40 Minutes

 Serves:
6

Ingredients

- Rice paper rounds (three sheets)
- Avocado (half one medium)
- Red onion (one slice)
- Carrots (two tablespoons grated)
- Red bell pepper (quarter one medium)
- Fresh mint leaves (six leaves)
- Fresh basil leaves (six leaves)
- Toasted sesame seeds (one teaspoon)
- Crunchy peanut butter (one tablespoon)
- Peanut oil (two tablespoons)
- Soy sauce (one tablespoon)
- Hot sauce (one teaspoon)
- Maple syrup (one teaspoon)

Directions

1. Prepare veggies and leave in individual piles on a plate. Slice avocado, bell pepper, and onion into lengthways slices. Grate the carrot, wash and de-stem the leaves.
2. In a bowl, put maple syrup, hot sauce, soy sauce, oil, and peanut butter and whisk together with a fork.
3. Run the rice paper under cool water until all parts have touched the water. Place on a clean work surface making sure they don't touch each other.
4. Layer the vegetables into the middle of each sheet lengthways, leaving a couple of inches away from each end. It should be a log laying in the middle of the round. Sprinkle the vegetables with the toasted sesame seeds. If the rice paper isn't 100% pliable, wait until it is. It should feel like stretchy fabric.
5. Fold one side over the vegetable log, then fold in both ends before rolling up like a burrito. Do this for all three, then put on a plate. Dip the roll into the peanut sauce and enjoy!

Easy hummus!

Preparation:
20 Minutes

Serves:
3

Ingredients

▶ Tahini (quarter cup)
▶ Extra virgin olive oil (three tablespoons))
▶ Garlic (one clove)
▶ Chickpeas (one can)
▶ Lemon juice (one medium lemon)
▶ Paprika (quarter teaspoon)
▶ Cumin (half teaspoon)
▶ Salt and pepper (to taste)

Directions

1. In a food processor put the lemon juice and tahini along with one tablespoon of olive oil and the garlic and blend for one minute.
2. Add another tablespoon of olive oil with the cumin and paprika, then spatula the sides clean of the mixture. Drain and rinse the chickpeas and put them into the mix before blending for another minute.
3. Add salt and pepper, the last tablespoon of oil and one tablespoon of cool water and blend again for another minute. Stop and have a little taste. If it needs more of anything, now is the time to do so.
4. On a low setting, blend the hummus again, but put one more tablespoon of water as it blends to make it as smooth as possible.
5. Scoop into a container and drizzle with more olive oil. Enjoy!

Spicy cheesy queso

Preparation:
30 Minutes

Serves:
3

Ingredients

- Paprika (quarter teaspoon)
- Canned jalapenos (two tablespoons)
- Garlic powder (quarter teaspoon)
- Onion powder (half teaspoon)
- Salt (halt teaspoon)
- Coconut milk (three-quarter cup)
- Nutritional yeast (three tablespoons)
- Tapioca starch (two tablespoons)
- Salsa (three tablespoons)

Directions

1. In a blender put the drained jalapenos, garlic and onion powders, salt, coconut milk, tapioca starch, and nutritional yeast. Pulse until combined, the jalapenos shouldn't be 100% blended.
2. Pour into a saucepan, add the salsa and bring to a boil while stirring. Turn heat down to low and let it simmer until it starts coming away from the sides and if you pull up the spoon, it pulls like a real cheese sauce.
3. Scrape into a serving bowl and enjoy with corn chips or whatever you'd like!

Holy guacamole

Preparation:
30 Minutes

Serves:
3

Ingredients

▶ Garlic (one clove)
▶ Ripe avocados (three medium)
▶ Red onion (half cup)
▶ Lime juice (one medium lime)
▶ Salt and pepper (to taste)
▶ Roma tomatoes (two medium)
▶ Cilantro (quarter cup)
▶ Jalapeno (one medium)
▶ Nutritional yeast (one tablespoon)

Directions

1. Scoop out the avocado flesh and dice into cubes. Put this in a bowl and cover with lime juice then mash with the back of a fork until it's a little chunky.
2. Finely dice the garlic, onion, jalapeno, and cilantro, then add to the avocado.
3. Cut the tomatoes in half and scoop out the seeds and pulp. Then dice the tomato and add to the avocado along with the nutritional yeast and salt and pepper to taste.
4. Mix together well but not too much as you don't want the guacamole to become too smooth. Enjoy with corn chips or anything else you like!

Happy granola bar

 Preparation:
20 Minutes

 Serves:
3

Ingredients

- Chia seeds (one tablespoon)
- Cinnamon (quarter teaspoon)
- Desiccated coconut (quarter cup)
- Almonds (three-quarter cup)
- Oats (two cups)
- Maple syrup (quarter cup)
- Blackstrap molasses (quarter cup)
- Almond butter (two-thirds cup)
- Hazelnuts (quarter cup)
- Cocoa powder (one teaspoon)

Directions

1. Heat a saucepan over medium heat and put in the almond butter, maple syrup and molasses. Stir until the almond butter has melted down.
2. Take off the heat and stir in everything except the nuts.
3. Using a large butcher's knife, roughly chop up the almonds and hazelnuts so that they are a variety of sizes and maybe a few are left whole.
4. Fold the nuts through the mix and have a taste to see if it needs anything else. You could add some salt or dried berries at this point if you think it needs it.
5. Line a slice pan with baking paper and press the mixture into it with pressure until it is firmly packed down and relatively even in the pan.
6. Put in the fridge until hardened, then cut into slices and store in a container in the fridge. Enjoy!

Peanut butter protein balls

Preparation:
30 Minutes

Serves:
2

Ingredients

- Almond milk (two tablespoons)
- Sesame seeds (one-third cup)
- Roasted sunflower seeds (one-third cup)
- Vanilla extract (one teaspoon)
- Maple syrup (three tablespoons)
- Smooth peanut butter (half cup)
- Cocoa powder (two teaspoons)
- Chia seeds (one tablespoon)
- Cinnamon (half teaspoon)
- Chocolate vegan protein powder (half cup)
- Rolled oats (one and a half cup)

Directions

1. Put everything into a large bowl except for the almond milk and mix well.
2. Using clean hands, add the almond milk one tablespoon at a time and knead the mixture together until you get a large sticky mass.
3. Roll into twenty same-sized balls, tossing each one in some cocoa powder to coat. Put into a container and keep in the fridge until ready to eat. Enjoy!

279

Super seedy cookie bites

 Preparation:
10 Minutes

 Serves:
3

Directions

1. Blend the dates and banana into a paste and put into a large bowl with the rest of the ingredients.
2. Mix together well using a little water if it needs help to combine.
3. Roll into twenty equal balls and lay out on a baking tray lined with baking paper. Squish each ball down slightly with your thumb to make a little cookie bite.
4. Cook for twenty-five minutes at 300f. Let them cool before you put in a container. Enjoy!

Ingredients

- Shredded coconut (one cup)
- Cacao nibs (two tablespoons)
- Hemp hearts (three tablespoons)
- Dried cranberries (quarter cup)
- Raisins (quarter cup)
- Pumpkin seeds (half cup)
- Flaxseed meal (half cup)
- Walnuts (half cup)
- Medjool dates (eight)
- Banana (one medium)

Bitty brownie fudge bites

Preparation:
30 Minutes

Serves:
3

Ingredients

- Cacao nibs (two tablespoons)
- Cacao powder (three-quarter cups)
- Salt (half teaspoon)
- Dates (two and a half cups)
- Coconut oil (two tablespoons)
- Icing sugar (quarter cup)
- Almond milk (quarter cup)
- Vegan dark chocolate chips (one cup)
- Raw almonds (one cup)
- Raw walnuts (one and a half cups)

Directions

1. In a food processor put one cup walnuts and all the almonds, pulse until a fine consistency. Then add a quarter teaspoon salt and the cacao powder. Pulse again put in a bowl.
2. Next, blend the dates into tiny pieces and put in a separate bowl.
3. Put the walnut mixture back into the processor and blend while adding tiny portions of the dates until it looks like a dough. You should be able to knead the dough and have it stick together. If it doesn't, add more dates.
4. Push the dough into a slice pan lined with baking paper then break up half of the remaining walnuts and sprinkle over the top along with some of the cacao nibs and press down to it's compacted and flat then put in the fridge.
5. Heat a saucepan over medium-low heat and put in the almond milk until it begins to simmer then take off the heat.
6. Add the chocolate chips and allow to melt into the milk then add a quarter teaspoon salt and the coconut oil and whisk.
7. Put this in the fridge for ten minutes to cool, then sift in the icing sugar and whisk it slowly to thicken the mixture, eventually whipping it like cream.
8. Spread the fudge over the brownie base then sprinkle with the remaining walnut pieces and cacao nibs.
9. Put back in the fridge to set before slicing and storing in a container either in the fridge or at room temperature. Enjoy!

Healthy salted caramel bar

 Preparation:
40 Minutes

 Serves:
3

Ingredients

- Almond milk (two tablespoons)
- Maple syrup (two tablespoons)
- Vanilla extract (one and quarter teaspoons)
- Cocoa powder (third cup)
- Coconut oil (half cup)
- Salt (quarter teaspoon)
- Cashew butter (quarter cup)
- Almond milk (two teaspoons)
- Medjool dates (one and a half cup)
- Shredded coconut (half cup)
- Almond flour (one cup)

Directions

1. In a food processor put coconut oil, four dates, shredded coconut, and almond flour and blend. Evenly push it into a baking paper lined slice pan and put it in the freezer.
2. Next, using the processor again, put the rest of the dates along with the salt, one teaspoon vanilla, almond milk, and cashew butter. Blend until smooth and add to the top of the slice pan and put back in the freezer.
3. Heat the coconut oil in a saucepan on low and mix in the cocoa powder, quarter teaspoon vanilla with the maple syrup and stir until a consistent texture.
4. Pour this over the slice pan once it has cooled off, top with a sprinkling of shredded coconut, and put it in the fridge for two hours. Slice and enjoy!

Tropical lemon slice

Preparation:
50 Minutes

Serves:
3

Ingredients

- Coconut oil (four tablespoons)
- Lemon juice (half one medium lemon)
- Lemon zest (one teaspoon)
- Maple syrup (quarter cu p)
- Salt (pinch)
- Vanilla extract (half teaspoon)
- Shredded coconut (two cups)

Directions

1. Heat a saucepan on low and put all the above ingredients into it. Stir until everything has melted together then pour into a baking tray that has been lined with baking paper.
2. Pack it down until it's even then put in the fridge for two hours before cutting into slices and serving. Enjoy!

Cranberry protein bars

Preparation:
20 Minutes

Serves:
3

Ingredients

- ¼ cup dried cranberries
- ¾ cup raw almonds
- ¼ cup date, pitted
- ¼ cup pistachios, unsalted with shells removed
- 1 tablespoon of chia seeds
- 2 tablespoons applesauce
- 1 tablespoon coconut oil
- 1 scoop vanilla protein powder

Directions

1. Add the almonds and pistachios to a food processor and pulse to coarse, sand-like texture.
2. Add dates and dried cranberries, and pulse for 30 seconds.
3. Add vanilla protein powder, chia seeds, applesauce, and coconut oil to the food processor. Pulse for 30 more seconds.
4. Transfer the mixture to a clean working surface. Place parchment paper over the mixture and roll into a ½ inch thickness.
5. Cut the mixture into 8 bars and transfer the working surface to the freezer. Freeze for 30 minutes.
6. Remove from the freezer and wrap the bars individually in plastic wrap to preserve shape and freshness. Can be stored in the refrigerator for 7 days or in the freezer for 2 months.

Mixed berry sorbet

 Preparation:
20 Minutes

 Serves:
3

Ingredients

▸ 6 cup mixed berries, frozen
▸ ¾ cup lemon juice
▸ 1 cup fresh basil
▸ 1 cup coconut sugar

Directions

1. Add water and coconut sugar to a medium saucepan. Place over high heat and stir occasionally as the sugar dissolves.
2. Add basil once the sugar has dissolved.
3. Remove the pan from the heat, cover with a lid and let stand for 15 minutes
4. Strain the liquid into a medium bowl. Discard basil. Refrigerate the liquid until cold.
5. In a blender, puree the frozen mixed berries. Add liquid to a blender along with lemon juice to the blender and blend until mixture achieves a smooth consistency.
6. Transfer mixture to a metal 8 inch baking pan. Cover with plastic wrap and free for 2 hours or until the sorbet is thick enough to scoop.

Peanut butter chocolate marble cake

Preparation:
40 Minutes

Serves:
3

Ingredients

- 1 ½ cup almond flour
- 1 teaspoon baking powder
- ¼ cup baking soda
- ¼ teaspoon salt
- 3 tablespoon natural creamy peanut butter
- 2 ½ tablespoon vegan cocoa powder
- 1 cup almond milk
- ⅔ cup coconut sugar
- 1 teaspoon vanilla extract
- ½ cup coconut oil, melted
- 1 tablespoon flax meal
- ⅓ cup vegan chocolate chips

Directions

1. Preheat your oven to 350 degrees f.
2. Prepare a 9 x 5 loaf pan by lining it with parchment paper.
3. Add almond flour, baking powder, baking soda and salt to a large bowl. Whisk.
4. Add almond milk, coconut sugar, vanilla extract, coconut oil, and flax meal to another bowl and mix until the sugar is dissolved.
5. Pout the dry ingredients into the wet mixture and mix until just combined.
6. Transfer half the batter to a medium bowl and add cocoa powder. Mix until just combined. Fold in chocolate chips.
7. In a microwave-safe bowl, melt the peanut butter and add to the other half batter bowl. Mix until just combined.
8. Pour each bowl into opposite sides of prepared loaf pan. Using a spatula, swirl it into the mixtures to form a marble pattern.
9. Bake for 50 minutes to until a toothpick inserted into the center comes out clean.
10. Remove from the oven. Allow the cake to cool for 30 minutes then remove from the pan and transfer to a wire rack. Allow to cool completely then slice and serve.

Vegan chocolate pudding

Preparation:
30 Minutes

Serves:
3

Ingredients

- ½ cup raw cacao powder
- 6 tablespoons maple syrup
- 2 teaspoon vanilla extract
- 1 ½ cup coconut cream
- Salt to taste

Directions

1. Add coconut cream, cacao powder, and maple syrup to a small saucepan. Place over low heat and whisk until a smooth consistency is achieved. Continue to cook for 2 minutes or until mixture just begins to form small bubbles.
2. Remove from the heat and stir in vanilla extract and salt.
3. Pour mixture into individual containers and chill overnight to set.

Coconut vanilla macaroons

Preparation:
35 Minutes

Serves:
3

Ingredients

- 1 teaspoon vanilla extract
- 2 cups unsweetened coconut, shredded
- 1 cup unsweetened almond milk
- 4 tablespoons maple syrup
- 1 tablespoon coconut flour
- 1 tablespoon almond flour

Directions

1. Preheat your oven to 350 degrees f.
2. Prepare a baking sheet by lining it with parchment paper.
3. Add coconut milk and maple syrup to us a saucepan. Place over medium heat and heat up. Do not bring to a boil. Whisk constantly.
4. Add coconut flour and almond flour, and stir to ensure they are clump-free and evenly combined.
5. Increase to medium heat and bring this mixture to a boil for 3 minutes or until the mixture obtains a thick consistency.
6. Remove from heat and mix in shredded coconut and vanilla extract.
7. Place spoonfuls of the mixture onto the baking sheet.
8. Bake for 15 minutes or until the macaroons are golden brown.
9. Cool and serve.

Avocado toasts

Preparation:
5 Minutes

Serves:
5

Directions

1. Arrange whole grain crackers in a food container.
2. Spread each cracker with mashed avocado.
3. Top with black olives and tomatoes.
4. Refrigerate until ready to eat.
5. Toast in the oven before serving.

Ingredients

- 5 whole grain crackers
- ¼ avocado, mashed
- 1 tablespoon black olives, sliced
- ¼ cup tomatoes, chopped

Sweet & spicy snack mix

Preparation:
5 Minutes

Cooking:
18 Minutes

Serves:
20

Ingredients

- 4 cups mixed vegetable sticks
- ½ cup whole almonds
- 2 cups corn square cereal
- 2 cups oat cereal, toasted
- 1 ¾ cups pretzel sticks
- 1 teaspoon packed brow n sugar
- 1 teaspoon paprika
- ½ teaspoon chili powder
- ½ teaspoon ground cumin
- ¼ teaspoon cayenne pepper
- Salt to taste
- Cooking spray

Directions

1. Preheat your oven to 300 degrees f.
2. In a roasting pan, add the vegetable sticks, almonds, corn and oat cereals and pretzel sticks.
3. In a bowl, mix the rest of the ingredients.
4. Coat the cereal mixture with cooking spray.
5. Sprinkle spice mixture on top of the cereals.
6. Bake in the oven for 18 minutes.
7. Store in an airtight container for up to 7 days.

Carrot & peppers with hummus

Preparation:
5 Minutes

Serves:
1

Directions

1. Arrange carrot and pepper slices in a food container.
2. Place hummus in a smaller food container and add to the big food container beside the carrot and peppers.

Ingredients

- ½ green bell pepper, sliced
- 2 carrots, sliced into sticks
- 3 tablespoons hummus

Roasted squash seeds

Preparation:
10 Minutes

Cooking:
15 Minutes

Serves:
2

Ingredients

- ½ cup spaghetti squash seeds
- ½ teaspoon olive oil
- 1 teaspoon maple syrup
- ½ teaspoon ground cumin
- ½ teaspoon ground cinnamon
- ⅛ teaspoon salt

Directions

1. Preheat your oven to 300 degrees f.
2. Toss seeds in the mixture of the rest of the ingredients.
3. Spread on a baking sheet.
4. Bake for 15 minutes.
5. Store in airtight container.

Chips with kiwi salsa

Preparation:
5 Minutes

Serves:
1

Directions

1. Combine the kiwi and salsa.
2. Serve with tortilla chips.

Ingredients

- ▸ 2 tablespoons kiwi, chopped
- ▸ 2 tablespoons tomato salsa
- ▸ 8 corn tortilla chips

Melon dessert

 Preparation:
5 Minutes

 Serves:
6

Directions

1. Mix sparkling water and vinegar in a bowl.
2. Toss melon balls in the mixture.
3. Transfer to a glass jar with lid.
4. Cover and refrigerate until ready to serve.
5. Garnish with lemon zest before serving.

Ingredients

- 4 cups melon balls
- ½ cup sparkling water (berry flavor)
- 3 tablespoons white balsamic vinegar
- Lemon zest

Mango & strawberry ice cream

Preparation:
10 Minutes

Serves:
4

Directions

1. Put all the ingredients in a food processor.
2. Blend until smooth.
3. Store in the freezer for up to 3 months.
4. Let it soften a little for 30 minutes before serving.

Ingredients

- 12 oz. Mango cubes
- 8 oz. Strawberry slices
- 1 tablespoon freshly squeeze lime juice

Watermelon pizza

 Preparation:
10 Minutes

 Serves:
8

Directions

1. Mix vanilla, maple and yogurt in a bowl.
2. Spread mixture on top of each watermelon slice.
3. Cut into 8 slices.
4. Top with blackberries and strawberries.
5. Sprinkle coconut flakes on top.

Ingredients

- ¼ teaspoon vanilla extract
- 1 teaspoon maple syrup
- ½ cup coconut-milk yogurt
- 2 large round slices watermelon from the center
- ⅔ cup strawberries, sliced
- ½ cup blackberries, sliced in half
- 2 tablespoons unsweetened coconut flakes, toasted

Roasted mango & coconut

Preparation:
5 Minutes

Cooking:
10 Minutes

Serves:
4

Ingredients

- 2 mangoes, cubed
- 2 tablespoons coconut flakes
- 2 teaspoons orange zest
- 2 teaspoons crystallized ginger, chopped

Directions

1. Preheat your oven to 350 degrees f.
2. Put the mango cubes in custard cups.
3. Top with coconut flakes, orange zest and ginger.
4. Bake in the oven for 10 minutes.

Fruit compote

Preparation:
15 Minutes

Cooking:
8 h

Serves:
10

Ingredients

- 3 pears, cubed
- 15 oz. Pineapple chunks
- ¾ cup dried apricots, sliced into quarters
- 3 tablespoons orange juice concentrate
- 1 tablespoon quick-cooking tapioca
- ½ teaspoon ground ginger
- 2 cups dark sweet cherries, pitted
- ¼ cup coconut flakes, toasted

Directions

1. In a slow cooker, add all the ingredients except the cherries and coconut flakes.
2. Cover the pot and cook on low setting for 8 hours.
3. Stir in the cherries.
4. Transfer to food containers.
5. Sprinkle with coconut flakes.
6. Refrigerate and serve when ready to eat.

Chapter 9.
Sauces and Dips

Cucumber Bites

Preparation:
10 Minutes +
Soaking 1-3 h

Serves:
14 Bites

Ingredients

- 1 cup almonds – soaked 1-3 hours
- ¼ Cup cashew nuts – soaked 1-3 hours
- Juice of 1 lemon
- 1 clove garlic –minced
- Salt & pepper
- 1 tsp. Olive oil
- 1 large cucumber – sliced into approximately 1 inch pieces
- 1 tomato – diced
- ½ Cup fresh parsley – roughly chopped

Directions

1. Soak almonds and cashew nuts in warm water for 1-3 hours. The longer you soak them, the softer and creamier they will be.
2. Put all Ingredients (except cucumber, parsley and tomato) into a blender or food processor.
3. Blend or process until you get a creamy paste.
4. If the mix is too thick for your likings you can add a little bit of water.
5. Remove the mixture from the blender.
6. Add the diced tomato and fresh parsley and gently mix with a spoon.
7. Scoop one spoonful of mixture onto each cucumber slice.
8. Sprinkle with black pepper and serve.

Broccoli Crispy Bread

Preparation:
5 Minutes

Cooking:
30 Minutes

Serves:
3-4

Ingredients

- 4 cups of broccoli florets – cut into chunks
- 3 tbsp. Nutritional yeast
- 1 tbsp. Extra virgin olive oil
- 2 tbsp. Chia seeds
- 1 tsp. Baking powder
- Salt & pepper
- ½ Cup fresh basil

Directions

1. Preheat oven to 375f.
2. Soak the chia seeds with 6 tablespoons of water for about 5 minutes.
3. Put broccoli into a food processor and pulse until you get a texture similar to rice.
4. Add Nutritional yeast, basil, salt and pepper, and pulse until Ingredients are well combined.
5. Transfer the mix into a bowl, add olive oil, baking powder, chia seeds and stir well.
6. Line a baking tray with a sheet of baking paper.
7. Pour the dough onto the baking paper and spread evenly. The thinner you make it, the crispier it will be.
8. Bake in the oven for approximately 30 minute until golden and crispy. Make sure it is cooked in the middle.
9. Remove from the oven and cut into bars.
10. Enjoy while still warm or cold.

Roasted Pumpkin Seeds

Preparation:
5 Minutes

Cooking:
25 Minutes

Serves:
as many as you'd like

Ingredients

▸ Pumpkin seeds
▸ Extra virgin olive oil
▸ Salt & pepper

Directions

1. Preheat oven to 350f.
2. Line a baking tray with baking paper or aluminium foil. Either will do.
3. Place the seeds into a bowl, drizzle with not too much oil but enough to evenly coat them.
4. Sprinkle with salt and pepper and toss well together.
5. Pour the seeds onto the baking tray and roast in the oven for approximately 20 minutes or until they become very lightly brown. Keep an eye on them not to burn them.
6. During cooking remove the tray a few times to stir the seeds.
7. When completely roasted, remove from oven and let them cool.
8. Enjoy as nibbles or sprinkle on your salad or soup.

Almond Cauliflower

Preparation:
5 Minutes

Cooking:
30 Minutes

Serves:
4

Ingredients

- 4 cups cauliflower florets – chopped into bite size chunks
- 1 tbsp. Extra virgin olive oil
- 2 tbsp. Almonds – chopped in very small pieces

Directions

1. Preheat oven to 425f.
2. Line a baking tray with baking paper.
3. Place cauliflower into a bowl, add olive oil, salt and pepper, almonds and toss everything well together.
4. Pour the cauliflower onto the baking paper.
5. Bake in oven for approximately 30 minutes or until golden brown and soft. Stir occasionally.
6. Remove from oven, sprinkle with ground black pepper and serve.

Tahini Dressing

 Preparation:
5 Minutes

 Serves:
4-5

Directions

1. Place all Ingredients into a blender (except for water).
2. Blend until creamy.
3. If the dressing is too thick, add a little bit of water until it reaches the desired consistency.

Ingredients

- ¼ Cup tahini paste
- Juice of 1 lemon
- 1 tbsp. Apple cider vinegar
- 2 tbsp. Extra virgin olive oil
- 2 clove of garlic – minced
- Salt & pepper

Lemon & Mustard Vinaigrette

Preparation:
5 Minutes

Serves:
6 tablespoons

Ingredients

- Juice of 1 lemon
- ½ Tsp. Dijon mustard
- 4 tbsp. Extra virgin olive oil
- Salt & pepper

Directions

1. Put lemon juice, mustard, salt and pepper into a bowl.
2. Whisk well until combined.
3. While whisking, drizzle in the extra virgin olive oil.
4. Keep whisking vigorously until all Ingredients are combined and you have a medium creamy dressing.
5. The dressing should be ready at this point. You can taste and adjust any of the Ingredients to taste.

Cheesy Sauce

 Preparation:
5 Minutes

 Serves:
4

Directions

1. Combine all Ingredients together into a bowl and whisk vigorously.
2. Serve as an accompaniment to your dishes.

Ingredients

- 2 tbsp. Extra virgin olive oil
- 2 tbsp. Nutritional yeast
- Juice of 1 lemon
- Salt & pepper

Chimichurri Style Sauce

Preparation:
1-2 Minutes

Cooking:
5 Minutes

Serves:
2-3 cups

Ingredients

- ½ Cup extra virgin olive oil
- 1 tsp. Fresh rosemary
- 1 tsp. Fresh oregano
- 2 medium cloves garlic – crushed
- 2 tsp. Smoked paprika
- 1 bay leaf
- ¼ Tsp. Sea salt
- 1 tbsp. Lemon juice
- Pinch of black pepper flakes

Directions

1. Put the herbs into a mortar and pestle and lightly pound them. If you do not have a mortar and pestle you can chop them very finely.
2. Pour olive oil into a pan and warm over medium-low heat.
3. When oil is hot, remove from heat.
4. Stir paprika, black pepper flakes, bay leaf and a pinch of salt into the oil.
5. Add herbs and lemon juice.
6. Put the sauce into a jar in the fridge and leave it to infuse for a couple of days before using.

Peanut Sauce

Preparation:
10 Minutes

Serves:
5

Ingredients

- ½ Cup creamy peanut butter
- 2 tbsp. Thai red curry paste
- ¾ Cup coconut milk
- 2tbsp. Apple cider vinegar
- 1/2 tbsp. Coconut palm sugar
- 2 tbsp. Ground peanuts
- Salt

Directions

1. Add all Ingredients together into a saucepan and whisk well.
2. Transfer the pan to the stove and heat up the mix over a low heat while continuing whisking.
3. Keep a constant eye on the sauce and as soon as it starts bubbling remove from heat. If you like the sauce more liquid, add a little bit of water and whisk. Keep adding water bit by bit until it reaches your desired consistency.
4. Move the sauce into a bowl and top with ground peanuts.

Spicy Almond & Garlic Dip

Preparation:
5 Minutes +
Soaking overnight

Serves:
1 large cup

Directions

1. Soak almonds overnight.
2. Put all Ingredients into a blender.
3. Blend until smooth and creamy.
4. You can use immediately or refrigerate covered.

Ingredients

▶ 1 cup raw almonds
▶ 1 cup almond milk
▶ 2 cloves garlic
▶ ½ Tsp. Chili powder
▶ ¼ Tsp. Smoked paprika
▶ Pinch of salt
▶ Pinch of cayenne pepper

Cauliflower Hummus

Preparation:
5 Minutes

Cooking:
5 Minutes

Serves:
2 cups

Ingredients

- 4 cups cauliflower stems and florets – chopped
- 2 tbsp. Tahini paste
- 5 tbsp. Extra virgin olive oil
- Juice of 2 lemons
- Salt & pepper
- Pinch of cumin

Directions

1. Steam or lightly boil cauliflower for approximately 5 minutes or until soft.
2. Drain and let it cool down completely.
3. Combine cauliflower, tahini paste, extra virgin olive oil, lemon juice and cumin into a food processor. Process until creamy. Alternatively, you can use a blender.
4. Add salt and pepper to taste.
5. You might want to taste it and add more lemon juice or olive oil according to taste.
6. Serve with raw vegetables.

Eggplant & Walnut Spread

Preparation:
10-15 Minutes

Cooking:
45 Minutes

Serves:
1 large cup

Ingredients

- 2 x medium round eggplants
- 1 tbsp. Extra virgin olive oil
- 1 cup walnuts – chopped
- 2 cloves garlic
- Juice of 1 large lemon
- Salt & pepper
- 1 tsp. Cumin
- 1/3 cup tahini paste
- ½ Cup fresh parsley leaves

Directions

1. Preheat oven to 375f.
2. Place eggplants on a baking tray and rub them with the olive oil.
3. Stab them with a knife a couple times.
4. Roast for 45 minutes until they look deflated and wrinkled.
5. In the meantime, toast the walnuts in a pan over medium-high heat for 3-4 minutes. Leave to cool.
6. When eggplant is cooked, remove from oven and let it cool down.
7. Cut the eggplants in half and scoop the flesh out into a food processor.
8. Add walnuts and all other Ingredients. Process until obtaining a paste.
9. Serve into a bowl with a drizzle of extra virgin olive oil accompanied by crackers or raw vegetables.

311

Coconut Yogurt Dip

Preparation:
10 Minutes

Serves:
2 Cups

Ingredients

- 1 ½ cup coconut yogurt
- 1 large cucumber – peeled and cut into chunks
- 3 cloves garlic
- Juice of 1 lemon
- 2 tbsp. Extra virgin olive oil
- ½ Cup fresh coriander – finely chopped
- Salt & pepper

Directions

1. Place all Ingredients (except coriander) into a blender and blend until smooth.
2. Add salt and pepper to taste and the coriander.
3. Mix well with a spoon.
4. Refrigerate for about 1 hour to let the flavors infuse.
5. Stir the dip well before serving.

Olive Tapenade

Preparation:
5 Minutes

Serves:
1 Cup

Directions

1. Put all Ingredients together into a food processor and process for few seconds. You basically want all Ingredients finely chopped and well mixed together. Be careful not processes for too long otherwise you will have a paste.
2. Serve to spread onto your favorite crackers.

Ingredients

- ½ Cup black olives
- ½ Cup green olives
- 2 cloves garlic
- 1tsp. Lemon juice
- Ground black pepper

Chunky Rocket Spread

Preparation:
15 Minutes

Serves:
1 cup

Ingredients

- 1 ½ cup roasted cashew nuts
- 1 clove garlic
- 3 cups rocket leaves
- ¼ Cup Nutritional yeast
- ¼ Cup extra virgin olive oil
- Juice of ½ lemon
- Salt & pepper

Directions

1. Place the cashew nuts, garlic and Nutritional yeast into a food processor.
2. Pulse gently until the nuts are still chunky and mixed well together with the other Ingredients.
3. Transfer the mix into a bowl.
4. Place olive oil and lemon juice into the food processor, then add rocket leaves and pulse to blend.
5. Transfer the rocket mixture into the bowl with the cashews, season with salt and pepper and mix together with a spoon.
6. Serve with crackers or other low carb breads.

Chapter 10.
Recipes Around the World

Fluffy Deep-Dish Pizza

 Preparation:
2 h 15 minutes

 Serves:
6

Ingredients

- 12 inch of frozen whole-wheat pizza crust, thawed
- 1 medium-sized red bell pepper, cored and sliced
- 5-ounce of spinach leaves, chopped
- 1 small red onion, peeled and chopped
- 1 1/2 teaspoons of minced garlic
- 1/4 teaspoon of salt
- 1/2 teaspoon of red pepper flakes
- 1/2 teaspoon of dried thyme
- 1/4 cup of chopped basil, fresh
- 14-ounce of pizza sauce
- 1 cup of shredded vegan mozzarella

Directions

1. Place a medium-sized non-stick skillet pan over an average heat, add the oil and let it heat.
2. Add the onion, garlic and let it cook for 5 minutes or until it gets soft.
3. Then add the red bell pepper and continue cooking for 4 minutes or until it becomes tender-crisp.
4. Add the spinach, salt, red pepper, thyme, basil and stir properly.
5. Cool off for 3 to 5 minutes or until the spinach leaves wilts, and then set it aside until it is called for.
6. Grease a 4-quarts slow cooker with a non-stick cooking spray and insert the pizza crust in it.
7. Press the dough into the bottom and spread 1 inch up along the sides.
8. Spread it with the pizza sauce, cover it with the spinach mixture and then garnish evenly with the cheese.
9. Sprinkle it with the red pepper flakes, basil leaves and cover it with the lid.
10. Plug in the slow cooker and let it cook for 1 1/2 hours to 2 hours at the low heat setting or until the crust turns golden brown and the cheese melts completely.
11. When done, transfer the pizza into the cutting board, let it rest for 10 minutes, then slice to serve.

Nutritions: *Calories:250 Cal, Carbohydrates:25g, Protein:5g, Fats:8g, Fiber:1g.*

Incredible Artichoke and Olives Pizza

 Preparation:
1 h 50 minutes

 Serves:
6

Ingredients

- 12 inch of frozen whole-wheat pizza crust, thawed
- 1 mushroom, sliced
- 1/2 cup of sliced char-grilled artichokes
- 1 small green bell pepper, cored and sliced
- 2 medium-sized tomatoes, sliced
- 2 tablespoons of sliced black olives
- 1/2 teaspoon of garlic powder
- 1 teaspoon of salt, divided
- 1/2 teaspoon of dried oregano
- 2 tablespoons of nutritional yeast
- 2-ounce cashews
- 2 teaspoons of lemon juice
- 3 tablespoon of olive oil, divided
- 8-ounce of tomato paste
- 4 fluid ounce of water

Directions

1. Place the cashews in a food processor; add the garlic powder, 1/2 teaspoon of salt, yeast, 2 tablespoons of oil, lemon juice, and water.
2. Mash it until it gets smooth and creamy, but add some water if need be.
3. Grease a 4 to 6 quarts slow cooker with a non-stick cooking spray and insert the pizza crust into it.
4. Press the dough in bottom and spread the tomato paste on top of it.
5. Sprinkle it with garlic powder, oregano and top it with the prepared cashew mixture.
6. Spray it with the mushrooms, bell peppers, tomato, artichoke slices, olives and then with the remaining olive oil.
7. Sprinkle it with the oregano, the remaining salt and cover it with the lid.
8. Plug in the slow cooker and let it cook for 1 to 1 1/2 hours at the low heat setting or until the crust turns golden brown.
9. When done, transfer the pizza to the cutting board, let it rest for 10 minutes and slice to serve.

Nutritions: *Calories:212 Cal, Carbohydrates:39g, Protein:16g, Fats:5g, Fiber:5g.*

Mushroom and Peppers Pizza

Preparation:
2 h

Serves:
6

Ingredients

- 12 inch of frozen whole-wheat pizza crust, thawed
- 1/2 cup of chopped red bell pepper
- 1/2 cup of chopped green bell pepper
- 1/2 cup of chopped orange bell pepper
- 3/4 cup of chopped button mushrooms
- 1 small red onion, peeled and chopped
- 1 teaspoon of garlic powder, divided
- 1 teaspoon of salt, divided
- 1/2 teaspoon of coconut sugar
- 1/2 teaspoon of red pepper flakes
- 1 teaspoon of dried basil, divided
- 1 1/2 teaspoon of dried oregano, divided
- 1 tablespoon of olive oil
- 6-ounce of tomato paste
- 1/2 cup of vegan Parmesan cheese

Directions

1. Place a large non-stick skillet pan over an average heat, add the oil and let it heat.
2. Add the onion, bell peppers and cook for 10 minutes or until it gets soft and lightly charred. Then add the mushroom, cook it for 3 minutes and set the pan aside until it is needed.
3. Pour the tomato sauce, sugar, 1/2 teaspoon of the garlic powder, salt, basil, oregano, into a bowl and stir properly.
4. Grease a 4 to 6 quarts slow cooker with a non-stick cooking spray and insert the pizza crust into it.
5. Press the dough in bottom and spread the already prepared tomato sauce on top of it. Sprinkle it with the Parmesan cheese and top it with the cooked vegetable mixture.
6. Cover it with the lid, plug in the slow cooker and let it cook for 1 to 1 1/2 hours at the low heat setting or until the crust turns golden brown.
7. When done, transfer the pizza to a cutting board, sprinkle it with the remaining oregano, basil, then let it rest for 10 minutes and then slice to serve.

Nutritions: *Calories:188 Cal, Carbohydrates:27g, Protein:5g, Fats:5g, Fiber:3g.*

Tangy Barbecue Tofu Pizza

 Preparation:
2 h

 Serves:
6

Ingredients

- 12 inch of frozen whole-wheat pizza crust, thawed
- 1 cup of tofu pieces
- 1 small red onion, peeled and sliced
- 1/4 cup of chopped cilantro
- 1 1/2 teaspoons of salt
- 3/4 teaspoon of ground black pepper
- 1 tablespoon of olive oil
- 1 cup of barbecue sauce
- 2 cups of vegan mozzarella

Directions

1. Place a large non-stick skillet pan over an average heat, add 1 tablespoon of oil and let it heat.
2. Add the tofu pieces in a single layer sprinkle it with 1 teaspoon of salt, black pepper and cook for 5 to 7 minutes or until it gets crispy with a golden brown on all sides.
3. Transfer the tofu pieces into a bowl, add 1/2 cup of the barbecue sauce and toss it properly to coat.
4. Grease a 4 to 6 quarts slow cooker with a non-stick cooking spray and insert the pizza crust in it.
5. Press the dough into the bottom and spread the remaining 1/2 cup of the barbecue sauce.
6. Evenly garnish it with tofu pieces and onion slices.
7. Sprinkle it with the mozzarella cheese and cover it with the lid.
8. Plug in the slow cooker and let it cook for 1 to 1 1/2 hours at the low heat setting or until the crust turns golden brown.
9. When done, transfer the pizza into the cutting board, let it rest for 10 minutes and slice to serve.

Nutritions: *Calories:135 Cal, Carbohydrates:15g, Protein:6g, Fats:5g, Fiber:1g.*

Tasty Tomato Garlic Mozzarella Pizza

Preparation:
2 h 30 minutes

Serves:
6

Ingredients

- 12 inch of frozen whole-wheat pizza crust, thawed
- 3/4 teaspoon of tapioca flour
- 2 teaspoons of minced garlic
- 2 teaspoons of agar powder
- 1 teaspoon of cornstarch
- 1 teaspoon of salt, divided
- 1/2 teaspoon of red pepper flakes
- 1/2 teaspoon of dried basil
- 1/2 teaspoon of dried parsley
- 2 tablespoons of olive oil
- 1/4 teaspoon of lemon juice
- 3/4 teaspoon of apple cider vinegar
- 8 fluid ounce of coconut milk, unsweetened

Directions

1. Start by preparing the mozzarella.
2. Place a small saucepan over a medium-low heat, pour in the milk and let it steam until it gets warm thoroughly.
3. With a whisker, pour in the agar powder and stir properly until it dissolves completely.
4. Switch the temperature to a low and pour in the salt, lemon juice, vinegar, and whisk them properly.
5. Mix the tapioca flour and cornstarch with 2 tablespoons of water before adding it to the milk mixture.
6. Whisk properly and transfer this mixture to a greased bowl.
7. Place the bowl in a refrigerator for 1 hour or until it is set.
8. Then grease a- 4 to 6 quarts of the slow cooker with a non-stick cooking spray and insert pizza crust into it.
9. Press the dough into the bottom and brush the top with olive oil.
10. Spread the garlic and then cover it with the tomato slices.
11. Sprinkle it with salt, red pepper flakes, basil, and the oregano.
12. Cut the mozzarella cheese into coins and place them across the top of the pizza.
13. Cover it with the lid, plug in the slow cooker, let it cook for 1 to 1 1/2 hours at the low heat setting or until the crust turns golden brown and the cheese melts completely. When done, transfer the pizza to the cutting board, then let it rest for 5 minutes, and slice to serve.

Nutritions: *Calories:113 Cal, Carbohydrates:10g, Protein:7g, Fats:5g, Fiber:1g.*

Delicious Chipotle Red Lentil Pizza

Preparation:
1 h 45 minutes

Serves:
4

Ingredients

- 12 inch of frozen whole-wheat pizza crust, thawed
- 1/4 cup of red lentils, uncooked and rinsed
- 1/4 cup of chopped carrot
- 1 cups of chopped tomato
- 1 medium-sized tomatoes, sliced
- 2 green onions, sliced
- 1 chipotle chili pepper in adobo sauce. Chopped
- 1/2 cup of sliced olives
- 1/4 cup of chopped red onion
- 1/2 teaspoon of minced garlic
- 1/2 teaspoon of salt
- 1/4 teaspoon of ground black pepper
- 1/2 teaspoon of cayenne pepper
- 1/2 teaspoon of dried oregano
- 1 teaspoon of dried basil, divided
- 1 tablespoon of tomato paste
- 1 teaspoon of olive oil
- 1/2 teaspoon of apple cider vinegar
- 1 cup of water
- 1 cup crumbled almond ricotta cheese

Directions

1. Place a medium-sized non-stick skillet pan over an average heat, add the oil and let it heat.
2. Add the onion, garlic and using the sauté button, heat it for 5 minutes or until the onions get soft.
3. Add the carrots, tomatoes, chipotle chile, oregano, 1/2 teaspoon of basil and stir properly.
4. Let it cook for 5 minutes before adding the lentils, salt, black pepper, cayenne pepper, vinegar, and water.
5. Stir properly, cook for 15 to 20 minutes or until the lentils get tender, thereafter, cover the pan partially with a lid.
6. In the meantime, grease a 4 to 6 quarts slow cooker with a non-stick cooking spray and insert pizza crust into it.
7. Press the dough into the bottom and spread the lentil mixture.
8. Spray it with the tomato slices, green onions, and olives.
9. Spread the cheese over the top and sprinkle it with the remaining 1/2 teaspoon of basil.
10. Cover it with the lid, plug in the slow cooker and let it cook for 1 hour or until the crust turns golden brown and allow the cheese to melt completely.
11. When done, transfer the pizza to the cutting board, then let it rest for 5 minutes, before slicing to serve.

Nutritions: *Calories:135 Cal, Carbohydrates:15g, Protein:6g, Fats:5g, Fiber:1g.*

Nourishing Whole-Grain Porridge

Preparation:
2 h 10 minutes

Serves:
4

Directions

1. Using a 6-quarts slow cooker, place all the ingredients and stir properly.
2. Cover it with the lid, plug in the slow cooker and let it cook for 2 hours or until grains get soft, while stirring halfway through.
3. Serve the porridge with fruits.

Ingredients

- 3/4 cup of steel-cut oats, rinsed and soaked overnight
- 3/4 cup of whole barley, rinsed and soaked overnight
- 1/2 cup of cornmeal
- 1 teaspoon of salt
- 3 tablespoons of brown sugar
- 1 cinnamon stick, about 3 inches long
- 1 teaspoon of vanilla extract, unsweetened
- 4 1/2 cups of water

Nutritions: *Calories:129 Cal, Carbohydrates:22g, Protein:5g, Fats:2g, Fiber:4g.*

Pungent Mushroom Barley Risotto

Preparation:
3 h 30 minutes

Serves:
4

Ingredients

- 1 1/2 cups of hulled barley, rinsed and soaked overnight
- 8 ounces of carrots, peeled and chopped
- 1 pound of mushrooms, sliced
- 1 large white onion, peeled and chopped
- 3/4 teaspoon of salt
- 1/2 teaspoon of ground black pepper
- 4 sprigs thyme
- 1/4 cup of chopped parsley
- 2/3 cup of grated vegetarian Parmesan cheese
- 1 tablespoon of apple cider vinegar
- 2 tablespoons of olive oil
- 1 1/2 cups of vegetable broth

Directions

1. Place a large non-stick skillet pan over a medium-high heat, add the oil and let it heat until it gets hot.
2. Add the onion along with 1/4 teaspoon of each the salt and black pepper.
3. Cook it for 5 minutes or until it turns golden brown.
4. Then add the mushrooms and continue cooking for 2 minutes.
5. Add the barley, thyme and cook for another 2 minutes.
6. Transfer this mixture to a 6-quarts slow cooker and add the carrots, 1/4 teaspoon of salt, and the vegetable broth.
7. Stir properly and cover it with the lid.
8. Plug in the slow cooker, let it cook for 3 hours at the high heat setting or until the grains absorb all the cooking liquid and the vegetables get soft.
9. Remove the thyme sprigs, pour in the remaining ingredients except for parsley and stir properly.
10. Pour in the warm water and stir properly until the risotto reaches your desired state.
11. Add the seasoning, then garnish it with parsley and serve.

Nutritions: *Calories:321 Cal, Carbohydrates:48g, Protein:12g, Fats:10g, Fiber:11g.*

Healthful Lentil and Rice Stew

 Preparation:
4 h 15 minutes

 Serves:
6

Ingredients

- 1/2 cup of brown rice, rinsed
- 1 cup of brown lentils, rinsed
- 1 cup of chopped white onion
- 3/4 teaspoon of salt
- 1 teaspoon of ground turmeric
- 1 tablespoon of ground cumin
- 1/2 teaspoon of ground cinnamon
- 1 1/2 tablespoons of olive oil
- 1 1/2 quarts of water

Directions

1. Place a medium-sized non-stick skillet pan over a medium heat, add the oil and let it heat.
2. Add the onion and using the sauté button, heat it for 5 minutes or until it turns golden brown.
3. Transfer this mixture to a 6-quarts slow cooker, pour in the remaining ingredients and cover it with the lid.
4. Plug in the slow cooker and let it cook for 3 to 4 hours at the high heat setting or until the grains get soft.
5. Garnish it with the cilantro and serve it with lemon wedges.

Nutritions: *Calories:369 Cal, Carbohydrates:56g, Protein:5g, Fats:15g, Fiber:5g.*

Remarkable Three-Grain Medley

Preparation:
3 h 15 minutes

Serves:
6

Directions

1. Place all the ingredients in a 6-quarts slow cooker and stir properly.
2. Cover it with the lid, plug in the slow cooker and let it cook for 2 to 3 hours at the high heat setting or until the grains absorbs all the liquid, as a result becoming soft.
3. Serve right away.

Ingredients

- 1/2 cup of uncooked hulled barley, rinsed and soaked overnight
- 1/2 cup of uncooked wild rice, rinse and soaked overnight
- 2/3 cup of uncooked wheat berries, rinsed and soaked overnight
- 1/2 cup of sliced green onions
- 1 teaspoon of minced garlic
- 1/4 cup of chopped parsley
- 2 teaspoons of shredded lemon peel
- 1/4 cup of olive oil
- 28-ounce of vegetable broth
- 2 ounces of diced cherry pepper

Nutritions: *Calories:200 Cal, Carbohydrates:38g, Protein:5g, Fats:3g, Fiber:3g.*

Hearty Millet Stew

 Preparation:
4 h 30 minutes

 Serves:
4

Ingredients

- 1 cup of millet, uncooked
- 2 medium-sized potatoes, peeled and chopped
- 2 medium-sized carrots, peeled and chopped
- 1 cup of celery, chopped
- 1/2 pound of mushrooms, chopped
- 2 medium-sized white onions, peeled and sliced
- 1 teaspoon of minced garlic
- 1 teaspoon of salt
- 1/2 teaspoon of ground black pepper
- 1/2 teaspoon of dried basil
- 1/2 teaspoon of dried thyme
- 2 bay leaves
- 4 cups of water

Directions

1. Place a medium-sized non-stick skillet pan over an average heat, add the millet and let it cook for 5 minutes or until it gets toasted, while stirring frequently.
2. Transfer the toasted millets to a 6-quarts slow cooker, and reserve the pan.
3. Add the potatoes, carrots, celery, mushrooms and onion to the pan and let it cook for 5 to 7 minutes or until it is properly toasted.
4. Transfer the veggies to the slow cooker, pour in the remaining ingredients, stir and cover it with the lid.
5. Then plug in the slow cooker and let it cook for 4 hours at the high heat setting or until the vegetables and grains are cooked thoroughly.
6. Serve right away.

Nutritions: *Calories:268 Cal, Carbohydrates:44g, Protein:8g, Fats:6g, Fiber:8g.*

Mushroom Steak

Preparation:
1 h 30 minutes

Serves:
8

Ingredients

- 1 tbsp. of the following:
- fresh lemon juice
- olive oil, extra virgin
- 2 tbsp. coconut oil
- 3 thyme sprigs
- 8 medium Portobello mushrooms

For Sauce:
- 1 ½ t. of the following:
- minced garlic
- minced peeled fresh ginger
- 2 tbsp. of the following:
- light brown sugar
- mirin
- ½ c. low-sodium soy sauce

Directions

1. For the sauce, combine all the sauce ingredients, along with ¼ cup water into a little pan and simmer to cook. Cook using a medium heat until it reduces to a glaze, approximately 15 to 20 minutes, then remove from the heat.
2. For the mushrooms, bring the oven to 350 heat setting.
3. Using a skillet, melt coconut oil and olive oil, cooking the mushrooms on each side for about 3 minutes.
4. Next, arrange the mushrooms in a single layer on a sheet for baking and season with lemon juice, salt, and pepper.
5. Carefully slide into the oven and roast for 5 minutes. Let it rest for 2 minutes.
6. Plate and drizzle the sauce over the mushrooms.
7. Enjoy.

Nutritions: *Calories: 87, Carbohydrates: 6.2 g, Proteins: 3 g, Fats: 6.2 g*

Spicy Grilled Tofu Steak

 Preparation:
20 Minutes

 Serves:
4

Ingredients

- 1 tbsp. of the following:
- chopped scallion
- chopped cilantro
- soy sauce
- hoisin sauce
- 2 tbsp. oil
- ¼ t. of the following:
- salt
- garlic powder
- red chili pepper powder
- ground Sichuan peppercorn powder
- ½ t. cumin
- 1 pound firm tofu

Directions

1. Place the tofu on a plate and drain the excess liquid for about 10 minutes.
2. Slice drained tofu into ¾ thick stakes.
3. Stir the cumin, Sichuan peppercorn, chili powder, garlic powder, and salt in a mixing bowl until well-incorporated.
4. In another little bowl, combine soy sauce, hoisin, and 1 teaspoon of oil.
5. Heat a skillet to medium temperature with oil, then carefully place the tofu in the skillet.
6. Sprinkle the spices over the tofu, distributing equally across all steaks. Cook for 3-5 minutes, flip, and put spice on the other side. Cook for an additional 3 minutes.
7. Brush with sauce and plate.
8. Sprinkle some scallion and cilantro and enjoy.

Nutritions: *Calories: 155, Carbohydrates: 7.6 g, Proteins: 9.9 g, Fats: 11.8 g*

Piquillo Salsa Verde Steak

Preparation:
25 Minutes

Serves:
8

Ingredients

- 4 – ½ inch thick slices of ciabatta
- 18 oz. firm tofu, drained
- 5 tbsp. olive oil, extra virgin
- Pinch of cayenne
- ½ t. cumin, ground
- 1 ½ tbsp. sherry vinegar
- 1 shallot, diced
- 8 piquillo peppers (can be from a jar) – drained and cut to ½ inch strips
- 3 tbsp. of the following:
- parsley, finely chopped
- capers, drained and chopped

Directions

1. Place the tofu on a plate to drain the excess liquid, and then slice into 8 rectangle pieces.
2. You can either prepare your grill or use a grill pan. If using a grill pan, preheat the grill pan.
3. Mix 3 tablespoons of olive oil, cayenne, cumin, vinegar, shallot, parsley, capers, and piquillo peppers in a medium bowl to make our salsa verde. Season to preference with salt and pepper.
4. Using a paper towel, dry the tofu slices.
5. Brush olive oil on each side, seasoning with salt and pepper lightly.
6. Place the bread on the grill and toast for about 2 minutes using medium-high heat.
7. Next, grill the tofu, cooking each side for about 3 minutes or until the tofu is heated through.
8. Place the toasted bread on the plate then the tofu on top of the bread.
9. Gently spoon out the salsa verde over the tofu and serve.

Nutritions: *Calories: 427, Carbohydrates: 67.5 g, Proteins: 14.2 g, Fats: 14.6 g*

Butternut Squash Steak

Preparation:
50 Minutes

Serves:
4

Ingredients

- 2 tbsp. coconut yogurt
- ½ t. sweet paprika
- 1 ¼ c. low-sodium vegetable broth
- 1 sprig thyme
- 1 finely chopped garlic clove
- 1 big thinly sliced shallot
- 1 tbsp. margarine
- 2 tbsp. olive oil, extra virgin
- Salt and pepper to liking

Directions

1. Bring the oven to 375 heat setting.
2. Cut the squash, lengthwise, into 4 steaks.
3. Carefully core one side of each squash with a paring knife in a crosshatch pattern.
4. Using a brush, coat with olive oil each side of the steak then season generously with salt and pepper.
5. In an oven-safe, non-stick skillet, bring 2 tablespoons of olive oil to a warm temperature.
6. Place the steaks on the skillet with the cored side down and cook at medium temperature until browned, approximately 5 minutes.
7. Flip and repeat on the other side for about 3 minutes.
8. Place the skillet into the oven to roast the squash for 7 minutes.
9. Take out from the oven, placing on a plate and covering with aluminum foil to keep warm.
10. Using the previously used skillet, add thyme, garlic, and shallot, cooking at medium heat. Stir frequently for about 2 minutes.
11. Add brandy and cook for an additional minute.
12. Next, add paprika and whisk the mixture together for 3 minutes.
13. Add in the yogurt seasoning with salt and pepper.
14. Plate the steaks and spoon the sauce over the top.
15. Garnish with parsley and enjoy!

Nutritions: *Calories: 300, Carbohydrates: 46 g, Proteins: 5.3 g, Fats: 10.6 g*

Cauliflower Steak Kicking Corn

Preparation:
60 Minutes

Serves:
6

Ingredients

- ► 2 t. capers, drained
- ► 4 scallions, chopped
- ► 1 red chili, minced
- ► ¼ c. vegetable oil
- ► 2 ears of corn, shucked
- ► 2 big cauliflower heads
- ► Salt and pepper to taste

Directions

1. Heat the oven to 375 degrees.
2. Boil a pot of water, about 4 cups, using the maximum heat setting available.
3. Add corn in the saucepan, cooking approximately 3 minutes or until tender.
4. Drain and allow the corn to cool, then slice the kernels away from the cob.
5. Warm 2 tablespoons of vegetable oil in a skillet.
6. Combine the chili pepper with the oil, cooking for approximately 30 seconds.
7. Next, combine the scallions, sautéing with the chili pepper until soft.
8. Mix in the corn and capers in the skillet and cook for approximately 1 minute to blend the flavors. Then remove from heat.
9. Warm 1 tablespoon of vegetable oil in a skillet. Once warm, begin to place cauliflower steaks to the pan, 2 to 3 at a time. Season to your liking with salt and cook over medium heat for 3 minutes or until lightly browned.
10. Once cooked, slide onto the cookie sheet and repeat step 5 with the remaining cauliflower.
11. Take the corn mixture and press into the spaces between the florets of the cauliflower.
12. Bake for 25 minutes.
13. Serve warm and enjoy!

Nutritions: *Calories: 153, Carbohydrates: 15 g, Proteins: 4 g, Fats: 10 g*

Pistachio Watermelon Steak

Preparation:
10 Minutes

Serves:
4

Ingredients

- Microgreens
- Pistachios chopped
- Malden sea salt
- 1 tbsp. olive oil, extra virgin
- 1 watermelon
- Salt to taste

Directions

1. Begin by cutting the ends of the watermelon.
2. Carefully peel the skin from the watermelon along the white outer edge.
3. Slice the watermelon into 4 slices, approximately 2 inches thick.
4. Trim the slices, so they are rectangular in shape approximately 2 x4 inches.
5. Heat a skillet to medium heat add 1 tablespoon of olive oil.
6. Add watermelon steaks and cook until the edges begin to caramelize.
7. Plate and top with pistachios and microgreens.
8. Sprinkle with Malden salt.
9. Serve warm and enjoy!

Nutritions: Calories: 67, Carbohydrates: 3.8 g, Proteins: 1.6 g, Fats: 5.9 g

Conclusion

Likely the most beneficial eating design you can follow is that of a veggie lover or vegetarian. Notwithstanding, individuals (particularly meat eaters) or people who will in general like inexpensive food often classify veggie lovers, or the individuals who practice the lifestyle, as being fragile in outline or frail.

Nonetheless, those are only two of the "legend originations" that are seen by individuals who are not familiar with eating veggie lover or vegetarian cooking. Actually, a large number of the vegetables and natural products that are included in veggie lover menu plans are nourishment rich and low in calories.

Plant diets offer tip top nourishment and an extraordinary aid in wellbeing impacts, for example, lower dangers for coronary illness, malignant growth, and type 2 diabetes. The Adventist Health Study 2 demonstrated that veggie lovers gauge a normal of 30 pounds not as much as meat eaters do. Eating from the earth has extraordinary advantages, and it is imperative to know the realities and overlook the bits of gossip.

PLANT BASED RECIPES FOR BEGINNERS

THE EASY GUIDE TO A DIET MEAL PLAN. HEALTHY
EATING AND WEIGHT LOSS COOKBOOK WITH THE
ULTIMATE MEAL PREP. HIGH PROTEIN RECIPES SUITABLE
ALSO FOR ATHLETES

Kevin Rinaldi

Table of Contents

Introduction

Whether you are already convinced that plant-based eating is the best way to go, or just plain curious about this increasingly popular diet, this book will guide you in understanding the what's, how's and why's of a plant-based diet.

Plant-based eating is not too restrictive nor is it difficult to follow. You will find an array of easy, affordable and inspirational ideas on how to include more plant-based foods into your diet—from main hearty meals and quick creative lunches to refreshing juices and smoothies and fun tasty desserts.

In contrast, most fad diets are very motivating at first but eventually fail because eliminating and restricting food groups may end up backfiring by increasing your risks of getting sick.

Still not sure if you can commit to eating plant-based foods 100 percent? Rest assured that every step you take is a step closer to lowered risks of developing chronic diseases, and higher energy levels through a plant-based diet that you can stick with for the rest of your longer and healthier life.

The availability of the variety of diet plans has made the choice of a perfect diet plan very perplexing. Almost all dietitians and nutritionists across the world recommend diet plans that support fresh and whole foods and restrict processed foods. The Plant-Based Diet is based on these unanimously preferred foods.

Plant-based diet patterns focus on foods predominantly from plants, including fruits, vegetables, nuts, oils, seeds, whole grains, beans, and legumes. This diet does not make you strictly a vegetarian or vegan who is not allowed to eat meat or dairy. Instead, you have to consume more of your foods from plant sources. This introduction emphasizes the importance and benefits of a plant-based diet. It will clear away all of your doubts and reservations regarding the plant-based diet plan.

You may still be reluctant about following the plant-based diet if you are not familiar with its benefits.

This is a primary benefit that draws many people toward this diet. Obesity and other weight issues have been increasing in alarming proportions over the years. This can be countered by making the right dietary choices and changing your lifestyle for the better. The plant-based diet helps you do that. The diet will help you consume a lot of fiber -and reduce the amount of processed foods you consume. This is automatically a way to shed extra weight from your body. Studies show that people following the plant-based diet lose more weight compared to those who follow a more animal food-based diet.

Other than the personal benefits you reap, you also have to appreciate the fact that this diet is good for the planet. The modern-day diet rich in processed foods and animal-based foods have a very negative effect on the environment over the last decade. A plant-based diet will allow you to leave a much smaller environmental footprint. Sustainability is allowed when you follow the plant-based diet. This will help in the reduction of greenhouse gas emissions, land use as well as water wastage. All of these factors play a big role in global warming.

As you can see, the plant-based diet has numerous benefits that will help you lose excess weight, reduce the risk of various diseases, and also help you lead a much more environmentally conscious life. All of this should definitely motivate you to try out the wholesome plant-based diet.

Chapter 1. Why Go Plant Based?

By now you know that you do not need to cut meat out completely from your diet if considering a plant-based diet, you are just required to make savvier choices when standing in the meat aisle and, of course, if purchasing animal products. I am sure there are many people breathing a sigh of relief regarding the above.

Meat is not bad for you, meat products are rich in vitamins, iron, and protein. However, processed meats such as hams are high in sodium, whereas red meats may be filled with saturated fats. When it comes to your health, both of these should be avoided. Rather, opt for white meats such as fish and chicken. These lower your risk remarkably in reference to chronic disease.

Apart from making more mindful decisions, choosing a plant-based diet will greatly improve your overall health. Filled with plenty of fresh fruits, vegetables, legumes, seeds, and nuts, one will always be left feeling satisfied after a meal.

The reason for considering a plant-based diet is the nutritional benefits it carries. Fresh foods are vital for overall health and provide us with much-needed vitamins, minerals, and fiber.

Health Benefits

Apart from the rainbow of nutritional benefits this diet holds, it has been suggested that it may help those who struggle with obesity and many other related illnesses such as reducing your chance of developing diabetes, cancer, inflammation, and heart disease. Obesity is on the rise, and studies have suggested that over 69 percent of Americans are either overweight or are considered obese.

Opting to go plant-based has also been known to keep the weight off for those who are eager to shed a few pounds and keep those numbers on the scale down in the long run. Filling your diet with color can also keep you mentally sharp.

It is best to avoid any form of processed foods, as they are no longer in their natural state and most of the nutrition has been sapped from them during production. Many contain added salts, sugars, and stabilizers to give them a longer shelf life too.

This does not mean that you have to toss all your canned or frozen goods, just make yourself aware of what has been added the next time you go grocery shopping.

Environmental Prosperity

The love of meat and animal products has impacted the world and also contributed significantly to climate change, totaling 14.5 percent of the world's greenhouse gasses. Animal oriented farming for mass consumption produces over 300 million tons of waste in America alone.

Other environmental benefits include:

• Saving water. It has been said that it takes 1000 gallons of water to make one gallon of milk and 4325 liters to produce 2.2 lbs of chicken.

• We have cleaner air. Waste from cattle emits ammonia and methane gas, both harmful to humans, animals, and the environment.

• No more dead zones. The toxins in manure are so high that their runoff can ruin sensitive marine ecosystems. In the Gulf of Mexico, there is an 8,500 square foot dead zone because of this.

• Saves all habitats. More farming means more land needed for livestock to roam and feed, leading to deforestation and thus greatly impacting natural wildlife.

For all the eco-warriors out there, the diet automatically reduces the environmental footprint we leave and is a wonderful choice to make with regards to preserving mother earth. Furthermore, it provides a way in which to support and uplift local farming operations and our communities.

Animal Welfare

Mass farming is unsustainable and also leads to animals suffering. As per the International Humane Society, over 80 billion animals are slaughtered worldwide, annually. A shocking figure, and hard to digest. The high consumption of meat means that the welfare and living conditions of these animals are hampered. Many are caged, unable to roam and socialize, and are handled very poorly.

Livestock is also medically treated with antibiotics and steroids

346

to promote growth and stave off infection, and we eat this meat. It cannot be healthy.

Start small by having one meat-free meal a week. The less demand there is for animal products the less the industry can grow, calling for more sustainable and welfare-orientated ways of farming. Free-range and grass-fed are options you can consider if you find it hard to cut out meat completely.

Adding a bit of color to your diet seems all the more worthwhile when considering the impact it can make on your health and overall well-being. All those who have ever been on a diet or multiple can agree that they all have one fundamental pillar, and that is a diet high in fresh fruits and vegetables.

Plants as Medicine

Medicine has always been made using plants. It is therefore crystal clear that the plant-based diet can serve as medicines to our bodies.

You may find that when a person is unwell, a health expert may recommend eating a particular plant-based food. This is because plants have always had medicinal properties.

Diet-Related Diseases

Some of the diseases that are diet-related include;

Diabetes

Cancer

Cardiac arrest

Plants and Other Benefits

If you already eat a fairly healthy diet, you will have no trouble incorporating these foods into your meals. In fact, you may already be enjoying them and just need a few tweaks to increase their presence in your meal planning. Some of the good foods that prevent and reduce chronic inflammation are as follows:

Omega 3 Fatty Acids

Omega 3 fatty acids are found in fish and fish oil. They calm the white blood cells and help them realize there is no danger, so they will return to dormancy.

Fruits And Vegetables

Most fruits and vegetables are anti-inflammatory. They are naturally rich in antioxidants, carotenoids, lycopene, and magnesium. Dark green leafy vegetables and colorful fruits and berries do much to inhibit white blood cell activity.

At least nine servings of fruits and vegetables each day are recommended. One serving is about a half-cup of cooked fruits and vegetables or a full cup if raw. The Mediterranean Diet, rich in fruits and vegetables, is often suggested to individuals suffering from chronic inflammation.

Protective Oils And Fats

Yes, there are a few oils and fats that are actually good for chronic inflammation sufferers. They include coconut oil and extra virgin olive oil.

Fiber

Fiber keeps waste moving through the body. Since the vast majority of our immune cells reside in the intestines, it is important to keep your gut happy. Eat at least 25 grams of fiber every day in the form of fresh vegetables, fruits, and whole grains. If that doesn't provide enough fiber, feel free to take a fiber supplement.

Flavor your food with spices and herbs instead of bad fats and unsafe oils. Spices like turmeric, cumin, cloves, ginger, and cinnamon can enhance the calming of white blood cells. Herbs like fennel, rosemary, sage, and thyme also aid in reducing inflammation while adding delicious new flavors to your food.

Healthy snacks would include a limited amount of unsweetened, plain yogurt with fruit mixed in, celery, carrots, pistachios, almonds, walnuts, and other fruits and vegetables.

Chapter 2. Benefits for Athletes

More and more people each year make the decisions to change to a vegan lifestyle and way of eating. Veganism can improve your life in so many ways, such as giving you marvelous health benefits and putting less stress on the environment. The reasons why someone might choose to switch to a vegan lifestyle are many and very personal. Whether you are changing just the way you eat or you are deciding to forego using any type of animal product is totally your decision. This book will address the vegan way of eating and how it will help you to live the healthy life you have always wanted to live.

One of the healthiest ways to live is by following a vegan diet. The plant-based diet will contain vegetables, fruits, seeds, nuts, legumes, beans, and whole-grains. Since the vegan diet relies heavily on these plant-based staples, it is a healthy diet higher in fiber, phytochemicals, minerals, and vitamins than the average diet. The healthy vegan diet is also full of iron, magnesium, folic acid, and various vitamins, while they are also relatively low in cholesterol and saturated fats.

Here are some of the most important benefits that switching to a vegan diet will offer you.

You will be eating a diet that is rich in nutrients. In the typical Western diet, meat and animal products are usually the stars of the show. They do not have a place in the plant-based diet, so they will be eliminated. You will need to rely heavily on plant-based foods. These foods will give you a higher daily consumption of certain vital nutrients that you will get from your food. Eating a vegan diet will give you more antioxidants, fiber, and other beneficial plant compounds. The diet will be richer in folate, magnesium, potassium, and Vitamins A, C, and E. It will be important for you to base your meals on whole foods and not vegan alternative pre-packaged and fast food options because these are severely lacking in nutrients and will not provide the sufficient amounts of nutrition that you need.

A plant-based vegan diet can help you lose weight. Even when people consuming a plant-based diet eat until they are full, they can still lose weight because the calorie counts are lower for fruits, veggies,

349

and whole-grains than they are for meat servings. Consider the following table:

Calories in one three-ounce chicken breast: 204

Calories in one three-ounce hamburger patty: 213

Calories in three ounces of green beans: 26

Calories in three ounces of peaches: 33

Calories in three ounces of oatmeal: 70

When your diet is made of plant-based foods like fruits, vegetables, and whole grains , you can eat until you are full and still not be consuming that many calories. Because of the foods that are eaten, the vegan diet has a natural tendency to reduce your intake of calories. This will automatically give you weight loss without the need to focus on cutting or counting calories.

Following a vegan diet can help you to lower your risk of heart disease. The vegan diet can benefit the health of your heart by significantly reducing those common risk factors that lead to heart disease, such as obesity. The vegan diet can also help to reduce cholesterol levels, blood sugar levels, and your overall blood pressure. All three of these are factors that contribute to the development of heart disease. Plant-based foods are naturally low in saturated fats and cholesterol while providing the good fats your body needs to function.

Reducing pain and inflammation is a benefit of the vegan diet. Plant-based foods contain compounds that will decrease the symptoms of inflammation and the effects of osteoarthritis, which is an inflammatory disease. As the compounds help to relieve inflammation, the diet itself will help you to lose weight, which is an added bonus because obesity will add to inflammation and the effects of osteoarthritis. Four pounds of extra pressure is put on the joints in the lower body with just one pound of excess body weight.

Certain cancers can be prevented by consuming a vegan diet. Eating seven portions of fresh vegetables and fruits each day may help to lower your risk of developing certain cancers. Lowering your consumption of animal products may reduce the risk of developing colon, breast, and prostate cancer. And legumes can help to reduce the risk of colorectal cancer. Fruits, vegetables, and whole-grains provide the fiber your body needs to cleanse itself of waste products. Seven servings each day may seem like a lot of food, but a serving of fruit is one small to medium piece or one cup, and a serving of vegetables is one-half cup.

Plant-based foods may improve kidney function and lower blood sugar levels. People who regularly follow a plant-based diet, like a vegan diet, usually have higher insulin sensitivity, lower blood sugar levels, and a significantly lower risk of developing Type 2 Diabetes. Your body produces insulin to move the blood sugar derived from the foods you eat into your cells to be used as energy. In obese people, the cells have stopped responding to the insulin so the excess blood sugar is stored as fat in the body. Reducing the number of calories will result in lower blood sugar levels, which will result in the cells being more sensitive to the call of the insulin and allowing the blood sugar to enter, reducing or eliminating the need to store it as fat.

The key to successfully switching to a plant-based diet, like the vegan diet, is careful planning. If your diet is going to be healthy for you, then you will need to consume the right kinds of foods that will give you the types and amounts of nutrition that your body needs. It is easy to get certain nutrients when your diet includes meat and dairy, but when you cut these out, then you will need to source out different ways to get the proper level of nutrition for your overall health.

Vitamin D – This is found naturally in fatty fish, cheese, egg yolks, and beef liver. These foods are not part of a vegan diet so you might need to look to other sources for your daily requirement of Vitamin D. Eating soy products, drinking fortified orange juice, or spending just ten to fifteen minutes in the sun each day will provide you with the Vitamin D your body needs.

Essential fatty acids – Problems that are related to brain health, such as depression and cognitive impairment, are related to a lack of dietary essential fatty acids. If you remove fish from your diet, then you are removing a natural source of Omega-3, which is an essential fatty acid your brain needs for good function. But these fats can also be found in seeds and nuts like walnuts, chia seeds, and flaxseed; and in plant-based oils like canola oil, soybean oil, and flaxseed oil. You can also add more collards, spinach, and kale to your diet.

Protein – We usually look to animal products for our sources of protein, but they are not the only source available to you. On a plant-based diet, your protein will come from lentils, chickpeas, soybeans, and tofu.

Iron – Egg yolks and red meat are the best sources of dietary iron, and these foods are high in dietary cholesterol. Fruits, tofu, and black-eyed peas are good sources of dietary iron. Quinoa, pumpkin seeds, spinach, and legumes are also good sources.

Vitamin B-12 – You will feel weak and tired if your body lacks this vitamin. It can be challenging for vegans to get enough Vitamin B-12 from their diets because it is not found in plants. You might either need to take a supplement or load up on soy drinks, fortified rice, and fortified cereals.

So knowing that you want to eat a more plant-based diet like the vegan diet and actually beginning to eat that way are two different things. Many people personally struggle with the idea of giving up animal products as part of their daily diets. After all, the typical Western meal is centered on some sort of meat dish. In many other countries, the meat is a side dish to the vegetable. Whether you just want to change to a more plant-based diet or move into a full vegan mode, there are things you can do to ease into a more plant-based diet that will make it easier for you to go fully vegan if you so desire.

The star of your meal are vegetables. Too often people think about what they are giving up, as in 'I am giving up beef' and not thinking about what they will be allowed to eat. Most people would not pair steak with pinto beans, but both are good sources of iron. If you don't eat the steak, then the pinto beans can become the main dish of the meal, and the beans will keep you fuller longer for fewer calories than the steak will.

Choose to eat a variety of whole-grains. If you change the white bread and white pasta in your diet to whole-grains like quinoa and brown rice, you will be eating extra fiber that will help you to lose weight. Also, quinoa and brown rice will add B vitamins and iron to your diet, where the white bread and pasta will not, as these essential items are stripped out during the refining process.

Always make good whole food choices. Vegan margarine on garlic bread is not any better for your heart than eating regular butter, and vegan cookies will expand your waistline just like regular cookies will. Never assume those food products that are labeled 'vegan' are healthier than their animal-product counterparts. These foods often contain coconut oil and palm oil, both of which are full of saturated fats. It is better to stick to nutritious whole foods that are vegan, like guacamole and whole-grain chips, dried fruit and nuts, or hummus with celery or carrots.

Make sure you get your vitamins from your food when possible. One vitamin that is often overlooked is Vitamin D because the typical Western diet will provide you with Vitamin D from yogurt, milk, and fish. On a more plant-based diet, you will need to spend some time in the sun every day, about ten minutes, or drink fortified non-dairy drinks such as orange juice, almond milk, or soy milk. Vitamin B-12 is also often overlooked because, in the Western diet, you get your amounts from dairy foods, eggs, poultry, fish, and meat. On a plant-based diet, a supplement may be needed. Vitamin B-12 can also be found in fortified energy bars and cereals.

Don't overlook your iron intake. Again, this is another nutrient that is readily found in the Western diet of chicken and red meat. Iron is available in plant sources like leafy greens, legumes, and beans, but the iron from those sources is not as easily absorbed by the body as the iron that comes from animal sources. A good way to boost your body's absorption of iron from plant-based foods is to pair a food rich in Vitamin C, such as citrus food, with a plant food rich in iron. Tossing slices of mandarin oranges with a bowl of leafy greens is one delicious way to do this. Just remember to keep the calcium-rich foods on your menu away from this combination because calcium inhibits the absorption of dietary iron.

You will need Omega-3 fatty acids to promote good health. These are important for the health of your heart and brain and are found in great quantities in fatty fish. You will also be able to get them from foods like walnuts and flaxseed, and from soy products and canola oils. You might also need to consider a supplement.

Investigate the world of plant-based protein. Protein is readily available in animal sources like cheese and meat, but it brings with it high amounts of unhealthy saturated fats. There are numerous sources of protein from plant-based foods available for the vegan diet, like beans, chickpeas, edamame (soybeans), tofu, tempeh, and lentils. You can also get supplies of protein from pumpkin seeds, sunflower seeds, walnuts, and almonds. It is also an easy matter to get protein from whole-wheat pasta, oatmeal, nut butters, and quinoa.

Eat more whole-grains that will keep you full and fit. If you change out your refined grain foods like white bread and white pasta for more whole-grains , you will add more fiber, iron, and B vitamins to your daily diet.

Consume a variety of foods from all colors of the rainbow. Eating the

353

rainbow is one of the newest ways that people are following to ensure that they are eating a well-balanced diet. It means adding foods to your diet, vegetables, and fruits, in all of the available colors so that you are adding in a variety of vitamins and minerals to your diet. Vegetables and fruits are full of water and fiber, and these two compounds will help you to feel fuller for longer periods and will also help rid your body of toxins through waste removal. Also, the colors that make the foods beautiful to look at are made naturally by compounds that are good for you, such as:

Red foods contain phytochemicals that fight cancer and heart disease and improve the quality of your skin

Yellow foods provide potassium, phosphorus, riboflavin, magnesium, folate, and fiber as well as Vitamins A, B-6, and C

Blue foods provide resveratrol and anthocyanins, both of which are powerful antioxidants

Orange foods support the health of your eyes as well as reducing blood pressure and cholesterol. They also help your joints and bones to be strong and healthy

Green foods help fight heart disease and diabetes by helping to fight obesity. They are full of fiber and antioxidants.

Adopting a more plant-based diet or even fully converting to a vegan diet is not difficult. You will need to make the personal choice of just how far you want to go with this. Will it be just adopting more of a plant-based diet or a full-on vegan lifestyle? The choice is yours. Just remember that when you are trying new foods, do so with an open mind but a bit of caution. Some of these you may never have eaten and would like to try, and you should. But for some things, it may be better to source out a vegan restaurant or friend and try a dish that they have made before you take the item home and prepare it yourself. There is no need to take home a whole zucchini or eggplants if you do not like the taste because you will never eat it. Don't be afraid to experiment, but do begin with those vegetables, fruits, whole-grains , seeds, and nuts that you already know you like and build meals around those items. Then begin adding in new food items. You will be surprised at the endless variety now available in your food choices.

Chapter 3. Shopping List

While this shopping list does not include everything for original recipes, this shopping list will help you to keep your pantry stocked with the basics.

Vegetables: Non-Starchy

These vegetables are excellent for your body because they are packed with nutrients and will help to get you the vitamins you need. This includes your leafy greens such as kale, spinach, butter lettuce, etc. You can also use eggplant, zucchini, tomatoes, and brocco li as your non-starchy basics.

Vegetables: Starchy

This includes all types of potatoes, whole corn, legumes of all kinds. This consists of all beans and lentils, root vegetables, and even quinoa. These are filling parts of your meals, which are packed with fiber.

Whole Grains

You need some sort of grain in your plant-based diet. Whole grains are always recommended, including whole wheat, brown rice, and oats. Over processed oats will not give you the nutrients you need.

Fruits

Any whole fruits are available on the plant-based diet. However, it is recommended that you avoid dried fruits and juiced fruits because of the sheer amount of sugar it'll pack into your diet.

Beverages

You can have almost any drinks on your plant-based diet. However, it's recommended that you drink unsweetened plant-based kinds of milk, decaffeinated tea, decaffeinated coffee, and green tea.

Spices

As far as spices are concerned, any spices are allowed. This includes dried spices and fresh herbs.

Omega 3 Sources

With an all plant-based diet, you'll need omega three sources. These include ground flax seed as well as chia seeds.

Nuts

Any nuts are recommended on the plant-based diet, but it's useful to have peanuts and walnuts on hand. You can also keep cashews and almonds since they are used regularly in different dishes.

Consume Sparingly

These are plant-based foods, but they aren't as healthy for you as other plants. So, while you can have them, it's recommended that you use these sparingly. This includes added sweeteners. Examples of added sweeteners are fruit juice concentrate, natural sugars, honey, and maple syrup. Pumpkin seeds, sesame seeds, sunflower seeds, and dried fruits should also be consumed on a limited basis. Coconuts and avocados as well. You should also limit your refined wheat protein or soy protein

Chapter 4.
Breakfast Recipes

Fruit and Nut Oatmeal

 Preparation:
5 Minutes

 Cooking:
10 Minutes

 Serves:
2

Ingredients

- ¾ cup rolled oats
- ¼ cup berries, fresh
- ½ ripe banana, sliced
- 2 tablespoons nuts, chopped
- ½ teaspoon cinnamon
- ¼ teaspoon salt
- 2 tablespoons Maple syrup

Directions

1. Put the oats in a small saucepan and add 1½ cups of water. Stir and over high heat, boil. Reduce to low heat and cook for about 5 minutes, or until the water has been absorbed.
2. Stir in the cinnamon and add the pinch of salt. Serve in 2 bowls and top each with the chopped fruit and nuts. You can also add a little bit of maple syrup if you want.

Nutritions: *Calories 257, Total Fat 6.6g, Saturated Fat 1g, Cholesterol 0mg, Sodium 352mg, Total Carbohydrate 45.7g, Dietary Fiber 5.6g, Total Sugars 17.5g, Protein 6g, Vitamin D 0mcg, Calcium 45mg, Iron 2mg, Potassium 334mg*

Amazing Almond & Banana Granola

Preparation:
5 Minutes

Cooking:
70 Minutes

Serves:
8

Ingredients

- 2 peeled and chopped ripe bananas
- 4 cups of rolled oats
- 1 teaspoon of salt
- 2 cups of freshly chopped and pitted dates
- 1 cup of slivered and toasted almonds
- 1 teaspoon of almond extract

Directions

1. Heat the oven to 275°F.
2. With parchment paper, line two 13 x 18-inch baking sheets.
3. In an average saucepan, add water, 1 cup and the dates, and boil. On medium heat, cook them for about 10 minutes. The dates will be soft and pulpy. Keep on adding water to the saucepan so that the dates do not stick to the pot.
4. After removing the dates from the high temperature, allow them to cool before you blend them with salt, bananas, almond extract.
5. You will have a creamy and smooth puree.
6. To the oats, add this mixture, and give it a thorough mix.
7. Divide the mixture into equal halves and spread over the baking sheets.
8. Bake for about 30-40 minutes, and stir every 10 minutes or so.
9. You will know that the granola is ready when it becomes crunchy.
10. After removing the baking sheets from the cooker, allow them to cool. Then, add the almonds.
11. You can store your granola in a container and enjoy it whenever you are hungry.

Nutritions: *Calories 603, Total Fat 14.2g, Saturated Fat 1.5g, Cholesterol 0mg, Sodium 471mg, Total Carbohydrate 112.7g, Dietary Fiber 15.9g, Total Sugars 52.4g, Protein 14.9g, Calcium 116mg, Iron 4mg, Potassium 1014mg*

Perfect Polenta with a Dose of Cranberries & Pears

Preparation:
5 Minutes

Cooking:
10 Minutes

Serves:
4

Ingredients

- 2 pears freshly cored, peeled, and diced
- 1 cup warm basic polenta
- ¼ cup of brown rice syrup
- 1 teaspoon of ground cinnamon
- 1 cup of dried or fresh cranberries

Directions

1. Warm the polenta in a medium-sized saucepan. Then, add the cranberries, pears, and cinnamon powder.
2. Cook everything, stirring occasionally. You will know that the dish is ready when the pears are soft.
3. The entire dish will be done within 10 minutes.
4. Divide the polenta equally among 4 bowls. Add some pear compote as the last finishing touch.
5. Now you can dig into this hassle-free breakfast bowl full of goodness.

Nutritions: *Calories 178, Total Fat 0.3g, Saturated Fat 0g, Cholesterol 0mg, Sodium 17mg, Total Carbohydrate 44.4g, Dietary Fiber 4.9g, Total Sugars 23.8g, Protein 1.9g, Calcium 20mg, Iron 0mg, Potassium 170mg*

Tempeh Bacon Smoked to Perfection

Preparation:
5 Minutes

Cooking:
10 Minutes

Serves:
4

Ingredients

- 3 tablespoons of maple syrup
- 8 ounce package of tempeh
- ¼ cup of soy sauce
- 2 teaspoons of liquid smoke

Directions

1. In a steamer basket, steam the block of tempeh.
2. Mix the tamari, maple syrup, and liquid smoke in a medium-sized bowl.
3. Once the tempeh cools down, slice into stripes and add to the prepared marinade. Remember: the longer the tempeh marinates, the better the flavor will be. If possible, refrigerate overnight. If not, marinate for at least half an hour.
4. In a sauté pan, cook the tempeh on medium-high heat with a bit of the marinade.
5. Once the strips get crispy on one side, turn them over so that both sides are evenly cooked.
6. You can add some more marinade to cook the tempeh, but they should be properly caramelized. It will take about 5 minutes for each side to cook.
7. Enjoy the crispy caramelized tempeh with your favorite dip.

Nutritions: *Calories 157, Total Fat 6.2g, Saturated Fat 1.3g, Cholesterol 0mg, Sodium 905mg, Total Carbohydrate 16.6g, Dietary Fiber 0.1g, Total Sugars 9.2g, Protein 11.5g, Calcium 76mg, Iron 2mg, Potassium 299mg*

Quiche with Cauliflower & Chickpea

 Preparation:
10 Minutes

 Cooking:
30 Minutes

 Serves:
3

Ingredients

- ½ teaspoon of salt
- 1 cup of grated cauliflower
- 1 cup of chickpea flour
- ½ teaspoon of baking powder
- ½ zucchini, thinly sliced into half moons
- 1 tablespoon of flax meal
- 1 cup of water
- 4 tbsp fresh rosemary
- ½ teaspoon of Italian seasoning
- ½ freshly sliced red onion

Directions

1. In a bowl, combine all the dry ingredients.
2. Chop the onion and zucchini.
3. Grate the cauliflower so that it has a rice-like consistency, and add it to the dry ingredients. Now, add the water and mix well.
4. Add the zucchini, onion, and rosemary last. You will have a clumpy and thick mixture, but you should be able to spoon it into a tin.
5. You can use either a silicone or a metal cake tin with a removable bottom. Now put the mixture in the tin and press it down gently.
6. The top should be left messy to resemble a rough texture.
7. Bake at 350o F for about half an hour. You will know your quiche is ready when the top is golden.
8. You can serve the quiche warm or cold, as per your preference.

Nutritions: *Calories 280, Total Fat 5.3g, Saturated Fat 0.5g, Cholesterol 1mg, Sodium 422mg, Total Carbohydrate 46.6g, Dietary Fiber 14.2g, Total Sugars 9.4g, Protein 14.7g, Calcium 136mg, Iron 5mg, Potassium 916mg*

Tasty Oatmeal and Carrot Cake

 Preparation:
5 Minutes

 Cooking:
10 Minutes

 Serves:
2

Ingredients

- 1 cup of water
- ½ teaspoon of cinnamon
- 1 cup of rolled oats
- Salt
- ¼ cup of raisins
- ½ cup of shredded carrots
- 1 cup of soy milk
- ¼ teaspoon of allspice
- ½ teaspoon of vanilla extract
- Toppings:
- ¼ cup of chopped walnuts
- 2 tablespoons of maple syrup
- 2 tablespoons of shredded coconut

Directions

1. Put a small pot on low heat and bring the non-dairy milk, oats, and water to a simmer.
2. Now, add the carrots, vanilla extract, raisins, salt, cinnamon and allspice. You need to simmer all of the ingredients, but do not forget to stir them. You will know that they are ready when the liquid is fully absorbed into all of the ingredients (in about 7-10 minutes).
3. Transfer the thickened dish to bowls. You can drizzle some maple syrup on top or top them with coconut or walnuts.
4. This nutritious bowl will allow you to kickstart your day.

Nutritions: *Calories 442, Total Fat 15.5g, Saturated Fat 2.7g, Cholesterol 0mg, Sodium 384mg, Total Carbohydrate 66.3g, Dietary Fiber 7.9g, Total Sugars 29g, Protein 13.6g, Vitamin D 1mcg, Calcium 224mg, Iron 5mg, Potassium 520mg*

Almond Butter Banana Overnight Oats

 Preparation:
5 Minutes

 Cooking:
10 Minutes

 Serves:
2

Directions

1. Take a large bowl and add the oats, milk, chia seeds, vanilla, cinnamon and honey.
2. Stir to combine then divide half of the mixture between two bowls.
3. Top with the banana and peanut butter then add the remaining mixture.
4. Cover then pop into the fridge overnight.
5. Serve and enjoy.

Ingredients

- ½ cup rolled oats
- 1 cup almond milk
- ½ oz chia seeds
- ¼ teaspoon vanilla extract
- ½ teaspoon ground cinnamon
- 1 tablespoon honey
- 1 banana, sliced
- ½ oz almond butter

Nutritions: *Calories 789, Total Fat 60.1g, Saturated Fat 28.1g, Cholesterol 0mg, Sodium 121mg, Total Carbohydrate 49.4g, Dietary Fiber 14.9g, Total Sugars 22.1g, Protein 20g, Vitamin D 0mcg, Calcium 234mg, Iron 4mg, Potassium 638mg*

Vegan Mango Almond Milkshake

Preparation:
4 Minutes

Cooking:
5 Minutes

Serves:
1

Directions

1. Grab your blender, add the ingredients and whizz until smooth.
2. Serve and enjoy.

Ingredients

- 1 ripe mango, pulp
- ¾ cup almond milk, unsweetened
- ½ cup Ice

Nutritions: *Calories 232, Total Fat 3.9g, Saturated Fat 0.5g, Cholesterol 0mg, Sodium 142mg, Total Carbohydrate 51.8g, Dietary Fiber 6.1g, Total Sugars 45.9g, Protein 3.5g, Vitamin D 1mcg, Calcium 266mg, Iron 1mg, Potassium 708mg*

Peach & Chia Seed Breakfast Parfait

Preparation:
5 Minutes

Cooking:
10 Minutes

Serves:
4

Directions

1. Find a small bowl and add the chia seeds, maple syrup and coconut milk.
2. Stir well then cover and pop into the fridge for at least one hour.
3. Find another bowl, add the peaches and sprinkle with the cinnamon. Pop to one side.
4. When it's time to serve, take two glasses and pour the chia mixture between the two.
5. Sprinkle the granola over the top, keeping a tiny amount to one side to use to decorate later.
6. Top with the peaches and top with the reserve granola and serve.

Ingredients

- ½ oz chia seeds
- 1 tablespoon pure maple syrup
- 1 cup coconut milk
- 1 teaspoon ground cinnamon
- 3 medium peaches, diced small
- 2/3 cup granola

Nutritions: *Calories 261, Total Fat 25.5g, Saturated Fat 14.5g, Cholesterol 0mg, Sodium 20mg, Total Carbohydrate 40.8g, Dietary Fiber 8.2g, Total Sugars 23.6g, Protein 9.1g, Vitamin D 0mcg, Calcium 73mg, Iron 3mg, Potassium 618mg*

Avocado Toast with White Beans

Preparation:
4 Minutes

Cooking:
6 Minutes

Serves:
4

Ingredients

- ½ cup canned white beans, drained and rinsed
- 2 teaspoons tahini paste
- 2 teaspoons lemon juice
- ½ teaspoon salt
- ½ avocado, peeled and pit removed
- 4 slices whole grain bread, toasted
- ½ cup grape tomatoes, cut in half

Directions

1. Grab a small bowl and add the beans, tahini, ½ the lemon juice and ½ the salt. Mash with a fork.
2. Take another bowl and add the avocado and the remaining lemon juice and salt. Mash together.
3. Place your toast onto a flat surface and add the mashed beans, spreading well.
4. Top with the avocado and the sliced tomatoes then serve and enjoy.

Nutritions: *Calories 245, Total Fat 8g, Saturated Fat 1.3g, Cholesterol 0mg, Sodium 431mg, Total Carbohydrate 33.8g, Dietary Fiber 10g, Total Sugars 3.3g, Protein 11g, Vitamin D 0mcg, Calcium 77mg, Iron 4mg, Potassium 642mg*

Homemade Granola

 Preparation:
5 Minutes

 Cooking:
1 h 15 minutes

 Serves:
7

Directions

1. Preheat oven to 250°F.
2. Mix all ingredients in a large bowl.
3. Spread granola evenly on two rimmed sheet pans.
4. Bake at 250°F for 1 hour 15 minutes, stirring every 20-25 min.
5. Let cool in pans, and serve.

Ingredients

- ▶ 5 cups rolled oats
- ▶ 1 cup almonds, slivered
- ▶ ¾ cup coconut, shredded
- ▶ ¾ tsp salt
- ▶ ¼ cup coconut oil
- ▶ ½ cup maple syrup

Nutritions: *Calories 456, Total Fat 21.3g, Saturated Fat 10.5g, Cholesterol 0mg, Sodium 255mg, Total Carbohydrate 58.9g, Dietary Fiber 8.4g, Total Sugars 15.1g, Protein 10.8g, Vitamin D 0mcg, Calcium 82mg, Iron 4mg, Potassium 387mg*

Country Breakfast Cereal

Preparation:
5 Minutes

Cooking:
40 Minutes

Serves:
6

Directions

1. Combine rice, butter, raisins, and cinnamon in a saucepan. Add 2 ¼ cups water. Bring to boil.
2. Simmer covered for 40 minutes until rice is tender.
3. Fluff with fork. Add honey and nuts to taste.

Ingredients

- 1 cup brown rice, uncooked
- ½ cup raisins, seedless
- 1 tsp cinnamon, ground
- ¼ Tbsp butter
- 2 ¼ cups water
- 1 tablespoon Honey, to taste
- ½ cup Nuts, toasted

Nutritions: *Calories 234, Total Fat 7.3g, Saturated Fat 1.3g, Cholesterol 1mg, Sodium 85mg, Total Carbohydrate 39.8g, Dietary Fiber 2.8g, Total Sugars 10.6g, Protein 4.8g, Vitamin D 0mcg, Calcium 31mg, Iron 1mg, Potassium 248mg*

Oatmeal Fruit Shake

Preparation:
10 Minutes

Cooking:
0 Minutes

Serves:
2

Directions

1. Add all ingredients to blender.
2. Blend from low to high for several minutes until smooth.

Ingredients

- 1 cup oatmeal, already prepared, cooled
- 1 apple, cored, roughly chopped
- 1 banana, halved
- 1 cup baby spinach
- 2 cups coconut water
- 2 cups ice, cubed
- ½ tsp ground cinnamon
- 1 tsp pure vanilla extract

Nutritions: *Calories 322, Total Fat 3.6g, Saturated Fat 1g, Cholesterol 0mg, Sodium 275mg, Total Carbohydrate 66.8g, Dietary Fiber 11.6g, Total Sugars 25.8g, Protein 8.5g, Vitamin D 0mcg, Calcium 110mg, Iron 4mg, Potassium 1170mg*

Amaranth Banana Breakfast Porridge

Preparation:
10 Minutes

Cooking:
25 Minutes

Serves:
8

Directions

1. Combine the amaranth, water, and cinnamon sticks, and banana in a pot. Cover and let simmer around 25 minutes.
2. Remove from heat and discard the cinnamon. Places into bowls, and top with pecans.

Ingredients

- 2 cup amaranth
- 2 cinnamon sticks
- 4 bananas, diced
- 10 pieces pecans
- 4 cups water

Nutritions: *Calories 390, Total Fat 8g, Saturated Fat 1.6g, Cholesterol 0mg, Sodium 114mg, Total Carbohydrate 72g, Dietary Fiber 6.9g, Total Sugars 15.5g, Protein 10.7g, Vitamin D 0mcg, Calcium 86mg, Iron 5mg, Potassium 391mg*

Breakfast Quinoa with Figs and Honey

Preparation:
5 Minutes

Cooking:
15 Minutes

Serves:
4

Directions

1. Rinse quinoa under cool water.
2. Combine it with water, cinnamon, and cloves. Bring to boil.
3. Simmer covered for 10-15 minutes.
4. Add dried figs, nuts, milk. Garnish with honey. Serve.

Ingredients

- 2 cups water
- 1 cup white quinoa
- 1 cup dried figs, sliced
- 1 cup walnuts, chopped
- 1 cup almond milk
- ½ tsp cinnamon, ground
- ¼ tsp cloves, ground
- 1 tablespoon Honey, to taste

Nutritions: *Calories 512, Total Fat 33.9g, Saturated Fat 13.8g, Cholesterol 0mg, Sodium 19mg, Total Carbohydrate 50.3g, Dietary Fiber 9.3g, Total Sugars 31.3g, Protein 12.1g, Vitamin D 0mcg, Calcium 122mg, Iron 3mg, Potassium 666mg*

Maple Walnut Teff Porridge

Preparation:
5 Minutes

Cooking:
20 Minutes

Serves:
2

Directions

1. Combine the water and coconut oil in a medium pot. Bring to boil, then stir in the teff.
2. Add the cardamom, and simmer uncovered for 15-20 minutes.
3. Mix in the maple syrup and walnuts. Serve.

Ingredients

- 1 ½ cups water
- 1 cup teff, whole grain
- ½ cup coconut milk
- ½ tsp cardamom, ground
- ¼ cup walnuts, chopped
- 1 tsp sea salt
- 1 Tbsp maple syrup

Nutritions: *Calories 352, Total Fat 24.1g, Saturated Fat 13.2g, Cholesterol 0mg, Sodium 954mg, Total Carbohydrate 30.4g, Dietary Fiber 4.5g, Total Sugars 8.1g, Protein 8.7g, Vitamin D 0mcg, Calcium 83mg, Iron 3mg, Potassium 267mg*

PB & J Overnight Oatmeal

Preparation:
25 Minutes

Cooking:
8 h 20 minutes

Serves:
4

Ingredients

- ► 1½ cups blueberries, frozen
- ► 1 oz chia seeds, divided
- ► 2 cups rolled oats
- ► 3 cups almond milk
- ► 4 pitted dates
- ► 2 Tbsp peanut butter

Directions

1. Microwave blueberries in 1 Tbsp water for 2-3 minutes.
2. Stir in 2 Tbsp chia seed to the blueberries. Refrigerate for 20 minutes.
3. Put ½ cup oats and ½ Tbsp chia seeds into 4 jars.
4. Blend milk, dates, and peanut butter. Pour it into the jars.
5. Add blueberry chia jam to the jars. Refrigerate for 6-8 hours.

Nutritions: *Calories 788, Total Fat 52.5g, Saturated Fat 39.6g, Cholesterol 0mg, Sodium 69mg, Total Carbohydrate 77.3g, Dietary Fiber 16.5g, Total Sugars 32.2g, Protein 14.4g, Vitamin D 0mcg, Calcium 100mg, Iron 9mg, Potassium 910mg*

Southwest Tofu Scramble

Preparation:
10 Minutes

Cooking:
15 Minutes

Serves:
4

Directions

1. Mix first four ingredients with a fork.
2. In a heavy skillet, combine the zucchini, pepper, shallot, and olive oil. Sauté for 5 minutes.
3. Stir in tofu and cook for another 10 minutes. Serve.

Ingredients

- 8 oz package firm tofu, crumbled
- 1-2 tsp ground cumin
- ½ cup nutritional yeast
- 2 tsp tamari
- 2 tsp extra-virgin olive oil
- 1 zucchini, diced
- 1 bell pepper, diced
- 1 onion, diced

Nutritions: *Calories 263, Total Fat 10.8g, Saturated Fat 1.5g, Cholesterol 0mg, Sodium 247mg, Total Carbohydrate 20g, Dietary Fiber 8.7g, Total Sugars 3.6g, Protein 26.8g, Vitamin D 0mcg, Calcium 337mg, Iron 8mg, Potassium 720mg*

Amaranth Polenta with Wild Mushrooms

Preparation:
10 Minutes

Cooking:
30 Minutes

Serves:
3

Ingredients

- ½ ounce dried porcini
- 1 Tbsp olive oil
- ¼ cup shallots, chopped
- 1 cup amaranth
- ¼ tsp salt
- 1 tsp fresh thyme, chopped
- ¼ tsp Ground pepper, to taste

Directions

1. Combine 1 ¾ cups boiling water and mushrooms. Leave for 10 minutes to soften.
2. In a saucepan, cook shallots in olive oil for 1 minutes. Add amaranth, mushrooms, and soaking liquid. Simmer for 15 minutes.
3. Add pepper, thyme, and salt. Simmer for another 15 minutes.
4. Serve in small bowls.

Nutritions: *Calories 306, Total Fat 9.1g, Saturated Fat 1.8g, Cholesterol 0mg, Sodium 209mg, Total Carbohydrate 46.9g, Dietary Fiber 7.3g, Total Sugars 1.4g, Protein 11.1g, Vitamin D 0mcg, Calcium 112mg, Iron 6mg, Potassium 287mg*

Berry Breakfast Bars

Preparation:
8 Minutes

Cooking:
27 Minutes

Serves:
9

Ingredients

- 1 ½ cup Rolled oats
- ½ cup Applesauce
- 1 tablespoon Flaxseed meal
- 2 cups Almond flour
- ¼ Salt
- ¼ cup Blackstrap molasses
- ½ teaspoon Baking powder
- 1 teaspoon Vanilla extract
- ¼ cup Almond butter
- 1 teaspoon Apple cider vinegar
- ½ cup Oat milk
- ¼ cup Maple syrup
- 1 tablespoon Agar agar
- 3 cups Mixed frozen berries
- 1 teaspoon Lemon juice

Directions

1. You'll need an oven-safe dish, preferably a baking dish. Square is better to get nine full-portioned squares from it, but any shape will do. Your oven should be heated to 350°F and your baking dish should be lined with baking paper.

2. Mix together the oat milk, applesauce, molasses, vanilla, and almond butter. Add the almond flour and flaxseed meal and mix. If it looks too thick at this point, add a little water (maybe a tablespoon or two) to ensure it is runny enough to accept the oats. Stir in the oats and baking powder then add the salt and mix really well to get a nice thick batter.

3. Spoon all but about one cup of mixture into the bottom of your dish and press it down with your fingers to get an even base and bake for 15 minutes.

4. While this is in the oven, get a saucepan and over medium-high heat, cook down the frozen berries and agar-agar with half a cup of cold water. Keep an eye on it and once it comes to a boil, you should turn down the heat to medium-low and let it simmer for around five minutes while stirring as it thickens. Then take it off the heat and add the lemon juice and maple syrup, stir again and then leave to thicken.

5. Pour this over the oat base and with your fingers, roughly crumble the cup of oat mixture you put aside over the top of the berry filling.

6. Put the baking dish back in the oven for another 12 minutes then take out. The oat mixture on top should be beautifully browned. Allow it to cool before you put it in the fridge to set for an hour or so.

7. Cut into squares or bars or whatever makes you happy. Then wrap individually in baking paper or cling film and keep in the fridge or freezer!

Nutritions: *Calories 188, Total Fat 5g, Saturated Fat 0.4g, Cholesterol 0mg, Sodium 19mg, Total Carbohydrate 33.1g, Dietary Fiber 5g, Total Sugars 16.8g, Protein 3.9g, Vitamin D 6mcg, Calcium 86mg, Iron 2mg, Potassium 252mg*

Tasty Oatmeal Muffins

Preparation:
10 Minutes

Cooking:
20 Minutes

Serves:
12

Ingredients

- ½ cup of hot water
- ½ cup of raisins
- ¼ cup of ground flaxseed
- 2 cups of rolled oats
- ¼ teaspoon of sea salt
- ½ cup of walnuts
- ¼ teaspoon of baking soda
- 1 banana
- 2 tablespoons of cinnamon
- ¼ cup of maple syrup

Directions

1. Whisk the flaxseed with water and allow the mixture to sit for about 5 minutes.
2. In a food processor, blend all the ingredients along with the flaxseed mix. Blend everything for 30 seconds, but do not create a smooth substance. To create rough-textured cookies, you need to have a semi-coarse batter.
3. Put the batter in cupcake liners and place them in a muffin tin. As this is an oil-free recipe, you will need cupcake liners. Bake everything for about 20 minutes at 350 degrees.
4. Enjoy the freshly-made cookies with a glass of warm milk.

Nutritions: *Calories 143, Total Fat 4.8g, Saturated Fat 0.4g, Cholesterol 0mg, Sodium 70mg, Total Carbohydrate 22.8g, Dietary Fiber 3.4g, Total Sugars 8.9g, Protein 3.8g, Vitamin D 0mcg, Calcium 30mg, Iron 2mg, Potassium 194mg*

Omelet with Chickpea Flour

Preparation:
10 Minutes

Cooking:
20 Minutes

Serves:
1

Ingredients

- ½ teaspoon, onion powder
- ¼ teaspoon, black pepper
- 1 cup, chickpea flour
- ½ teaspoon, garlic powder
- ½ teaspoon, baking soda
- 1/3 cup, nutritional yeast
- 3 finely chopped green onions
- 4 ounces, sautéed mushrooms

Directions

1. In a small bowl, mix the onion powder, white pepper, chickpea flour, garlic powder, black and white pepper, baking soda, and nutritional yeast.
2. Add 1 cup of water and create a smooth batter.
3. On medium heat, put a frying pan and add the batter just like the way you would cook pancakes.
4. On the batter, sprinkle some green onion and mushrooms. Flip the omelet and cook evenly on both sides.
5. Once both sides are cooked, serve the omelet with spinach, tomatoes, hot sauce, and salsa.
6. Enjoy a guilt-free meal.

Nutritions: *Calories 1006, Total Fat 15.4g, Saturated Fat 1.7g, Cholesterol 0mg, Sodium 722mg, Total Carbohydrate 168.1g, Dietary Fiber 52g, Total Sugars 28g, Protein 66.1g, Vitamin D 0mcg, Calcium 293mg, Iron 24mg, Potassium 3315mg*

Chapter 5.
Lunch Recipes

Vegan Mushroom Pho

Preparation:
10 Minutes

Cooking:
30 Minutes

Serves:
3

Ingredients

- 14-oz. block firm tofu, drained
- 6 cups vegetable broth
- 3 green onions, thinly sliced
- 1 tsp. minced ginger
- 1 tbsp. olive oil
- 3 cups mushrooms, sliced
- 2 tbsp. hoisin sauce
- 1 tbsp. sesame oil
- 2 cups gluten-free rice noodles
- 1 cup raw bean sprouts
- 1 cup matchstick carrots
- 1 cup bok choy, chopped
- 1 cup cabbage, chopped
- ¼ tsp Salt
- ¼ tsp pepper

Directions

1. Cut the tofu into ¼-inch cubes and set it aside.
2. Take a deep saucepan and heat the vegetable broth, green onions, and ginger over medium high heat.
3. Boil for 1 minute before reducing the heat to low; then cover the saucepan with a lid and let it simmer for 20 minutes.
4. Take another frying pan and heat the olive oil in it over medium-high heat.
5. Add the sliced mushrooms to the frying pan and cook until they are tender, for about 5 minutes.
6. Add the tofu, hoisin sauce, and sesame oil to the mushrooms.
7. Heat until the sauce thickens (around 5 minutes), and remove the frying pan from the heat.
8. Prepare the gluten-free rice noodles according to the package instructions.
9. Top the rice noodles with a scoop of the tofu mushroom mixture, a generous amount of broth, and the bean sprouts.
10. Add the carrots, and optional cabbage and/or bok choy (if desired), right before serving.
11. Top with salt and pepper to taste and enjoy, or, store ingredients separately!

Nutritions: *Calories 610, Total Fat 18.9g, Saturated Fat 3.5g, Cholesterol 0mg, Sodium 2098mg, Total Carbohydrate 83g, Dietary Fiber 5.4g, Total Sugars 9.4g, Protein 29.6g, Vitamin D 252mcg, Calcium 366mg, Iron 7mg, Potassium 1132mg*

Ruby Red Root Beet Burger

Preparation:
20 Minutes

Cooking:
21 Minutes

Serves:
6

Ingredients

- 1 cup dry chickpeas
- ½ cup dry quinoa
- 2 large beets
- 2 tbsp. olive oil
- 2 tbsp. garlic powder
- 1 tbsp. balsamic vinegar
- ¼ tsp Salt
- 2 tsp. onion powder
- 1 tsp. fresh parsley, chopped
- ¼ tsp pepper
- 2 cups spinach, fresh or frozen, washed and dried
- 6 buns or wraps of choice

Directions

1. Preheat the oven to 400°F.
2. Peel and dice the beets into ¼-inch or smaller cubes, put them in a bowl, and coat the cubes with 1 tablespoon of olive oil and the onion powder.
3. Spread the beet cubes out across a baking pan and put the pan in the oven.
4. Roast the beets until they have softened, approximately 10-15 minutes. Take them out and set aside so the beets can cool down.
5. After the beets have cooled down, transfer them into a food processor and add the cooked chickpeas and quinoa, vinegar, garlic, parsley, and a pinch of pepper and salt.
6. Pulse the ingredients until everything is crumbly, around 30 seconds.
7. Use your palms to form the mixture into 6 equal-sized patties and place them in a small pan.
8. Put them in a freezer, up to 1 hour, until the patties feel firm to the touch.
9. Heat up the remaining 1 tablespoon of olive oil in a skillet over medium-high heat and add the patties.
10. Cook them until they're browned on each side, about 4-6 minutes per side.
11. Store or serve the burgers with a handful of spinach, and if desired, on the bottom of the optional bun.
12. Top the burger with your sauce of choice.

Nutritions: *Calories 353, Total Fat 9.2g, Saturated Fat 1.5g, Cholesterol 0mg, Sodium 351mg, Total Carbohydrate 57.8g, Dietary Fiber 9g, Total Sugars 9.2g, Protein 13.9g, Vitamin D 0mcg, Calcium 103mg*

382

Creamy Squash Pizza

Preparation:
25 Minutes

Cooking:
21 Minutes

Serves:
4

Ingredients

- 3 cups butternut squash, fresh or frozen, cubed
- 2 tbsp. minced garlic
- 1 tbsp. olive oil
- 1 tsp. red pepper flakes
- 1 tsp. cumin
- 1 tsp. paprika
- 1 tsp. oregano

Crust:
- 2 cups dry French green lentils
- 2 cups water
- 2 tbsp. minced garlic
- 1 tbsp. Italian seasoning
- 1 tsp. onion powder

Toppings:
- 1 tbsp. olive oil
- 1 medium green bell pepper, pitted, diced
- 1 cup chopped broccoli
- 1 small purple onion, diced

Directions

1. Preheat the oven to 350°F.
2. Prepare the French green lentils according to the method.
3. Add all the sauce ingredients to a food processor or blender, and blend on low until everything has mixed and the sauce looks creamy. Set the sauce aside in a small bowl.
4. Clean the food processor or blender; then add all the ingredients for the crust and pulse on high speed until a dough-like batter has formed.
5. Heat a large deep-dish pan over medium-low heat and lightly grease it with 1 tablespoon of olive oil.
6. Press the crust dough into the skillet until it resembles a round pizza crust and cook until the crust is golden brown—about 5-6 minutes on each side.
7. Put the crust on a baking tray covered with parchment paper.
8. Coat the topside of the crust with the sauce using a spoon, and evenly distribute the toppings across the pizza.
9. Bake the pizza in the oven until the vegetables are tender and browned, for about 15 minutes.
10. Slice into 4 equal pieces and serve, or store.

Nutritions: *Calories 258, Total Fat 9.2g, Saturated Fat 1.2g, Cholesterol 2mg, Sodium 21mg, Total Carbohydrate 38.3g, Dietary Fiber 9.7g, Total Sugars 6.2g, Protein 9g, Vitamin D 0mcg, Calcium 111mg, Iron 4mg, Potassium 838mg*

Lasagna Fungo

Preparation:
20 Minutes

Cooking:
40 Minutes

Serves:
8

Ingredients

- 10 lasagna sheets
- 2 cups matchstick carrots
- 1 cup mushrooms, sliced
- 2 cups raw kale
- 1 14-oz. package extra firm tofu, drained
- 1 cup hummus
- ½ cup nutritional yeast
- 2 tbsp. Italian seasoning
- 1 tbsp. garlic powder
- 1 tbsp. olive oil
- 4 cups marinara sauce
- 1 tsp. salt

Directions

1. Preheat the oven to 400°F.
2. Cook the lasagna noodles or sheets according to method.
3. Take a large frying pan, put it over medium heat, and add the olive oil.
4. Throw in the carrots, mushrooms, and half a teaspoon of salt; cook for 5 minutes.
5. Add the kale, sauté for another 3 minutes, and remove the pan from the heat.
6. Take a large bowl, crumble in the tofu, and set the bowl aside for now.
7. Take another bowl and add the hummus, nutritional yeast, Italian seasoning, garlic, and ½ teaspoon salt; mix everything together.
8. Coat the bottom of an 8x8 baking dish with 1 cup of the marinara sauce.
9. Cover the sauce with a couple of the noodles or sheets, and top these with the tofu crumbles.
10. Add a layer of the vegetables on top of the tofu.
11. Continue to build up the lasagna by stacking layers of marinara sauce, noodles or sheets, tofu, and vegetables, and top it off with a cup of marinara sauce.
12. Cover the lasagna with aluminum foil, and bake in the oven for 20-25 minutes.
13. Remove the foil and put back in the oven for an additional 5 minutes.
14. Allow the lasagna to sit for 10 minutes before serving, or store for another day!

Nutritions: Calories 491, Total Fat 13.1g, Saturated Fat 2.2g, Cholesterol 30mg, Sodium 959mg, Total Carbohydrate 73.5g, Dietary Fiber 9g, Total Sugars 13.3g, Protein 23.3g, Vitamin D 32mcg, Calcium 176mg, Iron 5mg, Potassium 903mg

Sweet and Sour Tofu

Preparation:
40 Minutes

Cooking:
21 Minutes

Serves:
4

Ingredients

- 14-oz. package extra firm tofu, drained
- 2 tbsp. olive oil
- 1 large red bell pepper, pitted, chopped
- 1 medium white onion, diced
- 2 tbsp. minced garlic
- ½-inch minced ginger
- 1 cup pineapple chunks
- 1 tbsp. tomato paste
- 2 tbsp. rice vinegar
- 2 tbsp. low sodium soy sauce
- 1 tsp. cornstarch
- 1 tbsp. cane sugar
- ¼ tsp Salt
- ¼ tsp pepper

Directions

1. In a small bowl, whisk together the tomato paste, vinegar, soy sauce, cornstarch, and sugar.
2. Cut the tofu into ¼-inch cubes, place in a medium bowl, and marinate in the soy sauce mixture until the tofu has absorbed the flavors (up to 3 hours).
3. Heat 1 tablespoon of the olive oil in a frying pan over medium-high heat.
4. Add the tofu chunks and half of the remaining marinade to the pan, leaving the rest for later.
5. Stir frequently until the tofu is cooked golden brown, approximately 10-12 minutes. Remove the tofu from the heat and set aside in a medium-sized bowl.
6. Add the other tablespoon of olive oil to the same pan, then the garlic and ginger; heat for about 1 minute.
7. Add in the peppers and onions. Stir until the vegetables have softened, about 5 minutes.
8. Pour the leftover marinade into the pan with the vegetables and heat until the sauce thickens while continuously stirring, around 4 minutes.
9. Add the pineapple chunks and tofu cubes to the pan while stirring and continue to cook for 3 minutes.
10. Serve and enjoy right away, or, let the sweet and sour tofu cool down and store for later!

Nutritions: *Calories 290, Total Fat 16.9g, Saturated Fat 2.6g, Cholesterol 0mg, Sodium 512mg, Total Carbohydrate 19.5g, Dietary Fiber 3.3g, Total Sugars 9.1g, Protein 15.9g, Vitamin D 0mcg, Calcium 138mg, Iron 1mg, Potassium 434mg*

Stuffed Sweet Potatoes

Preparation:
30 Minutes

Cooking:
1 h 16 minutes

Serves:
3

Ingredients

- ½ cup dry black beans
- 3 small or medium sweet potatoes
- 2 tbsp. olive oil
- 1 large red bell pepper, pitted, chopped
- 1 small sweet yellow onion, chopped
- 2 tbsp. garlic, minced or powdered
- 1 8-oz. package tempeh, diced into ¼" cubes
- ½ cup marinara sauce
- ½ cup water
- 1 tbsp. chili powder
- 1 tsp. parsley
- ½ tsp. cayenne
- ¼ tsp Salt
- ¼ tsp pepper

Directions

1. Preheat the oven to 400°F.
2. Using a fork, poke several holes in the skins of the sweet potatoes.
3. Wrap the sweet potatoes tightly with aluminum foil and place them in the oven until soft and tender, or for approximately 45 minutes.
4. While sweet potatoes are cooking, heat the olive oil in a deep pan over medium-high heat. Add the onions, bell peppers, and garlic; cook until the onions are tender, for about 10 minutes.
5. Add the water, together with the cooked beans, marinara sauce, chili powder, parsley, and cayenne. Bring the mixture to a boil and then lower the heat to medium or low. Allow the mixture to simmer until the liquid has thickened, for about 15 minutes.
6. Add the diced tempeh cubes and heat until warmed, around 1 minute.
7. Blend in salt and pepper to taste.
8. When the potatoes are done baking, remove them from the oven. Cut a slit across the top of each one, but do not split the potatoes all the way in half.
9. Top each potato with a scoop of the beans, vegetables, and tempeh mixture. Place the filled potatoes back in the hot oven for about 5 minutes.
10. Serve after cooling for a few minutes, or, store for another day!

Nutritions: *Calories 548, Total Fat 19.7g, Cholesterol 1mg, Sodium 448mg, Total Carbohydrate 76g, Dietary Fiber 12.4g, Total Sugars 15.2g, Protein 25.3g, Vitamin D 0mcg, Calcium 185mg, Iron 5mg, Potassium 1132mg*

Sweet Potato Quesadillas

Preparation:
30 Minutes

Cooking:
1 h 9 minutes

Serves:
3

Ingredients

- ▸ 1 cup dry black beans
- ▸ ½ cup dry rice of choice
- ▸ 1 large sweet potato, peeled and diced
- ▸ ½ cup salsa
- ▸ 4 tortilla wraps
- ▸ 1 tbsp. olive oil
- ▸ ½ tsp. garlic powder
- ▸ ½ tsp. onion powder
- ▸ ½ tsp. paprika

Directions

1. Preheat the oven to 350°F.
2. Line a baking pan with parchment paper.
3. Cut the sweet potato into ½-inch cubes and drizzle these with olive oil. Transfer the cubes to the baking pan.
4. Place the pan in the oven and bake the potatoes until tender, for around 1 hour.
5. Allow the potatoes to cool for 5 minutes and then add them to a large mixing bowl with the salsa and cooked rice. Use a fork to mash the ingredients together into a thoroughly combined mixture.
6. Heat a saucepan over medium-high heat and add the potato/rice mixture, cooked black beans, and spices to the pan.
7. Cook everything for about 5 minutes or until it is heated through.
8. Take another frying pan and put it over medium-low heat. Place a tortilla in the pan and fill half of it with a heaping scoop of the potato, bean, and rice mixture.
9. Fold the tortilla in half to cover the filling, and cook the tortilla until both sides are browned—about 4 minutes per side.
10. Serve the tortillas with some additional salsa on the side.

Nutritions: *Calories 683, Total Fat 12.7g, Saturated Fat 2.3g, Cholesterol 0mg, Sodium 980mg, Total Carbohydrate 121g, Dietary Fiber 18.5g, Total Sugars 8.3g, Protein 24.9g, Vitamin D 0mcg, Calcium 184mg, Iron 9mg, Potassium 1425mg*

Satay Tempeh with Cauliflower Rice

Preparation:
60 Minutes

Cooking:
15 Minutes

Serves:
4

Ingredients

- ¼ cup water
- 4 tbsp. peanut butter
- 3 tbsp. low sodium soy sauce
- 2 tbsp. coconut sugar
- 1 garlic clove, minced
- 1 tbsp ginger, minced
- 2 tsp. rice vinegar
- 1 tsp. red pepper flakes
- 4 tbsp. olive oil
- 2 8-oz. packages tempeh, drained
- 2 cups cauliflower rice
- 1 cup purple cabbage, diced
- 1 tbsp. sesame oil
- 1 tsp. agave nectar

Directions

1. Take a large bowl, combine all the ingredients for the sauce, and then whisk until the mixture is smooth and any lumps have dissolved.
2. Cut the tempeh into ½-inch cubes and put them into the sauce, stirring to make sure the cubes get coated thoroughly.
3. Place the bowl in the refrigerator to marinate the tempeh for up to 3 hours.
4. Before the tempeh is done marinating, preheat the oven to 400°F.
5. Spread the tempeh out in a single layer on a baking sheet lined with parchment paper or lightly greased with olive oil.
6. Bake the marinated cubes until browned and crisp—about 15 minutes.
7. Heat the cauliflower rice in a saucepan with 2 tablespoons of olive oil over medium heat until it is warm.
8. Rinse the large bowl with water, and then mix the cabbage, sesame oil, and agave together.
9. Serve a scoop of the cauliflower rice topped with the marinated cabbage and cooked tempeh on a plate or in a bowl and enjoy. Or, store for later.

Nutritions: Calories 554, Total Fat 38.8g, Saturated Fat 7.1g, Cholesterol 0mg, Sodium 614mg, Total Carbohydrate 32.3g, Dietary Fiber 2.1g, Total Sugars 13.9g, Protein 28.1g, Vitamin D 0mcg, Calcium 140mg, Iron 5mg, Potassium 655mg

Teriyaki Tofu Wraps

Preparation:
30 Minutes

Cooking:
15 Minutes

Serves:
3

Ingredients

- 1 14-oz. drained, package extra firm tofu
- 1 small white onion, diced
- 1 cup chopped pineapple
- ¼ cup soy sauce
- 2 tbsp. sesame oil
- 1 garlic clove, minced
- 1 tsp. coconut sugar
- 4 large lettuce leaves
- 1 tbsp. roasted sesame seeds
- ¼ tsp Salt
- ¼ tsp pepper

Directions

1. Take a medium-sized bowl and mix the soy sauce, sesame oil, coconut sugar, and garlic.
2. Cut the tofu into ½-inch cubes, place them in the bowl, and transfer the bowl to the refrigerator to marinate, up to 3 hours.
3. Meanwhile, cut the pineapple into rings or cubes.
4. After the tofu is adequately marinated, place a large skillet over medium heat, and pour in the tofu with the remaining marinade, pineapple cubes, and diced onions; stir.
5. Add salt and pepper to taste, making sure to stir the ingredients frequently, and cook until the onions are soft and translucent—about 15 minutes.
6. Divide the mixture between the lettuce leaves and top with a sprinkle of roasted sesame seeds.
7. Serve right away, or, store the mixture and lettuce leaves separately.

Nutritions: *Calories 247, Total Fat 16.2g, Saturated Fat 2.6g, Cholesterol 0mg, Sodium 1410mg, Total Carbohydrate 16.1g, Dietary Fiber 3.1g, Total Sugars 9g, Protein 13.4g, Vitamin D 0mcg, Calcium 315mg, Iron 4mg, Potassium 371mg*

Tex-Mex Tofu & Beans

 Preparation:
25 Minutes

 Cooking:
12 Minutes

 Serves:
2

Ingredients

- ▶ 1 cup dry black beans
- ▶ 1 cup dry brown rice
- ▶ 1 14-oz. package firm tofu, drained
- ▶ 2 tbsp. olive oil
- ▶ 1 small purple onion, diced
- ▶ 1 medium avocado, pitted, peeled
- ▶ 1 garlic clove, minced
- ▶ 1 tbsp. lime juice
- ▶ 2 tsp. cumin
- ▶ 2 tsp. paprika
- ▶ 1 tsp. chili powder
- ▶ ¼ tsp Salt
- ▶ ¼ tsp pepper

Directions

1. Cut the tofu into ½-inch cubes.
2. Heat the olive oil in a large skillet over high heat. Add the diced onions and cook until soft, for about 5 minutes.
3. Add the tofu and cook an additional 2 minutes, flipping the cubes frequently.
4. Meanwhile, cut the avocado into thin slices and set aside.
5. Lower the heat to medium and mix in the garlic, cumin, and cooked black beans.
6. Stir until everything is incorporated thoroughly, and then cook for an additional 5 minutes.
7. Add the remaining spices and lime juice to the mixture in the skillet. Mix thoroughly and remove the skillet from the heat.
8. Serve the Tex-Mex tofu and beans with a scoop of rice and garnish with the fresh avocado.
9. Enjoy immediately, or, store the rice, avocado, and tofu mixture separately.

Nutritions: *Calories 1175, Total Fat 46.8g, Saturated Fat 8.8g, Cholesterol 0mg, Sodium 348mg, Total Carbohydrate 152.1g, Dietary Fiber 28.8g, Total Sugars 5.7g, Protein 47.6g, Vitamin D 0mcg, Calcium 601mg, Iron 13mg, Potassium 2653mg*

Vegan Friendly Fajitas

Preparation:
30 Minutes

Cooking:
19 Minutes

Serves:
6

Ingredients

- 1 cup dry black beans
- 1 large green bell pepper, seeded, diced
- 1 poblano pepper, seeded, thinly sliced
- 1 large avocado, peeled, pitted, mashed
- 1 medium sweet onion, chopped
- 3 large portobello mushrooms
- 2 tbsp. olive oil
- 6 tortilla wraps
- 1 tsp. lime juice
- 1 tsp. chili powder
- 1 tsp. garlic powder
- ¼ tsp. cayenne pepper
- ¼ tsp Salt

Directions

1. Prepare the black beans according to the method.
2. Heat 1 tablespoon of olive oil in a large frying pan over high heat.
3. Add the bell peppers, poblano peppers, and half of the onions.
4. Mix in the chili powder, garlic powder, and cayenne pepper; add salt to taste.
5. Cook the vegetables until tender and browned, around 10 minutes.
6. Add the black beans and continue cooking for an additional 2 minutes; then remove the frying pan from the stove.
7. Add the portobello mushrooms to the skillet and turn heat down to low. Sprinkle the mushrooms with salt.
8. Stir/flip the ingredients often, and cook until the mushrooms have shrank down to half their size, around 7 minutes. Remove the frying pan from the heat.
9. Mix the avocado, remaining 1 tablespoon of olive oil, and the remaining onions together in a small bowl to make a simple guacamole. Mix in the lime juice and add salt and pepper to taste.
10. Spread the guacamole on a tortilla with a spoon and then top with a generous scoop of the mushroom mixture.
11. Serve and enjoy right away, or, allow the prepared tortillas to cool down and wrap them in paper towels to store!

Nutritions: *Calories 429, Total Fat 16.8g, Saturated Fat 3.2g, Cholesterol 0mg, Sodium 627mg, Total Carbohydrate 59.2g, Dietary Fiber 12.7g, Total Sugars 4.2g, Protein 14.8g, Vitamin D 0mcg, Calcium 113mg, Iron 4mg, Potassium 899mg*

Tofu Cacciatore

Preparation:
45 Minutes

Cooking:
35 Minutes

Serves:
3

Ingredients

- 1 14-oz. package extra firm tofu, drained
- 1 tbsp. olive oil
- 1 cup matchstick carrots
- 1 medium sweet onion, diced
- 1 medium green bell pepper, seeded, diced
- 1 28-oz. can diced tomatoes
- 1 4-oz. can tomato paste
- ½ tbsp. balsamic vinegar
- 1 tbsp. soy sauce
- 1 tbsp. maple syrup
- 1 tbsp. garlic powder
- 1 tbsp. Italian seasoning
- ¼ tsp Salt
- ¼ tsp pepper

Directions

1. Chop the tofu into ¼- to ½-inch cubes.
2. Heat the olive oil in a large skillet over medium-high heat.
3. Add the onions, garlic, bell peppers, and carrots; sauté until the onions turn translucent, around 10 minutes. Make sure to stir frequently to prevent burning.
4. Now add the balsamic vinegar, soy sauce, maple syrup, garlic powder and Italian seasoning.
5. Stir well while pouring in the diced tomatoes and tomato paste; mix until all ingredients are thoroughly combined.
6. Add the cubed tofu and stir one more time.
7. Cover the pot, turn the heat to medium-low, and allow the mixture to simmer until the sauce has thickened, for around 20-25 minutes.
8. Serve the tofu cacciatore in bowls and top with salt and pepper to taste, or, store for another meal!

Nutritions: *Calories 319, Total Fat 12g, Saturated Fat 2.1g, Cholesterol 3mg, Sodium 1156mg, Total Carbohydrate 43.1g, Dietary Fiber 10.4g, Total Sugars 27.1g, Protein 17.6g, Vitamin D 0mcg, Calcium 359mg, Iron 5mg, Potassium 961mg*

Portobello Burritos

Preparation:
50 Minutes

Cooking:
40 Minutes

Serves:
4

Ingredients

- 3 large portobello mushrooms
- 2 medium potatoes
- 4 tortilla wraps
- 1 medium avocado, pitted, peeled, diced
- ¾ cup salsa
- 1 tbsp. cilantro
- ½ tsp salt
- 1/3 cup water
- 1 tbsp. lime juice
- 1 tbsp. minced garlic
- ¼ cup teriyaki sauce

Directions

1. Preheat the oven to 400°F.
2. Lightly grease a sheet pan with olive oil (or alternatively, line with parchment paper) and set it aside.
3. Combine the water, lime juice, teriyaki, and garlic in a small bowl.
4. Slice the portobello mushrooms into thin slices and add these to the bowl. Allow the mushrooms to marinate thoroughly, for up to three hours.
5. Cut the potatoes into large matchsticks, like French fries. Sprinkle the fries with salt and then transfer them to the sheet pan. Place the fries in the oven and bake them until crisped and golden, around 30 minutes. Flip once halfway through for even cooking.
6. Heat a large frying pan over medium heat. Add the marinated mushroom slices with the remaining marinade to the pan. Cook until the liquid has absorbed, around 10 minutes. Remove from heat.
7. Fill the tortillas with a heaping scoop of the mushrooms and a handful of the potato sticks. Top with salsa, sliced avocados, and cilantro before serving.
8. Serve right away and enjoy, or, store the tortillas, avocado, and mushrooms separately for later!

Nutritions: *Calories 391, Total Fat 14.9g, Saturated Fat 3.1g, Cholesterol 0mg, Sodium 1511mg, Total Carbohydrate 57g, Dietary Fiber 10.8g, Total Sugars 5.1g, Protein 11.2g, Vitamin D 0mcg, Calcium 85mg, Iron 3mg, Potassium 956mg*

Mushroom Madness Stroganoff

 Preparation:
30 Minutes

 Cooking:
25 Minutes

 Serves:
4

Ingredients

- 2 cups gluten-free noodles
- 1 small onion, chopped
- 2 cups vegetable broth
- 2 tbsp. almond flour
- 1 tbsp. tamari
- 1 tsp. tomato paste
- 1 tsp. lemon juice
- 3 cups mushrooms, chopped
- 1 tsp. thyme
- 3 cups raw spinach
- 1 tbsp. apple cider vinegar
- 1 tbsp. olive oil
- ¼ tsp Salt
- ¼ tsp pepper
- 2 tbsp. fresh parsley

Directions

1. Prepare the noodles according to the package instructions.
2. Heat the olive oil in a large skillet over medium heat.
3. Add the chopped onion and sauté until soft—for about 5 minutes.
4. Stir in the flour, vegetable broth, tamari, tomato paste, and lemon juice; cook for an additional 3 minutes.
5. Blend in the mushrooms, thyme, and salt to taste, then cover the skillet.
6. Cook until the mushrooms are tender, for about 7 minutes, and turn the heat down to low.
7. Add the cooked noodles, spinach, and vinegar to the pan and top the ingredients with salt and pepper to taste.
8. Cover the skillet again and let the flavors combine for another 8-10 minutes.
9. Serve immediately, topped with the optional parsley if desired, or, store and enjoy the stroganoff another day of the week!

Nutritions: *Calories 240, Total Fat 11.9g, Saturated Fat 1.3g, Cholesterol 0mg, Sodium 935mg, Total Carbohydrate 26.1g, Dietary Fiber 4.3g, Total Sugars 4.9g, Protein 9.9g, Vitamin D 189mcg, Calcium 71mg, Iron 4mg, Potassium 463mg*

VEGAN COOKBOOK FOR ATHLETES

Chapter 6.
Dinner Recipes

Broccoli & black beans stir fry

Preparation:
60 Minutes

Serves:
6

Ingredients

- 4 cups broccoli florets
- 2 cups cooked black beans
- 1 tablespoon sesame oil
- 4 teaspoons sesame seeds
- 2 cloves garlic, finely minced
- 2 teaspoons ginger, finely chopped
- A large pinch red chili flakes
- A pinch turmeric powder
- Salt to taste
- Lime juice to taste (optional)

Directions

1. Steam broccoli for 6 minutes. Drain and set aside.
2. Warm the sesame oil in a large frying pan over medium heat. Add sesame seeds, chili flakes, ginger, garlic, turmeric powder, and salt. Sauté for a couple of minutes.
3. Add broccoli and black beans and sauté until thoroughly heated.
4. Sprinkle lime juice and serve hot.

Sweet 'n spicy tofu

Preparation:
45 Minutes

Serves:
8

Ingredients

- 14 ounces extra firm tofu; press the excess liquid and chop into cubes.
- 3 tablespoons olive oil
- 2 2-3 cloves garlic, minced
- 4 tablespoons sriracha sauce or any other hot sauce
- 2 tablespoons soy sauce
- 1/4 cup sweet chili sauce
- 5-6 cups mixed vegetables of your choice (like carrots, cauliflower, broccoli, potato, etc.)
- Salt to taste (optional)

Directions

1. Place a nonstick pan over medium-high heat. Add 1 tablespoon oil. When oil is hot, add garlic and mixed vegetables and stir-fry until crisp and tender. Remove and keep aside.
2. Place the pan back on heat. Add 2 tablespoons oil. When oil is hot, add tofu and sauté until golden brown. Add the sautéed vegetables. Mix well and remove from heat.
3. Make a mixture of sauces by mixing together all the sauces in a small bowl.
4. Serve the stir fried vegetables and tofu with sauce.

Eggplant & mushrooms in peanut sauce

 Preparation:
32 Minutes

 Serves:
6

Directions

1. Place the eggplants and mushroom in a steamer. Steam the eggplant and mushrooms until tender. Transfer to a bowl.
2. To a small bowl, add peanut butter and vinegar and whisk.
3. Add rest of the ingredients and whisk well. Add this to the bowl of eggplant slices. Add scallions and mix well.
4. Serve hot.

Ingredients

- 4 Japanese eggplants cut into 1-inch thick round slices
- 3/4 pounds of shiitake mu shrooms, stems discarded, halved
- 3 tablespoons smooth peanut butter
- 2 1/2 tablespoons rice vinegar
- 1 1/2 tablespoons soy sauce
- 1 1/2 tablespoons, peeled, fresh ginger, finely grated
- 1 1/2 tablespoons light brown sugar
- Coarse salt to taste
- 3 scallions, cut into 2-inch lengths, thinly sliced lengthwise

Green beans stir fry

Preparation:
30 Minutes

Serves:
6-8

Ingredients

- 1 1/2 pounds of green beans, stringed, chopped into 1 ½-inch pieces
- 1 large onion, thinly sliced
- 4 star anise (optional)
- 3 tablespoons avocado oil
- 1 1/2 tablespoons tamari sauce or soy sauce
- Salt to taste
- 3/4 cup water

Directions

1. Place a wok over medium heat. Add oil. When oil is heated, add onions and sauté until onions are translucent.
2. Add beans, water, tamari sauce, and star anise and stir. Cover and cook until the beans are tender.
3. Uncover, add salt and raise the heat to high. Cook until the water dries up in the wok. Stir a couple of times while cooking.

Collard greens 'n tofu

Preparation:
15 Minutes

Serves:
4

Directions

1. Place a large skillet over medium-high heat. Add oil. When the oil is heated, add tofu and cook until brown.
2. Add rest of the ingredients and mix well.
3. cook until greens wilts and almost dry.

Ingredients

- 2 pounds of collard greens, rinsed, chopped
- 1 cup water
- 1/2 pound of tofu, chopped
- Salt to taste
- Pepper powder to taste
- Crushed red chili to taste

Double-garlic bean and vegetable soup

Preparation:
25 Minutes

Serves:
4

Ingredients

- 1 tablespoon (15 ml) olive oil
- 1 teaspoon fine sea salt
- 1 (240 g) minced onion 5 cloves garlic, minced
- 2 cups (220 g) chopped red potatoes
- ⅔ cup (96 g) sliced carrots
- Protein content per serving cup (60 g) chopped celery
- 1 teaspoon italian seasoning blend
- Protein content per serving teaspoon red pepper flakes, or to taste
- Protein content per serving teaspoon celery seed
- 4 cups water (940 ml), divided
- 1 can (14.5 ounces, or 410 g) crushed tomatoes or tomato puree
- 1 head roasted garlic
- 2 tablespoons (30 g) prepared vegan pesto, plus more for garnish
- 2 cans (each 15 ounces, or 425 g) different kinds of white beans, drained and rinsed
- Protein content per serving cup (50 g)
- 1-inch (2.5 cm) pieces green beans
- Salt and pepper

Directions

1. Heat the oil and salt in a large soup pot over medium heat. Add the onion, garlic, potatoes, carrots, and celery. Cook for 4 to 6 minutes, occasionally stirring, until the onions are translucent. Add the seasoning blend, red pepper flakes, and celery seed and stir for 2 minutes. Add 3 cups (705 ml) of the water and the crushed tomatoes.
2. Combine the remaining 1 cup (235 ml) water and the roasted garlic in a blender. Process until smooth. Add to the soup mixture and bring to a boil. Reduce the heat to simmer and cook for 30 minutes.
3. Stir in the pesto, beans, and green beans. Simmer for 15 minutes. Taste and adjust the seasonings. Serve each bowl with a dollop of pesto, if desired.

Nutritions: *Protein content per serving: 21 g*

Mean bean minestrone

 Preparation:
45 Minutes

 Serves:
6

Ingredients

- 1 tablespoon (15 ml) olive oil
- 1/3 cup (80 g) chopped red onion
- 4 cloves garlic, grated or pressed
- 1 leek, white and light green parts, trimmed and chopped (about 4 ounces, or 113 g)
- 2 carrots, peeled and minced (about 4 ounces, or 113 g)
- 2 ribs of celery, minced (about 2 ounces, or 57 g)
- 2 yellow squashes, trimmed and chopped (about 8 ounces, or 227 g)
- 1 green bell pepper, trimmed and chopped (about 8 ounces, or 227 g)
- 1 tablespoon (16 g) tomato paste
- 1 teaspoon dried oregano
- 1 teaspoon dried basil
- ⅓ teaspoon smoked paprika
- '¼ To ¼ teaspoon cayenne pepper, or to taste
- 2 cans (each 15 ounces, or 425 g) diced fire-roasted tomatoes
- 4 cups (940 ml) vegetable broth, more if needed
- 3 cups (532 g) cannellini beans, or other white beans
- 2 cups (330 g) cooked farro, or other whole grain or pasta
- Salt, to taste
- Nut and seed sprinkles, for garnish, optional and to taste

Directions

1. In a large pot, add the oil, onion, garlic, leek, carrots, celery, yellow squash, bell pepper, tomato paste, oregano, basil, paprika, and cayenne pepper. Cook on medium-high heat, stirring often until the vegetables start to get tender, about 6 minutes.
2. Add the tomatoes and broth. Bring to a boil, lower the heat, cover with a lid, and simmer 15 minutes.
3. Add the beans and simmer another 10 minutes. Add the farro and simmer 5 more minutes to heat the farro.
4. Note that this is a thick minestrone. If there are leftovers (which taste even better, by the way), the soup will thicken more once chilled.
5. Add extra broth if you prefer a thinner soup and adjust seasoning if needed. Add nut and seed sprinkles on each portion upon serving, if desired.
6. Store leftovers in an airtight container in the refrigerator for up to 5 days. The minestrone can also be frozen for up to 3 months.

Nutritions: *Protein content per serving: 9 g*

Sushi rice and bean stew

Preparation:
45 Minutes

Serves:
6

Ingredients

For the sushi rice:
- 1 cup (208 g) dry sushi rice, thoroughly rinsed until water runs clear and drained
- 1¾ cups (295 ml) water
- 1 tablespoon (15 ml) fresh lemon juice
- 1 teaspoon toasted sesame oil
- 1 teaspoon sriracha
- 1 teaspoon tamari
- 1 teaspoon agave nectar or brown rice syrup

For the stew:
- 1 tablespoon (15 ml) toasted sesame oil
- 9 ounces (255 g) minced carrot (about 4 medium carrots)
- 1/3 cup (80 g) chopped red onion or ¼ cup (40 g) minced shallot
- 2 teaspoons grated fresh ginger or ⅓ teaspoon ginger powder 4 cloves garlic, grated or pressed
- 1½ cups (246 g) cooked chickpeas
- 1 cup (155 g) frozen, shelled edamame
- 3 tablespoons (45 ml) seasoned rice vinegar
- 2 tablespoons (30 ml) tamari
- 2 teaspoons sriracha, or to taste
- 1 cup (235 ml) mushroom-soaking broth
- 2 cups (470 ml) vegetable broth
- 2 tablespoons (36 g) white miso
- 2 tablespoons (16 g) toasted white sesame seeds

Directions

1. To make the sushi rice: combine the rice and water in a rice cooker, cover with the lid, and cook until the water is absorbed without lifting the lid. (alternatively, cook the rice on the stove top, following the directions on the package.) While the rice is cooking, combine the remaining sushi rice ingredients in a large bowl.

2. Let the rice steam for 10 minutes in the rice cooker with the lid still on. Gently fold the cooked rice into the dressing. Set aside.

3. To make the stew: heat the oil in a large pot on medium-high heat. Add the carrots, onion, ginger, and garlic. Lower the temperature to medium and cook until the vegetables start to get tender, stirring often about 4 minutes.

4. Add the chickpeas, edamame, vinegar, tamari, and sriracha. Stir and cook for another 4 minutes. Add the broths, and bring back to a slow boil. Cover with a lid, lower the heat, and simmer

for 10 minutes.

5. Place the miso in a small bowl and remove 3 tablespoons (45 ml) of the broth from the pot. Stir into the miso to thoroughly combine. Stir the miso mixture back into the pan, and remove from the heat.

6. Divide the rice among 4 to 6 bowls, depending on your appetite. Add approximately 1 cup (235 ml) of the stew on top of each portion of rice. Add 1 teaspoon of sesame seeds on top of each serving, and serve immediately.

7. If you do not plan on eating this dish in one shot, keep the rice and stew separated and store in the refrigerator for up to 4 days.

8. When reheating the stew, do not bring to a boil. Slowly warm the rice with the stew on medium heat in a small saucepan until heated through.

Giardiniera chili

Preparation:
35 Minutes

Serves:
6

Ingredients

- 1 tablespoon (15 ml) neutral-flavored oil
- 1 medium red onion, chopped
- 4 carrots, peeled and minced (9 ounces, or 250 g)
- 2 zucchini, trimmed and minced (11 ounces, or 320 g)
- 4 roma tomatoes, diced (14 ounces, or 400 g)
- 4 cloves garlic, grated or pressed
- 1 tablespoon (8 g) mild to medium chili powder
- 1 teaspoon ground cumin
- ½ teaspoon smoked paprika
- ½ teaspoon liquid smoke
- ¼ teaspoon fine sea salt, or to taste
- ¼ teaspoon cayenne pepper, or to taste
- 2 tablespoons (32 g) tomato paste
- 1 can (15 ounces, or 425 g) diced fire-roasted tomatoes
- ½ cup (120 ml) vegetable broth
- ½ cup (120 ml) mushroom-soaking broth or extra vegetable broth
- 1 can (15 ounces, or 425 g) pinto beans, drained and rinsed
- 1 can (15 ounces, or 425 g) black beans, drained and rinsed
- ½ cup (60 g) nutritional yeast

Directions

1. Heat the oil on medium-high in a large pot and add the onion, carrots, zucchini, tomatoes, and garlic. Cook for 6 minutes, stirring occasionally until the carrots start to get tender. Add the chili powder, cumin, paprika, liquid smoke, salt, cayenne pepper, and tomato paste, stirring to combine. Cook another 2 minutes. Add the diced tomatoes, broths, beans, and nutritional yeast. Bring to a low boil. Lower the heat, cover with a lid, and simmer 15 minutes, stirring occasionally. Remove the lid and simmer for another 5 minutes.
2. Serve on top of a cooked whole grain of choice or with your favorite chili accompaniments.
3. Leftovers can be stored in an airtight container in the refrigerator for up to 4 days or frozen for up to 3 months.

Nutritions: *Protein content per serving: 28 g*

Shorba (lentil soup)

 Preparation:
30 Minutes

 Serves:
6

Ingredients

- 1 tablespoon (15 ml) olive oil
- 1 medium onion, minced
- 1 large carrot, peeled and chopped
- 1 fist-size russet potato, cut into small cubes (about 7 ounces, or 198 g)
- 4 large cloves garlic, minced
- 2 teaspoons grated fresh ginger root
- 1 to 2 teaspoons berbere, to taste
- 1/3 teaspoon turmeric
- 1 cup (192 g) brown lentils, picked over and rinsed
- 6 cups (1.4 l) water, more if desired
- 1 tablespoon (16 g) tomato paste
- 1 tablespoon (18 g) vegetable bouillon paste, or 2 bouillon cubes
- Salt and pepper

Directions

1. Heat the oil in a large soup pot over medium heat. Add the onion, carrot, and potato. Cook for 5 to 7 minutes, stirring occasionally until the onions are translucent. Stir in the garlic, ginger, berbere, turmeric, and lentils and cook and stir for 1 minute until fragrant. Add the water, tomato paste, and bouillon. Bring to a boil, and then reduce the heat to a simmer. Cook for 30 minutes, stirring occasionally until the lentils are tender. Taste and adjust the seasonings.

Nutritions: *Protein content per serving: 10 g*

The whole enchilada

 Preparation:
20 Minutes

 Serves:
6

Ingredients

For the sauce:

► 2 tablespoons (30 ml) olive oil 1/3 cup (80 g) chopped red onion 4 ounces (113 g) tomato paste
► 1 tablespoon (15 ml) adobo sauce
► 1 tablespoon (8 g) mild to medium chili powder
► 1 teaspoon ground cumin
► 3 cloves garlic, grated or pressed
► ⅓ teaspoon fine sea salt, or to taste
► 2 tablespoons (15 g) whole wheat pastry flour or (16 g) all-purpose flour
► 2 cups (470 ml) water

For the filling:

► 1 protein content per serving teaspoons olive oil
► ⅓ cup (53 g) chopped red onion
► 1 sweet potato, trimmed and peeled, chopped (about 8.8 ounces, or 250 g)
► 1 yellow squash, trimmed and chopped (about 5.3 ounces, or 150 g)
► 2 cloves garlic, grated or pressed
► 1 tablespoon (8 g) nutritional yeast
► 1 smoked paprika
► ¼ teaspoon liquid smoke
► Pinch of fine sea salt, or to taste
► 1 (258 g) cooked black beans
► 3 tablespoons (45 ml) enchilada sauce
► 12 to 14 corn tortillas
► 1 recipe creamy cashew sauce
► Chopped fresh cilantro, to taste hot sauce, to taste

Directions

1. To make the sauce: heat the oil on medium heat in a large skillet. Add the onion and cook until fragrant while occasionally stirring, about 2 minutes. Add the tomato paste, adobo sauce, chili powder, cumin, garlic, and salt. Saute for 2 minutes, stirring frequently. Sprinkle the flour on top and cook 2 minutes, stirring frequently. Slowly whisk in the water and cook until slightly thickened, about 6 minutes, frequently whisking to prevent clumps. Remove from the heat and set aside.

2. To make the filling: heat the oil in a large skillet on medium heat. Add the onion and sweet potato and cook 6 minutes or until the potato starts

to get tender, stirring occasionally. Add the squash and garlic and cook for 4 minutes, stirring occasionally. Add the nutritional yeast, paprika, liquid smoke, and salt, stir to combine, and cook for another minute. Add the beans and enchilada sauce and stir to combine. Cover the pan and simmer until the vegetables are completely tender about 4 minutes. Add a little water if the plants stick to the skillet. Adjust the seasonings if needed.

3. Preheat the oven to 350°f (180°c, or gas mark 4).

4. Place the sauce in a large shallow bowl. If you aren't using pre-shaped, uncooked tortillas, follow the direction in the recipe notes to soften the tortillas so that they are easier to work with. Ladle about 1/3 cup (80 ml) of enchilada sauce on the bottom of a 9 x 13-inch (23 x 33 cm) baking dish. Dip each tortilla in the sauce to coat only lightly. Don't be too generous and gently scrape off the excess sauce with a spatula; otherwise, you will run out of sauce. Add a scant ¼ cup (about 45 g) of the filling in each tortilla. Fold the tortilla over the filling, rolling like a cigar. Place the enchiladas in the pan, seam side down. Make sure to squeeze them in tight so that there's room in the dish for all of them. Top evenly with the remaining enchilada sauce. Add the creamy cashew sauce consistently on top.

5. Bake for 20 to 25 minutes or until the top is set, and the enchiladas are heated through. Garnish with cilantro and serve with hot sauce.

Nutritions: *Protein content per serving: 6 g*

Black bean and avocado salad

Preparation:
45 Minutes

Serves:
6

Ingredients

- 1 cup (172 g) cooked black beans
- ⅓ cup (82 g) frozen corn (run under hot water, drained)
- 3 tablespoons (15 g) minced scallion
- 2 cloves garlic, minced
- 6 cherry tomatoes, cut into quarters
- 1 teaspoon minced fresh cilantro, or to taste
- Pinch of dried oregano 1 chipotle in adobo
- 1 tablespoon (15 ml) fresh lemon juice
- 1 tablespoon (15 ml) apple cider vinegar 1 tablespoon (15 ml) vegetable broth
- 1 teaspoon nutritional yeast
- 2 tablespoons (15 g) roasted salted pepitas (hulled pumpkin seeds)
- 2 avocados, pitted, peeled, and chopped
- Salt and pepper

Directions

1. Combine the beans, corn, scallion, cherry tomatoes, garlic, cilantro, and oregano in a medium-size bowl. Using a small blender or a mortar and pestle, thoroughly combine the chipotle, lemon juice, vinegar, broth, and nutritional yeast to form a dressing. Pour over the bean mixture and stir in the pepitas. Gently stir in the avocados. Season to taste with salt and pepper. Serve promptly so that the avocado doesn't discolor.

Nutritions: *Protein content per serving: 8 g*

Mediterranean quinoa and bean salad

Preparation:
35 Minutes

Serves:
6

Ingredients

▸ 1¾ cups (213 g) dry ivory quinoa, rinsed
▸ 2 (590 ml) vegetable broth
▸ 2 tablespoons (30 ml) apple cider vinegar
▸ 2 tablespoons (30 ml) fresh lemon juice
▸ 3 tablespoons (45 ml) extra-virgin olive oil
▸ ⅔ cup (40 g) finely chopped red onion
▸ 2 to 3 cloves garlic, minced, or to taste
▸ Protein content per serving teaspoon red pepper flakes, or to taste
▸ Salt and pepper
▸ 1 (266 g) cooked cannellini beans
▸ 24 jumbo pitted kalamata olives, minced
▸ Half of red bell pepper, cored and diced
▸ Half of yellow bell pepper, cored and diced
▸ 8 ounces (227 g) mini heirloom tomatoes, halved or quartered depending on size
▸ 6 tablespoons (24 g) minced fresh parsley
▸ 15 leaves fresh basil, cut in chiffonade

Directions

1. Combine the quinoa with the broth in a medium saucepan. Bring to a boil and then reduce the heat to a simmer. Cover and cook until all liquid is absorbed, 12 to 15 minutes. The quinoa should be tender and translucent, and the germ ring should be visible along the outside edge of the grain. Set aside to cool completely.

2. In a large bowl, combine the vinegar, lemon juice, oil, onion, garlic, red pepper flakes, salt, and pepper. Stir the beans into the dressing. Add the cooled quinoa, olives, bell peppers, tomatoes, and parsley into the bowl with the beans. Fold with a rubber spatula to thoroughly yet gently combine.

3. Cover and chill for an hour to let the flavors meld. Garnish with basil upon serving. Leftovers can be stored in an airtight container in the refrigerator for up to 4 days.

Nutritions: *Protein content per serving: 6 g*

Chapter 7.
Smoothies and Beverages

Pear Lemonade

 Preparation:
5 Minutes

 Cooking:
30 Minutes

 Serves:
2

Ingredients

- ½ cup of pear, peeled and diced
- 1 cup of freshly squeezed lemon juice
- ½ cup of chilled water

Directions

1. Add all the ingredients into a blender and pulse until it has all been combined. The pear does make the lemonade frothy, but this will settle.
2. Place in the refrigerator to cool and then serve.

Tips:
Keep stored in a sealed container in the refrigerator for up to four days.
Pop the fresh lemon in the microwave for ten minutes before juicing, you can extract more juice if you do this.

Colorful Infused Water

Preparation:
5 Minutes

Cooking:
1 h

Serves:
8

Ingredients

- 1 cup of strawberries, fresh or frozen
- 1 cup of blueberries, fresh or frozen
- 1 tablespoon of baobab powder
- 1 cup of ice cubes
- 4 cups of sparkling water

Directions

1. In a large water jug, add in the sparkling water, ice cubes, and baobab powder. Give it a good stir.
2. Add in the strawberries and blueberries and cover the infused water, store in the refrigerator for one hour before serving.

Tips:
Store for 12 hours for optimum taste and nutritional benefits.
Instead of using strawberries and blueberries, add slices of lemon and six mint leaves, one cup of mangoes or cherries, or half a cup of leafy greens such as kale and/or spinach.

413

Hibiscus Tea

 Preparation:
1 Minutes

 Cooking:
5 Minutes

 Serves:
2

Ingredients

- 1 tablespoon of raisins, diced
- 6 Almonds, raw and unsalted
- ½ teaspoon of hibiscus powder
- 2 cups of water

Directions

1. Bring the water to a boil in a small saucepan, add in the hibiscus powder and raisins. Give it a good stir, cover and let simmer for a further two minutes.
2. Strain into a teapot and serve with a side helping of almonds.

Tips:
As an alternative to this tea, do not strain it and serve with the raisin pieces still swirling around in the teacup.
You could also serve this tea chilled for those hotter days.
Double or triple the recipe to provide you with iced-tea to enjoy during the week without having to make a fresh pot each time.

Lemon and Rosemary Iced Tea

Preparation:
5 Minutes

Cooking:
10 Minutes

Serves:
4

Ingredients

- 4 cups of water
- 4 earl grey tea bags
- ¼ cup of sugar
- 2 lemons
- 1 sprig of rosemary

Directions

1. Peel the two lemons and set the fruit aside.
2. In a medium saucepan, over medium heat combine the water, sugar, and lemon peels. Bring this to a boil.
3. Remove from the heat and place the rosemary and tea into the mixture. Cover the saucepan and steep for five minutes.
4. Add the juice of the two peeled lemons to the mixture, strain, chill, and serve.

Tips:
Skip the sugar and use honey to taste.
Do not squeeze the tea bags as they can cause the tea to become bitter.

Lavender and Mint Iced Tea

Preparation:
5 Minutes

Cooking:
10 Minutes

Serves:
8

Ingredients

- 8 cups of water
- ⅓ cup of dried lavender buds
- ¼ cup of mint

Directions

1. Add the mint and lavender to a pot and set this aside.
2. Add in eight cups of boiling water to the pot. Sweeten to taste, cover and let steep for ten minutes. Strain, chill, and serve.

Tips:
Use a sweetener of your choice when making this iced tea.
Add spirits to turn this iced tea into a summer cocktail.

Thai Iced Tea

Preparation:
5 Minutes

Cooking:
10 Minutes

Serves:
4

Ingredients

- 4 cups of water
- 1 can of light coconut milk (14 oz.)
- ¼ cup of maple syrup
- ¼ cup of muscovado sugar
- 1 teaspoon of vanilla extract
- 2 tablespoons of loose-leaf black tea

Directions

1. In a large saucepan, over medium heat bring the water to a boil.
2. Turn off the heat and add in the tea, cover and let steep for five minutes.
3. Strain the tea into a bowl or jug. Add the maple syrup, muscovado sugar, and vanilla extract. Give it a good whisk to blend all the ingredients together.
4. Set in the refrigerator to chill. Upon serving, pour ¾ of the tea into each glass, top with coconut milk and stir.

Tips:
Add a shot of dark rum to turn this iced tea into a cocktail.
You could substitute the coconut milk for almond or rice milk too.

Hot Chocolate

 Preparation:
5 Minutes

 Cooking:
15 Minutes

 Serves:
2

Ingredients

- Pinch of brown sugar
- 2 cups of milk, soy or almond, unsweetened
- 2 tablespoons of cocoa powder
- ½ cup of vegan chocolate

Directions

1. In a medium saucepan, over medium heat gently bring the milk to a boil. Whisk in the cocoa powder.
2. Remove from the heat, add a pinch of sugar and chocolate. Give it a good stir until smooth, serve and enjoy.

Tips:
You may substitute the almond or soy milk for coconut milk too.

Preparation:
5 Minutes

Cooking:
15 Minutes

Serves:
2

Directions

1. Add all the ingredients to a blender except for the ice-cubes. Pulse until smooth and creamy, add the ice-cubes, pulse a few more times and serve.

Tips:
The dates provide enough sweetness to the recipe, however, you are welcome to add maple syrup or honey for a sweeter drink.

Ingredients

- 1 and ½ cups of almond milk, sweetened or unsweetened
- 3 bananas, peeled and frozen 12 hours before use
- 4 dates, pitted
- 1 and ½ teaspoons of chocolate powder, sweetened or unsweetened
- ½ teaspoon of vanilla extract
- ½ teaspoon of cinnamon
- ¼ teaspoon of ground ginger
- Pinch of ground cardamom
- Pinch of ground cloves
- Pinch of ground nutmeg
- ½ cup of ice cubes

Mango Lassi

 Preparation:
5 Minutes

 Cooking:
5 Minutes

 Serves:
2-4

Ingredients

- Pinch of salt
- ½ teaspoon of turmeric, finely ground
- 1 cup of coconut milk
- 1 tablespoon of lemon juice
- 3 tablespoons of maple syrup
- 2 cups of mango, frozen
- ½ cup of ice

Directions

1. Add all the ingredients into a blender, pulse until smooth, pour into glasses, top with mint and serve.

Tips:
As an alternative, you may use honey instead of maple syrup.

Health Boosting Juices

Preparation:
10 Minutes

Cooking:
15 Minutes

Serves:
2

Directions

1. Juice all ingredients in a juicer, chill and serve.

Ingredients

- 4 beetroots, quartered
- 2 cups of strawberries
- 2 cups of blueberries
- Ingredients for an orange juice:
- 4 green or red apples, halved
- 10 carrots
- ½ lemon, peeled
- 1" of ginger
- Ingredients for a yellow juice:
- 2 green or red apples, quartered
- 4 oranges, peeled and halved
- ½ lemon, peeled
- 1" of ginger
- Ingredients for a lime juice:
- 6 stalks of celery
- 1 cucumber
- 2 green apples, quartered
- 2 pears, quartered
- Ingredients for a green juice:
- ½ a pineapple, peeled and sliced
- 8 leaves of kale
- 2 fresh bananas, peeled

Coffee Smoothie

Preparation:
5 Minutes

Cooking:
5 Minutes

Serves:
2

Directions

1. Add all the ingredients into a blender, pulse until combined and smooth, serve in two tall glasses.

Tips:
You may use instant espresso powder for a stronger hint of coffee.

Ingredients

- 1 ½ cups of lite coconut milk
- 2 tablespoons of maple syrup
- 2 tablespoons of peanut butter or almond butter
- 2 teaspoons of instant coffee
- 3 frozen bananas, peeled and halved, freeze for 12 hours prior to use

Mint Choc Chip Smoothie

Preparation:
5 Minutes

Cooking:
5 Minutes

Serves:
2

Ingredients

- 1 and ½ cups of almond, soy or coconut milk, unsweetened
- 2 bananas, peeled and frozen 12 hours before use
- ½ teaspoon of vanilla essence
- ¼ cup of mint leaves
- 1 cup of spinach
- 1 tablespoon of vegan choc chips

Directions

1. Add all the ingredients into a blender, pulse until smooth and serve.

Tips:
If you want a more subtle mint smoothie opt for ⅛ cups of mint instead so it won't be as fragrant.

Peanut Butter Smoothie

 Preparation:
5 Minutes

 Cooking:
5 Minutes

 Serves:
2

Directions

1. Add all the ingredients into a blender, pulse until smooth and serve.

Tips:
You may substitute the peanut butter for any other nut butter.

Ingredients

- 1 and ½ cups of almond, soy or coconut milk, unsweetened
- 2 bananas, peeled and frozen 12 hours before use
- ½ teaspoon of vanilla essence
- 1 tablespoon of cocoa powder
- 2 tablespoons of peanut butter

Cinnamon Smoothie

Preparation:
5 Minutes

Cooking:
5 Minutes

Serves:
2

Directions

1. Add all the ingredients into a blender, pulse until smooth and serve.

Tips:
Feel free to add more cinnamon or oats for a more filling smoothie.

Ingredients

▶ 1 and ½ cups of almond, soy or coconut milk, unsweetened
▶ 2 bananas, peeled and frozen 12 hours before use
▶ ½ teaspoon of vanilla essence
▶ ½ teaspoon of cinnamon
▶ ½ cup of oats, rolled
▶ 3 dated, pitted and halved

Green Smoothie

 Preparation:
5 Minutes

 Cooking:
5 Minutes

 Serves:
2

Directions

1. Add all the ingredients into a blender, pulse until smooth and serve.

Tips:
You may substitute the almond milk for another milk of your choice.

Ingredients

- 2 cups of almond milk
- 1 banana, peeled and frozen 12 hours before use
- 1 cup of spinach
- ½ an avocado
- 2 tablespoons hemp hearts
- 2 tablespoons of chia seeds

Green Piña Colada Smoothie

 Preparation:
5 Minutes

 Cooking:
5 Minutes

 Serves:
2

Ingredients

- 2 cups of light coconut milk
- 1 banana, peeled and frozen 12 hours before use
- 1 cup of pineapple, frozen
- 1 teaspoon of vanilla extract

Directions

1. Add all the ingredients into a blender, pulse until smooth and serve.

Tips:
For a creamier option, opt to use 1 cup of light coconut milk with 1 cup of full-fat coconut milk.

Ginger and Berry Smoothie

 Preparation:
5 Minutes

 Cooking:
5 Minutes

 Serves:
2

Ingredients

- ▸ 2 cups of almond milk
- ▸ 1 knob of ginger
- ▸ 1 cup of strawberries, frozen
- ▸ 1 cup of raspberries, frozen
- ▸ 1 cup of cauliflower, steam before use in recipe

Directions

1. Add all the ingredients into a blender, pulse until smooth and serve.

Tips:
The reason the cauliflower is steamed before use is because it is easier on digestion.
Frozen fruits thicken a smoothie more than fresh fruits.

Lime and Raspberry Smoothie

Preparation:
5 Minutes

Cooking:
5 Minutes

Serves:
2

Directions

1. Add all the ingredients into a blender, pulse until smooth and serve.

Tips:
Add blocks of ice to the blender for added texture.

Ingredients

- 1 cup of water
- 1 banana, peeled and frozen 12 hours before use
- 1 cup of raspberries, frozen
- 1 teaspoon of coconut oil
- 2 teaspoons of lime juice
- 1 teaspoon of sweetener of your choice

Avocado, Blueberry, and Chia Smoothie

Preparation:
5 Minutes

Cooking:
5 Minutes

Serves:
2

Ingredients

- 2 cups of almond milk
- 2 cups of blueberries, frozen
- 1 avocado, peeled and pitted
- 2 dates, pitted
- 2 tablespoons of flax or chia
- ½ teaspoon of vanilla extract

Directions

1. Add the blueberries, avocado, dates, chia or flax, and vanilla extract to a blender. Pulse until smooth.
2. Add in the almond milk and pulse until combined with the rest of the mixture, serve.

Tips:
Substitute the almond milk for coconut milk if you'd prefer.

430

Coconut, Raspberry, and Quinoa Smoothie

Preparation:
5 Minutes

Cooking:
5 Minutes

Serves:
2

Directions

1. Add all the ingredients into a blender, pulse until smooth and serve.

Tips:
Substitute the coconut milk for almond milk for a different taste.

Ingredients

- 2 cups of coconut milk
- 2 cups of raspberries, frozen
- 4 tablespoons of goji berries
- 2 dates, pitted
- 1 cup of quinoa, cooked
- 4 tablespoons of coconut, shredded

Chapter 8.
Snacks and Desserts

Snickerdoodle Energy Balls

Preparation:
10 Minutes

Cooking:
0 Minutes

Serves:
20

Ingredients

- Medjool Dates (1 C.)
- Ground Cinnamon (2 t.)
- Cashews (1 C.)
- Vanilla Extract (1/4 t.)
- Almonds (1/2 C.)
- Salt (to Taste)

Directions

1. These little snacks are great op hand because they offer a boost of protein and are easy to grab on the go! To start out, you will want to place your Medjool dates into a food processor and blend until the Medjool dates become soft and sticky.
2. Next, you can add the nuts and seasoning along with the vanilla extract and blend until completely combined.
3. Now that you have your dough use your hand to create bite-sized balls and place onto a plate. You can enjoy them instantly or place them in the fridge for thirty minutes and wait for them to harden up a bit.

Nutritions: *Calories: 100, Carbs: 15g, Fats: 5g, Proteins: 3g*

Baked Carrot Chips

 Preparation:
10 Minutes

 Cooking:
30 Minutes

 Serves:
8

Ingredients

- Olive Oil (1/4 C.)
- Ground Cinnamon (1 t.)
- Ground Cumin (1 t.)
- Salt (to Taste)
- Carrots (3 Pounds)

Directions

1. As you begin a plant-based diet, you may find yourself craving something crunchy. This recipe offers the best of both worlds by giving you a crunch and something nutritious to snack on. You can begin this recipe by heating your oven to 425 and setting up a baking sheet with some parchment paper.
2. Next, you will want to chop the top off each carrot and slice the carrot up paper-thin. You can complete this task by using a knife, but it typically is easier if you have a mandolin slicer.
3. With your carrot slices all prepared, next, you will want to toss them in a small bowl with the cinnamon, cumin, olive oil, and a touch of salt. When the carrot slices are well coated, go ahead and lay them across your baking sheet.
4. Finally, you are going to pop the carrots into the oven for fifteen minutes. After this time, you may notice that the edges are going to start to curl and get crispy. At this point, remove the dish from the oven and flip all of the chips over. Place the dish back into the oven for six or seven minutes, and then your chips will be set!

Nutritions: *Calories: 100, Carbs: 12g, Fats: 8g, Proteins: 1g*

Sweet Cinnamon Chips

Preparation:
5 Minutes

Cooking:
15 Minutes

Serves:
5

Ingredients

- Whole Wheat Tortillas (10)
- Ground Cinnamon (1 t.)
- Sugar (3 T.)
- Olive Oil (2 C.)

Directions

1. If you are looking for a snack that is sweet and simple, these chips should do the trick! You are going to want to start out by getting out a small bowl so you can mix the cinnamon and sugar together. When this is complete, set it to the side.
2. Next, you will want to get out your frying pan and bring the olive oil to a soft simmer. While the oil gets to a simmer, take some time to slice your tortillas up into wedges. When these are set, carefully place them into your simmering olive oil and cook for about two minutes on each side, or until golden.
3. Once the chips are all set, pat them down with a paper towel and then generously coat each chip with the cinnamon mixture you made earlier. After that, your chips will be set for your enjoyment.

Nutritions: *Calories: 70, Carbs: 5g, Fats: 5g, Proteins: 1g*

Creamy Avocado Hummus

 Preparation:
5 Minutes

 Cooking:
0 Minutes

 Serves:
4

Ingredients

- Olive Oil (1 T.)
- Avòcado (1)
- White Beans (1 Can)
- Cayenne Pepper (1/4 t.)
- Lime Juice (2 t.)

Directions

1. When you are looking for something smooth and creamy to dip your vegetables or chips in, this is the perfect recipe to give a try! All you will have to do is place the ingredients from the list above into the food processor and process until smooth.
2. Place the avocado hummus into a serving bowl, and you are ready to dip.

Nutritions: *Calories: 120, Carbs: 5g, Fats: 10g, Proteins: 1g*

Cauliflower Popcorn

Preparation:
10 Minutes

Cooking:
0 Minutes

Serves:
4

Ingredients

- Olive Oil (2 T.)
- Chili Powder (2 t.)
- Cumin (2 t.)
- Nutritional Yeast (1 T.)
- Cauliflower (1 Head)
- Salt (to Taste)

Directions

1. Before you begin making this recipe, you will want to take a few moments to cut your cauliflower into bite-sized pieces, like popcorn!
2. Once your cauliflower is set, place it into a mixing bowl and coat with the olive oil. Once coated properly, add in the nutritional yeast, salt, and the rest of the spices.
3. You can enjoy your snack immediately or place into a dehydrator at 115 for 8 hours. By doing this, it will make the cauliflower crispy! You can really enjoy it either way.

Nutritions: *Calories: 100, Carbs: 10g, Fats: 5g, Proteins: 5g*

Banana and Strawberry Oat Bars

 Preparation:
10 Minutes

 Cooking:
1 h

 Serves:
5

Ingredients

- Rolled Oats (2 C.)
- Chia Seeds (2 T.)
- Maple Syrup (1/4 C.)
- Strawberries (2 C.)
- Vanilla Extract (2 t.)
- Bananas (2, Mashed)
- Maple Syrup (2 T.)
- Baking Powder (1 t.)

Nutritions:
*Calories: 250,
Carbs: 50g, Fats: 5g,
Proteins: 5g*

Directions

1. These oat bars take a few different steps, but they are a great snack to have when you are short on time! You are going to start off by making the strawberry jam for the bars. You can do this by placing the strawberries and two tablespoons of maple syrup into a pan and place it over medium heat. After about fifteen minutes, the strawberries should be releasing their liquid and will come to a boil. You will want to boil for an additional ten minutes.

2. As a final touch for the jam, gently stir in the one teaspoon of the vanilla extract and the chia seeds. Be sure that you continue stirring for an additional five minutes before removing from the heat and setting to the side.

3. Now, it is time to make the bars! You can start this part out by prepping the oven to 375 and getting together a baking dish and lining it with parchment paper.

4. Next, you are going to want to add one cup of your oats into a food processor and blend until they look like flour. At this point, you can pour the oats into a mixing bowl and place it in the rest of the oats along with the baking powder.

5. Once these ingredients are blended well, throw in the other teaspoon of vanilla, maple syrup, and your mashed bananas. As you mix everything together, you will notice that you are now forming a dough.

6. When you are ready to assemble the bars, you will want to take half of the mixture and press it into the bottom of your baking dish and carefully spoon the jam over the surface. Once these are set, add the rest of the dough over the top and press down ever so slightly.

7. Finally, you are going to want to place the dish into the oven and cook for about thirty minutes. By the end of this time, the top of your bars should be golden, and you can remove the dish from the oven. Allow the bars to cool slightly before slicing and enjoying.

PB Cookie Dough Balls

Preparation:
10 Minutes

Cooking:
0 Minutes

Serves:
8

Ingredients

- Whole Wheat Flour (2 C.)
- Maple Syrup (1 C.)
- Peanuts (1/2 C.)
- Peanut Butter (1 C.)
- Rolled Oats (1/2 C.)

Directions

1. Is this recipe a snack or dessert? That is completely up to you! To start this recipe, you will want to get out a large mixing bowl and combine all of the ingredients from the list above.
2. Once they are well blended, take your hands and carefully roll the dough into bite-sized balls before you enjoy! For easier handling, you will want to place the balls into the fridge for about twenty minutes before enjoying.

Nutritions: *Calories: 70, Carbs: 10g, Fats: 4g, Proteins: 4g*

Almond Millet Chews

 Preparation:
15 Minutes

 Cooking:
0 Minutes

 Serves:
10

Ingredients

- Millet (1 C.)
- Almond Butter (1/2 C.)
- Raisins (1/4 C.)
- Brown Rice Syrup (1/4 C.)

Directions

1. This dessert is perfect for when you want something small after dinner. You will want to begin by melting the almond butter in the microwave for about twenty seconds. When this step is complete, place it into a mixing bowl with the brown rice syrup, raisins, and millets.
2. Once everything is blended well, use your hands to roll balls and place onto a plate. If needed, you can add a touch more syrup to keep everything together. Place into the fridge for twenty minutes and then enjoy your dessert.

Nutritions: *Calories: 100, Carbs: 15g, Fats: 5g, Proteins: 2g*

Simple Banana Cookies

Preparation:
5 Minutes

Cooking:
20 Minutes

Serves:
4

Ingredients

- Peanut Butter (3 T.)
- Banana (2)
- Walnuts (1/4 C.)
- Rolled Oats (1 C.)

Directions

1. For a simple but delicious cookie, start by prepping the oven to 350. As the oven warms up, take out your mixing bowl and first mash the bananas before adding in the oats.
2. When you have folded the oats in, add in the walnuts and peanut butter before using your hands to layout small balls onto a baking sheet. Once this is set, pop the dish into the oven for fifteen minutes and bake your cookies.
3. By the end of fifteen minutes, remove the dish from the oven and allow them to cool for five minutes before enjoying.

Nutritions: *Calories: 250, Carbs: 30g, Fats: 10g, Proteins: 5g*

Basic Chocolate Cookies

Preparation:
5 Minutes

Cooking:
15 Minutes

Serves:
10

Ingredients

- Cocoa Powder (1/2 C.)
- Almond Butter (1/2 C.)
- Bananas (2, Mashed)
- Salt (to Taste)

Directions

1. These chocolate cookies are a great way to get a touch of sweetness without overdoing the calories! To begin, prep the oven to 350.
2. As that heats, take out a mixing bowl so you can completely mash your bananas. When this is complete, carefully stir in the almond butter and the cocoa powder.
3. Once your mixture is created, place tablespoons of the mix onto a lined cookie sheet and sprinkle a touch of salt over the top. When these are set, pop the dish into the oven for about fifteen minutes.
4. Finally, remove the dish from the oven and cool before enjoying.

Nutritions: *Calories: 100, Carbs: 10g, Fats: 5g, Proteins: 5g*

Quick Brownie Bites

Preparation:
10 Minutes

Cooking:
0 Minutes

Serves:
10

Ingredients

- Cocoa Powder (1/4 C.)
- Medjool Dates (10)
- Vanilla Extract (1 t.)
- Walnut Halves (1 ½ C.)
- Water (1 T.)

Directions

1. To be honest, who isn't guilty of eating cookie dough raw? Now, you can do it on purpose! To begin this recipe, you will first need to get out a food processor so you can break down the Medjool dates. Once these are broken down, add in the rest of the ingredients and blend until combined.
2. Now that you have your batter, roll it into small balls, and your dessert is ready in an instant!

Nutritions: *Calories: 150, Carbs: 15g, Fats: 10g, Proteins: 5g*

Peach Crisp

Preparation:
5 Minutes

Cooking:
15 Minutes

Serves:
2

Ingredients

- Rolled Oats (2 T.)
- Flour (1 t.)
- Brown Sugar (2 T.)
- Peaches (2, Diced)
- Sugar (1 t.)
- Coconut Oil (3 t.)
- Flour (3 t.)

Directions

1. This recipe is built for two! You can begin by prepping the oven to 375 and getting out two small baking dishes.
2. As the oven begins to warm, take one of the mixing bowls and toss the peach pieces with the sugar, cinnamon, and a teaspoon of flour. When this is set, pour the peaches into a baking dish.
3. In the other bowl, mix together the three teaspoons of flour with the oats and the sugar. Once these are blended, pour in coconut oil and continue mixing. Now that you have your crumble, place it over the peaches in the baking dish.
4. Finally, you are going to pop the dish into the oven for fifteen minutes or until the top is a nice golden color. If it looks finished, remove and cool before slicing your dessert up.

Nutritions: *Calories: 110, Carbs: 20g, Fats: 5g, Proteins: 2g*

Chocolate Dessert Dip

Preparation:
10 Minutes

Cooking:
0 Minutes

Serves:
6

Directions

1. Do you need to whip up dessert quickly? This is an excellent recipe to have on hand, especially if you want to impress your guests! All you have to do is place the three ingredients into a food processor and mix until blended.
2. Simply place the dip into a serving dish, and you are ready to go.

Ingredients

- Date Paste (1/2 C.)
- Cocoa (1/4 C.)
- Cashew Butter (1/2 C.)

Nutritions: *Calories: 150, Carbs: 15g, Fats: 10g, Proteins: 5g*

Lemon Coconut Cookies

 Preparation:
15 Minutes

 Cooking:
0 Minutes

 Serves:
4

Ingredients

- Coconut Flour (1/3 C.)
- Shredded Coconut (1 ½ C.)
- Agave (6 T.)
- Almond Flour (1 ½ C.)
- Lemon Zest (1 T.)
- Lemon Juice (4 T.)
- Coconut Oil (1 T.)
- Vanilla Extract (2 t.)
- Salt (to Taste)

Directions

1. If you enjoy dessert but are looking for something that isn't chocolate, this recipe will be perfect for you! To make these incredible cookies, you will want to place all of the ingredients from the list, minus the shredded coconut, into the food processor, and blend until you have created a dough.
2. Once your dough is set, take your hands and roll the dough into small, bite-sized balls.
3. As a final touch, roll the balls in your shredded coconut and then place into the fridge for twenty minutes. After this time has passed, go ahead and enjoy your dessert!

Nutritions: *Calories: 450, Carbs: 30g, Fats: 20g, Proteins: 10g*

Watermelon Pizza

Preparation:
15 Minutes

Cooking:
0 Minutes

Serves:
4

Ingredients

- Watermelon (1, Sliced)
- Banana (1, Sliced)
- Blueberries (1 C.)
- Coconut Flakes (1/2 C.)
- Chopped Walnuts (1/4 C.)

Directions

1. This dessert is pretty simple, but it can be a lot of fun to make and eat if you have kids in the house! You will begin this recipe by taking the watermelon and chopping it up to look like pizza slices.
2. When the watermelon slices are set, you can then add the chopped fruit on top of the watermelon, followed by any chopped nuts and coconut flakes. For this recipe, we chose to use bananas and blueberries, but you can use any fruit that you like!
3. Just like that, you have watermelon pizza for dessert!

Nutritions: *Calories: 50, Carbs: 10g, Fats: 3g, Proteins: 1g*

Chapter 9.
Sauces, Dressing and Dips

Enchilada Sauce

Preparation:
15 Minutes

Cooking:
12 Minutes

Serves:
6

Directions

1. Heat the oil over pan on a medium flame and add flour and chili powder to it, stirring well.
2. Cook for about 2 minutes and add all other ingredients.
3. Cook for about 10 minutes and remove from the flame.
4. Allow it to cool down and serve to enjoy.

Ingredients

- 1½ cups water
- 1 can tomato sauce
- ¼ teaspoon ground cumin
- ¼ teaspoon onion salt
- ¼ teaspoon garlic powder
- ¼ cup vegetable oil
- ¼ cup red chili powder
- 2 tablespoons self-rising flour
- Salt, as required

Nutritions: *Calories: 117, Net Carbs: 2.6g, Fat: 10.1g, Carbohydrates: 7g, Fiber: 2.4g, Sugar: 2g, Protein: 1.5g, Sodium: 341mg*

BBQ Sauce

Preparation:
15 Minutes

Cooking:
28 Minutes

Serves:
20

Directions

1. Put all the ingredients to a pan and cook for about 3 minutes over medium heat, stirring occasionally.
2. Turn the heat to low and let the ingredients simmer for 25 more minutes.
3. Remove from the heat, cool and serve.

Ingredients

- 1¼ cups red wine vinegar
- 1¼ cups brown sugar
- ½ teaspoon celery seeds
- ½ teaspoon onion powder
- ½ teaspoon garlic powder
- 4 teaspoons hickory-flavored liquid smoke
- ½ cup molasses
- 1 teaspoon paprika
- ½ teaspoon cayenne pepper
- ¼ teaspoon chili powder
- ¼ teaspoon ground cinnamon
- 2 cups ketchup
- 2 tablespoons coconut oil
- 2 cups tomato sauce
- Salt and ground black pepper, as required

Nutritions: *Calories: 111, Net Carbs: 22.1g, Fat: 1.5g, Carbohydrates: 24.6g, Fiber: 0.5g, Sugar: 21.7g, Protein: 0.8g, Sodium: 413mg*

Marinara Sauce

 Preparation:
15 Minutes

 Cooking:
22 Minutes

 Serves:
8

Ingredients

- 1/3 cup olive oil
- 1 can tomato paste
- 2 cans stewed tomatoes
- ½ cup white wine
- ¼ cup fresh parsley, chopped
- 1 teaspoon dried oregano, crushed
- Salt and ground black pepper, as required
- 1/3 cup olive oil
- 1/3 cup onion, chopped finely
- 1 garlic clove, minced

Directions

1. Add the tomato paste, stewed tomatoes, garlic, parsley and oregano to a blender and blend until smooth.
2. Heat oil over medium heat and sauté chopped onions for 2 minutes.
3. Add the tomato mixture and wine and cook for about 20 minutes, stirring constantly.
4. Remove from the flame and serve when cool.

Nutritions: *Calories: 194, Net Carbs: 10g, Fat: 14.2g, Carbohydrates: 14g, Fiber: 2g, Sugar: 5.2g, Protein: 2.4g, Sodium: 260mg*

Raspberry Sauce

Preparation:
15 Minutes

Cooking:
10 Minutes

Serves:
8

Directions

1. Put water and cornstarch in a bowl and beat well.
2. Add the cornstarch mixture and rest of the ingredients to a pan and cook over medium-low heat for about 5 minutes.
3. Let the ingredients simmer for about 5 more minutes to have a thick consistency.
4. Remove from the heat and cool to serve.

Ingredients

- ¼ cup white sugar
- 2 cups fresh raspberries
- 2 tablespoons cornstarch
- 2 tablespoons fresh orange juice
- ¼ cup white sugar
- 1 cup cold water

Nutritions: *Calories: 49, Net Carbs: 8.2g, Fat: 0.2g, Carbohydrates: 12.2g, Fiber: 2g, Sugar: 7.9g, Protein: 0.4, gSodium: 1mg*

Baba Ganoush

Preparation:
15 Minutes

Cooking:
20 Minutes

Serves:
4

Ingredients

- 1 garlic clove, chopped
- ¼ teaspoon salt
- 2 tablespoons tahini
- ¼ cup fresh parsley, chopped
- 1 large eggplant, pricked with a fork
- 2 tablespoons fresh lemon juice

Directions

1. Preheat the oven to 450 degrees F and line a baking sheet with foil paper.
2. Place the eggplant on the baking sheet and roast for about 20 minutes.
3. Remove from the oven and allow to cool.
4. Scoop out the pulp after cutting the eggplant.
5. Put this pulp to a food processor along rest of the ingredients.
6. Dish out in a bowl and serve warm.

Nutritions: *Calories: 78, Net Carbs: 2.1g, Fat: 4.3g, Carbohydrates: 9g, Fiber: 4.9g, Sugar: 3.7g, Protein: 2.6g, Sodium: 162g*

Basil Pesto

Preparation:
15 Minutes

Serves:
8

Directions

1. Grind the basil, garlic, and walnuts in a food processor
2. Add olive oil to it while the motor is running and combine well.
3. Add the nutritional yeast, lemon juice, salt and black pepper to it.
4. Mix well and dish out to serve and enjoy.

Ingredients

- 3 tablespoons nutritional yeast
- ½ cup extra-virgin olive oil
- 2 cups tightly packed fresh basil
- 1 tablespoon fresh lemon juice
- 2 garlic cloves, roughly chopped
- ½ cup walnuts
- Pinch of salt and ground black pepper

Nutritions: *Calories: 173, Net Carbs: 0g, Fat: 17.5g, Carbohydrates: 2.9g, Fiber: 1.6g, Sugar: 0.2g, Protein: 3.9g, Sodium: 3mg*

Poppy Seed Dressing

Preparation:
15 Minutes

Serves:
12

Ingredients

- 2/3 cup unsweetened cashew milk
- ½ teaspoon red palm oil
- ½ cup fresh lemon juice
- ¼ cup maple syrup
- ¾ teaspoon salt
- ½ teaspoon Dijon mustard
- 1 cup raw cashews
- 1 tablespoon poppy seeds

Directions

1. Put the cashews in a spice grinder and pulse until smooth.
2. Put the cashew milk, lemon juice, maple syrup, mustard, palm oil and salt along with ground cashews in a blender.
3. Pulse until smooth and dish out in a container.
4. Stir in the poppy seeds and refrigerate to chill for about 2 hours.
5. Drizzle over your favorite salad and serve to enjoy.

Nutritions: *Calories: 92, Net Carbs: 6.1g, Fat: 6g, Carbohydrates: 8.6g, Fiber: 0.5g, Sugar: 4.8g, Protein: 2g, Sodium: 163mg*

Cranberry Dressing

Preparation:
15 Minutes

Serves:
18

Directions

1. Put rice vinegar, Dijon mustard, cranberry sauce, apple cider vinegar, garlic, salt and black pepper in a blender and pulse until smooth.
2. Add walnut oil and vegetable and pulse to form a creamy mixture.
3. Dish out in a bowl and serve to enjoy.

Ingredients

- ¼ cup rice vinegar
- ¼ cup Dijon mustard
- ¼ cup cranberry sauce
- ¼ cup apple cider vinegar
- ¼ cup walnut oil
- 1 cup vegetable oil
- 1 garlic clove, chopped
- Salt and ground black pepper, as required

Nutritions: *Calories: 124, Net Carbs: 0g, Fat: 13.3g, Carbohydrates: 0.6g, Fiber: 0.3g, Sugar: 0.1g, Protein: 0.6g, Sodium: 40mg*

Preparation:
10 Minutes

 Serves:
20

Directions

1. Put all the ingredients in a blender and blend until smooth.
2. Transfer to a bowl and serve to enjoy.

Ingredients

- 1 cup ketchup
- ½ teaspoon salt
- ½ cup vinegar
- 1 small onion, chopped
- ¾ cup white sugar
- 1 teaspoon paprika
- 1½ cups vegetable oil
- 1 teaspoon fresh lemon juice

Nutritions: *Calories: 187, Net Carbs: 8.8g, Fat: 16.4g, Carbohydrates: 11g, Fiber: 0.2g, Sugar: 10.4g, Protein: 0.3g, Sodium: 194g*

Olive and Pumpkin Seed Tapenade

Preparation:
10 Minutes

Serves:
1

Directions

1. Put all the ingredients except water to a food processor and blend until smooth.
2. Add water to the ingredients and blend again.
3. Take out the contents from the food processor and serve to enjoy.

Ingredients

- ¼ cup fresh basil leaves, chopped
- ¼ teaspoon red chili flakes
- ½ teaspoon black pepper
- 2 tablespoons water
- ½ cup black and green olives, pitted
- ½ cup pumpkin seeds
- 1 tablespoon lemon juice
- 2 garlic cloves, minced
- 2 tablespoons olive oil

Nutritions: *Calories: 740, Net Carbs: 12.6g, Fat: 68.6g, Carbohydrates: 20g, Fiber: 5.4g, Sugar: 1.1g, Protein: 22.7g, Sodium: 713mg*

Pink Peppercorn Pickled Swiss Chard Stem

Preparation:
15 Minutes

Serves:
2

Ingredients

- 2 tablespoons coconut palm sugar
- 1 tablespoon pink peppercorns
- ¼ red onion, diced
- 1 teaspoon coriander seeds
- 1 cup Swiss chard stems, sliced
- ½ teaspoon salt
- ¼ cup apple cider vinegar
- ¼ cup white vinegar

Directions

1. Cut the Swiss chard stem into slices and season with salt.
2. Toast coriander seeds in a saucepan and add apple cider vinegar, white vinegar, and coconut palm sugar.
3. Let the ingredients in the saucepan to boil and allow to simmer to dissolve the sugar.
4. Put onion and Swiss chard stems to a jar and pour the vinegar mixture over the contents of jar.
5. Refrigerate overnight and serve with foods you like.

Nutritions: *Calories: 59, Net Carbs: 21.3g, Fat: 0g, Carbohydrates: 23.1g, Fiber: 0.8g, Sugar: 10.2g, Protein: 0.2g, Sodium: 711mg*

Creamy Jalapeño Dip

 Preparation:
50 Minutes

 Serves:
4

Directions

1. Put the cashews, lemon juice, water and apple cider vinegar to a high speed blender.
2. Blend for about 2 minutes and scrape off the sides of blender.
3. Add the remaining ingredients and chill to serve.

Ingredients

- 2 lemons, juiced
- 2/3 teaspoon garlic powder
- 2½ tablespoons apple cider vinegar
- 2 tablespoons sauerkraut
- 1 teaspoon onion powder
- 1 teaspoon salt
- 1 jalapeño, chopped
- 2 teaspoons black pepper
- 2 tablespoons chives
- 2 cups cashews, soaked in boiled water for 30 minutes and drained

Nutritions: *Calories: 410, Net Carbs: 0.7g, Fat: 31.9g, Carbohydrates: 26.5g, Fiber: 3.2g, Sugar: 4.8g, Protein: 11.1g, Sodium: 623g*

Easy Mayonnaise

 Preparation:
5 Minutes

 Cooking:
5 Minutes

 Serves:
4

Ingredients

- ½ teaspoon salt
- ½ teaspoon mustard powder
- 2 tablespoons olive oil
- 2 cups silken tofu
- 2 tablespoons lemon juice
- 1 teaspoon maple syrup
- 2 tablespoons apple cider vinegar

Directions

1. Blend all ingredients in a blender except olive oil and mustard powder.
2. Add mustard powder and blend for a minute.
3. Drizzle olive oil in the mixture and blend using a food processor.
4. Put the mayonnaise in a sealed container and store.

Nutritions: *Calories: 96, Net Carbs: 0.4g, Fat: 8.3g, Carbohydrates: 2.5g, Fiber: 0.1g, Sugar: 1.7g, Protein: 3.1, gSodium: 308mg*

Almond Dip

 Preparation:
10 Minutes

 Cooking:
10 Minutes

 Serves:
2

Directions

1. Take a blender and all the ingredients to it.
2. Blend them at a high speed for about 1 minute.
3. Take it out in a jar and cover the lid to store.
4. Enjoy whenever you like.

Ingredients

- ½ cup raw almonds
- ½ teaspoon cumin
- ½ teaspoon chili powder
- ¼ teaspoon ground coriander
- ¼ teaspoon paprika
- ¼ teaspoon cayenne pepper
- ½ cup water
- ¼ cup grapeseed oil
- ¼ cup lemon juice
- 2 tablespoons garlic infused oil
- ¼ teaspoon salt
- 3½ tablespoons nutritional yeast

Nutritions: *Calories: 424, Net Carbs: 4.8g, Fat: 40g, Carbohydrates: 12g, Fiber: 5.2g, Sugar: 1.8g, Protein: 8.7g, Sodium: 311mg*

Rainbow Ketchup

Preparation:
5 Minutes

Cooking:
15 Minutes

Serves:
4

Directions

1. Take a saucepan and add all the ingredients to it.
2. Cover it and cook for 15 minutes on medium heat.
3. Uncover it and cook for another 15 minutes.
4. Remove from heat, store and enjoy.

Ingredients

- ¾ teaspoon salt
- 1 cup strawberries, fresh
- 1 big bay leaf
- 1 teaspoon garlic, grated
- 1 cup onion, chopped
- ¼ cup apple cider vinegar
- 1/3 cup brown sugar

Nutritions: *Calories: 74, Net Carbs: 14.4g, Fat: 0.2g, Carbohydrates: 17.8g, Fiber: 1.4g, Sugar: 14.8g, Protein: 0.6g, Sodium: 444mg*

Harissa Paste

 Preparation:
5 Minutes

 Cooking:
5 Minutes

 Serves:
2

Ingredients

- ► 1 teaspoon smoked paprika
- ► 2 teaspoons cumin seeds
- ► ½ teaspoon salt
- ► 1 tablespoon tomato paste
- ► 1 teaspoon coriander seeds
- ► 1 teaspoon caraway seeds
- ► 1 teaspoon red chili flakes
- ► 1 green bell pepper, chopped
- ► 4 tablespoons extra virgin olive oil

Directions

1. Take a saucepan, heat it and roast caraway and cumin seeds in it along coriander.
2. Crush the seeds using a mortar and pestle.
3. Blend all the ingredients until a smooth texture is obtained.
4. Scrape off the harissa and store in a jar.
5. Add a layer of oil over the harissa to store it for a long time.

Nutritions: *Calories: 337, Net Carbs: 2.5g, Fat: 32.1g, Carbohydrates: 6.2g, Fiber: 1.7g, Sugar: 2.3g, Protein: 10.4g, Sodium: 813g*

Preparation:
15 Minutes

Cooking:
5 Minutes

Serves:
4

Directions

1. Put all the ingredients in a blender and process until smooth.
2. Dish out the dip in a platter and serve with nachos.

Ingredients

- ½ fresh lime, juiced
- 1 avocado, ripe
- ¼ cup cilantro, chopped
- ½ teaspoon cumin
- ¾ cup buttermilk
- Seasoning salt, to taste

Nutritions: *Calories: 125, Net Carbs: 2.1g, Fat: 10.3g, Carbohydrates: 7.7g, Fiber: 3.7g, Sugar: 2.7g, Protein: 2.6g, Sodium: 53mg*

Chapter 10. 21 Days Meal Plan

Week 1
Monday

Breakfast: Creamy Chocolate Shake

 Preparation:
10 Minutes

 Cooking:
0 Minutes

 Serves:
2

Ingredients

- 2 frozen ripe bananas, chopped
- 1/3 cup frozen strawberries
- 2 tbsp cocoa powder
- 2 tbsp salted almond butter
- 2 cups unsweetened vanilla almond milk
- 1 dash Stevia or agave nectar
- 1/3 cup ice

Directions

1. Add all ingredients in a blender and blend until smooth.
2. Take out and serve.

Nutritions: *Calories 312, Total Fat 14 g, Saturated Fat 1 g, Cholesterol 0 mg, Sodium 0 mg, Total Carbs 48 g, Fiber 7.5 g, Sugar 27 g, Protein 6.2 g, Potassium 311 mg*

Lunch:
Asian Chilled Cucumber and Seaweed Soup

 Ready in:
15 Minutes

 Serves:
6

Directions

1. Soak seaweed in water to cover overnight.
2. When soft, drain and cut into 2-inch pieces.
3. Boil water with a little salt in a pot.
4. Blanch drained seaweed for 20 to 25 seconds; plunge into the ice water.
5. In a bowl, combine together cucumber, seaweed, and all remaining ingredients; stir well.
6. Refrigerate to chill well.
7. Taste and adjust salt to taste.
8. Serve in chilled bowls.

Ingredients

- 1 cup soaked seaweed, rinsed * see note
- 2 cucumbers cut into thin slices
- Seasonings
- 4 Tbsp of soy sauce
- 1/4 cup fresh lemon juice
- 1/2 tsp garlic minced
- 1 Tbsp red pepper flakes
- 2 tsp sesame seeds toasted
- 1 tsp brown sugar
- 4 cups of water
- Sea salt to taste

Nutritions: *Calories 49.06, Calories From Fat (15%) 7.18, Total Fat 0.86g 1%, Saturated Fat 0.2g 1%, Cholesterol 0mg 0%, Sodium 440.87mg 18%, Potassium 238,19mg 7%, Total Carbohydrates 10.11g 3%, Fiber 1.29g 5%, Sugar 3.41g, Protein 3g 6%*

467

Dinner: Fung Tofu

 Ready in:
25 Minutes

 Serves:
4

Ingredients

- ¼ Cup Soy Sauce
- ½ Cup Black Vinegar
- 1 Tablespoon Sesame Oil
- 2 Inches Ginger, Fresh, Peeled & Minced
- ¼ Cup Maple Syrup
- 3 Cloves Garlic, Minced
- 2 Blocks Tofu, Firm, Pressed & Sliced into 4 Slices
- 1 Tablespoon Sesame Seeds

Directions

1. Mix your black vinegar, ginger, garlic, soy sauce, sesame oil, and maple syrup in a bowl. Toss in the tofu to coat, and then put the slices on a baking sheet to marinate for an hour.
2. Heat your grill to medium-high heat and grill for three minutes per side. Garnish using sesame seeds.

Tuesday

Breakfast: Hidden Kale Smoothie

Preparation:
5 Minutes

Cooking:
0 Minutes

Serves:
2

Directions

1. Add all ingredients in a blender and blend until smooth.
2. Take out and serve.

Ingredients

- 1 medium ripe banana, peeled and sliced
- ½ cup frozen mixed berries
- 1 tbsp hulled hemp seeds
- 2 cups frozen or fresh kale
- 2/3 cup 100% pomegranate juice
- 2¼ cups filtered water

Nutritions: *Calories 178, Total Fat 1.8 g, Saturated Fat 0.3 g, Cholesterol 0 mg, Sodium 33 mg, Total, Carbs 37.8 g, Fiber 4.3 g, Sugar 20.4 g, Protein 4.1 g, Potassium 785 mg*

Lunch: Baked "Hasselback" Sweet Potatoes

Ready in:
1h 15 Minutes

Serves:
4

Ingredients

- 1/2 cup olive oil
- 1 Tbsp of fresh rosemary finely chopped
- 4 large sweet potatoes, chopped
- 1/2 tsp ground mustard
- Kosher salt and freshly ground black pepper
- 1 cup Tofu grated (optional)

Directions

1. Preheat oven to 425 F.
2. Wash and rub potatoes; cut trough potatoes about halfway into thin slices (as Hasselback potatoes).
3. Combine olive, rosemary, and ground mustard; generously brush potatoes.
4. Place sweet potatoes on a greased baking sheet.
5. Bake for 60 minutes or until soft.
6. Remove from the oven, and let cool for 10 minutes.
7. Serve with grated Tofu (optional).

Nutritions: *Calories 285.21, Calories From Fat (92%) 263.44, Total Fat 30g 46%, Saturated Fat 4g 20%, Cholesterol 0mg 0%, Sodium 12.48mg <1%, Potassium 69.92mg 2%, Total Carbohydrates 1.13g <1%, Sugar 0.25g, Protein 5g 10%*

Ready in:
40 Minutes

Serves:
4

Ingredients

- ½ Tablespoon Olive
- 4 Cloves Garlic, Minced
- 2 Tablespoons Lemongrass, Minced
- 2 Tablespoons Red Curry Paste
- 1 Tablespoon Ginger, Fresh & created
- 1 Tablespoon Brown Sugar
- 2 Tablespoons Soy Sauce
- 2 Tablespoons Lime Juice, Fresh
- 1 Tablespoon Hot Chili Paste
- 12 Ounces Linguine
- 2 Cups Broccoli Florets
- 1 Cup Carrots, Shredded
- 1 Cup Edamame, Shelled
- 1 Red Bell Pepper, Sliced

Directions

1. Get out a large pot and fill it with water. Salt it before bringing it to a boil using high heat.
2. Add in the pasta and cook to an al dente texture. Rinse under cold water to stop the cooking.
3. Get out a saucepan and place it over medium heat, heating your oil.
4. Throw in the garlic, lemongrass, and ginger. Cook for another half a minute.
5. Add in soy sauce, coconut milk, curry paste, brown sugar, chili paste, and lime juice. Stir in your curry mixture, cooking for ten minutes until it thickens.
6. Toss in the broccoli, edamame, bell pepper, carrots, and cooked pasta. Mix well before serving warm.

471

Wednesday

Breakfast: Blueberry Protein Shake

Preparation:
5 Minutes

Cooking:
0 Minutes

Serves:
1

Directions

1. Add all ingredients in a blender and blend until smooth.
2. Take out and serve.

Ingredients

- ½ cup cottage cheese or low-fat yogurt
- 3 tbsp vanilla protein powder
- ½ cup frozen blueberries
- ½ tsp maple extract
- ¼ tsp vanilla extract
- 2 tsp flaxseed meal
- Sweetener of choice (to taste)
- 10-15 ice cubes
- ¼ cup water

Nutritions: *Calories 230, Total Fat 5 g, Saturated Fat 1.9 g, Cholesterol 0 mg, Sodium 0 mg, Total Carbs 18 g, Fiber 3.1 g, Sugar 9 g, Protein 27.5 g, Potassium 210 mg*

Ready in:
30 Minutes

Serves:
4

Ingredients

- 2 Tbsp olive oil
- 1 cup of soy milk
- 1 cup soy flour
- 2 tsp garlic powder
- 1 head of cauliflower, chopped into flowerets
- 1 cup Red Hot Sauce (or vegan Buffalo sauce)
- 2 Tbsp of avocado oil

Directions

1. Preheat the oven to 450 F/225 C.
2. Grease a shallow baking dish with olive oil; set aside.
3. In a bowl, stir together soy milk, soy flour, and garlic powder until well combined.
4. Coat the cauliflower florets with the soy flour mixture and place in a prepared baking dish.
5. Bake for 18 to 20 minutes.
6. In a meanwhile, heat Red Hot Sauce or vegan Buffalo sauce with avocado oil in a saucepan.
7. Pour the hot sauce over the baked cauliflower and bake for an additional 6 to 8 minutes.
8. Serve hot.

Nutritions: *Calories 360.35, Calories From Fat (63%) 225.7, Total Fat 25.93g 40%, Saturated Fat 3.54g 18%, Cholesterol 0mg 0%, Sodium 953.78mg 40%, Potassium 1286.29mg 37%, Total Carbohydrates 23.49g 8%, Fiber 7.32g 29%, Sugar 8g, Protein 14g 28%*

Dinner: Mushroom & Bean Soup

 Ready in:
45 Minutes

 Serves:
4

Ingredients

- 1 Tablespoon Olive Oil
- 16 Ounces Bella Mushrooms, Sliced
- ½ Red Onion, Chopped
- 3 Cloves Garlic, Minced
- 15 Ounces White Beans, Canned & Drained
- 1 Tablespoon Italian Seasoning, Dried
- 3 Cups Vegetable Broth
- 1 Teaspoon Rosemary, Fresh or Dried
- Pinch Hot Red Pepper Flakes
- Sea Salt & Black Pepper to Taste

Directions

1. Get out a medium saucepan over medium heat. Heat your olive oil and add in your garlic and onions. Cook for two or three minutes or until golden brown. Add in your spices, salt, pepper, mushrooms and white beans now.
2. Cook for an additional five minutes and then add in your broth. Allow it to come to a boil. Stir in the chili flakes, reducing your heat to a simmer.
3. Allow your soup to cook for another half hour.
4. Puree with an immersion blender and serve garnished with hemp seeds, scallions, olive oil, or mushrooms as desired.

Thursday

Breakfast: Peppermint Monster Smoothie

 Preparation:
5 Minutes

 Cooking:
0 Minutes

 Serves:
1

Directions

1. Add all ingredients in a blender and blend until smooth.
2. Take out and serve

Ingredients

- 1 large frozen banana, peeled
- 1½ cups non-dairy milk
- A handful of fresh mint leaves, stems removed
- 1-2 handfuls spinach

Nutritions: *Calories 451, Total Fat 18.6 g, Saturated Fat 10.2 g, Cholesterol 40 mg, Sodium 271 mg, Total Carbs 54.8 g, Fiber 4.8 g, Sugar 38.7 g, Protein 18.4 g, Potassium 1,511 mg*

Lunch:
Baked Creamy Corn with Shredded Tofu

 Ready in:
25 Minutes

 Serves:
4

Ingredients

- 4 Tbsp rice oil
- 3 cups sweet corn kernels (frozen or fresh)
- 2 green onions, thinly sliced
- 1 cup vegan mayonnaise
- 1 Tbsp brown sugar
- Salt and pepper to taste
- 8 oz silken tofu shredded

Directions

1. Preheat oven to 400 F/200 C.
2. Grease a baking dish with rice oil.
3. In a bowl, combine together corn kernels, green onions. Vegan mayonnaise, brown sugar, and salt and pepper; stir to combine well.
4. Pour the corn mixture into a prepared baking dish.
5. Sprinkle evenly with shredded tofu.
6. Bake for 14 to 16 minutes.
7. Remove from the oven and allow it to cool.
8. Serve.

Nutritions: Calories 482, Calories From Fat (65%) 312.49, Total Fat 35.37g 54%, Saturated Fat 5.86g 29%, Cholesterol 15.28mg 5%, Sodium 425.49mg 18%, Potassium 338.68mg 10%, Total Carbohydrates 40.56g 14%, Fiber 2.4g 10%, Sugar 10.48g, Protein 7.16g 14%

Ready in:
1 h 15 minutes

Serves:
6

Ingredients

- 4 Cups Vegetable Broth
- 3 Cups Water
- 15 Ounces Chickpeas, Canned
- 1 Cup Green Beans, Frozen
- 14.5 Ounces Coconut Milk, Full Fat
- Sea Salt & Black Pepper to Taste
- ½ Teaspoon Ground Ginger
- ½ Teaspoon Cumin
- 1 Teaspoon Turmeric
- ½ Teaspoon Curry Powder
- 1 Tablespoon Tomato Paste
- 1 Cup Wild Rice
- 4 Cloves Garlic, Grated
- 1 ½ Cups Mushrooms, Chopped
- ½ Cup Carrots, Chopped
- 1 Cup White Onions, Chopped
- 1 Tablespoon Coconut Oil

Directions

1. Get out a stockpot and place it over medium heat. Add in your coconut oil and add in the onions and carrots. Sauté until soft.
2. Stir in the mushrooms and garlic cooking for three minutes.
3. Add in the spices, wild rice, tomato paste, and liquids.
4. Once it boils, you can reduce it to a simmer and allow it to simmer for an hour. Add in the green beans and chickpeas and then serve warm.

477

Friday

Breakfast: Almond Banana Granola

 Preparation:
15 Minutes

 Cooking:
50 Minutes

 Serves:
8

Ingredients

- 8 cups rolled oats
- 2 cups dates, pitted and chopped
- 2 ripe bananas, peeled and chopped
- 1 tsp almond extract
- 1 tsp salt

Directions

1. Preheat oven to 275 degrees F.
2. Add oats to a bowl.
3. Take a baking sheet and line it with parchment paper.
4. Take a saucepan and add 1 cup water to it.
5. Place dates in the saucepan and heat them for 10 minutes.
6. Remove from heat.
7. Add heated mixture, bananas, almond extract, and salt to a blender.
8. Blend until smooth.
9. Add this mixture to the bowl with the oats and mix well.
10. Transfer the mixture to the lined baking sheets and spread it out evenly.
11. Bake for 40 to 50 minutes until crispy, stirring after 10 minutes.
12. Let cool and serve.

Nutritions: *Calories 463, Total Fat 5.6 g, Saturated Fat 1 g, Cholesterol 0 mg, Sodium 297 mg, Total Carbs 95.6 g, Fiber 12.6 g, Sugar 32.7 g, Protein 12.2 g, Potassium 695 mg*

Ready in:
45 Minutes

Serves:
4

Directions

1. Preheat the oven to 375 degrees F.
2. Grease a baking sheet with some oil and set aside.
3. Toss Tofu slabs with 1/4 cup of the tamari sauce.
4. Arrange the tofu on the prepared baking sheet and bake for 25 to 30 minutes.
5. Remove from the oven and set aside to cool.
6. In a large bowl, combine the cabbage, carrots, and onion; season with the salt and pepper, and set aside.
7. In a separate bowl, combine sesame oil, ginger, chili paste, and remaining 1/4 cup of tamari sauce, vinegar, garlic, and water.
8. Pour the garlic-ginger mixture over the cabbage mixture and toss to combine.
9. Taste and adjust seasonings.
10. Serve topped with tofu.

Ingredients

- 1 lb firm tofu, drained and cut into 1/2-inch slabs
- 1/2 cup tamari sauce
- 1 lb shredded cabbage
- 2 shredded carrots
- 1 onion finely sliced
- Sea salt and ground pepper to taste
- 4 Tbsp sesame oil
- 1 Tbsp fresh ginger grated
- 1 tsp hot chili paste
- 3 Tbsp rice vinegar or apple cider vinegar
- 2 cloves garlic minced
- 4 Tbsp water

Nutritions: *Calories 386, Calories From Fat (55%) 213.87, Total Fat 24.8g 38%, Saturated Fat 3.58g 18%, Cholesterol 0mg 0%, Sodium 2080mg 87%, Potassium 759.94mg 22%, Total Carbohydrates 21.52g 7%, Fiber 7.1g 31%, Sugar 7.54g, Protein 25.8g 52%*

Dinner:
Wild Rice Lemon Soup

 Ready in:
1 h 5 Minutes

 Serves:
6

Ingredients

- 1 Cup Carrots, Chopped
- ½ Cup White Onion
- 1 Tablespoon Olive Oil
- 1Cup Celery, Sliced
- 6 Cloves Garlic, Minced
- 1 Tablespoon Lemon Zest
- Sea Salt & Black Pepper to Taste
- 1 Tablespoon Italian Seasoning
- ½ Cup Wild Rice
- 4 Cups Vegetable Broth
- 1 Cup Almond Milk
- ¼ Cup Lemon Juice, Fresh
- 1 Cup Spinach, Fresh

Directions

1. Get out a Dutch oven and add your oil to it. Place it over medium heat, and then toss in the carrots, garlic, celery, and onion. Cook for five minutes.
2. Stir in your zest and the remaining seasoning, cooking for three minutes. Add in the wild rice and vegetable broth.
3. Allow it to come to a boil and then reduce the heat to a simmer.
4. Cover and allow it to cook for forty minutes.
5. Add the spinach, milk, and lemon juice.
6. Leave it covered for five minutes and allow it to serve warm.

Saturday

 Preparation:
10 Minutes

 Cooking:
15 Minutes

 Serves:
3

Directions

1. Add all ingredients to a bowl and mix well.
2. Heat a frying pan on medium heat.
3. Pour batter into the frying pan.
4. As it cooks, flip the omelet.
5. When the underside is cooked, flip it again and cook for 1 minute.
6. Serve and enjoy.

Ingredients

- 1 cup chickpea flour
- ½ tsp onion powder
- ½ tsp garlic powder
- ¼ tsp white pepper
- ¼ tsp black pepper
- 1/3 cup nutritional yeast
- ½ tsp baking soda
- 3 green onions (white and green parts), chopped

Nutritions: *Calories 314, Total Fat 5.1 g, Saturated Fat 0.6 g, Cholesterol 0 mg, Sodium 240 mg, Total Carbs 50.5 g, Fiber 16.6 g, Sugar 7.7 g, Protein 21.5 g, Potassium 1,063 mg*

Lunch: High-Protein Minestrone Soup (Crock Pot)

 Ready in:
8 h

 Serves:
6

Ingredients

- 1 cup dried beans, soaked
- 1 onion finely chopped
- 2 cloves garlic finely chopped
- 1 large carrot peeled and cut into 1/2-inch slices
- 1 cup shredded cabbage
- 1 stalk celery cut into 1-inch chunks
- 1 cup fresh chard chopped
- 1 zucchini sliced
- 1 large potato peeled and diced
- 1 cup tomato paste
- 2 cups vegetable broth
- 1/2 cup olive oil
- Salt and ground pepper to taste

Directions

1. Soak beans overnight.
2. Place all ingredients into your 6 quarts Crock-Pot.
3. Give a good stir and cover.
4. Cook on HIGH for 4 to 5 hours or on LOW heat for 8 hours.
5. Taste, and adjust salt and pepper.
6. Serve hot.

Nutritions: *Calories 263.29, Calories From Fat (6%) 16.82, Total Fat 2g 3%, Saturated Fat 0.45g 2%, Cholesterol 0.2mg <1%, Sodium 751.11mg 31%, Potassium 1435.7mg 41%, Total Carbohydrates 50.7g 17%, Fiber 10.12g 40%, Sugar 5.39g, Protein 13.19g 26%*

Ready in:
1 h

Serves:
4

Ingredients

- 1 Tablespoon Olive Oil
- 1 Cup Fennel, Chopped
- 1 Leek, Sliced Thin
- 3 Cups Carrots, Chopped
- 1 Cup Butternut Squash, Chopped
- 3 Cloves Garlic, Minced
- 1 Tablespoon Ginger, Grated
- 1 Tablespoon Turmeric Powder
- Sea Salt & Black Pepper to Taste
- 3 Cups Vegetable Broth
- 14.5 Ounces Coconut Milk, Canned

Directions

1. Get out a Dutch oven and place it over medium heat to heat your olive oil.
2. Stir in your fennel, carrots, leeks, and squash. Cook for five minutes. Toss your garlic, ginger, salt, pepper, and turmeric in next. Stir and cook for another two minutes. Pour in your broth and coconut milk next.
3. Once it comes to a boil, cover it and reduce it to a simmer. Allow it to simmer for twenty minutes.
4. Once it's cooked, puree it using an immersion blender and garnish with coconut yogurt.

Sunday

Breakfast: Polenta

Preparation:
5 Minutes

Cooking:
10 Minutes

Serves:
4

Directions

1. Take a saucepan and heat the brown rice syrup.
2. Add in the pears, polenta, cranberries, and cinnamon and cook for 10 minutes, stirring occasionally.
3. Serve and enjoy.

Ingredients

- ¼ cup brown rice syrup
- 2 pears, peeled, cored, and diced
- 1 cup fresh or dried cranberries
- 1 tsp ground cinnamon
- 1 cup Basic Polenta, kept warm

Nutritions: *Calories 178, Total Fat 0.3 g, Saturated Fat 0 g, Cholesterol 0 mg, Sodium 17 mg, Total Carbs 44.4 g, Fiber 4.9 g, Sugar 23.9 g, Protein 1.9 g, Potassium 170 mg*

Lunch: Hot Sour and Spicy Bok Choy Salad

Ready in:
20 Minutes

Serves:
4

Ingredients

- 1/3 cup sesame oil
- 1 onion finely chopped
- 2 cloves garlic, minced
- Salt and ground pepper to taste
- 1 1/2 lbs Bok Choy (chopped)
- 2 Tbsp of lime juice
- 1 tsp crushed red pepper
- 1/2 tsp hot chili pepper finely chopped
- 1 tsp garlic powder
- 1/2 cup water

Directions

1. Trim the Bok Choy stems off and rinse under cold water; place into a colander to drain.
2. Heat oil in a large frying skillet over medium heat.
3. Sauté onion and garlic with a pinch of salt until soft or for 3 to 4 minutes.
4. Add Bok Choy and slightly stir.
5. Cover and cook for about 3 to 4 minutes.
6. Add fresh lime juice, crushed pepper, chili pepper, and garlic powder.
7. Pour water and simmer for a further 4 to 5 minutes.
8. Taste and adjust salt and pepper to taste.
9. Serve hot.

Nutritions: *Calories 183.95, Calories From Fat (88%) 161, Total Fat 18.22g 28%, Saturated Fat 2.6g 13%, Cholesterol 0mg 0%, Sodium 342.5mg 14%, Potassium 92.71mg 3%, Total Carbohydrates 5g 2%, Fiber 0.77g 3%, Sugar 1.6g, Protein 2g 4%*

Dinner:
Blackeye Pea Burritos

 Ready in:
50 Minutes

 Serves:
6

Ingredients

- 1 Teaspoon Olive Oil
- 1 Red Onion, Diced
- 2 Cloves Garlic, Minced
- 1 Zucchini, Chopped
- 1 Bell Pepper, Seeded & Diced
- 2 Teaspoons Chili Powder
- Sea Salt to Taste
- 14 Ounces Blackeye Peas, Rinsed & Drained
- 6 Tortillas, Whole Grain
- 1 Tomato, Diced

Directions

1. Start by turning your oven to 325, and then get out a skillet. Put it over medium heat, and add in the oil and onion. Cook for five minutes before adding the garlic. Cook for less than a minute more. Add the bell pepper and tomato, and cook for two to three more minutes.
2. When your tomato is warmed, add in your slat, blackeye peas, and chili powder. Stir well.
3. Place in the center of tortillas and roll like a burrito.
4. Place these burritos in a baking dish and pour in the vegetable juice. Continue cooking for twenty to thirty minutes.

Week 2
Monday

Breakfast: Blueberry Overnight Oats

Preparation:
5 Minutes

Cooking:
8 h

Serves:
1

Ingredients

- Almond Milk (1/4 C.)
- Quick Oats (1/4 C.)
- Blueberries (1/2 C.)
- Banana (1/4, Sliced)
- Chia Seeds (1/2 T.)
- Cinnamon (1/8 t.)
- Pecans (1 T.)
- Stevia (to Taste)

Directions

1. While this meal does need to soak overnight, it is easy to do the night before you need a quick breakfast! All you have to do is place all of the ingredients into a jar or bowl and set in the fridge.
2. When you are ready to enjoy, top it however you would like and then enjoy your breakfast.

Nutritions: *Calories: 230, Carbs: 35g, Fats: 6g, Proteins: 4g*

Lunch: Integral Rotini Pasta with Vegetables

 Ready in:
35 Minutes

 Serves:
4

Ingredients

- 1 lb whole-grain pasta rotini
- 4 Tbsp olive oil
- 2 cups zucchini - cut into small cubes
- 1 red onion, cut into cubes
- 1 red bell pepper sliced
- 1 cup of vegetable broth
- 1 cup cherry tomatoes halved
- 2 cloves garlic finely sliced
- 1/2 cup fresh basil finely chopped
- 2 Tbsp lemon juice (freshly squeezed)
- Salt and ground pepper to taste

Directions

1. Cook rotini pasta according to the instructions on the package.
2. Rinse and drain into a colander; set aside.
3. Heat oil in a wok or deep frying pan over medium heat.
4. Add zucchini, onion, and red peppers; sauté for about 6 to 7 minutes.
5. Add sliced garlic, a pinch of salt, and stir for 2 minutes.
6. Add cherry tomatoes and vegetable broth; cook for a further 3 to 4 minutes.
7. Add rotini pasta and fresh basil; toss to combine well.
8. Taste and adjust salt and pepper to taste.
9. Serve with lemon juice.

Nutritions: *Calories 348.77, Calories From Fat (50%) 174.3, Total Fat 19.81g 30%, Saturated Fat 3.81g 19%, Cholesterol 0mg 0%, Sodium 103.66mg 4%, Potassium 690.39mg 20%, Total Carbohydrates 37.38g 12%, Fiber 6.07g 24%, Sugar 3.51g, Protein 9g 18%*

Ready in:
20 Minutes

Serves:
3

Ingredients

- 1 Tablespoon Ginger, Peeled & Grated
- 8 Ounces Firm Tofu, Chopped into Slices
- 4 Green Onions, Sliced Thin
- Toasted Sesame Oil to Taste
- 1 Bunch Asparagus, Trimmed & Chopped
- 1 Handful Cashew Nuts, Chopped & Toasted
- 2 Tablespoons Hoisin Sauce
- 1 Lime, Juiced & Zested
- 1 Handful Mint, Fresh & Chopped
- 1 Handful Basil, Fresh & Chopped
- 3 Cloves Garlic, Chopped
- 3 Handfuls Spinach, Chopped
- Pinch Sea Salt

Directions

1. Get out a wok and heat up your oil. Add in your tofu, cooking for a few minutes.
2. Put your tofu to the side, and then sauté your red pepper flakes, ginger, salt, onions and asparagus for a minute.
3. Mix in your spinach, garlic, and cashews, cooking for another two minutes.
4. Add your tofu back in, and then drizzle in your lime juice, lime zest, hoisin sauce, cooking for another half a minute.
5. Remove it from heat, adding in your mint and basil.

Nutritions: *Calories: 380, Protein: 22 Grams, Fat: 24 Grams, Carbs: 27 Grams*

Tuesday

Breakfast: Carrot Pancakes

 Preparation:
5 Minutes

 Cooking:
25 Minutes

 Serves:
1

Ingredients

- Shredded Carrots (1/4 C.)
- Pancake Mix (1/2 C.)
- Water (1/2 C.)
- Ground Cloves (1/8 t.)
- Nutmeg (1/8 t.)
- Cinnamon (1/4 t.)

Directions

1. Yes, you will still be able to enjoy pancakes while following a plant-based diet! Before you prep your meal, you can start out by heating a skillet over medium-low heat.
2. As the skillet warms, take out a mixing bowl so you can combine all of your ingredients. You may find you need to use different amounts of water, depending on how you like your pancakes!
3. When your mix is all set, scoop out the mixture about pancake-sized, and place on the skillet. These will cook just like regular pancakes, so when it begins to bubble on the top, toss and bake the other side.
4. Finally, serve up with some maple syrup and enjoy your pancakes.

Nutritions: *Calories: 260, Carbs: 50g, Fats: 3g, Proteins: 5g*

Ready in:
30 Minutes

 Serves:
4

Directions

1. Heat oil in a deep skillet over medium-high heat.
2. Sauté the onion and rice for 2-3 minutes; stir frequently.
3. Pour the broth, water, sliced mushrooms, turmeric, and boiled chickpeas; stir well.
4. Bring to boil, reduce heat to medium, cover and cook for 18 minutes; stir occasionally.
5. Remove from the heat and let it cool for 5 minutes.
6. Taste and adjust salt and pepper to taste; stir.
7. Serve.

Ingredients

- 1/2 cup olive oil
- 1 onion finely diced
- 1 1/2 cups rice basmati
- 2 cups fresh mushrooms sliced
- 2 cups vegetable broth
- 2 cups of water
- 1/2 lb canned chickpeas, drained and rinsed
- 1/4 tsp turmeric ground
- Salt and pepper to taste

Nutritions: *Calories 630.4, Calories From Fat (41%) 257.56, Total Fat 29.19g 45%, Saturated Fat 4.17g 21%, Cholesterol 0.62mg <1%, Sodium 582.12mg 24%, Potassium 417.22mg 12%, Total Carbohydrates 81.5g 27%, Fiber 4.19g 17%, Sugar 1.9g, Protein 11g 22%*

Dinner: Cauliflower Steaks

 Ready in:
30 Minutes

 Serves:
4

Ingredients

- ¼ Teaspoon Black Pepper
- ½ Teaspoon Sea Salt, Fine
- 1 Tablespoon Olive Oil
- 1 Head Cauliflower, Large
- ¼ Cup Creamy Hummus
- 2 Tablespoons Lemon Sauce
- ½ Cup Peanuts, Crushed (Optional)

Directions

1. Start by heating your oven to 425.
2. Cut your cauliflower stems, and then remove the leaves. Put the cut side down, and then slice half down the middle. Cut into ¾ inch steaks. If you cut them thinner, they could fall apart.
3. Arrange them in a single layer on a baking sheet, drizzling with oil. Season with salt and pepper, and bake for twenty to twenty-five minutes. They should be lightly browned and tender.
4. Spread your hummus on the steaks, drizzling with your lemon sauce. Top with peanuts if you're using it.

Nutritions: *Calories: 167, Protein: 6 Grams, Fat: 13 Grams, Carbs: 10 Grams*

Wednesday

Breakfast: Potato Pancakes

Preparation:
5 Minutes

Cooking:
40 Minutes

Serves:
4

Ingredients

- Olive Oil (2 t.)
- Potatoes (2)
- Salt (to Taste)

Directions

1. These pancakes are simple and to make and delicious to enjoy! You will want to start off by peeling your potatoes and then grate them into a mixing bowl. Once in the mixing bowl, be sure to use a paper towel to squeeze out any excess moisture.
2. Next, you will want to warm a skillet over middle heat. Once warm, insert in the olive oil and then place a patty of your mixture down. You'll want to cook the pancake on each side for about seven or eight minutes. By the end of this time, the pancake should be browned and crispy.
3. Finally, season with pepper and salt, and your pancakes are set.

Nutritions: *Calories: 150, Carbs: 30g, Fats: 3g, Proteins: 5g*

Lunch:
Pasta Salad with Marinated Artichoke Hearts and Tofu

Ready in:
20 Minutes

Serves:
4

Ingredients

- 1 lb medium pasta shape, uncooked
- 1 can (15 oz) marinated artichoke hearts, drained, chopped
- 1 cup Tofu firm cut into small cubes
- 1 cup fresh mushrooms, sliced
- 1/2 cup onion finely diced
- 1/3 cup chopped fresh basil
- Salt and freshly ground black pepper to taste
- 2/3 cup vegan salad dressing

Directions

1. Prepare pasta according to package directions.
2. In a large salad bowl, combine artichoke hearts, Tofu, mushrooms, onion, basil, and the salt and pepper.
3. Rinse pasta with cold water, and drain well.
4. Add pasta and vegan dressing to a salad bowl; toss well.
5. Taste and adjust salt and pepper to taste.
6. Serve or keep refrigerated.

Nutritions: *Calories 587.57, Calories From Fat (15%) 90.63, Total Fat 10.39g 16%, Saturated Fat 1.59g 8%, Cholesterol 0mg 0%, Sodium 405mg 17%, Potassium 557mg 16%, Total Carbohydrates 101.69g 34%, Fiber 10.91g 44%, Sugar 3.78g, Protein 22.28g 45%*

Ready in:
30 Minutes

Serves:
4

Ingredients

- ¾ Cup Scallions, Sliced Thin
- 1 ½ Tablespoon Mirin
- ¼ Cup Tamari
- 1 ½ Tablespoon Dark Sesame Oil, Toasted
- 1 Tablespoon Sesame Seeds, Toasted (Optional)
- 2 Teaspoons Ginger, fresh & Grated
- ½ Teaspoon Red Pepper, crushed
- 12 Ounces Extra Firm Tofu, Drained & Cut into ½ Inch Pieces
- 4 Cups Zucchini Noodles
- 2 Tablespoons Rice Vinegar
- 2 Cups Carrots, Shredded
- 2 Cups Pea Shoots
- ¼ Cup Basil, Fresh & Chopped
- ¼ Cup Peanuts, Toasted & Chopped (Optional)

Directions

1. Wisk your tamari, mirin, sesame seeds, oil, ginger, red pepper, and scallion greens in a bowl. Set two tablespoons of this sauce aside, and add the tofu to the remaining sauce. Toss to coat.
2. Combine your vinegar and zucchini noodles in a bowl.
3. Divide it between four bowls, topping with tofu, carrots, and a tablespoon of basil and peanuts.
4. Drizzle with sauce before serving.

Nutritions: *Calories: 262, Protein: 16 Grams, Fat: 15 Grams, Carbs: 19 Grams*

Thursday

Breakfast: Soft Granola Bars

 Preparation:
10 Minutes

 Cooking:
30 Minutes

 Serves:
6

Ingredients

- Medjool Dates (3/4 C.)
- Salt (to taste)
- Cinnamon (1 t.)
- Vanilla (1 t.)
- Chia Seeds (1/2 C.)
- Pumpkin Seeds (1/4 C.)
- Sunflower Seeds (1/4 C.)
- Water (1 C.)
- Rolled Oats (3/4 C.)

Directions

1. Before you begin prepping this recipe, save yourself some time by prepping the stove to 325 and lining a cooking pane with parchment paper.
2. To start your granola bars, you will first need to take out your blender and blend the rolled oats until you form a flour. When you have this, place it into a separate bowl.
3. Next, you are going to want to add the dates and water to your blender. If possible, allow for the dates to soak about thirty minutes. This will help the blending process so you can a smooth texture once blended.
4. Next, you are going to combine all of your ingredients in the mixing bowl and stir until the seeds are spread out evenly.
5. When you are ready, place the mixture onto your baking sheet and then pop it into the oven for twenty-five minutes. By the end of this time, the bar should be firm. If it is, eliminate the dish from the stove and permit to cool off for about ten minutes before slicing and serving.

Nutritions: *Calories: 250, Carbs: 30g, Fats: 10g, Proteins: 6g*

Ready in:
10 Minutes

Serves:
2

Directions

1. Combine ingredients (except coconut milk and mint) in a blender.
2. Blend on high until smooth.
3. Pour in coconut milk, and blend again until combined well.
4. Pour into bowls, sprinkle with fresh mint and serve.
5. Keep refrigerated.

Ingredients

- 4 Tbsp sesame oil
- 1/4 cup coconut aminos or soy sauce
- 1 Tbsp curry powder
- 1/4 cup fresh lime juice
- 1/2 cup of tomato sauce
- 2 Tbsp grated ginger
- 2 cloves of garlic
- Salt, to taste
- 1 cup of canned mushrooms
- 3 cups coconut milk canned
- 2 Tbsp fresh chopped mint, to garnish

Nutritions: *Calories 649.42, Calories From Fat (85%) 550.12, Total Fat 64.2g 99%, Saturated Fat 36g 180%, Cholesterol 0mg 0%, Sodium 1361mg 48%, Potassium 934.65mg 27%, Total Carbohydrates 18.3g 6%, Fiber 3.16g 13%, Sugar 4.9g, Protein 10.39g 21%*

Dinner: Ratatouille

Ready in:
1 h 15 Minutes

Serves:
10

Ingredients

- 2 Tablespoons Olive Oil
- 2 Eggplants, Peeled & Cubed
- 8 Zucchini, Chopped
- 4 Tomatoes, Chopped
- ¼ Cup Basil, Chopped
- 4 Thyme Sprigs
- 2 Yellow Onions, Diced
- 3 Cloves Garlic, Minced
- 3 Bell Peppers, Chopped
- 1 Bay Leaf
- Sea Salt to Taste

Directions

1. Salt your eggplant and leave it in a strainer.
2. Heat a teaspoon of oil in a Dutch oven, cooking your onions for ten minutes. Season with salt.
3. Mix your peppers in, cooking for five more minutes.
4. Place this mixture in a bowl.
5. Heat your oil and sauté zucchini, sprinkling with salt. Cook for five minutes, and place it in the same bowl.
6. Rinse your eggplant, squeezing the water out, and heat another two teaspoons of oil in your Dutch oven. Cook your eggplant for ten minutes, placing it in your vegetable bowl.
7. Heat the remaining oil and cook your garlic. Add in your tomatoes, thyme sprigs and bay leaves to deglaze the bottom.
8. Toss your vegetables back in, and then bring it to a simmer.
9. Simmer for forty-five minutes, and make sure to stir. Discard your thyme and bay leaf. Mix in your basil and serve warm.

Nutritions: *Calories: 90, Protein: 3 Grams, Fat: 25 Grams, Carbs: 13 Grams*

Friday

Breakfast: Build Your Own Oatmeal Square

 Preparation:
5 Minutes

 Cooking:
20 Minutes

 Serves:
4

Ingredients

- Water (4 C.)
- Old-fashioned Oats (2 C.)

Directions

1. This recipe is for the base of your breakfast! By building the oatmeal squares, you can top; however, you desire! To start off, you are going to boil your water and add in the oats.
2. Once the oats are in the water, reduce the heat and cook for about five minutes without a cover and then place the lid and cook for another five minutes.
3. Now that the oatmeal is set take out a baking dish and pour it in. Throw a cover over the top and position in the fridge for the night.
4. The following morning, you will have oatmeal squares to cut up and enjoy your own way.

Nutritions: *Calories: 250, Carbs: 44g, Fats: 5g, Proteins: 10g*

Lunch:
Slow-Cooked Navy Bean Soup

Ready in:
8 h

Serves:
8

Directions

1. Soak beans overnight.
2. Rinse beans and add in your 6 Quart Slow Cooker.
3. Add all remaining ingredients and stir well.
4. Cover and cook on LOW for 8 hours.
5. Adjust the salt and pepper to taste.
6. Serve hot.

Ingredients

- 1 lb dry navy beans, soaked, rinsed
- 4 Tbsp olive oil
- 1/4 cup onion finely diced
- 2 cloves garlic finely chopped
- 2 carrots sliced
- 1/2 cup tomato sauce (canned)
- 1 tsp mustard
- 1/2 tsp curry powder
- 6 cups of water
- Salt and ground black pepper to taste

Nutritions: *Calories 191.2, Calories From Fat (4%) 7.6, Total Fat 0.91g 1%, Saturated Fat 0.11g <1%, Cholesterol 0mg 0%, Sodium 146.67mg 6%, Potassium 746.42mg 21%, Total Carbohydrates 35.18g 12%, Fiber 13.64g 55%, Sugar 3.85g, Protein 12.15g 24%*

Ready in:
2 h 25 minutes

Serves:
6

Ingredients

- 2 Tablespoons + 1 Teaspoon Red Wine Vinegar, Divided
- ½ Teaspoon Pepper
- 1 Teaspoon Sea Salt
- 1 Avocado,
- ¼ Cup Basil, Fresh & Chopped
- 3 Tablespoons + 2 Teaspoons Olive Oil, Divided
- 1 Clove Garlic, crushed
- 1 Red Bell Pepper, Sliced & Seeded
- 1 Cucumber, Chunked
- 2 ½ lbs. Large Tomatoes, Cored & Chopped

Directions

1. Place half of your cucumber, bell pepper, and ¼ cup of each tomatoes in a bowl, covering. Set it in the fried.
2. Puree your remaining tomatoes, cucumber and bell pepper with garlic, three tablespoons oil, two tablespoons of vinegar, sea salt and black pepper into a blender, blending until smooth. Transfer it to a bowl, and chill for two hours.
3. Chop the avocado, adding it to your chopped vegetables, adding your remaining oil, vinegar, salt, pepper and basil.
4. Ladle your tomato puree mixture into bowls, and serve with chopped vegetables as a salad.

Nutritions: *Calories: 181, Protein: 3 Grams, Fat: 14 Grams, Carbs: 14 Grams*

Saturday

Breakfast: Spiced Breakfast Potatoes

 Preparation:
5 Minutes

 Cooking:
25 Minutes

 Serves:
4

Ingredients

- Olive Oil (2 T.)
- Potatoes (1 Lb., Diced)
- Pepper (to taste)
- Garlic Powder (1/2 t.)
- Salt (to taste)
- Paprika (1/2 t.)

Directions

1. Potatoes are nice comfort food to have on hand, especially in the morning. Before you begin making up the potatoes, you will want to prep the oven to 400.
2. Now, dice up the potatoes to bite-sized fragments and set them into a mixing bowl. Once in place, coat the potatoes with olive oil and season to your liking. When they are set, you can place them onto a baking dish and pop them into the oven for thirty minutes.
3. By the end of this time, the potatoes should be golden and set to serve.

Nutritions: *Calories: 150, Carbs: 20g, Fats: 6g, Proteins: 3g*

Ready in:
40 minutes

Serves:
6

Directions

1. Heat oil in a large pot over medium-high heat.
2. Add artichokes and sauté for 5 minutes.
3. Add carrots and sprinkle with a pinch of the salt and pepper.
4. Sauté and stir for 2 to 3 minutes.
5. Add rice and stir for one minute.
6. Pour water, and add dill and parsley; stir.
7. Bring to a boil and reduce heat to simmer.
8. Cover and cook for 25 minutes.
9. Taste and adjust seasonings.
10. Pour apple cider vinegar and stir.
11. Serve hot.

Ingredients

- 1 cup of olive oil
- 10 canned artichoke hearts, chopped
- 2 carrots cut into thin slices
- 1 cup of long-grain rice
- 3 cups vegetable broth
- 2 Tbsp of fresh parsley finely chopped
- 2 Tbsp fresh dill finely chopped
- 2 Tbsp apple cider vinegar (optional)
- Salt and ground pepper to taste

Nutritions: *Calories 445.53, Calories From Fat (40%) 180.14, Total Fat 20.41g 31%, Saturated Fat 3g 15%, Cholesterol 1.23mg <1%, Sodium 1025.47mg 43%, Potassium 854.8mg 24%, Total Carbohydrates 58.7g 20%, Fiber 10.55g 42%, Sugar 1.31g, Protein 11g 22%*

Dinner: Simple Chili

Ready in:
30 Minutes

Serves:
4

Ingredients

- 1 Onion, Diced
- 1 Teaspoon Olive Oil
- 3 Cloves Garlic, Minced
- 28 Ounces Tomatoes, Canned
- ¼ Cup Tomato Paste
- 14 Ounces Kidney Beans, Canned, Rinsed & Dried
- 2-3 Teaspoons Chili Powder
- ¼ Cup Cilantro, Fresh (or Parsley)
- ¼ Teaspoon Sea Salt, Fine

Directions

1. Get out a pot, and sauté your onion and garlic in your oil at the bottom cook for five minutes. Add in your tomato paste, tomatoes, beans, and chili powder. Season with salt.
2. Allow it to simmer for ten to twenty minutes.
3. Garnish with cilantro or parsley to serve.

Nutritions: *Calories: 160, Protein: 8 Grams, Fat: 3 Grams, Carbs: 29 Grams*

VEGAN COOKBOOK FOR ATHLETES

Sunday

Breakfast: Breakfast Energy Balls

 Preparation:
2 Minutes

 Cooking:
20 Minutes

 Serves:
16

Ingredients

- Rolled Oats (1/2 C.)
- Apple (1/2)
- Almonds (1/2 C.)
- Dates (12)
- Cacao Powder (1/4 C.)
- Almond Extract (2 t.)
- Sunflower Seeds (1/2 C.)
- Flax Seed (1 T.)

Directions

1. The morning can be an extremely busy time. If this sounds like you, this recipe is perfect to prep for the whole week. That way, you just grab a couple of energy balls, and you are out the door with breakfast in hand.
2. If you have time, soak the dates for about twenty minutes before starting the recipe.
3. When the dates are set, place all of the ingredients from the list into your blender and blend on high for about thirty seconds. By the end, you should have a slightly sticky dough.
4. Next, you will want to portion the mixture out about one tablespoon per ball and place onto a plate.
5. For extra flavor and variety, roll the balls in cacao powder, crushed nuts, or crushed seeds. When they are set, place them in the fridge and allow to harden for at least thirty minutes before enjoying!

Nutritions: *Calories: 70, Carbs: 5g, Fats: 5g, Proteins: 3g*

Lunch:
Spring Greens and Rice Stew

 Ready in:
35 miutes

 Serves:
4

Ingredients

- ► 1/3 cup of olive oil
- ► 2 cups lettuce salad, chopped
- ► 2 cups dandelion leaves chopped
- ► 1 cup rice short grain
- ► 3 cups vegetable broth
- ► 1 tsp fresh basil finely chopped
- ► 2 Tbsp fresh dill chopped
- ► Table salt and ground black pepper to taste

Directions

1. Heat oil in a large pot over medium-high heat.
2. Sauté lettuce and dandelion leaves for about 4 to 5 minutes.
3. Add rice, cook for one minute; pour rice, and stir.
4. Add in basil, dill, and the salt and ground pepper.
5. Reduce heat to medium-low, cover and cook for about 40 minutes or until all liquid has been absorbed
6. Taste, adjust seasoning, and serve.

Nutritions: *Calories 470.95, Calories From Fat (42%) 199.52, Total Fat 22.66g 35%, Saturated Fat 3.2g 16%, Cholesterol 1.85mg <1%, Sodium 1246.8mg 52%, Potassium 499mg 14%, Total Carbohydrates 63.81g 21%, Fiber 7g 28%, Sugar 0.2g, Protein 9g 18%*

Ready in:
20 minutes

Serves:
4

Directions

1. Get out a bowl and combine your cauliflower rice, tomatoes, mint, parsley, cucumbers, scallions and snap peas together. Toss until combined.
2. Add your olive oil and lemon juice before tossing again. Season with salt and pepper.

Ingredients

- 4 Cups Cauliflower Rice
- 1 ½ Cups Cherry Tomatoes, Quartered
- 3-4 Tablespoons Olive Oil
- 1 Cup Parsley, Fresh & Chopped
- 1 Cup Mint, Fresh & Chopped
- 1 Cup Snap Peas, Sliced Thin
- 1 Small Cucumber, Cut into ¼ Inch Pieces
- ¼ Cup Scallions, Sliced Thin
- 3-4 Tablespoons Lemon Juice, Fresh
- 1 Teaspoon Sea Salt, Fine
- ½ Teaspoon Black Pepper

Nutritions: *Calories: 220, Protein: 7 Grams, Fat: 15 Grams, Carbs: 20 Grams*

Week 3
Monday

Breakfast: Pumpkin Porridge

 Preparation:
5 Minutes

 Cooking:
50 Minutes

 Serves:
2

Ingredients

- Pumpkin Puree (1/2 C.)
- Soaked Quinoa (1 C.)
- Maple Syrup (4 T.)
- Ground Ginger (1/2 t.)
- Ground Cinnamon (1 t.)
- Ground Cloves (1/8 t.)

Directions

1. Before you begin, it is vital that you soak the quinoa for at least an hour. Once the quinoa is done, you will want to drain any excess water before placing it into a pan over moderate heat on the stove.
2. When this is done, add in .75 cup of water and get everything to a boil. Once the pot is bubbling, reduce the high temperature and allow the quinoa to simmer for about fifteen minutes. At the end of this time, all of the liquid should be gone and absorbed.
3. Once the quinoa is cooked properly, you can then add in the pumpkin, maple syrup, and all of the seasonings. At this point, feel open to insert more or less seasoning to your liking!

Nutritions: *Calories: 430, Carbs: 80g, Fats: 5g, Proteins: 10g*

Ready in:
30 minutes

Serves:
4

Ingredients

► 2 Tablespoons Olive Oil
► 4 Cloves Garlic, Minced
► 8 Ounces Whole Wheat Pasta
► ½ Cup Panko Bread Crumbs
► 1 Tablespoon Nutritional Yeast
► 1 Teaspoon Red Pepper Flakes
► 1 Large Lemon, Juiced & Zested
► 1 Bunch Collard Greens, Large

Directions

1. Fill a pot with water and salt it. Bring it to a boil using high heat. Add in the pasta and cool al dente before rinsing under cold water to stop the cooking.
2. Reserve half a cup of the cooking liquid from the pasta and set it to the side.
3. Place it over medium heat and add in a tablespoon of olive oil. Stir in half of your garlic, sautéing for a half a minute.
4. Add in the breadcrumbs and then sauté, cooking for five more minutes.
5. Toss in the red pepper flakes and nutritional yeast, mixing well.
6. Transfer the breadcrumbs in the pan.
7. Add the remaining olive oil and then stir in your salt, pepper, garlic clove, and greens.
8. Cook for five minutes. Cook until wilted.
9. Add in the pasta, mix in the reserved pasta liquid, and then mix well. Add in the lemon juice, zest, and garlic crumbs. Toss before serving.

Dinner:
Dijon Maple Burgers

Ready in:
50 minutes

Serves:
12

Ingredients

- 1 Red Bell Pepper
- 19 Ounces Can Chickpeas, Rinsed & Drained
- 1 Cup Almonds, Ground
- 2 Teaspoons Dijon Mustard
- 1 Teaspoon Oregano
- ½ Teaspoon Sage
- 1 Cup Spinach, Fresh
- 1 – ½ Cups Rolled Oats
- 1 Clove Garlic, Pressed
- ½ Lemon, Juiced
- 2 Teaspoons Maple Syrup, Pure

Directions

1. Start by heating your oven to 350, and then get out a baking sheet. Line it with parchment paper.
2. Cut your red pepper in half and then take the seeds out. Place it on your baking sheet, and roast in the oven while you prepare your other ingredients.
3. Process your chickpeas, almonds, mustard and maple syrup together in a food processor.
4. Add in your lemon juice, oregano, sage, garlic and spinach, processing again. Make sure it's combined, but don't puree it.
5. Once your red bell pepper is softened, which should roughly take ten minutes, add this to the processor as well. Add in your oats, mixing well.
6. Form twelve patties, cooking in the oven for a half hour. They should be browned.

Nutritions: *Calories: 200, Protein: 8 Grams, Fat: 11 Grams, Carbs: 21 Grams*

Tuesday

Breakfast: Easy PBB Breakfast Cookies

 Preparation:
2 Minutes

 Cooking:
10 Minutes

 Serves:
2

Ingredients

- Rolled Oats (1 C.)
- Peanut Butter (1/4 C.)
- Bananas (2)

Directions

1. Who said cookies were inappropriate for breakfast? These simple peanut butter and banana cookies are a much healthier option and will be set to go when you need a quick breakfast. Start off by prepping the oven to 350.
2. Next, take out a mixing bowl and combine your oats, peanut butter, and some mashed bananas.
3. Now that you have your mixture done take out a baking sheet and lay down some parchment paper. With this in place, you can now roll the mixture into 12 small cookies and lay them evenly across the baking sheet.
4. Finally, pop the dish into the oven for 12 minutes, and your cookies should come out golden-brown and delicious!

Nutritions: *Calories: 250, Carbs: 40g, Fats: 11g, Proteins: 10g*

Lunch: Plant Pad Thai

Ready in:
20 Minutes

Serves:
4

Ingredients

- 2 Teaspoons Coconut Oil
- 1 Red Pepper, Sliced
- 2 Carrots, Sliced
- ½ White Onion, Sliced
- 1 Thai Chili, Chopped
- 8 Ounces Brown Rice Noodles
- ½ Cup Peanuts, Chopped
- ½ Cup Cilantro, Chopped

Sauce:
- 3 Tablespoons Soy Sauce
- 3 Tablespoons Lime Juice, Fresh
- 3 Tablespoons Brown Sugar
- 1 Tablespoon Sriracha
- 3 Tablespoons Vegetable Broth
- 1 Teaspoon Chili Garlic Paste
- 2 Cloves Garlic, Minced

Tofu:
- 1 lb. Extra Firm Tofu, Sliced
- 1 Tablespoon Peanut Butter
- 2 Tablespoons Sriracha
- 3 Tablespoons Soy Sauce
- 2 Tablespoons Rice Vinegar
- 2 Teaspoons Sesame Oil
- 2 Teaspoons Ginger, Grated

Directions

1. Get out a large pot of water and soak the rice noodles in it. Press your tofu to get out the excess liquid. Get out a nonstick pan and heat it over medium-high heat. Add in the tofu, searing for three minutes per side.
2. Whisk all ingredients for the tofu in a bowl, stirring in the tofu, and mixing well to marinate.
3. Separately mix your Thai sauce in a bowl, adding the tofu in.
4. Get a wok and put it over medium heat, adding in a teaspoon of oil.
5. Toss in the carrots, onion, red pepper, and chili. Cook for three minutes.
6. Transfer the vegetables to the tofu bowl and add in more oil. Stir the drained noodles in, and then cook for an additional minute.
7. Transfer the noodles to your tofu, and toss before serving warm. Garnish with cilantro and peanuts.

Ready in:
40 Minutes

Serves:
1

Directions

1. Steam your edamame beans, and then assemble your edamame, rice, avocado, spinach, cilantro, scallions and bell pepper into a bowl.
2. Cut the nori into ribbons, sprinkling it on top, drizzling with tamari and sesame seeds before serving.

Ingredients

- ½ Cup Edamame Beans, Shelled & Fresh
- ¾ Cup Brown Rice, Cooked
- ½ Cup Spinach, Chopped
- ¼ Cup Bell Pepper, Sliced
- ¼ Cup Avocado, Sliced
- ¼ Cup Cilantro, Fresh & Chopped
- 1 Scallion, Chopped
- ¼ Nori Sheet
- 1-2 Tablespoons Tamari
- 1 Tablespoon Sesame Seeds, Optional

Nutritions: *Calories: 467, Protein: 22 Grams, Fat: 20 Grams, Carbs: 56 Grams*

Wednesday

Breakfast: Oatmeal and Berry Smoothie Bowl

 Preparation:
1 Minutes

 Cooking:
5 Minutes

 Serves:
2

Ingredients

- Almond Milk (1/4 C.)
- Frozen Mixed Berries (1 C.)
- Frozen Acai (1 C.)
- Peanut Butter (1 T.)
- Old-Fashioned Oats (1/4 C.)

Directions

1. This recipe is meant for when you have more time on your hands to make a pretty dish. You will want to start out by placing the nut butter, oats, and fruits into your blender.
2. Once everything is blended smooth, go ahead and pour it into a bowl.
3. At this point, you can top your smoothie bowl however you would like! You can use fresh berries, slices of banana, more oats, or even treat yourself with some shredded coconut! The options are limitless.

Nutritions: *Calories: 300, Carbs: 58g, Fats: 8g, Proteins: 10g*

Ready in:
40 Minutes

Serves:
4

Directions

1. Rinse your quinoa and then throw it in a saucepan over medium heat. Cook for five minutes before adding the water.
2. Bring it to a boil before reducing your pot to a simmer. Cover and cook for thirteen minutes.
3. Toss all remaining ingredients into a salad bowl and mix with quinoa. Serve fresh.

Ingredients

- 1 Cup Dry Quinoa
- 1 ½ Cups Water
- ½ cup Cranberries, Dried
- 4 Tablespoon Cilantro, Fresh & Chopped
- 1 Lime, Juiced
- 1 ½ Teaspoon Curry Powder
- 1/8 Teaspoon Cumin
- ¼ Cup Green Onion, Chopped
- ½ Cup Bell Pepper, Diced
- 1/3 Cup Toasted Almonds, Sliced
- ½ Carrots, Shredded
- 4 Tablespoons Pepitas
- Sea Salt & Black Pepper to Taste
- Olive Oil for Drizzling
- Lime Wedges to Garnish

Dinner: Pesto & Tomato Quinoa

Ready in:
25 Minutes

Serves:
1

Ingredients

- ▶ 1 Teaspoon Olive Oil
- ▶ 1 Cup Onion, Chopped
- ▶ 1 Cup Zucchini, Chopped
- ▶ 1 Clove Garlic, Minced
- ▶ 1 Tomato, Chopped
- ▶ Pinch Sea Salt
- ▶ 2 Tablespoons Sun Dried Tomatoes, Chopped
- ▶ 2-3 Tablespoons Basil Pesto
- ▶ 1 Cup Spinach, Chopped
- ▶ 2 Cups Quinoa, Cooked
- ▶ 1 Tablespoon Nutritional Yeast, Optional

Directions

1. Heat your oil in a skillet, and sauté your onion over medium-high heat. This should take five minutes, and then add in your garlic, cooking for another minute. Add in your sea salt and zucchini.
2. Cook for about five-minute and then add in your sun dried tomatoes, and mix well.
3. Toss your pesto in, and then mix well.
4. Layer your spinach, quinoa and then zucchini mixture on a plate, topping with nutritional yeast if desired.

Nutritions: *Protein: 20 Grams, Fat: 23 Grams, Carbs: 69 Grams*

Thursday

Breakfast: Classic Green Morning Smoothie

Preparation:
2 Minutes

Cooking:
5 Minutes

Serves:
1

Ingredients

- Almond Milk (1 C.)
- Kale (1 C.)
- Banana (1)
- Poppy Seeds (2 t.)
- Peanut Butter (2 T.)

Directions

1. This is the smoothie everyone turns their nose up to, but it is packed with flavor and nutrients! Simply place everything into your blender with ice, blend on high for thirty seconds or so, then you are all set to go.

Nutritions: *Calories: 350, Carbs: 40g, Fats: 20g, Proteins: 20g*

Lunch: Eggplant Pasta

Ready in:
30 Minutes

Serves:
4

Ingredients

- 12 Ounces Dry Pasta
- 2 Cups Cremini Mushrooms, Sliced
- ½ Eggplant, Small & Cubed
- 1 ½ Cups Marinara Sauce, Preferably Vegan
- 2 Cups Water
- Sea Salt & Black Pepper to Taste
- 3 Tablespoons Olive Oil
- Basil, Fresh to Garnish

Directions

1. Put your eggplant in a colander before sprinkling with salt. They will drain as it rests for half an hour. Rinse thoroughly after the thirty-minute mark.
2. Put a saucepan over medium-high heat with your eggplant, olive oil, ½ teaspoon of salt, and a third of your minced garlic. Stir and then cook for an additional six minutes. It should be golden brown and then add n the mushrooms. Sauté for two minutes before putting it in a bowl.
3. Cook your pasta according to package instructions and drain. Add in the marinara sauce and garlic into the saucepan with your pasta. Season with salt and pepper as necessary.
4. Toss in the eggplant and garnish with basil.

Ready in:
13 minutes

Serves:
4

Directions

1. Cut the stems and tops of your bok choy into one inch pieces.
2. Mix together all remaining ingredients in a bowl.
3. Add your bok choy, and top with your dressing.
4. Fry until tender, which should take eight to ten minutes.

Ingredients

- 1 Head Bok Choy
- 1 Teaspoon Canola Oil
- 1/3 Cup Green Onion, Chopped
- 1 Tablespoon Brown Sugar
- 1 ½ Tablespoon Soy Sauce, Light
- 1 Tablespoon Rice Wine
- ½ Teaspoon Ginger, Ground
- 1 Tablespoon Sesame Seeds

Nutritions: *Calories: 76, Protein: 4.4 Grams, Fat: 2.7 Grams, Carbs: 9.8 Grams*

Friday

Breakfast: Zoom Energy Smoothie

 Preparation:
2 Minutes

 Cooking:
5 Minutes

 Serves:
2

Ingredients

- Almond Milk (1 C.)
- Banana (1)
- Orange (1)
- Pineapple (1 C.)
- Raspberries (1 C.)

Directions

1. This is another delicious recipe, meant to give you a pep in your step through the power of fruit! Easily set all of the items into your blender with ice, combine on high, and go!

Nutritions: *Calories: 120, Carbs: 25g, Fats: 2g, Proteins: 4g*

Ready in:
25 Minutes

Serves:
6

Ingredients

- 2 Celery Stalks, Diced
- ¼ Teaspoon Thyme
- 1 Carrot, Peeled & Diced
- 2 Broccoli Heads, Chopped
- 2 Bay Leaves
- 1 Can Cannellini Beans
- 4 Cups Vegetable Broth
- 2 Cups Water
- 2 Tablespoons Nutritional Yeast
- 1 Packet Vegetable Powder

Directions

1. Get out a pot and add the carrot, celery, and thyme.
2. Cover and cook for five minutes using medium heat.
3. Pour in a dash of water, then take it off of the heat. Chop the florets and stalks again after peeling. Add the stock, water, bay leaf, beans, broccoli to your carrot mixture.
4. Cover the soup, and bring it all to a boil.
5. Allow it to simmer for ten minutes, and then discard the bay leaf before taking it off of the heat.
6. Stir in the vegetable powder and nutritional powder. Blend using an immersion blender before serving.

Saturday

Breakfast: Sweet Strawberry and Mango Smoothie

 Preparation:
1 Minutes

 Cooking:
5 Minutes

 Serves:
1

Directions

1. A smoothie is a perfect way to start the morning, especially if you are in a rush! Simply put all of the components into your mixer, add a desired amount of ice, and blend on high until everything is smooth.
2. Pour and go!

Ingredients

- Almond Milk (6 T.)
- Strawberries (4)
- Mango (1)
- Blueberries (1 C.)
- Banana (2)

Nutritions: *Calories: 440, Carbs: 100g, Fats: 2g, Proteins: 8g*

Ready in:
40 Minutes

Serves:
6

Ingredients

- 1 Tablespoon Oregano
- 1 Tablespoon Basil
- 6 Cloves Garlic, Minced
- 1 Sweet Onion, Chopped
- ¼ Cup Olive Oil
- 2 Teaspoons Turmeric
- Salt & Pepper to Taste
- 28 Ounces Fire Roasted Tomatoes
- ½ Cup Sundried Tomatoes, Oil Packed & Chopped
- 8 Ounces Red Lentil Pasta
- 1 Tablespoon Apple Cider Vinegar
- 2 Handfuls Baby Spinach, Large

Directions

1. Get out a large pot and heat the oil over medium heat. Add your onion and cook for ten minutes.
2. Stir in the turmeric, oregano, salt, pepper, basil, and garlic, cooking for another minute. Add in the tomatoes with the juices, sundried tomatoes, and vinegar. Cook for fifteen minutes, and then use an immersion blender. Toss the spinach into your sauce, and cook for another five minutes. Boil your pasta according to the box, and serve with the spinach mixture and garnish as desired.

Dinner: Stuffed Bell Pepper

 Ready in:
25 Minutes

 Serves:
4

Directions

1. Bake your peppers at 400 for ten minutes, and then mix the rest of your ingredients in a bowl.
2. Stuff your peppers with the quinoa mixture.

Ingredients

- 4 Bell Peppers, Halved & Hollowed
- ½ Cup Quinoa, Cooked
- 12 Black Olives, Halved
- 1/3 Cup Tomatoes, Sun Dried
- ½ Cup Baby Spinach
- 2 Cloves Garlic, Minced
- Sea Salt & Black Pepper to Taste

Nutritions: *Calories: 126, Protein: 3 Grams, Fat: 5 Grams, Carbs: 19 Grams*

Sunday

Breakfast: Chia and Peanut Butter Oatmeal

Preparation:
5 Minutes

Cooking:
10 Minutes

Serves:
2

Ingredients

- Water (3 C.)
- Rolled Oats (1 C.)
- Chia Seeds (1 T.)
- Salt (1/8 t.)
- Peanut Butter (2 T.)
- Cinnamon (1 t.)
- Banana (1)

Directions

1. Oatmeal is an excellent way to start the day, especially when it involves peanut butter! You will want to begin this recipe by taking out a pot and placing it over medium heat. As it warms up, you can add in the sliced-up banana, oats, chia seeds, salt, and the cinnamon. When these items are in place, carefully pour in the water and stir everything up well.
2. You will want to cook these ingredients for about ten minutes or until all of the liquid is gone. As this cooks, be sure to whisk the pot to avoid anything smoldering to the underside of the pot.
3. When everything is cooked, portion out your oatmeal and serve with sliced banana and peanut butter on top.

Nutritions: *Calories: 370, Carbs: 70g, Fats: 15g, Proteins: 15g*

Lunch:
White Wine Pasta

Ready in:
30 Minutes

Serves:
4

Ingredients

Brussels:
- 16 Ounce Brussels Sprouts, Halved
- 2 Tablespoons Olive Oil
- Sea Salt & Black Pepper to Taste

Pasta:
- 4 Cloves Garlic, Chopped
- 3 Tablespoons Olive Oil
- 1/3 Cup Dry White Wine
- 4 Tablespoons Arrowroot Starch
- 1 ¾ Cup Almond Milk
- 4 Tablespoons Nutritional Yeast
- Sea Salt & Black Pepper to Taste
- 10 Ounces Vegan Pasta
- ¼ Cup Parmesan Cheese

Serving:
- Simple Greens
- Garlic Bread

Directions

1. Heat the oven to 400, and then get a baking tray out. Spread the sprouts out, and then add the oil. Season with salt and pepper before tossing.
2. Boil the pasta al dente and then drain.
3. Heat a skillet using medium heat. Add the oil. Once it shimmers, add the garlic. Cook for an additional three minutes.
4. Stir the wine in to deglaze and then cook for an additional two minutes.
5. Whisk the almond milk and arrowroot powder, and then blend with the cheese in a food processor. Season with salt and pepper if desired.
6. Het the almond milk sauce in your skillet until it bubbles. Bake your sprouts for fifteen minutes, and then toss in the drained pasta, cheese sauce and sprouts together in a bowl before serving.

Dinner: Cabbage & Beet Stew

Ready in:
30 minutes

Serves:
4

Directions

1. Start by heating up your oil in a pot, and then sauté your vegetables.
2. Pour your broth in, mixing in your seasoning. Simmer until it's cooked through, and then top with dill.

Ingredients

- 2 Tablespoons Olive Oil
- 3 Cups Vegetable Broth
- 2 Tablespoons Lemon Juice, Fresh
- ½ Teaspoon Garlic Powder
- ½ Cup Carrots, Shredded
- 2 Cups Cabbage, Shredded
- 1 Cup Beets, Shredded
- Dill for Garnish
- ½ Teaspoon Onion Powder
- Sea Salt & Black Pepper to Taste

Nutritions: Calories: 95, Protein: 1 Gram, Fat: 7 Grams, Carbs: 10 Grams

Conclusion

Plants are a good source of all nutrients and minerals. They have low cholesterol, good lipids, and antioxidant characteristics which help to detoxify the body from pollutants. A plant-based diet has a significant impact on health, skin, and the environment. Plant-based diet improves and provides shine to the skin. This book is a complete guide for beginners who intend to reduce weight, strengthen muscles and bones, and health-related problems such as heart diseases, obesity, and metabolic syndromes.

PLANT BASED DIET PLAN

THE BEGINNER'S GUIDE FOR HEALTHY EATING TO WEIGHT LOSS. EASY COOKBOOK WITH QUICK RECIPES ON A BUDGET. HIGH PROTEIN MEAL PLAN AND KEEP FIT LIKE AN ATHLETE

Kevin Rinaldi

Table of Contents

Introduction

Choosing to live a plant based lifestyle is one of the most important decisions you will ever make. Plant-based diets contain lots of fresh vegetables and fruits, along with nuts, seeds, and whole-grains. There are massive amounts of food just waiting for you to discover them and how delicious they really can be. And you will be leaving behind all of the saturated fats and other toxic substances that are holding back your health now.

It really should not be thought of as a diet plan or a manner of eating because deciding to 'go vegan' will affect all the parts of your life. It will dictate what you buy at the grocery store, where you go to eat out, and may even dictate who you decide to hang out with in your private life. But this is a decision that you are making to benefit your life.

So, let us take a journey together. I shall be your food guide, taking you through some of the most incredible plant-based and vegan recipes.

Research also shows that plant-based eating is related to healthy weight management, lower mortality risk, and lower heart disease risk. It is also related to hypertension prevention and treatment, high cholesterol, and lower risk of certain cancers.

Chapter 1. Basics About the Plants Based Diet and Your Health

The plant is a good source of closely all the nutrients required by the human body. Plant based diets include fruits, vegetables, nuts, whole grain, and legumes. These are basically plant based foods and hole foods. With the realization of the various health benefits attributed to plant proteins, people have shifted from consuming animal foods to plant-based foods. Plant based diet includes all unprocessed plant foods. It excludes the consumption of processed foods such as pasta and sugars. It excludes processed fruit juices, milk and milk products, all forms of meat (white and red), and eggs.

Foods to keep off when on a plant-based diet are as follows;

Avoid eating processed foods such as pasta and canned foods. Instead, go for fresh and whole foods. Processed foods are low in their fiber content; they also have other additives such as sugar, salt, preservatives, excess oils, and fats. These foods are linked to the development of chronic illnesses such as cancer, diabetes, hypertension, kidney disease, and heart problems, among others. These foods are also a significant contributor to obesity and weight challenges.

Plant based diet excludes all animal products such as eggs, milk products, poultry, red meat, fish, and any other foods obtained from animals. Animal products are linked to the development of cancers in the human body, especially the heme iron contained in red meat. When animal products are cooked up to certain temperatures, they emit carcinogenic compounds that lead the development of cancer cells. These foods are also a major contributor to weight gain. Research has shown that it is rather a difficulty to watch weight while still on animal products. Animal related foods are also high in their fat contents and have zero fiber. Consumption of animal products leads to heart problems and hypertension as a result of clogged blood vessels. Their low fiber content makes it a cause of stomach problems such as indigestion and diarrhea.

Avoid the consumption of fast foods such as fries, burgers, cakes, ice cream, and pizza, among others. Fast foods have contents such as processed sugars and high sodium content, high fat content. These foods induce cravings in your body that lead to excessive eating and obesity. The foods are also very unhealthy as they contribute to increased risk of chronic illnesses such as cancer, hypertension, diabetes, heart problems, among others. Fast foods are also low in their nutrient content. Being addictive, when a person forms a habit of consuming fast foods, their bodies go low on some essential nutrients such as vitamins and minerals. They also contain additives that you do not want to put in your bodies due to their toxic nature.

Health benefits of plant diets

Plant foods offer a wide range of advantages over animal foods. They are scientifically recommended for healthy living as they promote a person's wellbeing. By eating plant-based foods, a person is able to reduce the risk of certain illnesses and avoid problems associated with overweight/obesity.

Plant foods are advantageous in their low fat and calorie load. They are also dense in their protein content. Proteins are excellent in helping a person watch weight as they prevent the gaining of body fat. By consuming plant proteins, a person produces more weight limiting hormones. Proteins also help in weight reduction by reducing the feelings of hunger while at the same time increasing the metabolic rate of the body.

By consuming plant products, a person reduces the risk of being overweight. Plants offer excellent sources of fiber, antioxidants, minerals, and vitamins. Plant foods are mainly high in fiber which is helpful in digestion as it limits the amount of sugars absorbed in the digestion process. The fiber in plant foods is also helpful in reducing cholesterol by preventing the absorption of fats in the foods we take. Fiber also helps in preventing constipation in enhancing the digestion of foods. It helps in the stimulation of the various digestive organs to produce important digestive juices. Enough intake of dietary fiber prolongs the amount of time food takes to move through the canal, increasing the absorption of minerals and vitamins in the food. It also prevents diarrhea and excessive hardening of stool.

Research has also confirmed that people who take foods high in fiber are at a lower risk of gaining weight. By consuming foods high in fiber, a person reduces the chances of developing type 2 diabetes. The reason behind the fiber preventing the occurrence of type 2 diabetes is the ability of the fiber to reduce the amounts of sugar the body absorbs maintaining a healthy blood sugar level.

It is also attributed to lowered cholesterol and reduced risk of developing heart disease. The fiber in the digestive system also clumps fats reducing the rate at which they are digested and absorbed in the body. Healthy bacteria in the gut thrive on soluble fiber. The bacteria microbiome feeds on the remains of fermented fiber in the digestive system. These bacteria help in the production of short-chain fatty-acids that help in reducing cholesterol in the body. The short chain fatty-acids also promote good health by reducing inflammation in the body. Inflammation is a risky condition linked to the development of serious illnesses such as cancer among others.

Plant foods reduce the risk of cancers, such as colorectal cancer. While animal foods are found to increase the risk of cancer, plants contain phytochemicals and antioxidants that reduce the risk of developing cancer while at the same time fighting the progress of cancer cells. The fiber found in plant foods is also helpful in detoxification of the body. The detoxification process is aided by both soluble and insoluble fiber. The soluble fiber absorbs the excess hormones and toxins within the body, preventing them from being taken up by the cells. Insoluble fiber works by preventing the absorptions of toxins found in the foods we consume from the digestive tract. It also increases the time which food takes to go through the digestive tract. The process is said to reduce the body's demands for more food. The soluble fiber also stimulates the production of certain components that reduce the feelings of hunger which include peptide YY, peptide-1, and cholecystokinin.

When a person is on a plant-based diet, they cut on their consumption of processed foods and refined sugars that are harmful to the body. These sugars promote weight gain by increased food cravings and the production of certain hormones that induce the body to crave for food. These sugars and other additives found in processed food also increase the risk of cancer and among other illnesses.

Plant foods are also rich in certain components that are found to possess anti-oxidation properties while also working in reducing cholesterol levels in the body. These components are polyphenols, such as flavonoids, stilbenoids, and lignans.

For instance, green tea, which is most commonly used for its anti-oxidation properties is rich in (epigallocatechin gallate) a flavonoid responsible for the production of the fat burning hormone.

Another beauty of eating plant foods is that you worry less about overeating. The plant foods contain limited calories and negligible levels of harmful fats. According to research, persons who eat plant foods live longer as compared to those that feed on animal foods. Plants foods not only improve the quality of life by protecting a person from illnesses but also lower the risk of early deaths resulting from these illnesses and health conditions.

Plant based foods are also friendly to the environment. Eating plant foods encourages the planting of more plants to give more foods that protect the ozone layer by absorbing excess harmful carbon dioxide from the atmosphere. Plants based diet discourages the industrial practices associated with processing foods. These practices promote the release of harmful gases into the atmosphere, and the packaging of the foods makes use of materials that are not environmentally friendly.

What to Eat and What to Avoid

These are the things you should be eating in a plant-based diet:

Veggies: spinach, potatoes, kale, squash, cauliflower, and tomatoes

Legumes: lentils, chickpeas, beans, peas, and peanuts

Nut butters and nuts

Whole grains like quinoa, brown rice, barley, and oats

Tempeh or tofu

Seeds

Plant-based oils

Herbs

Spices

Fruits

Any kind of unsweetened beverage like sparkling water, coffee, and tea

These are the things you should avoid in a plant-based diet:

Packaged food items like sugary cereals, chips, and cookies

Fast food

Sweetened beverages and desserts

Processed meat like sausage and bacon

Refined grains like refined pasta, white bread, and white rice

You can eat non-vegetarian food in moderation.

Chapter 2. Plant Based Vs Vegan Vs Vegetarian

A plant-based diet is all about easy healthy plant food option that includes fruits, vegetables, lentils, beans, and more. Other than the hardcore plant diet options, it allows the intake of low-fat dairy products that include low-fat milk, low-fat cottage, mozzarella and cheddar cheese as well. Having a plant-based diet doesn't require that you avoid all the animal-based products.

A vegan diet states that one should eat all the vegetables and avoid any meat products. It is simply that a person prefers eating vegetables and fruits instead of meat and other fats. Vegan culture involves not using any other animal products not in food nor any daily use.

A vegetarian diet is about focusing on plant foods but also eating animal products such as honey and milk. The main difference with veganism is that vegans avoid any form of animal products while vegetarians do not eat meat but they eat animal products like honey and milk.

Benefits of a Plant-Based Diet

Environmentally friendly: Plant-based diet is all environmentally friendly. When masses are following the plant-based diet that means there will be more plants and no more packing food. No processed or packaged food means there won't be any disposal or trash out there. On the other hand, more plants will provide more oxygen for people and give them nutrients through food. It is an overall a good package for the ultimate healthy and happy society.

Better organ health: Plant-based diet is good for not only a specific organ like liver, heart or kidneys, but it helps your overall body to have a perfect mechanism. It gives proper attention to all the organs and make it possible for a person to have the best of health in any manner. Other than organs, the diet helps to increase muscular strength, make bones stronger, hair longer and many more. It is all about how you are managing the diet and you will be able to get the best results within a few days of

547

starting with it.

Benefits beyond health: The benefits of plant-based diet are not limited to the health and fitness only. It is a complete package of ultimate benefits that prolong in society and help each aspect of the society to grow better. Since the diet is all about plants, it means one needs to have fresh vegetables and fruits available in surroundings. Moreover, it enhances the consumption and utilization of all the products and bi-products. Here are some of the value-added benefits of the plant-based diet that is commendable:

Lowers Blood Pressure: One of the reasons why plant-based foods contribute to low blood pressure is that they tend to have high amount of potassium, which in turn helps you manage your blood pressure (Physicians Committee for Responsible Medicine, n.d.). Additionally, potassium has also been known to reduce anxiety and stress. Now, guess what meat has little of? That's right. Potassium. Some foods that have a high amount of potassium are fruits, whole grains, nuts, and legumes.

Prevents Chronic Diseases: Obesity? Cancer? Diabetes? These are illnesses that you can avoid or minimize the risk of with a plant-based diet. People who are already suffering from chronic diseases are asked to live on plant-based food because they help improve lifespans (Nordqvist, 2012).

Lowers Blood Sugar Levels: One thing that plant-based diets are rich in is fiber. When you consume fiber, your body reduces the amount of sugar it absorbs into the bloodstream. Additionally, fiber does not make you feel hungry really fast. When you do not feel full, you end up consuming more food than necessary. Plant-based foods help prevent such a situation from arising.

Ideal for Weight Loss: When you are consuming a plant-based diet, you are cutting down on excess fats and maintaining a healthy level of weight. You don't even have to worry about calorie restrictions! It helps you manage your hunger, and you also receive the necessary amount of minerals, proteins, and vitamins from your green meal.

Saves Time and Money: Plant-based foods are not as difficult to prepare as meat-based foods. In fact, you will take less time to prepare an organic meal. When you really need, you can easily put together some healthy ingredients and make a quick salad. Furthermore, you spend less money by preparing food using plant-based ingredients. When you source local and organic products, you end up shelling out less cash for the items that you would like to buy.

Lowers Cholesterol Level: This might sound like a myth, but plants contain no cholesterol. Even if you pick out coconut and cocoa plants, they do not contain any cholesterol. Hence, when you are at risk of having a high level of cholesterol, a plant-based diet will help you bring it back down to a much healthier level.

Chapter 3. Plant Based Is Not Just a Diet. It is a Lifestyle

Before you even begin thinking about starting a new diet, it is vital that you set yourself up for success. Many people fail any diet because they fail to make a plan!

The best way to set yourself up for success is to make a meal plan. When you plan your meals for the week, you will have a good idea of how many meals you need to make and if any events are coming up that you will need to plan for. With a meal plan in hand, you will know exactly what you need to buy for the week and what you are going to eat. With a plan, this leaves very little room for failure. So, how do you make a meal plan?

Creating a Meal Plan

The primary issue with most diets is that they are "cookie-cutter" plans. The truth is, there is no one way to follow a diet. For this reason, learning how to create a meal plan is going to be the best way to stick to your new diet! All you will have to do is follow a few simple steps, use some of the delicious recipes provided in this book, and you will be on your merry way of losing, gaining, or even maintaining your weight!

Step One: Nutritional Requirements

The first step you will need to take when developing a meal plan will be determining how many calories you need. This number will range from person to person as it depends upon your height, weight, sex, age, and activity level. If an individual is on the more active side, they will generally need more calories!

If you want to lose weight on your diet, you will need to cut anywhere from 500-750 calories from your diet. By doing this, you will be able to lose about a pound a week. In general, the average calories per day for an adult can be between 1,600 and 3,200 calories per day. You can find your average and subtract from that number by using an online calculator.

Once you have your calorie recommendation in hand, it is time to find the variety and balance to a proper diet. While following a plant-based diet, this should come relatively easy! Your main focus is going to be on fruits, vegetables, nuts, seeds, and whole-grain foods! Through the proper foods, you will be getting all of your recommended vitamins and minerals.

Knowing your macronutrients is going to be important as you make up your meal plan. As you might already know, there is a common misconception that a plant-based diet means you will lack in protein. We will be going over this a bit later, but all you need to know is that it is not true! While following your new diet, you will still have plenty of protein-rich foods such as beans, legumes, nuts, and soy products. Generally, you will want anywhere from 200-700 of your calories coming from a protein source!

Another critical macronutrient to keep in mind is fat. Unfortunately, fat tends to have a bad rep when it comes to diet. On the market, you will see a ton of products labeled "Non-fat" or "Low-Fat." Spoiler alert: these are just as bad for you! The key here is to realize that there are good fats, and they are necessary for a balanced diet. Generally, you will want to keep your fat intake to 30% or less of your total calories. Good fats can come from sources such as olives, soybeans, and nuts. What it comes down to is avoiding trans fats and saturated fats; these are the fats that are associated with diabetes and cardiovascular disease.

Just like with fat, carbohydrates are thought of as an "enemy" for individuals who are trying to lose weight. The truth is, carbohydrates play a crucial role in your health! If you want to provide your body with clean energy, it will be important that you choose the right type of carbs. As you create your meal plan, try your best to choose complex carbs. Complex carbs are whole and unprocessed. Some sources of these carbs include legumes, whole-grain bread, vegetables, and some fruits. It is the simple carbs that you will want to avoid! Anything like white bread, white pasta, or white rice has sugars processed and separated from any nutrients.

As you plan out your meals, you will also want to limit your sugar and salt intake. By cutting processed foods, this will happen mostly automatically, but you will still need to be careful of the salt and sugar when you are cooking your own foods. When you have too much sodium in your diet, this leads to fluid retention. Fluid retention is poor because the risk of stroke, heart disease, and high blood pressure can be increased. Generally, you will want to keep sodium to 2,300 mg a day or less.

Step Two: Make Your Diet Your Own

The problem with many diets is that not one size fits all. We all have different goals, different body types, and completely different lifestyles. For this reason, you will need to set your goals and develop a meal plan around that.

First, you will want to decide how much weight you would like to lose or gain, but remember to keep that goal within a reasonable time frame. On average, a person can safely lose about a pound a week. Drastic weight loss is not only unhealthy but also fairly unachievable. Remember to set goals for yourself that are in your reach. By setting attainable goals this can help motivate you to stick to your diet.

Keep in mind that there is no reason you need to change your habits overnight! If you want to lose weight, you will want to make these changes gradually. One of the best ways to do this is by learning how to slow down your meals. Generally, it takes the brain up to twenty minutes to let your body know that you are full. If you consciously eat slower, you will probably feel full quicker!

Step Three: Creating Your Meals

The final step in creating your own meal plan will be choosing out your meals! If you are just getting started, I highly suggest you try to keep your meal plan as simple as possible. There is absolutely no reason you need to complicate your meals by making separate meals every day of the week!

Instead, consider starting small. If this is your first time, try planning for just breakfast! All you will have to do is take a look at the breakfast recipes provided in this book, choose one or two, and you will be on your way! Once you become more comfortable with the concept of meal planning, you can add more meals to your plan. As you create your meal plans, you will eventually want to include breakfast, lunch, dinner, and some snacks. Luckily, there are many ways to add variety in your meals, so you can really start to get creative!

Week 1
Monday

Breakfast: Creamy Chocolate Shake

 Preparation:
10 Minutes

 Cooking:
0 Minutes

 Serves:
2

Ingredients

- 2 frozen ripe bananas, chopped
- 1/3 cup frozen strawberries
- 2 tbsp cocoa powder
- 2 tbsp salted almond butter
- 2 cups unsweetened vanilla almond milk
- 1 dash Stevia or agave nectar
- 1/3 cup ice

Directions

1. Add all ingredients in a blender and blend until smooth.
2. Take out and serve.

Lunch:
Asian Chilled Cucumber and Seaweed Soup

 Ready in:
15 Minutes

 Serves:
6

Ingredients

- 1 cup soaked seaweed, rinsed * see note
- 2 cucumbers cut into thin slices
- Seasonings
- 4 Tbsp of soy sauce
- 1/4 cup fresh lemon juice
- 1/2 tsp garlic minced
- 1 Tbsp red pepper flakes
- 2 tsp sesame seeds toasted
- 1 tsp brown sugar
- 4 cups of water
- Sea salt to taste

Directions

1. Soak seaweed in water to cover overnight.
2. When soft, drain and cut into 2-inch pieces.
3. Boil water with a little salt in a pot.
4. Blanch drained seaweed for 20 to 25 seconds; plunge into the ice water.
5. In a bowl, combine together cucumber, seaweed, and all remaining ingredients; stir well.
6. Refrigerate to chill well.
7. Taste and adjust salt to taste.
8. Serve in chilled bowls.

Dinner: Fung Tofu

 Ready in:
25 Minutes

 Serves:
4

Directions

1. Mix your black vinegar, ginger, garlic, soy sauce, sesame oil, and maple syrup in a bowl. Toss in the tofu to coat, and then put the slices on a baking sheet to marinate for an hour.
2. Heat your grill to medium-high heat and grill for three minutes per side. Garnish using sesame seeds.

Ingredients

- ¼ Cup Soy Sauce
- ½ Cup Black Vinegar
- 1 Tablespoon Sesame Oil
- 2 Inches Ginger, Fresh, Peeled & Minced
- ¼ Cup Maple Syrup
- 3 Cloves Garlic, Minced
- 2 Blocks Tofu, Firm, Pressed & Sliced into 4 Slices
- 1 Tablespoon Sesame Seeds

Tuesday

Breakfast: Hidden Kale Smoothie

 Preparation:
5 Minutes

 Cooking:
0 Minutes

 Serves:
2

Directions

1. Add all ingredients in a blender and blend until smooth.
2. Take out and serve.

Ingredients

- 1 medium ripe banana, peeled and sliced
- ½ cup frozen mixed berries
- 1 tbsp hulled hemp seeds
- 2 cups frozen or fresh kale
- 2/3 cup 100% pomegranate juice
- 2¼ cups filtered water

Nutritions: *Calories 178, Total Fat 1.8 g, Saturated Fat 0.3 g, Cholesterol 0 mg, Sodium 33 mg, Total, Carbs 37.8 g, Fiber 4.3 g, Sugar 20.4 g, Protein 4.1 g, Potassium 785 mg*

Lunch: Baked "Hasselback" Sweet Potatoes

 Ready in:
1h 15 Minutes

 Serves:
4

Ingredients

- ▶ 1/2 cup olive oil
- ▶ 1 Tbsp of fresh rosemary finely chopped
- ▶ 4 large sweet potatoes, chopped
- ▶ 1/2 tsp ground mustard
- ▶ Kosher salt and freshly ground black pepper
- ▶ 1 cup Tofu grated (optional)

Directions

1. Preheat oven to 425 F.
2. Wash and rub potatoes; cut trough potatoes about halfway into thin slices (as Hasselback potatoes).
3. Combine olive, rosemary, and ground mustard; generously brush potatoes.
4. Place sweet potatoes on a greased baking sheet.
5. Bake for 60 minutes or until soft.
6. Remove from the oven, and let cool for 10 minutes.
7. Serve with grated Tofu (optional).

Nutritions: *Calories 285.21, Calories From Fat (92%) 263.44, Total Fat 30g 46%, Saturated Fat 4g 20%, Cholesterol 0mg 0%, Sodium 12.48mg <1%, Potassium 69.92mg 2%, Total Carbohydrates 1.13g <1%, Sugar 0.25g, Protein 5g 10%*

Ready in:
40 Minutes

Serves:
4

Directions

1. Get out a large pot and fill it with water. Salt it before bringing it to a boil using high heat.
2. Add in the pasta and cook to an al dente texture. Rinse under cold water to stop the cooking.
3. Get out a saucepan and place it over medium heat, heating your oil.
4. Throw in the garlic, lemongrass, and ginger. Cook for another half a minute.
5. Add in soy sauce, coconut milk, curry paste, brown sugar, chili paste, and lime juice. Stir in your curry mixture, cooking for ten minutes until it thickens.
6. Toss in the broccoli, edamame, bell pepper, carrots, and cooked pasta. Mix well before serving warm.

Ingredients

- ½ Tablespoon Olive
- 4 Cloves Garlic, Minced
- 2 Tablespoons Lemongrass, Minced
- 2 Tablespoons Red Curry Paste
- 1 Tablespoon Ginger, Fresh & created
- 1 Tablespoon Brown Sugar
- 2 Tablespoons Soy Sauce
- 2 Tablespoons Lime Juice, Fresh
- 1 Tablespoon Hot Chili Paste
- 12 Ounces Linguine
- 2 Cups Broccoli Florets
- 1 Cup Carrots, Shredded
- 1 Cup Edamame, Shelled
- 1 Red Bell Pepper, Sliced

Wednesday

Breakfast: Blueberry Protein Shake

Preparation:
5 Minutes

Cooking:
0 Minutes

Serves:
1

Directions

1. Add all ingredients in a blender and blend until smooth.
2. Take out and serve.

Ingredients

- ½ cup cottage cheese or low-fat yogurt
- 3 tbsp vanilla protein powder
- ½ cup frozen blueberries
- ½ tsp maple extract
- ¼ tsp vanilla extract
- 2 tsp flaxseed meal
- Sweetener of choice (to taste)
- 10-15 ice cubes
- ¼ cup water

Nutritions: *Calories 230, Total Fat 5 g, Saturated Fat 1.9 g, Cholesterol 0 mg, Sodium 0 mg, Total Carbs 18 g, Fiber 3.1 g, Sugar 9 g, Protein 27.5 g, Potassium 210 mg*

Ready in:
30 Minutes

 Serves:
4

Ingredients

- ▸ 2 Tbsp olive oil
- ▸ 1 cup of soy milk
- ▸ 1 cup soy flour
- ▸ 2 tsp garlic powder
- ▸ 1 head of cauliflower, chopped into flowerets
- ▸ 1 cup Red Hot Sauce (or vegan Buffalo sauce)
- ▸ 2 Tbsp of avocado oil

Directions

1. Preheat the oven to 450 F/225 C.
2. Grease a shallow baking dish with olive oil; set aside.
3. In a bowl, stir together soy milk, soy flour, and garlic powder until well combined.
4. Coat the cauliflower florets with the soy flour mixture and place in a prepared baking dish.
5. Bake for 18 to 20 minutes.
6. In a meanwhile, heat Red Hot Sauce or vegan Buffalo sauce with avocado oil in a saucepan.
7. Pour the hot sauce over the baked cauliflower and bake for an additional 6 to 8 minutes.
8. Serve hot.

Nutritions: *Calories 360.35, Calories From Fat (63%) 225.7, Total Fat 25.93g 40%, Saturated Fat 3.54g 18%, Cholesterol 0mg 0%, Sodium 953.78mg 40%, Potassium 1286.29mg 37%, Total Carbohydrates 23.49g 8%, Fiber 7.32g 29%, Sugar 8g, Protein 14g 28%*

Dinner: Mushroom & Bean Soup

 Ready in:
45 Minutes

 Serves:
4

Ingredients

- 1 Tablespoon Olive Oil
- 16 Ounces Bella Mushrooms, Sliced
- ½ Red Onion, Chopped
- 3 Cloves Garlic, Minced
- 15 Ounces White Beans, Canned & Drained
- 1 Tablespoon Italian Seasoning, Dried
- 3 Cups Vegetable Broth
- 1 Teaspoon Rosemary, Fresh or Dried
- Pinch Hot Red Pepper Flakes
- Sea Salt & Black Pepper to Taste

Directions

1. Get out a medium saucepan over medium heat. Heat your olive oil and add in your garlic and onions. Cook for two or three minutes or until golden brown. Add in your spices, salt, pepper, mushrooms and white beans now.
2. Cook for an additional five minutes and then add in your broth. Allow it to come to a boil. Stir in the chili flakes, reducing your heat to a simmer.
3. Allow your soup to cook for another half hour.
4. Puree with an immersion blender and serve garnished with hemp seeds, scallions, olive oil, or mushrooms as desired.

Thursday

Breakfast: Peppermint Monster Smoothie

 Preparation:
5 Minutes

 Cooking:
0 Minutes

 Serves:
1

Directions

1. Add all ingredients in a blender and blend until smooth.
2. Take out and serve

Ingredients

- 1 large frozen banana, peeled
- 1½ cups non-dairy milk
- A handful of fresh mint leaves, stems removed
- 1-2 handfuls spinach

Nutritions: *Calories 451, Total Fat 18.6 g, Saturated Fat 10.2 g, Cholesterol 40 mg, Sodium 271 mg, Total Carbs 54.8 g, Fiber 4.8 g, Sugar 38.7 g, Protein 18.4 g, Potassium 1,511 mg*

Lunch:
Baked Creamy Corn with Shredded Tofu

Ready in:
25 Minutes

Serves:
4

Ingredients

- 4 Tbsp rice oil
- 3 cups sweet corn kernels (frozen or fresh)
- 2 green onions, thinly sliced
- 1 cup vegan mayonnaise
- 1 Tbsp brown sugar
- Salt and pepper to taste
- 8 oz silken tofu shredded

Directions

1. Preheat oven to 400 F/200 C.
2. Grease a baking dish with rice oil.
3. In a bowl, combine together corn kernels, green onions. Vegan mayonnaise, brown sugar, and salt and pepper; stir to combine well.
4. Pour the corn mixture into a prepared baking dish.
5. Sprinkle evenly with shredded tofu.
6. Bake for 14 to 16 minutes.
7. Remove from the oven and allow it to cool.
8. Serve.

Nutritions: Calories 482, Calories From Fat (65%) 312.49, Total Fat 35.37g 54%, Saturated Fat 5.86g 29%, Cholesterol 15.28mg 5%, Sodium 425.49mg 18%, Potassium 338.68mg 10%, Total Carbohydrates 40.56g 14%, Fiber 2.4g 10%, Sugar 10.48g, Protein 7.16g 14%

Dinner: Yellow Wild Rice Soup

Directions

Ready in:
1 h 15 minutes

Serves:
6

1. Get out a stockpot and place it over medium heat. Add in your coconut oil and add in the onions and carrots. Sauté until soft.
2. Stir in the mushrooms and garlic cooking for three minutes.
3. Add in the spices, wild rice, tomato paste, and liquids.
4. Once it boils, you can reduce it to a simmer and allow it to simmer for an hour. Add in the green beans and chickpeas and then serve warm.

Ingredients

- 4 Cups Vegetable Broth
- 3 Cups Water
- 15 Ounces Chickpeas, Canned
- 1 Cup Green Beans, Frozen
- 14.5 Ounces Coconut Milk, Full Fat
- Sea Salt & Black Pepper to Taste
- ½ Teaspoon Ground Ginger
- ½ Teaspoon Cumin
- 1 Teaspoon Turmeric
- ½ Teaspoon Curry Powder
- 1 Tablespoon Tomato Paste
- 1 Cup Wild Rice
- 4 Cloves Garlic, Grated
- 1 ½ Cups Mushrooms, Chopped
- ½ Cup Carrots, Chopped
- 1 Cup White Onions, Chopped
- 1 Tablespoon Coconut Oil

Friday

Breakfast: Almond Banana Granola

Preparation:
15 Minutes

Cooking:
50 Minutes

Serves:
8

Ingredients

- 8 cups rolled oats
- 2 cups dates, pitted and chopped
- 2 ripe bananas, peeled and chopped
- 1 tsp almond extract
- 1 tsp salt

Directions

1. Preheat oven to 275 degrees F.
2. Add oats to a bowl.
3. Take a baking sheet and line it with parchment paper.
4. Take a saucepan and add 1 cup water to it.
5. Place dates in the saucepan and heat them for 10 minutes.
6. Remove from heat.
7. Add heated mixture, bananas, almond extract, and salt to a blender.
8. Blend until smooth.
9. Add this mixture to the bowl with the oats and mix well.
10. Transfer the mixture to the lined baking sheets and spread it out evenly.
11. Bake for 40 to 50 minutes until crispy, stirring after 10 minutes.
12. Let cool and serve.

Nutritions: *Calories 463, Total Fat 5.6 g, Saturated Fat 1 g, Cholesterol 0 mg, Sodium 297 mg, Total Carbs 95.6 g, Fiber 12.6 g, Sugar 32.7 g, Protein 12.2 g, Potassium 695 mg*

Ready in:
45 Minutes

Serves:
4

Ingredients

- 1 lb firm tofu, drained and cut into 1/2-inch slabs
- 1/2 cup tamari sauce
- 1 lb shredded cabbage
- 2 shredded carrots
- 1 onion finely sliced
- Sea salt and ground pepper to taste
- 4 Tbsp sesame oil
- 1 Tbsp fresh ginger grated
- 1 tsp hot chili paste
- 3 Tbsp rice vinegar or apple cider vinegar
- 2 cloves garlic minced
- 4 Tbsp water

Directions

1. Preheat the oven to 375 degrees F.
2. Grease a baking sheet with some oil and set aside.
3. Toss Tofu slabs with 1/4 cup of the tamari sauce.
4. Arrange the tofu on the prepared baking sheet and bake for 25 to 30 minutes.
5. Remove from the oven and set aside to cool.
6. In a large bowl, combine the cabbage, carrots, and onion; season with the salt and pepper, and set aside.
7. In a separate bowl, combine sesame oil, ginger, chili paste, and remaining 1/4 cup of tamari sauce, vinegar, garlic, and water.
8. Pour the garlic-ginger mixture over the cabbage mixture and toss to combine.
9. Taste and adjust seasonings.
10. Serve topped with tofu.

Nutritions: *Calories 386, Calories From Fat (55%) 213.87, Total Fat 24.8g 38%, Saturated Fat 3.58g 18%, Cholesterol 0mg 0%, Sodium 2080mg 87%, Potassium 759.94mg 22%, Total Carbohydrates 21.52g 7%, Fiber 7.1g 31%, Sugar 7.54g, Protein 25.8g 52%*

Dinner:
Wild Rice Lemon Soup

 Ready in:
1 h 5 Minutes

 Serves:
6

Ingredients

- 1 Cup Carrots, Chopped
- ½ Cup White Onion
- 1 Tablespoon Olive Oil
- 1Cup Celery, Sliced
- 6 Cloves Garlic, Minced
- 1 Tablespoon Lemon Zest
- Sea Salt & Black Pepper to Taste
- 1 Tablespoon Italian Seasoning
- ½ Cup Wild Rice
- 4 Cups Vegetable Broth
- 1 Cup Almond Milk
- ¼ Cup Lemon Juice, Fresh
- 1 Cup Spinach, Fresh

Directions

1. Get out a Dutch oven and add your oil to it. Place it over medium heat, and then toss in the carrots, garlic, celery, and onion. Cook for five minutes.
2. Stir in your zest and the remaining seasoning, cooking for three minutes. Add in the wild rice and vegetable broth.
3. Allow it to come to a boil and then reduce the heat to a simmer.
4. Cover and allow it to cook for forty minutes.
5. Add the spinach, milk, and lemon juice.
6. Leave it covered for five minutes and allow it to serve warm.

Saturday

Preparation:
10 Minutes

Cooking:
15 Minutes

Serves:
3

Directions

1. Add all ingredients to a bowl and mix well.
2. Heat a frying pan on medium heat.
3. Pour batter into the frying pan.
4. As it cooks, flip the omelet.
5. When the underside is cooked, flip it again and cook for 1 minute.
6. Serve and enjoy.

Ingredients

- 1 cup chickpea flour
- ½ tsp onion powder
- ½ tsp garlic powder
- ¼ tsp white pepper
- ¼ tsp black pepper
- 1/3 cup nutritional yeast
- ½ tsp baking soda
- 3 green onions (white and green parts), chopped

Nutritions: *Calories 314, Total Fat 5.1 g, Saturated Fat 0.6 g, Cholesterol 0 mg, Sodium 240 mg, Total Carbs 50.5 g, Fiber 16.6 g, Sugar 7.7 g, Protein 21.5 g, Potassium 1,063 mg*

Lunch: High-Protein Minestrone Soup (Crock Pot)

Ready in:
8 h

Serves:
6

Directions

1. Soak beans overnight.
2. Place all ingredients into your 6 quarts Crock-Pot.
3. Give a good stir and cover.
4. Cook on HIGH for 4 to 5 hours or on LOW heat for 8 hours.
5. Taste, and adjust salt and pepper.
6. Serve hot.

Ingredients

- 1 cup dried beans, soaked
- 1 onion finely chopped
- 2 cloves garlic finely chopped
- 1 large carrot peeled and cut into 1/2-inch slices
- 1 cup shredded cabbage
- 1 stalk celery cut into 1-inch chunks
- 1 cup fresh chard chopped
- 1 zucchini sliced
- 1 large potato peeled and diced
- 1 cup tomato paste
- 2 cups vegetable broth
- 1/2 cup olive oil
- Salt and ground pepper to taste

Nutritions: *Calories 263.29, Calories From Fat (6%) 16.82, Total Fat 2g 3%, Saturated Fat 0.45g 2%, Cholesterol 0.2mg <1%, Sodium 751.11mg 31%, Potassium 1435.7mg 41%, Total Carbohydrates 50.7g 17%, Fiber 10.12g 40%, Sugar 5.39g, Protein 13.19g 26%*

Ready in:
1 h

Serves:
4

Ingredients

- 1 Tablespoon Olive Oil
- 1 Cup Fennel, Chopped
- 1 Leek, Sliced Thin
- 3 Cups Carrots, Chopped
- 1 Cup Butternut Squash, Chopped
- 3 Cloves Garlic, Minced
- 1 Tablespoon Ginger, Grated
- 1 Tablespoon Turmeric Powder
- Sea Salt & Black Pepper to Taste
- 3 Cups Vegetable Broth
- 14.5 Ounces Coconut Milk, Canned

Directions

1. Get out a Dutch oven and place it over medium heat to heat your olive oil.
2. Stir in your fennel, carrots, leeks, and squash. Cook for five minutes. Toss your garlic, ginger, salt, pepper, and turmeric in next. Stir and cook for another two minutes. Pour in your broth and coconut milk next.
3. Once it comes to a boil, cover it and reduce it to a simmer. Allow it to simmer for twenty minutes.
4. Once it's cooked, puree it using an immersion blender and garnish with coconut yogurt.

Sunday

Breakfast: Polenta

 Preparation:
5 Minutes

 Cooking:
10 Minutes

 Serves:
4

Directions

1. Take a saucepan and heat the brown rice syrup.
2. Add in the pears, polenta, cranberries, and cinnamon and cook for 10 minutes, stirring occasionally.
3. Serve and enjoy.

Ingredients

- ¼ cup brown rice syrup
- 2 pears, peeled, cored, and diced
- 1 cup fresh or dried cranberries
- 1 tsp ground cinnamon
- 1 cup Basic Polenta, kept warm

Nutritions: *Calories 178, Total Fat 0.3 g, Saturated Fat 0 g, Cholesterol 0 mg, Sodium 17 mg, Total Carbs 44.4 g, Fiber 4.9 g, Sugar 23.9 g, Protein 1.9 g, Potassium 170 mg*

Lunch: Hot Sour and Spicy Bok Choy Salad

 Ready in:
20 Minutes

 Serves:
4

Directions

1. Trim the Bok Choy stems off and rinse under cold water; place into a colander to drain.
2. Heat oil in a large frying skillet over medium heat.
3. Sauté onion and garlic with a pinch of salt until soft or for 3 to 4 minutes.
4. Add Bok Choy and slightly stir.
5. Cover and cook for about 3 to 4 minutes.
6. Add fresh lime juice, crushed pepper, chili pepper, and garlic powder.
7. Pour water and simmer for a further 4 to 5 minutes.
8. Taste and adjust salt and pepper to taste.
9. Serve hot.

Ingredients

- 1/3 cup sesame oil
- 1 onion finely chopped
- 2 cloves garlic, minced
- Salt and ground pepper to taste
- 1 1/2 lbs Bok Choy (chopped)
- 2 Tbsp of lime juice
- 1 tsp crushed red pepper
- 1/2 tsp hot chili pepper finely chopped
- 1 tsp garlic powder
- 1/2 cup water

Nutritions: *Calories 183.95, Calories From Fat (88%) 161, Total Fat 18.22g 28%, Saturated Fat 2.6g 13%, Cholesterol 0mg 0%, Sodium 342.5mg 14%, Potassium 92.71mg 3%, Total Carbohydrates 5g 2%, Fiber 0.77g 3%, Sugar 1.6g, Protein 2g 4%*

Dinner: Blackeye Pea Burritos

 Ready in:
50 Minutes

 Serves:
6

Ingredients

- ► 1 Teaspoon Olive Oil
- ► 1 Red Onion, Diced
- ► 2 Cloves Garlic, Minced
- ► 1 Zucchini, Chopped
- ► 1 Bell Pepper, Seeded & Diced
- ► 2 Teaspoons Chili Powder
- ► Sea Salt to Taste
- ► 14 Ounces Blackeye Peas, Rinsed & Drained
- ► 6 Tortillas, Whole Grain
- ► 1 Tomato, Diced

Directions

1. Start by turning your oven to 325, and then get out a skillet. Put it over medium heat, and add in the oil and onion. Cook for five minutes before adding the garlic. Cook for less than a minute more. Add the bell pepper and tomato, and cook for two to three more minutes.
2. When your tomato is warmed, add in your slat, blackeye peas, and chili powder. Stir well.
3. Place in the center of tortillas and roll like a burrito.
4. Place these burritos in a baking dish and pour in the vegetable juice. Continue cooking for twenty to thirty minutes.

Week 2
Monday

Breakfast: Blueberry Overnight Oats

 Preparation:
5 Minutes

 Cooking:
8 h

 Serves:
1

Ingredients

- Almond Milk (1/4 C.)
- Quick Oats (1/4 C.)
- Blueberries (1/2 C.)
- Banana (1/4, Sliced)
- Chia Seeds (1/2 T.)
- Cinnamon (1/8 t.)
- Pecans (1 T.)
- Stevia (to Taste)

Directions

1. While this meal does need to soak overnight, it is easy to do the night before you need a quick breakfast! All you have to do is place all of the ingredients into a jar or bowl and set in the fridge.
2. When you are ready to enjoy, top it however you would like and then enjoy your breakfast.

Nutritions: *Calories: 230, Carbs: 35g, Fats: 6g, Proteins: 4g*

Lunch: Integral Rotini Pasta with Vegetables

Ready in:
35 Minutes

Serves:
4

Ingredients

- 1 lb whole-grain pasta rotini
- 4 Tbsp olive oil
- 2 cups zucchini - cut into small cubes
- 1 red onion, cut into cubes
- 1 red bell pepper sliced
- 1 cup of vegetable broth
- 1 cup cherry tomatoes halved
- 2 cloves garlic finely sliced
- 1/2 cup fresh basil finely chopped
- 2 Tbsp lemon juice (freshly squeezed)
- Salt and ground pepper to taste

Directions

1. Cook rotini pasta according to the instructions on the package.
2. Rinse and drain into a colander; set aside.
3. Heat oil in a wok or deep frying pan over medium heat.
4. Add zucchini, onion, and red peppers; sauté for about 6 to 7 minutes.
5. Add sliced garlic, a pinch of salt, and stir for 2 minutes.
6. Add cherry tomatoes and vegetable broth; cook for a further 3 to 4 minutes.
7. Add rotini pasta and fresh basil; toss to combine well.
8. Taste and adjust salt and pepper to taste.
9. Serve with lemon juice.

Nutritions: *Calories 348.77, Calories From Fat (50%) 174.3, Total Fat 19.81g 30%, Saturated Fat 3.81g 19%, Cholesterol 0mg 0%, Sodium 103.66mg 4%, Potassium 690.39mg 20%, Total Carbohydrates 37.38g 12%, Fiber 6.07g 24%, Sugar 3.51g, Protein 9g 18%*

Ready in:
20 Minutes

Serves:
3

Ingredients

- 1 Tablespoon Ginger, Peeled & Grated
- 8 Ounces Firm Tofu, Chopped into Slices
- 4 Green Onions, Sliced Thin
- Toasted Sesame Oil to Taste
- 1 Bunch Asparagus, Trimmed & Chopped
- 1 Handful Cashew Nuts, Chopped & Toasted
- 2 Tablespoons Hoisin Sauce
- 1 Lime, Juiced & Zested
- 1 Handful Mint, Fresh & Chopped
- 1 Handful Basil, Fresh & Chopped
- 3 Cloves Garlic, Chopped
- 3 Handfuls Spinach, Chopped
- Pinch Sea Salt

Directions

1. Get out a wok and heat up your oil. Add in your tofu, cooking for a few minutes.
2. Put your tofu to the side, and then sauté your red pepper flakes, ginger, salt, onions and asparagus for a minute.
3. Mix in your spinach, garlic, and cashews, cooking for another two minutes.
4. Add your tofu back in, and then drizzle in your lime juice, lime zest, hoisin sauce, cooking for another half a minute.
5. Remove it from heat, adding in your mint and basil.

Nutritions: *Calories: 380, Protein: 22 Grams, Fat: 24 Grams, Carbs: 27 Grams*

Tuesday

Breakfast: Carrot Pancakes

 Preparation:
5 Minutes

 Cooking:
25 Minutes

 Serves:
1

Ingredients

- Shredded Carrots (1/4 C.)
- Pancake Mix (1/2 C.)
- Water (1/2 C.)
- Ground Cloves (1/8 t.)
- Nutmeg (1/8 t.)
- Cinnamon (1/4 t.)

Directions

1. Yes, you will still be able to enjoy pancakes while following a plant-based diet! Before you prep your meal, you can start out by heating a skillet over medium-low heat.
2. As the skillet warms, take out a mixing bowl so you can combine all of your ingredients. You may find you need to use different amounts of water, depending on how you like your pancakes!
3. When your mix is all set, scoop out the mixture about pancake-sized, and place on the skillet. These will cook just like regular pancakes, so when it begins to bubble on the top, toss and bake the other side.
4. Finally, serve up with some maple syrup and enjoy your pancakes.

Nutritions: *Calories: 260, Carbs: 50g, Fats: 3g, Proteins: 5g*

Lunch: Mushrooms and Chickpeas Risotto

Ready in:
30 Minutes

Serves:
4

Ingredients

- 1/2 cup olive oil
- 1 onion finely diced
- 1 1/2 cups rice basmati
- 2 cups fresh mushrooms sliced
- 2 cups vegetable broth
- 2 cups of water
- 1/2 lb canned chickpeas, drained and rinsed
- 1/4 tsp turmeric ground
- Salt and pepper to taste

Directions

1. Heat oil in a deep skillet over medium-high heat.
2. Sauté the onion and rice for 2-3 minutes; stir frequently.
3. Pour the broth, water, sliced mushrooms, turmeric, and boiled chickpeas; stir well.
4. Bring to boil, reduce heat to medium, cover and cook for 18 minutes; stir occasionally.
5. Remove from the heat and let it cool for 5 minutes.
6. Taste and adjust salt and pepper to taste; stir.
7. Serve.

Nutritions: *Calories 630.4, Calories From Fat (41%) 257.56, Total Fat 29.19g 45%, Saturated Fat 4.17g 21%, Cholesterol 0.62mg <1%, Sodium 582.12mg 24%, Potassium 417.22mg 12%, Total Carbohydrates 81.5g 27%, Fiber 4.19g 17%, Sugar 1.9g, Protein 11g 22%*

Dinner: Cauliflower Steaks

Ready in:
30 Minutes

Serves:
4

Ingredients

- ¼ Teaspoon Black Pepper
- ½ Teaspoon Sea Salt, Fine
- 1 Tablespoon Olive Oil
- 1 Head Cauliflower, Large
- ¼ Cup Creamy Hummus
- 2 Tablespoons Lemon Sauce
- ½ Cup Peanuts, Crushed (Optional)

Directions

1. Start by heating your oven to 425.
2. Cut your cauliflower stems, and then remove the leaves. Put the cut side down, and then slice half down the middle. Cut into ¾ inch steaks. If you cut them thinner, they could fall apart.
3. Arrange them in a single layer on a baking sheet, drizzling with oil. Season with salt and pepper, and bake for twenty to twenty-five minutes. They should be lightly browned and tender.
4. Spread your hummus on the steaks, drizzling with your lemon sauce. Top with peanuts if you're using it.

Nutritions: *Calories: 167, Protein: 6 Grams, Fat: 13 Grams, Carbs: 10 Grams*

Wednesday

Breakfast: Potato Pancakes

 Preparation:
5 Minutes

 Cooking:
40 Minutes

 Serves:
4

Ingredients

- Olive Oil (2 t.)
- Potatoes (2)
- Salt (to Taste)

Directions

1. These pancakes are simple and to make and delicious to enjoy! You will want to start off by peeling your potatoes and then grate them into a mixing bowl. Once in the mixing bowl, be sure to use a paper towel to squeeze out any excess moisture.
2. Next, you will want to warm a skillet over middle heat. Once warm, insert in the olive oil and then place a patty of your mixture down. You'll want to cook the pancake on each side for about seven or eight minutes. By the end of this time, the pancake should be browned and crispy.
3. Finally, season with pepper and salt, and your pancakes are set.

Nutritions: *Calories: 150, Carbs: 30g, Fats: 3g, Proteins: 5g*

Lunch:
Pasta Salad with Marinated Artichoke Hearts and Tofu

Ready in:
20 Minutes

Serves:
4

Ingredients

- 1 lb medium pasta shape, uncooked
- 1 can (15 oz) marinated artichoke hearts, drained, chopped
- 1 cup Tofu firm cut into small cubes
- 1 cup fresh mushrooms, sliced
- 1/2 cup onion finely diced
- 1/3 cup chopped fresh basil
- Salt and freshly ground black pepper to taste
- 2/3 cup vegan salad dressing

Directions

1. Prepare pasta according to package directions.
2. In a large salad bowl, combine artichoke hearts, Tofu, mushrooms, onion, basil, and the salt and pepper.
3. Rinse pasta with cold water, and drain well.
4. Add pasta and vegan dressing to a salad bowl; toss well.
5. Taste and adjust salt and pepper to taste.
6. Serve or keep refrigerated.

Nutritions: *Calories 587.57, Calories From Fat (15%) 90.63, Total Fat 10.39g 16%, Saturated Fat 1.59g 8%, Cholesterol 0mg 0%, Sodium 405mg 17%, Potassium 557mg 16%, Total Carbohydrates 101.69g 34%, Fiber 10.91g 44%, Sugar 3.78g, Protein 22.28g 45%*

Ready in:
30 Minutes

 Serves:
4

Ingredients

- ¾ Cup Scallions, Sliced Thin
- 1 ½ Tablespoon Mirin
- ¼ Cup Tamari
- 1 ½ Tablespoon Dark Sesame Oil, Toasted
- 1 Tablespoon Sesame Seeds, Toasted (Optional)
- 2 Teaspoons Ginger, fresh & Grated
- ½ Teaspoon Red Pepper, crushed
- 12 Ounces Extra Firm Tofu, Drained & Cut into ½ Inch Pieces
- 4 Cups Zucchini Noodles
- 2 Tablespoons Rice Vinegar
- 2 Cups Carrots, Shredded
- 2 Cups Pea Shoots
- ¼ Cup Basil, Fresh & Chopped
- ¼ Cup Peanuts, Toasted & Chopped (Optional)

Directions

1. Wisk your tamari, mirin, sesame seeds, oil, ginger, red pepper, and scallion greens in a bowl. Set two tablespoons of this sauce aside, and add the tofu to the remaining sauce. Toss to coat.
2. Combine your vinegar and zucchini noodles in a bowl.
3. Divide it between four bowls, topping with tofu, carrots, and a tablespoon of basil and peanuts.
4. Drizzle with sauce before serving.

Nutritions: *Calories: 262, Protein: 16 Grams, Fat: 15 Grams, Carbs: 19 Grams*

Thursday

Breakfast: Soft Granola Bars

 Preparation:
10 Minutes

 Cooking:
30 Minutes

 Serves:
6

Ingredients

- Medjool Dates (3/4 C.)
- Salt (to taste)
- Cinnamon (1 t.)
- Vanilla (1 t.)
- Chia Seeds (1/2 C.)
- Pumpkin Seeds (1/4 C.)
- Sunflower Seeds (1/4 C.)
- Water (1 C.)
- Rolled Oats (3/4 C.)

Directions

1. Before you begin prepping this recipe, save yourself some time by prepping the stove to 325 and lining a cooking pane with parchment paper.
2. To start your granola bars, you will first need to take out your blender and blend the rolled oats until you form a flour. When you have this, place it into a separate bowl.
3. Next, you are going to want to add the dates and water to your blender. If possible, allow for the dates to soak about thirty minutes. This will help the blending process so you can a smooth texture once blended.
4. Next, you are going to combine all of your ingredients in the mixing bowl and stir until the seeds are spread out evenly.
5. When you are ready, place the mixture onto your baking sheet and then pop it into the oven for twenty-five minutes. By the end of this time, the bar should be firm. If it is, eliminate the dish from the stove and permit to cool off for about ten minutes before slicing and serving.

Nutritions: *Calories: 250, Carbs: 30g, Fats: 10g, Proteins: 6g*

Ready in:
10 Minutes

 Serves:
2

Directions

1. Combine ingredients (except coconut milk and mint) in a blender.
2. Blend on high until smooth.
3. Pour in coconut milk, and blend again until combined well.
4. Pour into bowls, sprinkle with fresh mint and serve.
5. Keep refrigerated.

Ingredients

- 4 Tbsp sesame oil
- 1/4 cup coconut aminos or soy sauce
- 1 Tbsp curry powder
- 1/4 cup fresh lime juice
- 1/2 cup of tomato sauce
- 2 Tbsp grated ginger
- 2 cloves of garlic
- Salt, to taste
- 1 cup of canned mushrooms
- 3 cups coconut milk canned
- 2 Tbsp fresh chopped mint, to garnish

Nutritions: *Calories 649.42, Calories From Fat (85%) 550.12, Total Fat 64.2g 99%, Saturated Fat 36g 180%, Cholesterol 0mg 0%, Sodium 1361mg 48%, Potassium 934.65mg 27%, Total Carbohydrates 18.3g 6%, Fiber 3.16g 13%, Sugar 4.9g, Protein 10.39g 21%*

Dinner: Ratatouille

Ready in:
1 h 15 Minutes

Serves:
10

Ingredients

- 2 Tablespoons Olive Oil
- 2 Eggplants, Peeled & Cubed
- 8 Zucchini, Chopped
- 4 Tomatoes, Chopped
- ¼ Cup Basil, Chopped
- 4 Thyme Sprigs
- 2 Yellow Onions, Diced
- 3 Cloves Garlic, Minced
- 3 Bell Peppers, Chopped
- 1 Bay Leaf
- Sea Salt to Taste

Directions

1. Salt your eggplant and leave it in a strainer.
2. Heat a teaspoon of oil in a Dutch oven, cooking your onions for ten minutes. Season with salt.
3. Mix your peppers in, cooking for five more minutes.
4. Place this mixture in a bowl.
5. Heat your oil and sauté zucchini, sprinkling with salt. Cook for five minutes, and place it in the same bowl.
6. Rinse your eggplant, squeezing the water out, and heat another two teaspoons of oil in your Dutch oven. Cook your eggplant for ten minutes, placing it in your vegetable bowl.
7. Heat the remaining oil and cook your garlic. Add in your tomatoes, thyme sprigs and bay leaves to deglaze the bottom.
8. Toss your vegetables back in, and then bring it to a simmer.
9. Simmer for forty-five minutes, and make sure to stir. Discard your thyme and bay leaf. Mix in your basil and serve warm.

Nutritions: *Calories: 90, Protein: 3 Grams, Fat: 25 Grams, Carbs: 13 Grams*

Friday

Breakfast: Build Your Own Oatmeal Square

Preparation:
5 Minutes

Cooking:
20 Minutes

Serves:
4

Ingredients

▶ Water (4 C.)
▶ Old-fashioned Oats (2 C.)

Directions

1. This recipe is for the base of your breakfast! By building the oatmeal squares, you can top; however, you desire! To start off, you are going to boil your water and add in the oats.
2. Once the oats are in the water, reduce the heat and cook for about five minutes without a cover and then place the lid and cook for another five minutes.
3. Now that the oatmeal is set take out a baking dish and pour it in. Throw a cover over the top and position in the fridge for the night.
4. The following morning, you will have oatmeal squares to cut up and enjoy your own way.

Nutritions: *Calories: 250, Carbs: 44g, Fats: 5g, Proteins: 10g*

Lunch:
Slow-Cooked Navy Bean Soup

 Ready in:
8 h

 Serves:
8

Directions

1. Soak beans overnight.
2. Rinse beans and add in your 6 Quart Slow Cooker.
3. Add all remaining ingredients and stir well.
4. Cover and cook on LOW for 8 hours.
5. Adjust the salt and pepper to taste.
6. Serve hot.

Ingredients

- 1 lb dry navy beans, soaked, rinsed
- 4 Tbsp olive oil
- 1/4 cup onion finely diced
- 2 cloves garlic finely chopped
- 2 carrots sliced
- 1/2 cup tomato sauce (canned)
- 1 tsp mustard
- 1/2 tsp curry powder
- 6 cups of water
- Salt and ground black pepper to taste

Nutritions: *Calories 191.2, Calories From Fat (4%) 7.6, Total Fat 0.91g 1%, Saturated Fat 0.11g <1%, Cholesterol 0mg 0%, Sodium 146.67mg 6%, Potassium 746.42mg 21%, Total Carbohydrates 35.18g 12%, Fiber 13.64g 55%, Sugar 3.85g, Protein 12.15g 24%*

Ready in:
2 h 25 minutes

 Serves:
6

Ingredients

- 2 Tablespoons + 1 Teaspoon Red Wine Vinegar, Divided
- ½ Teaspoon Pepper
- 1 Teaspoon Sea Salt
- 1 Avocado,
- ¼ Cup Basil, Fresh & Chopped
- 3 Tablespoons + 2 Teaspoons Olive Oil, Divided
- 1 Clove Garlic, crushed
- 1 Red Bell Pepper, Sliced & Seeded
- 1 Cucumber, Chunked
- 2 ½ lbs. Large Tomatoes, Cored & Chopped

Directions

1. Place half of your cucumber, bell pepper, and ¼ cup of each tomatoes in a bowl, covering. Set it in the fried.
2. Puree your remaining tomatoes, cucumber and bell pepper with garlic, three tablespoons oil, two tablespoons of vinegar, sea salt and black pepper into a blender, blending until smooth. Transfer it to a bowl, and chill for two hours.
3. Chop the avocado, adding it to your chopped vegetables, adding your remaining oil, vinegar, salt, pepper and basil.
4. Ladle your tomato puree mixture into bowls, and serve with chopped vegetables as a salad.

Nutritions: *Calories: 181, Protein: 3 Grams, Fat: 14 Grams, Carbs: 14 Grams*

Saturday

Breakfast: Spiced Breakfast Potatoes

 Preparation:
5 Minutes

 Cooking:
25 Minutes

 Serves:
4

Ingredients

- Olive Oil (2 T.)
- Potatoes (1 Lb., Diced)
- Pepper (to taste)
- Garlic Powder (1/2 t.)
- Salt (to taste)
- Paprika (1/2 t.)

Directions

1. Potatoes are nice comfort food to have on hand, especially in the morning. Before you begin making up the potatoes, you will want to prep the oven to 400.
2. Now, dice up the potatoes to bite-sized fragments and set them into a mixing bowl. Once in place, coat the potatoes with olive oil and season to your liking. When they are set, you can place them onto a baking dish and pop them into the oven for thirty minutes.
3. By the end of this time, the potatoes should be golden and set to serve.

Nutritions: *Calories: 150, Carbs: 20g, Fats: 6g, Proteins: 3g*

Ready in:
40 minutes

Serves:
6

Ingredients

- 1 cup of olive oil
- 10 canned artichoke hearts, chopped
- 2 carrots cut into thin slices
- 1 cup of long-grain rice
- 3 cups vegetable broth
- 2 Tbsp of fresh parsley finely chopped
- 2 Tbsp fresh dill finely chopped
- 2 Tbsp apple cider vinegar (optional)
- Salt and ground pepper to taste

Directions

1. Heat oil in a large pot over medium-high heat.
2. Add artichokes and sauté for 5 minutes.
3. Add carrots and sprinkle with a pinch of the salt and pepper.
4. Sauté and stir for 2 to 3 minutes.
5. Add rice and stir for one minute.
6. Pour water, and add dill and parsley; stir.
7. Bring to a boil and reduce heat to simmer.
8. Cover and cook for 25 minutes.
9. Taste and adjust seasonings.
10. Pour apple cider vinegar and stir.
11. Serve hot.

Nutritions: *Calories 445.53, Calories From Fat (40%) 180.14, Total Fat 20.41g 31%, Saturated Fat 3g 15%, Cholesterol 1.23mg <1%, Sodium 1025.47mg 43%, Potassium 854.8mg 24%, Total Carbohydrates 58.7g 20%, Fiber 10.55g 42%, Sugar 1.31g, Protein 11g 22%*

Dinner: Simple Chili

Ready in:
30 Minutes

Serves:
4

Ingredients

- 1 Onion, Diced
- 1 Teaspoon Olive Oil
- 3 Cloves Garlic, Minced
- 28 Ounces Tomatoes, Canned
- ¼ Cup Tomato Paste
- 14 Ounces Kidney Beans, Canned, Rinsed & Dried
- 2-3 Teaspoons Chili Powder
- ¼ Cup Cilantro, Fresh (or Parsley)
- ¼ Teaspoon Sea Salt, Fine

Directions

1. Get out a pot, and sauté your onion and garlic in your oil at the bottom cook for five minutes. Add in your tomato paste, tomatoes, beans, and chili powder. Season with salt.
2. Allow it to simmer for ten to twenty minutes.
3. Garnish with cilantro or parsley to serve.

Nutritions: *Calories: 160, Protein: 8 Grams, Fat: 3 Grams, Carbs: 29 Grams*

Sunday

Breakfast: Breakfast Energy Balls

 Preparation:
2 Minutes

 Cooking:
20 Minutes

 Serves:
16

Ingredients

- Rolled Oats (1/2 C.)
- Apple (1/2)
- Almonds (1/2 C.)
- Dates (12)
- Cacao Powder (1/4 C.)
- Almond Extract (2 t.)
- Sunflower Seeds (1/2 C.)
- Flax Seed (1 T.)

Directions

1. The morning can be an extremely busy time. If this sounds like you, this recipe is perfect to prep for the whole week. That way, you just grab a couple of energy balls, and you are out the door with breakfast in hand.
2. If you have time, soak the dates for about twenty minutes before starting the recipe.
3. When the dates are set, place all of the ingredients from the list into your blender and blend on high for about thirty seconds. By the end, you should have a slightly sticky dough.
4. Next, you will want to portion the mixture out about one tablespoon per ball and place onto a plate.
5. For extra flavor and variety, roll the balls in cacao powder, crushed nuts, or crushed seeds. When they are set, place them in the fridge and allow to harden for at least thirty minutes before enjoying!

Nutritions: *Calories: 70, Carbs: 5g, Fats: 5g, Proteins: 3g*

Lunch:
Spring Greens and Rice Stew

Ready in:
35 miutes

Serves:
4

Ingredients

- ▸ 1/3 cup of olive oil
- ▸ 2 cups lettuce salad, chopped
- ▸ 2 cups dandelion leaves chopped
- ▸ 1 cup rice short grain
- ▸ 3 cups vegetable broth
- ▸ 1 tsp fresh basil finely chopped
- ▸ 2 Tbsp fresh dill chopped
- ▸ Table salt and ground black pepper to taste

Directions

1. Heat oil in a large pot over medium-high heat.
2. Sauté lettuce and dandelion leaves for about 4 to 5 minutes.
3. Add rice, cook for one minute; pour rice, and stir.
4. Add in basil, dill, and the salt and ground pepper.
5. Reduce heat to medium-low, cover and cook for about 40 minutes or until all liquid has been absorbed
6. Taste, adjust seasoning, and serve.

Nutritions: *Calories 470.95, Calories From Fat (42%) 199.52, Total Fat 22.66g 35%, Saturated Fat 3.2g 16%, Cholesterol 1.85mg <1%, Sodium 1246.8mg 52%, Potassium 499mg 14%, Total Carbohydrates 63.81g 21%, Fiber 7g 28%, Sugar 0.2g, Protein 9g 18%*

Ready in:
20 minutes

Serves:
4

Directions

1. Get out a bowl and combine your cauliflower rice, tomatoes, mint, parsley, cucumbers, scallions and snap peas together. Toss until combined.
2. Add your olive oil and lemon juice before tossing again. Season with salt and pepper.

Ingredients

- 4 Cups Cauliflower Rice
- 1 ½ Cups Cherry Tomatoes, Quartered
- 3-4 Tablespoons Olive Oil
- 1 Cup Parsley, Fresh & Chopped
- 1 Cup Mint, Fresh & Chopped
- 1 Cup Snap Peas, Sliced Thin
- 1 Small Cucumber, Cut into ¼ Inch Pieces
- ¼ Cup Scallions, Sliced Thin
- 3-4 Tablespoons Lemon Juice, Fresh
- 1 Teaspoon Sea Salt, Fine
- ½ Teaspoon Black Pepper

Nutritions: *Calories: 220, Protein: 7 Grams, Fat: 15 Grams, Carbs: 20 Grams*

Week 3
Monday

Breakfast: Pumpkin Porridge

 Preparation:
5 Minutes

 Cooking:
50 Minutes

 Serves:
2

Ingredients

- Pumpkin Puree (1/2 C.)
- Soaked Quinoa (1 C.)
- Maple Syrup (4 T.)
- Ground Ginger (1/2 t.)
- Ground Cinnamon (1 t.)
- Ground Cloves (1/8 t.)

Directions

1. Before you begin, it is vital that you soak the quinoa for at least an hour. Once the quinoa is done, you will want to drain any excess water before placing it into a pan over moderate heat on the stove.
2. When this is done, add in .75 cup of water and get everything to a boil. Once the pot is bubbling, reduce the high temperature and allow the quinoa to simmer for about fifteen minutes. At the end of this time, all of the liquid should be gone and absorbed.
3. Once the quinoa is cooked properly, you can then add in the pumpkin, maple syrup, and all of the seasonings. At this point, feel open to insert more or less seasoning to your liking!

Nutritions: *Calories: 430, Carbs: 80g, Fats: 5g, Proteins: 10g*

Ready in:
30 minutes

Serves:
4

Ingredients

- ▸ 2 Tablespoons Olive Oil
- ▸ 4 Cloves Garlic, Minced
- ▸ 8 Ounces Whole Wheat Pasta
- ▸ ½ Cup Panko Bread Crumbs
- ▸ 1 Tablespoon Nutritional Yeast
- ▸ 1 Teaspoon Red Pepper Flakes
- ▸ 1 Large Lemon, Juiced & Zested
- ▸ 1 Bunch Collard Greens, Large

Directions

1. Fill a pot with water and salt it. Bring it to a boil using high heat. Add in the pasta and cool al dente before rinsing under cold water to stop the cooking.
2. Reserve half a cup of the cooking liquid from the pasta and set it to the side.
3. Place it over medium heat and add in a tablespoon of olive oil. Stir in half of your garlic, sautéing for a half a minute.
4. Add in the breadcrumbs and then sauté, cooking for five more minutes.
5. Toss in the red pepper flakes and nutritional yeast, mixing well.
6. Transfer the breadcrumbs in the pan.
7. Add the remaining olive oil and then stir in your salt, pepper, garlic clove, and greens.
8. Cook for five minutes. Cook until wilted.
9. Add in the pasta, mix in the reserved pasta liquid, and then mix well. Add in the lemon juice, zest, and garlic crumbs. Toss before serving.

Dinner:
Dijon Maple Burgers

 Ready in:
50 minutes

 Serves:
12

Ingredients

- 1 Red Bell Pepper
- 19 Ounces Can Chickpeas, Rinsed & Drained
- 1 Cup Almonds, Ground
- 2 Teaspoons Dijon Mustard
- 1 Teaspoon Oregano
- ½ Teaspoon Sage
- 1 Cup Spinach, Fresh
- 1 – ½ Cups Rolled Oats
- 1 Clove Garlic, Pressed
- ½ Lemon, Juiced
- 2 Teaspoons Maple Syrup, Pure

Directions

1. Start by heating your oven to 350, and then get out a baking sheet. Line it with parchment paper.
2. Cut your red pepper in half and then take the seeds out. Place it on your baking sheet, and roast in the oven while you prepare your other ingredients.
3. Process your chickpeas, almonds, mustard and maple syrup together in a food processor.
4. Add in your lemon juice, oregano, sage, garlic and spinach, processing again. Make sure it's combined, but don't puree it.
5. Once your red bell pepper is softened, which should roughly take ten minutes, add this to the processor as well. Add in your oats, mixing well.
6. Form twelve patties, cooking in the oven for a half hour. They should be browned.

Nutritions: *Calories: 200, Protein: 8 Grams, Fat: 11 Grams, Carbs: 21 Grams*

Tuesday

Breakfast: Easy PBB Breakfast Cookies

Preparation:
2 Minutes

Cooking:
10 Minutes

Serves:
2

Ingredients

- Rolled Oats (1 C.)
- Peanut Butter (1/4 C.)
- Bananas (2)

Directions

1. Who said cookies were inappropriate for breakfast? These simple peanut butter and banana cookies are a much healthier option and will be set to go when you need a quick breakfast. Start off by prepping the oven to 350.
2. Next, take out a mixing bowl and combine your oats, peanut butter, and some mashed bananas.
3. Now that you have your mixture done take out a baking sheet and lay down some parchment paper. With this in place, you can now roll the mixture into 12 small cookies and lay them evenly across the baking sheet.
4. Finally, pop the dish into the oven for 12 minutes, and your cookies should come out golden-brown and delicious!

Nutritions: *Calories: 250, Carbs: 40g, Fats: 11g, Proteins: 10g*

Lunch: Plant Pad Thai

Ready in:
20 Minutes

Serves:
4

Ingredients

- 2 Teaspoons Coconut Oil
- 1 Red Pepper, Sliced
- 2 Carrots, Sliced
- ½ White Onion, Sliced
- 1 Thai Chili, Chopped
- 8 Ounces Brown Rice Noodles
- ½ Cup Peanuts, Chopped
- ½ Cup Cilantro, Chopped

Sauce:
- 3 Tablespoons Soy Sauce
- 3 Tablespoons Lime Juice, Fresh
- 3 Tablespoons Brown Sugar
- 1 Tablespoon Sriracha
- 3 Tablespoons Vegetable Broth
- 1 Teaspoon Chili Garlic Paste
- 2 Cloves Garlic, Minced

Tofu:
- 1 lb. Extra Firm Tofu, Sliced
- 1 Tablespoon Peanut Butter
- 2 Tablespoons Sriracha
- 3 Tablespoons Soy Sauce
- 2 Tablespoons Rice Vinegar
- 2 Teaspoons Sesame Oil
- 2 Teaspoons Ginger, Grated

Directions

1. Get out a large pot of water and soak the rice noodles in it. Press your tofu to get out the excess liquid. Get out a nonstick pan and heat it over medium-high heat. Add in the tofu, searing for three minutes per side.
2. Whisk all ingredients for the tofu in a bowl, stirring in the tofu, and mixing well to marinate.
3. Separately mix your Thai sauce in a bowl, adding the tofu in.
4. Get a wok and put it over medium heat, adding in a teaspoon of oil.
5. Toss in the carrots, onion, red pepper, and chili. Cook for three minutes.
6. Transfer the vegetables to the tofu bowl and add in more oil. Stir the drained noodles in, and then cook for an additional minute.
7. Transfer the noodles to your tofu, and toss before serving warm. Garnish with cilantro and peanuts.

Ready in:
40 Minutes

 Serves:
1

Directions

1. Steam your edamame beans, and then assemble your edamame, rice, avocado, spinach, cilantro, scallions and bell pepper into a bowl.
2. Cut the nori into ribbons, sprinkling it on top, drizzling with tamari and sesame seeds before serving.

Ingredients

- ½ Cup Edamame Beans, Shelled & Fresh
- ¾ Cup Brown Rice, Cooked
- ½ Cup Spinach, Chopped
- ¼ Cup Bell Pepper, Sliced
- ¼ Cup Avocado, Sliced
- ¼ Cup Cilantro, Fresh & Chopped
- 1 Scallion, Chopped
- ¼ Nori Sheet
- 1-2 Tablespoons Tamari
- 1 Tablespoon Sesame Seeds, Optional

Nutritions: *Calories: 467, Protein: 22 Grams, Fat: 20 Grams, Carbs: 56 Grams*

Wednesday

Breakfast: Oatmeal and Berry Smoothie Bowl

 Preparation:
1 Minutes

 Cooking:
5 Minutes

 Serves:
2

Ingredients

▸ Almond Milk (1/4 C.)
▸ Frozen Mixed Berries (1 C.)
▸ Frozen Acai (1 C.)
▸ Peanut Butter (1 T.)
▸ Old-Fashioned Oats (1/4 C.)

Directions

1. This recipe is meant for when you have more time on your hands to make a pretty dish. You will want to start out by placing the nut butter, oats, and fruits into your blender.
2. Once everything is blended smooth, go ahead and pour it into a bowl.
3. At this point, you can top your smoothie bowl however you would like! You can use fresh berries, slices of banana, more oats, or even treat yourself with some shredded coconut! The options are limitless.

Nutritions: *Calories: 300, Carbs: 58g, Fats: 8g, Proteins: 10g*

Ready in:
40 Minutes

Serves:
4

Directions

1. Rinse your quinoa and then throw it in a saucepan over medium heat. Cook for five minutes before adding the water.
2. Bring it to a boil before reducing your pot to a simmer. Cover and cook for thirteen minutes.
3. Toss all remaining ingredients into a salad bowl and mix with quinoa. Serve fresh.

Ingredients

- 1 Cup Dry Quinoa
- 1 ½ Cups Water
- ½ cup Cranberries, Dried
- 4 Tablespoon Cilantro, Fresh & Chopped
- 1 Lime, Juiced
- 1 ½ Teaspoon Curry Powder
- 1/8 Teaspoon Cumin
- ¼ Cup Green Onion, Chopped
- ½ Cup Bell Pepper, Diced
- 1/3 Cup Toasted Almonds, Sliced
- ½ Carrots, Shredded
- 4 Tablespoons Pepitas
- Sea Salt & Black Pepper to Taste
- Olive Oil for Drizzling
- Lime Wedges to Garnish

Dinner:
Pesto & Tomato Quinoa

Ready in:
25 Minutes

Serves:
1

Ingredients

- 1 Teaspoon Olive Oil
- 1 Cup Onion, Chopped
- 1 Cup Zucchini, Chopped
- 1 Clove Garlic, Minced
- 1 Tomato, Chopped
- Pinch Sea Salt
- 2 Tablespoons Sun Dried Tomatoes, Chopped
- 2-3 Tablespoons Basil Pesto
- 1 Cup Spinach, Chopped
- 2 Cups Quinoa, Cooked
- 1 Tablespoon Nutritional Yeast, Optional

Directions

1. Heat your oil in a skillet, and sauté your onion over medium-high heat. This should take five minutes, and then add in your garlic, cooking for another minute. Add in your sea salt and zucchini.
2. Cook for about five-minute and then add in your sun dried tomatoes, and mix well.
3. Toss your pesto in, and then mix well.
4. Layer your spinach, quinoa and then zucchini mixture on a plate, topping with nutritional yeast if desired.

Nutritions: *Protein: 20 Grams, Fat: 23 Grams, Carbs: 69 Grams*

Thursday

Breakfast: Classic Green Morning Smoothie

Preparation:
2 Minutes

Cooking:
5 Minutes

Serves:
1

Directions

1. This is the smoothie everyone turns their nose up to, but it is packed with flavor and nutrients! Simply place everything into your blender with ice, blend on high for thirty seconds or so, then you are all set to go.

Ingredients

- Almond Milk (1 C.)
- Kale (1 C.)
- Banana (1)
- Poppy Seeds (2 t.)
- Peanut Butter (2 T.)

Nutritions: *Calories: 350, Carbs: 40g, Fats: 20g, Proteins: 20g*

Lunch: Eggplant Pasta

Ready in:
30 Minutes

Serves:
4

Ingredients

- 12 Ounces Dry Pasta
- 2 Cups Cremini Mushrooms, Sliced
- ½ Eggplant, Small & Cubed
- 1 ½ Cups Marinara Sauce, Preferably Vegan
- 2 Cups Water
- Sea Salt & Black Pepper to Taste
- 3 Tablespoons Olive Oil
- Basil, Fresh to Garnish

Directions

1. Put your eggplant in a colander before sprinkling with salt. They will drain as it rests for half an hour. Rinse thoroughly after the thirty-minute mark.
2. Put a saucepan over medium-high heat with your eggplant, olive oil, ½ teaspoon of salt, and a third of your minced garlic. Stir and then cook for an additional six minutes. It should be golden brown and then add n the mushrooms. Sauté for two minutes before putting it in a bowl.
3. Cook your pasta according to package instructions and drain. Add in the marinara sauce and garlic into the saucepan with your pasta. Season with salt and pepper as necessary.
4. Toss in the eggplant and garnish with basil.

Ready in:
13 minutes

Serves:
4

Directions

1. Cut the stems and tops of your bok choy into one inch pieces.
2. Mix together all remaining ingredients in a bowl.
3. Add your bok choy, and top with your dressing.
4. Fry until tender, which should take eight to ten minutes.

Ingredients

- 1 Head Bok Choy
- 1 Teaspoon Canola Oil
- 1/3 Cup Green Onion, Chopped
- 1 Tablespoon Brown Sugar
- 1 ½ Tablespoon Soy Sauce, Light
- 1 Tablespoon Rice Wine
- ½ Teaspoon Ginger, Ground
- 1 Tablespoon Sesame Seeds

Nutritions: *Calories: 76, Protein: 4.4 Grams, Fat: 2.7 Grams, Carbs: 9.8 Grams*

Friday

Breakfast: Zoom Energy Smoothie

 Preparation:
2 Minutes

 Cooking:
5 Minutes

 Serves:
2

Ingredients

- Almond Milk (1 C.)
- Banana (1)
- Orange (1)
- Pineapple (1 C.)
- Raspberries (1 C.)

Directions

1. This is another delicious recipe, meant to give you a pep in your step through the power of fruit! Easily set all of the items into your blender with ice, combine on high, and go!

Nutritions: *Calories: 120, Carbs: 25g, Fats: 2g, Proteins: 4g*

Ready in:
25 Minutes

Serves:
6

Ingredients

▶ 2 Celery Stalks, Diced
▶ ¼ Teaspoon Thyme
▶ 1 Carrot, Peeled & Diced
▶ 2 Broccoli Heads, Chopped
▶ 2 Bay Leaves
▶ 1 Can Cannellini Beans
▶ 4 Cups Vegetable Broth
▶ 2 Cups Water
▶ 2 Tablespoons Nutritional Yeast
▶ 1 Packet Vegetable Powder

Directions

1. Get out a pot and add the carrot, celery, and thyme.
2. Cover and cook for five minutes using medium heat.
3. Pour in a dash of water, then take it off of the heat. Chop the florets and stalks again after peeling. Add the stock, water, bay leaf, beans, broccoli to your carrot mixture.
4. Cover the soup, and bring it all to a boil.
5. Allow it to simmer for ten minutes, and then discard the bay leaf before taking it off of the heat.
6. Stir in the vegetable powder and nutritional powder. Blend using an immersion blender before serving.

Saturday

Breakfast: Sweet Strawberry and Mango Smoothie

 Preparation:
1 Minutes

 Cooking:
5 Minutes

 Serves:
1

Directions

1. A smoothie is a perfect way to start the morning, especially if you are in a rush! Simply put all of the components into your mixer, add a desired amount of ice, and blend on high until everything is smooth.
2. Pour and go!

Ingredients

► Almond Milk (6 T.)
► Strawberries (4)
► Mango (1)
► Blueberries (1 C.)
► Banana (2)

Nutritions: *Calories: 440, Carbs: 100g, Fats: 2g, Proteins: 8g*

Ready in:
40 Minutes

 Serves:
6

Directions

1. Get out a large pot and heat the oil over medium heat. Add your onion and cook for ten minutes.
2. Stir in the turmeric, oregano, salt, pepper, basil, and garlic, cooking for another minute. Add in the tomatoes with the juices, sundried tomatoes, and vinegar. Cook for fifteen minutes, and then use an immersion blender. Toss the spinach into your sauce, and cook for another five minutes. Boil your pasta according to the box, and serve with the spinach mixture and garnish as desired.

Ingredients

- 1 Tablespoon Oregano
- 1 Tablespoon Basil
- 6 Cloves Garlic, Minced
- 1 Sweet Onion, Chopped
- ¼ Cup Olive Oil
- 2 Teaspoons Turmeric
- Salt & Pepper to Taste
- 28 Ounces Fire Roasted Tomatoes
- ½ Cup Sundried Tomatoes, Oil Packed & Chopped
- 8 Ounces Red Lentil Pasta
- 1 Tablespoon Apple Cider Vinegar
- 2 Handfuls Baby Spinach, Large

Dinner: Stuffed Bell Pepper

Ready in:
25 Minutes

Serves:
4

Directions

1. Bake your peppers at 400 for ten minutes, and then mix the rest of your ingredients in a bowl.
2. Stuff your peppers with the quinoa mixture.

Ingredients

- 4 Bell Peppers, Halved & Hollowed
- ½ Cup Quinoa, Cooked
- 12 Black Olives, Halved
- 1/3 Cup Tomatoes, Sun Dried
- ½ Cup Baby Spinach
- 2 Cloves Garlic, Minced
- Sea Salt & Black Pepper to Taste

Nutritions: *Calories: 126, Protein: 3 Grams, Fat: 5 Grams, Carbs: 19 Grams*

Sunday

Breakfast: Chia and Peanut Butter Oatmeal

 Preparation:
5 Minutes

 Cooking:
10 Minutes

 Serves:
2

Ingredients

▶ Water (3 C.)
▶ Rolled Oats (1 C.)
▶ Chia Seeds (1 T.)
▶ Salt (1/8 t.)
▶ Peanut Butter (2 T.)
▶ Cinnamon (1 t.)
▶ Banana (1)

Directions

1. Oatmeal is an excellent way to start the day, especially when it involves peanut butter! You will want to begin this recipe by taking out a pot and placing it over medium heat. As it warms up, you can add in the sliced-up banana, oats, chia seeds, salt, and the cinnamon. When these items are in place, carefully pour in the water and stir everything up well.
2. You will want to cook these ingredients for about ten minutes or until all of the liquid is gone. As this cooks, be sure to whisk the pot to avoid anything smoldering to the underside of the pot.
3. When everything is cooked, portion out your oatmeal and serve with sliced banana and peanut butter on top.

Nutritions: *Calories: 370, Carbs: 70g, Fats: 15g, Proteins: 15g*

Lunch: White Wine Pasta

Ready in:
30 Minutes

Serves:
4

Ingredients

Brussels:
- 16 Ounce Brussels Sprouts, Halved
- 2 Tablespoons Olive Oil
- Sea Salt & Black Pepper to Taste

Pasta:
- 4 Cloves Garlic, Chopped
- 3 Tablespoons Olive Oil
- 1/3 Cup Dry White Wine
- 4 Tablespoons Arrowroot Starch
- 1 ¾ Cup Almond Milk
- 4 Tablespoons Nutritional Yeast
- Sea Salt & Black Pepper to Taste
- 10 Ounces Vegan Pasta
- ¼ Cup Parmesan Cheese

Serving:
- Simple Greens
- Garlic Bread

Directions

1. Heat the oven to 400, and then get a baking tray out. Spread the sprouts out, and then add the oil. Season with salt and pepper before tossing.
2. Boil the pasta al dente and then drain.
3. Heat a skillet using medium heat. Add the oil. Once it shimmers, add the garlic. Cook for an additional three minutes.
4. Stir the wine in to deglaze and then cook for an additional two minutes.
5. Whisk the almond milk and arrowroot powder, and then blend with the cheese in a food processor. Season with salt and pepper if desired.
6. Het the almond milk sauce in your skillet until it bubbles. Bake your sprouts for fifteen minutes, and then toss in the drained pasta, cheese sauce and sprouts together in a bowl before serving.

Dinner: Cabbage & Beet Stew

Ready in:
30 minutes

Serves:
4

Directions

1. Start by heating up your oil in a pot, and then sauté your vegetables.
2. Pour your broth in, mixing in your seasoning. Simmer until it's cooked through, and then top with dill.

Ingredients

- 2 Tablespoons Olive Oil
- 3 Cups Vegetable Broth
- 2 Tablespoons Lemon Juice, Fresh
- ½ Teaspoon Garlic Powder
- ½ Cup Carrots, Shredded
- 2 Cups Cabbage, Shredded
- 1 Cup Beets, Shredded
- Dill for Garnish
- ½ Teaspoon Onion Powder
- Sea Salt & Black Pepper to Taste

Nutritions: Calories: 95, Protein: 1 Gram, Fat: 7 Grams, Carbs: 10 Grams

Chapter 4.
Breakfast and Brunch Recipes

White Sandwich Bread

Preparation:
10 Minutes

Cooking:
20 Minutes

Serves:
16

Ingredients

- 1 cup warm water
- 2 tablespoons active dry yeast
- 4 tablespoons oil
- 2 ½ teaspoons salt
- 2 tablespoons raw sugar
- 1 cup warm almond milk
- 6 cups all-purpose flour

Directions

1. Add warm water, yeast and sugar into a bowl and stir. Set aside for 5 minutes or until lots of tiny bubbles are formed, sort of frothy.
2. Add flour and salt into a mixing bowl and stir. Pour the oil, yeast mix and milk and mix into dough. If the dough is too hard, add a little water, a tablespoon at a time and mix well each time. If the dough is too sticky, add more flour, a tablespoon at a time. Knead the dough for 8 minutes until soft and supple. You can use your hands or use the dough hook attachment of the stand mixer.
3. Now spray some water on top of the dough. Keep the bowl covered with a towel. Let it rest until it doubles in size.
4. Remove the dough from the bowl and place on your countertop. Punch the dough.
5. Line a loaf pan with parchment paper. You can also grease with some oil if you prefer. You can use 2 smaller loaf pans if you want to make smaller loaves, like I did.
6. Place the dough in the loaf pan. Now spray some more water on top of the dough. Keep the loaf pan covered with a towel. Let it rest until the dough doubles in size.
7. Bake in a preheated oven at 370° F for about 40 – 50 minutes or a toothpick when inserted in the center of the bread comes out without any particles stuck on it.
8. Let it cool to room temperature.
9. Cut into 16 equal slices and use as required. Store in a breadbox at room temperature.

Nutritions: Calories 245, Total Fat 7.5g, Saturated Fat 3.7g, Cholesterol 0mg, Sodium 369mg, Total Carbohydrate 38.7g, Dietary Fiber 1.9g, Total Sugars 2.1g, Protein 5.8g, Vitamin D 0mcg, Calcium 11mg, Iron 3mg, Potassium 120mg

A Toast to Remember

Preparation:
10 Minutes

Cooking:
15 Minutes

Serves:
4

Ingredients

- 8 oz black beans
- ¼ teaspoon sea salt
- 2 pieces whole-wheat toast
- ¼ teaspoon chipotle spice
- ¼ teaspoon black pepper
- 1 teaspoon garlic powder
- 1 freshly juiced lime
- 1 freshly diced avocado
- ¼ cup corn
- 3 tablespoons, finely diced onion
- ½ freshly diced tomato
- ¼ cup Fresh cilantro

Directions

1. Mix the chipotle spice with the beans, salt, garlic powder, and pepper. Stir in the lime juice.
2. Boil all of these until you have a thick and starchy mix.
3. In a bowl, mix the corn, tomato, avocado, red onion, cilantro, and juice from the rest of the lime. Add some pepper and salt.
4. Toast the bread and first spread the black bean mixture followed by the avocado mix.
5. Take a bite of wholesome goodness!

Nutritions: Calories 355, Total Fat 12g, Saturated Fat 2.4g, Cholesterol 0mg, Sodium 215mg, Total Carbohydrate 50.7g, Dietary Fiber 13.1g, Total Sugars 3g, Protein 14.6g, Vitamin D 0mcg, Calcium 82mg, Iron 4mg, Potassium 1167mg

Preparation:
5 Minutes

Cooking:
0 Minutes

Serves:
1

Directions

1. In a bowl, mix the cinnamon, hot water, raisins, and cacao powder.
2. Spread the peanut butter on the bread.
3. Cut the bananas and put them on the toast.
4. Mix the raisin mixture in a blender and spread it on the sandwich.

Ingredients

- ¼ cup hot water
- 1 teaspoon cinnamon
- ¼ cup raisins
- 2 teaspoons cacao powder
- 1 ripe banana
- 2 slices whole-grain bread
- ¼ cup natural peanut butter

Nutritions: Calories 807, Total Fat 34.2g, Saturated Fat 6.6g, Cholesterol 0mg, Sodium 269mg, Total Carbohydrate 103.2g, Dietary Fiber 20.6g, Total Sugars 45.9g, Protein 31.2g, Vitamin D 0mcg, Calcium 252mg, Iron 12mg, Potassium 704mg

Tasty Oatmeal and Carrot Cake

Preparation:
10 Minutes

Cooking:
10 Minutes

Serves:
1

Ingredients

- 1 cup water
- ½ teaspoon cinnamon
- 1 cup rolled oats
- ¼ teaspoon salt
- ¼ cup raisins
- ½ cup shredded carrots
- 1 cup almond milk
- ¼ teaspoon allspice
- ½ teaspoon vanilla extract

Toppings:
- ¼ cup chopped walnuts
- 2 tablespoons maple syrup
- 2 tablespoons shredded coconut

Directions

1. Put a small pot on low heat and bring the non-dairy milk, oats, and water to a simmer.
2. Now, add the carrots, vanilla extract, raisins, salt, cinnamon and allspice. You need to simmer all of the ingredients, but do not forget to stir them. You will know that they are ready when the liquid is fully absorbed into all of the ingredients (in about 7-10 minutes).
3. Transfer the thickened dish to bowls. You can drizzle some maple syrup on top or top them with coconut or walnuts.

Nutritions: Calories 1336, Total Fat 84.6g, Saturated Fat 55.7g, Cholesterol 0mg, Sodium 678mg, Total Carbohydrate 135.8g, Dietary Fiber 20g, Total Sugars 58.1g, Protein 25.8g, Vitamin D 0mcg, Calcium 186mg, Iron 11mg, Potassium 1671mg

Onion & Mushroom Tart with a Nice Brown Rice Crust

Preparation:
10 Minutes

Cooking:
55 Minutes

Serves:
1

Ingredients

- 1 ½ pounds mushrooms
- 1 cup short-grain brown rice
- 2 ¼ cups water
- ½ teaspoon ground black pepper
- 1 large onion
- 7 ounces extra-firm tofu
- 1 cup almond milk
- 2 teaspoons onion powder
- 1 tablespoon low-sodium soy
- 1 teaspoon molasses
- ¼ teaspoon ground turmeric
- ¼ cup white wine
- ¼ cup tapioca

Directions

1. Cook the brown rice and put it aside for later use.
2. Slice the onions into thin strips and sauté them in water until they are soft. Then, add the molasses, and cook them for a few minutes.
3. Next, sauté the mushrooms in water. Once the mushrooms are cooked and they are soft, add the white wine or sherry. Cook everything for a few more minutes.
4. In a blender, combine milk, tofu, arrowroot, turmeric, and onion powder till you have a smooth mixture
5. On a pie plate, create a layer of rice, spreading evenly to form a crust. The rice should be warm and not cold. It will be easy to work with warm rice. You can also use a pastry roller to get an even crust. With your fingers, gently press the sides.
6. Take half of the tofu mixture and the mushrooms and spoon them over the tart dish. Smooth the level with your spoon.
7. Now, top the layer with onions followed by the tofu mixture. You can smooth the surface again with your spoon.
8. Sprinkle some black pepper on top.
9. Bake the pie at 350°F for about 45 minutes. Toward the end, you can cover it loosely with tin foil. This will help the crust to remain moist.
10. Allow the pie crust to cool down, so that you can slice it. If you are in love with vegetarian dishes, there is no way that you will not love this pie.

Nutritions: Calories 1375, Total Fat 72.7g, Saturated Fat 51.9g, Cholesterol 0mg, Sodium 647mg, Total Carbohydrate 140.8g, Dietary Fiber 20.1g, Total Sugars 36.2g, Protein 54.9g, Vitamin D 2449mcg, Calcium 485mg, Iron 29mg, Potassium 3514mg

Perfect Breakfast Shake

 Preparation:
5 Minutes

 Cooking:
0 Minutes

 Serves:
2

Directions

1. Use a powerful blender to combine all the ingredients.
2. Process everything until you have a smooth shake.
3. Enjoy a hearty shake to kickstart your day.

Ingredients

- 3 tablespoons raw cacao powder
- 1 cup almond milk
- 2 bananas
- 3 tablespoons natural peanut butter

Nutritions: Calories 546, Total Fat 41.3g, Saturated Fat 27.9g, Cholesterol 0mg, Sodium 27mg, Total Carbohydrate 40.4g, Dietary Fiber 8.6g, Total Sugars 19.9g, Protein 12.2g, Vitamin D 0mcg, Calcium 25mg, Iron 5mg, Potassium 738mg

Beet Gazpacho

 Preparation:
10 Minutes

 Cooking:
2 Minutes

 Serves:
4

Ingredients

- ½ large bunch young beets with stems, roots and leaves
- 2 small cloves garlic, peeled,
- ¼ teaspoon Salt
- ¼ teaspoon Pepper
- ½ teaspoon liquid stevia
- ½ cup coconut milk kefir
- 1 teaspoon chopped dill
- ½ tablespoon canola oil
- 1 small red onion, chopped
- 1 tablespoon apple cider vinegar
- 2 cups vegetable broth or water
- 1 tablespoon chopped chives
- 1 scallion, sliced
- 1 cup Roasted baby potatoes

Directions

1. Cut the roots and stems of the beets into small pieces. Thinly slice the beet greens.
2. Place a saucepan over medium heat. Add oil. When the oil is heated, add onion and garlic and cook until onion turns translucent.
3. Stir in the beets, roots and stem and cook for a minute.
4. Add broth, salt and water and cover with a lid. Simmer until tender.
5. Add stevia and vinegar and mix well. Taste and adjust the stevia and vinegar if required.
6. Turn off the heat. Blend with an immersion blender until smooth.
7. Place the saucepan back over it. When it begins to boil, add beet greens and cook for a minute. Turn off the heat.
8. Cool completely. Chill if desired.
9. Add rest of the ingredients and stir.
10. Serve in bowls with roasted potatoes if desired.

Nutritions: Calories 97, Total Fat 3.8g, Saturated Fat 1.2g, Cholesterol 1mg, Sodium 580mg, Total Carbohydrate 12.4g, Dietary Fiber 2g, Total Sugars 2.6g, Protein 4g, Vitamin D 0mcg, Calcium 97mg, Iron 1mg, Potassium 198mg

Vegetable Rice

 Preparation:
7 Minutes

 Cooking:
15 Minutes

 Serves:
4

Ingredients

- ½ cup brown rice, rinsed
- 1 cup water
- ½ teaspoon dried basil
- 1 small onion, chopped
- 2 tablespoons raisins
- 5 ounces frozen peas, thawed
- 10 pieces pecans, halves and toasted
- 1 medium carrot, cut into matchsticks
- 4 green onions, cut into 1-inch pieces
- 1 tablespoon olive oil
- ½ teaspoon salt or to taste
- ¼ teaspoon Ground pepper or to taste

Directions

1. Place a small saucepan with water over medium heat.
2. When it begins to boil, add rice and basil. Stir.
3. When it again begins to boil, lower the heat and cover with a lid. Cook for 15 minutes until all the water is absorbed and rice is cooked. Add more water if you think the rice is not cooked well.
4. Meanwhile, place a skillet over medium high heat. Add carrots, raisins and onions and sauté until the vegetables are crisp as well as tender.
5. Stir in the peas, salt, and pepper.
6. Add pecans and rice and stir.
7. Serve.

Nutritions: Calories 419, Total Fat 29.3g, Saturated Fat 3.2g, Cholesterol 0mg, Sodium 333mg, Total Carbohydrate 36g, Dietary Fiber 7.9g, Total Sugars 7.4g, Protein 8.1g, Vitamin D 0mcg, Calcium 66mg, Iron 2mg, Potassium 400mg

Courgette Risotto

Preparation:
10 Minutes

Cooking:
5 Minutes

Serves:
8

Ingredients

- 2 tablespoons olive oil
- 4 cloves garlic, finely chopped
- 1.5 pounds Arborio rice
- 6 tomatoes, chopped
- 2 teaspoons chopped rosemary
- 6 courgettes, finely diced
- 1 ¼ cups peas, fresh or frozen
- 12 cups hot vegetable stock
- ¼ teaspoon Salt to taste
- ¼ teaspoon Freshly ground pepper

Directions

1. Place a large heavy bottomed pan over medium heat. Add oil. When the oil is heated, add onion and sauté until translucent.
2. Stir in the tomatoes and cook until soft.
3. Next stir in the rice and rosemary. Mix well.
4. Add half the stock and cook until dry. Stir frequently.
5. Add remaining stock and cook for 3-4 minutes.
6. Add courgette and peas and cook until rice is tender. Add salt and pepper to taste.
7. Stir in the basil. Let it sit for 5 minutes.
8. Serve hot.

Nutritions: Calories 422, Total Fat 7.6g, Saturated Fat 3.7g, Cholesterol 0mg, Sodium 1180mg, Total Carbohydrate 85g, Dietary Fiber 6.5g, Total Sugars 9.3g, Protein 9.7g, Vitamin D 0mcg, Calcium 53mg, Iron 3mg, Potassium 734mg

Cinnamon Peanut Butter Banana Overnight Oats

Preparation:
15 Minutes

Cooking:
0 Minutes

Serves:
5

Ingredients

- ½ cup Sliced Ripe Bananas
- 1 cup almond Milk
- ½ tsp Cinnamon
- 1 cup Oats
- 1 tbsp Peanut Butter

Directions

1. Use any glass container or jar.
2. Add milk, oats, and cinnamon to the container.
3. Mix well. You can add more liquid or more oats depending on how thin or thick you may want it.
4. Cover with lid or plastic wrap.
5. Place in refrigerator for at least 3 hours.
6. Add sliced bananas and peanut butter on top. Enjoy!

Nutritions: Calories 205, Total Fat 14.2g, Saturated Fat 10.7g, Cholesterol 0mg, Sodium 23mg, Total Carbohydrate 18g, Dietary Fiber 3.4g, Total Sugars 3.9g, Protein 4.2g, Vitamin D 0mcg, Calcium 19mg, Iron 2mg, Potassium 261mg

Savory Sweet Potato Hash with Black Beans

Preparation:
5 Minutes

Cooking:
15 Minutes

Serves:
3

Ingredients

- 1 cup Black Beans, cooked
- ¼ cup Chopped green onions
- 2 cups Diced Sweet Potatoes
- 1 cup Chopped Onion
- 2 cloves Minced Garlic
- 2 tsp Chili Powder
- 1/3 cup Vegetable Broth
- 4 tbsp Cilantro

Directions

1. Sauté onions and garlic in non-stick skillet.
2. Add one to two teaspoons of broth, and then add sweet potatoes and chili powder, Coat everything well.
3. Cook until potatoes are soft and cooked through. Mix to keep from sticking by adding broth as needed.
4. Add green onions and black beans. Cook for 15 minutes until beans are heated through.
5. Adjust seasoning to personal preferences.
6. Serve with cilantro on top. Enjoy!

Nutritions: Calories 370, Total Fat 1.6g, Saturated Fat 0.4g, Cholesterol 0mg, Sodium 118mg, Total Carbohydrate 74.2g, Dietary Fiber 15.6g, Total Sugars 3.9g, Protein 17g, Vitamin D 0mcg, Calcium 122mg, Iron 4mg, Potassium 1925mg

Nutty Breakfast Cookies

Preparation:
5 Minutes

Cooking:
10 Minutes

Serves:
12

Ingredients

- 1 tsp Vanilla
- 1 tsp Cinnamon
- ½ cup filtered water
- 1 tsp Sunflower Seeds
- ¼ cup Maple syrup
- ½ cup Nut Butter
- 2 cups Rolled or Old Fashion Oats
- ¼ cup Raisins

Directions

1. Heat oven to 350 degrees.
2. Use parchment paper on a cookie sheet.
3. Mix your warm water, and raisins. Let sit for five minutes.
4. Lightly blend one cup of oats. In large bowl, add the other cup of oats with this mixture.
5. Add nut butter to dry mixture. Make sure to create an even mix.
6. Mix in chia/raisin and water mixture. Using a wooden spoon, blend well.
7. Add sunflower seeds, maple syrup, cinnamon, and vanilla. Mix well.
8. Use a scooper to scoop even amounts onto cookie sheet. Or with wet hands, form into small balls and flatten with a spoon.
9. Let bake for 10 minutes. Once cool, keep in airtight container. Enjoy!

Nutritions: Calories 117, Total Fat 6.3g, Saturated Fat 1.3g, Cholesterol 0mg, Sodium 51mg, Total Carbohydrate 11.6g, Dietary Fiber 2.1g, Total Sugars 1.2g, Protein 4.5g, Vitamin D 0mcg, Calcium 10mg, Iron 2mg, Potassium 121mg

Super Protein Chia Pudding

Preparation:
5 Minutes

Cooking:
0 Minutes

Serves:
4

Ingredients

- ¼ tsp Vanilla
- 1/5 tsp Cinnamon
- ¼ cup Cooked Quinoa
- ¼ oz Chia Seeds
- ¾ cup almond Milk
- 2 tsps. Maple syrup
- ½ cup Hemp Seeds for topping
- ½ cup Chopped peanuts
- 1 mango

Directions

1. Mix together, chia seeds, cooked quinoa, almond milk, cinnamon, and maple syrup.
2. Put in a glass container, small mason jar or bowl
3. Place in refrigerator and leave for about 2 hours.
4. Once already set, add the mango toppings that you like. Enjoy!

Nutritions: Calories 442, Total Fat 28.1g, Saturated Fat 11.4g, Cholesterol 0mg, Sodium 14mg, Total Carbohydrate 40.2g, Dietary Fiber 5.8g, Total Sugars 13.7g, Protein 13.2g, Vitamin D 0mcg, Calcium 61mg, Iron 4mg, Potassium 596mg

Cinnamon Apple Muffins

Preparation:
10 Minutes

Cooking:
25 Minutes

Serves:
12

Ingredients

- ½ cup Apples, peeled and chopped
- ½ cup Raisins
- 1 tsp Apple Cider Vinegar
- ½ cup almond Milk
- 1 tsp Vanilla
- 1 tsp Cinnamon
- 1.5 cups Apple Sauce
- ½ cup Brown Sugar
- ¼ tsp All Spice
- ¼ tsp Salt
- 1 tsp Baking Powder
- 1 tsp Baking Soda
- 2 cups Whole Wheat Flour

Directions

1. Heat oven to 350°F
2. Mix together all dry ingredients into a big bowl. Set aside flour, sugar, salt, baking powder and soda, allspice, cinnamon.
3. Mix together all wet ingredients in a smaller bowl using a whisk. Set aside apple sauce, milk, vanilla, and vinegar.
4. Mix together both mixtures until smooth.
5. Add apples and raisins; coat well.
6. Scoop batter into silicone or non-stick muffin pan.
7. Let bake for 25 minutes. Let cool. Enjoy!

Nutritions: Calories 153, Total Fat 2.6g, Saturated Fat 2.1g, Cholesterol 0mg, Sodium 165mg, Total Carbohydrate 30.3g, Dietary Fiber 1.5g, Total Sugars 12.2g, Protein 2.6g, Vitamin D 0mcg, Calcium 33mg, Iron 1mg, Potassium 165mg

Carrot Cake-Like Overnight Oats

Preparation:
15 Minutes

Cooking:
0 Minutes

Serves:
5

Ingredients

- ½ cup Shredded carrots
- 1 cup almond Milk
- ¼ tsp Cinnamon
- 1 cup Oats
- 1 tsp Pitted dates
- ¼ tsp Nutmeg
- 1/3 tsp Grated or dried Ginger
- ¼ tsp Vanilla
- ¼ tbsp Hemp Seeds

Directions

1. Use any glass container or jar.
2. Add all ingredients together in a container.
3. Mix well. You can add more liquid or more oats depending on how thin or thick you may want it.
4. Cover with lid or plastic wrap.
5. Place in refrigerator for at least 3 hours.
6. Once set, mix together. Enjoy!

Nutritions: Calories 185, Total Fat 12.9g, Saturated Fat 10.4g, Cholesterol 0mg, Sodium 16mg, Total Carbohydrate 15.7g, Dietary Fiber 3.2g, Total Sugars 2.8g, Protein 3.6g, Vitamin D 0mcg, Calcium 22mg, Iron 2mg, Potassium 235mg

Fruity Muesli

 Preparation:
5 Minutes

 Cooking:
0 Minutes

 Serves:
3

Directions

1. In a bowl mix together milk, maple syrup, oats, fruit, and nuts.
2. Add milk to eat immediately like cereal.
3. Add milk and refrigerate for an overnight version.
4. Enjoy!

Ingredients

- ½ cup Plant-Based Milk
- 2 tsp Maple Syrup
- ¼ cup Chopped Nuts
- ½ cup mango
- 1 cup sliced bananas
- 1 cup Rolled Oats

Nutritions: Calories 336, Total Fat 17.5g, Saturated Fat 9.6g, Cholesterol 0mg, Sodium 85mg, Total Carbohydrate 42.1g, Dietary Fiber 6.4g, Total Sugars 14.7g, Protein 7.3g, Vitamin D 0mcg, Calcium 37mg, Iron 2mg, Potassium 506mg

Easy Oat and Waffles

 Preparation:
30 Minutes

 Cooking:
0 Minutes

 Serves:
10

Directions

1. Using a food processor, mix oats, flax seeds, cinnamon, and lemon zest. Form a powder.
2. Add milk and mashed bananas to make a thick batter.
3. Using a preheated waffle iron add some of the batter and close lid.
4. Repeat until finish batter. Top with fresh sliced fruit. Enjoy!

Ingredients

- 1/3 cup Ripe Mashed Bananas
- ½ tsp Cinnamon
- ¼ cup ground flax Seeds
- ½ cup unsweetened Almond Milk
- 2 cups Rolled Oats
- ¼ cup Lemon Zest
- 1 cup Sliced Bananas
- 1 cup Strawberries

Nutritions: Calories 115, Total Fat 2.3g, Saturated Fat 0.4g, Cholesterol 0mg, Sodium 11mg, Total Carbohydrate 21.1g, Dietary Fiber 3.6g, Total Sugars 5.6g, Protein 3.2g, Vitamin D 0mcg, Iron 2mg, Potassium 221mg

Quick Chickpea Omelet

Preparation:
30 Minutes

Cooking:
5 Minutes

Serves:
5

Ingredients

- ¾ cup sautéed mushrooms
- ½ cup green Onions
- ½ tsp Baking Soda
- 1/3 cup Nutritional Yeast
- ¾ tsp Black Pepper
- ½ tsp Garlic Powder
- ½ tsp Onion Powder
- 1 cup Chickpea Flour

Directions

1. In a small bowl mix together: Baking soda, yeast, both types of pepper, garlic powder, onion powder, and chickpea flour.
2. Add one cup of water to the mixture and mix well. Make a smooth batter.
3. Heat up a non-stick skillet. Add plant-based oil if desired.
4. Using the same method as making pancakes, do add batter into the pan.
5. Add green onions and mushrooms in the middle of the omelet.
6. Flip twice once each side is a golden brown color.
7. Let it cool. Enjoy!

Nutritions: Calories 196, Total Fat 3.2g, Saturated Fat 0.3g, Cholesterol 0mg, Sodium 199mg, Total Carbohydrate 31.7g, Dietary Fiber 10.5g, Total Sugars 5.1g, Protein 13.4g, Vitamin D 5mcg, Calcium 61mg, Iron 5mg, Potassium 726mg

Ayurvedic oatmeal

 Preparation:
5 Minutes

 Cooking:
10 Minutes

 Serves:
4

Ingredients

- ½ tsp turmeric powder
- ¼ tsp cardamom
- ¼ tsp ground cloves
- 4 Cinnamon sticks
- 11 ounces soy milk
- 3 ounces Oatmeal flakes
- ½ tablespoons raisins
- ½ tablespoons pumpkin seeds
- 1 oz Sliced fresh pumpkin
- 7 ounces tap water

Directions

1. Boil the shredded pumpkin in water in low heat till soft and well done.
2. Put in the soy milk then bring the mixture to boil once again.
3. Include the turmeric, cardamom powder, cinnamon sticks, and the oatmeal in the mixture.
4. Let the food cook for 10minutes.
5. Include the pumpkin seeds by sprinkling them in the dish.
6. It is now ready to serve.

Nutritions: Calories 133, Total Fat 2.7g, Saturated Fat 0.3g, Cholesterol 0mg, Sodium 177mg, Total Carbohydrate 23.2g, Dietary Fiber 3g, Total Sugars 9g, Protein 5.1g, Vitamin D 0mcg, Calcium 26mg, Iron 8mg, Potassium 134mg

Cantaloupe with dates oatmeal and mint-melon relish

Preparation:
5 Minutes

Cooking:
109 Minutes

Serves:
5

Ingredients

- ¼ tsp Salt
- ¼ cup quick cook steel cut oats
- ¼ cup coconut milk
- ¼ tsp coconut oil
- 2 dates pitted and chopped
- 1 cup cantaloupe
- 1 tsp minced mint leaves
- 2 blackberries, fresh

Directions

1. Puree the coconut oil, dates and cantaloupe in a food processor.
2. Pour the puree in a pan and add the coconut milk, and simmer the mixture for 10 minutes.
3. Include salt and oats and simmer.
4. As the moisture simmers, start on the mint-melon relish.
5. Slice the blackberries and cantaloupe into a quarter inch sized piece.
6. With fresh mint, toss the blackberries and cantaloupe mixture.
7. Put the cooked oatmeal in a bowl once it is cooked to your satisfaction.
8. Add the mint-melon relish on top of the oatmeal and splash some coconut milk over the dish.

Nutritions: Calories 82, Total Fat 3.6g, Saturated Fat 2.8g, Cholesterol 0mg, Sodium 124mg, Total Carbohydrate 12.6g, Dietary Fiber 4.1g, Total Sugars 7.9g, Protein 1.7g, Vitamin D 0mcg, Calcium 24mg, Iron 1mg, Potassium 233mg

Granola bars

Preparation:
6 Minutes

Cooking:
30 Minutes

Serves:
5

Ingredients

- 1 stick dark chocolate, melted
- 1 tsp almond extract
- 1/3 organic coconut oil
- ½ glass pure maple syrup
- ½ glass pure natural almond butter
- ¾ tsp sea salt
- 2 tbsps. cinnamon
- ¼ cup natural desiccated coconut
- ½ cup raw pumpkin seeds
- ¼ cup raw sunflower seeds
- ¼ hemp seeds
- ½ cup raw walnuts, chopped
- 1 cup dried cherries
- 1 cup raw almonds, chopped
- 2 ½ cups rolled gluten free oats

Directions

1. Line your oven with a standard parchment cookie sheet and preheat to 325F.
2. Mix the salt, cinnamon, hemp seeds, coconut, pumpkin seeds, sunflower seeds, walnuts, the presoaked cherries, almonds, and oats, in a bowl and put aside.
3. In low heat and in a small pot, put the coconut oil, almond butter, and the maple syrup. Keep stirring as it melts. Remove from the heat and mix in the almond extract.
4. To the dry ingredients, you had set aside, add the wet mixture, and keep mixing until satisfied with the outcome.
5. Firmly on the baking sheet, press the granola in a layer and make it spread evenly.
6. In the preheated oven, let it cook for a maximum of 30 minutes then remove it and let it cool down.
7. Once cold, cut into pieces of your liking.
8. Drizzle the pieces with the melted chocolate.

Nutritions: Calories 611, Total Fat 46.5g, Saturated Fat 9.4g, Cholesterol 0mg, Sodium 341mg, Total Carbohydrate 38.4g, Dietary Fiber 11g, Total Sugars 10.8g, Protein 19.9g, Vitamin D 0mcg, Calcium 167mg, Iron 6mg, Potassium 419mg

Chapter 5.
Main Course Recipes

Broccoli & black beans stir fry

Preparation:
60 Minutes

Serves:
6

Directions

1. Steam broccoli for 6 minutes. Drain and set aside.
2. Warm the sesame oil in a large frying pan over medium heat. Add sesame seeds, chili flakes, ginger, garlic, turmeric powder, and salt. Sauté for a couple of minutes.
3. Add broccoli and black beans and sauté until thoroughly heated.
4. Sprinkle lime juice and serve hot.

Ingredients

- 4 cups broccoli florets
- 2 cups cooked black beans
- 1 tablespoon sesame oil
- 4 teaspoons sesame seeds
- 2 cloves garlic, finely minced
- 2 teaspoons ginger, finely chopped
- A large pinch red chili flakes
- A pinch turmeric powder
- Salt to taste
- Lime juice to taste (optional)

Sweet 'n spicy tofu

 Preparation:
45 Minutes

 Serves:
8

Ingredients

- 14 ounces extra firm tofu; press the excess liquid and chop into cubes.
- 3 tablespoons olive oil
- 2 2-3 cloves garlic, minced
- 4 tablespoons sriracha sauce or any other hot sauce
- 2 tablespoons soy sauce
- 1/4 cup sweet chili sauce
- 5-6 cups mixed vegetables of your choice (like carrots, cauliflower, broccoli, potato, etc.)
- Salt to taste (optional)

Directions

1. Place a nonstick pan over medium-high heat. Add 1 tablespoon oil. When oil is hot, add garlic and mixed vegetables and stir-fry until crisp and tender. Remove and keep aside.
2. Place the pan back on heat. Add 2 tablespoons oil. When oil is hot, add tofu and sauté until golden brown. Add the sautéed vegetables. Mix well and remove from heat.
3. Make a mixture of sauces by mixing together all the sauces in a small bowl.
4. Serve the stir fried vegetables and tofu with sauce.

Eggplant & mushrooms in peanut sauce

Preparation:
32 Minutes

Serves:
6

Directions

1. Place the eggplants and mushroom in a steamer. Steam the eggplant and mushrooms until tender. Transfer to a bowl.
2. To a small bowl, add peanut butter and vinegar and whisk.
3. Add rest of the ingredients and whisk well. Add this to the bowl of eggplant slices. Add scallions and mix well.
4. Serve hot.

Ingredients

- 4 Japanese eggplants cut into 1-inch thick round slices
- 3/4 pounds of shiitake mu shrooms, stems discarded, halved
- 3 tablespoons smooth peanut butter
- 2 1/2 tablespoons rice vinegar
- 1 1/2 tablespoons soy sauce
- 1 1/2 tablespoons, peeled, fresh ginger, finely grated
- 1 1/2 tablespoons light brown sugar
- Coarse salt to taste
- 3 scallions, cut into 2-inch lengths, thinly sliced lengthwise

Green beans stir fry

 Preparation:
30 Minutes

 Serves:
6-8

Ingredients

- 1 1/2 pounds of green beans, stringed, chopped into 1 ½-inch pieces
- 1 large onion, thinly sliced
- 4 star anise (optional)
- 3 tablespoons avocado oil
- 1 1/2 tablespoons tamari sauce or soy sauce
- Salt to taste
- 3/4 cup water

Directions

1. Place a wok over medium heat. Add oil. When oil is heated, add onions and sauté until onions are translucent.
2. Add beans, water, tamari sauce, and star anise and stir. Cover and cook until the beans are tender.
3. Uncover, add salt and raise the heat to high. Cook until the water dries up in the wok. Stir a couple of times while cooking.

Collard greens 'n tofu

 Preparation:
15 Minutes

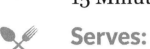 **Serves:**
4

Directions

1. Place a large skillet over medium-high heat. Add oil. When the oil is heated, add tofu and cook until brown.
2. Add rest of the ingredients and mix well.
3. cook until greens wilts and almost dry.

Ingredients

- 2 pounds of collard greens, rinsed, chopped
- 1 cup water
- 1/2 pound of tofu, chopped
- Salt to taste
- Pepper powder to taste
- Crushed red chili to taste

Double-garlic bean and vegetable soup

Preparation:
25 Minutes

Serves:
4

Ingredients

- 1 tablespoon (15 ml) olive oil
- 1 teaspoon fine sea salt
- 1 (240 g) minced onion 5 cloves garlic, minced
- 2 cups (220 g) chopped red potatoes
- ⅔ cup (96 g) sliced carrots
- Protein content per serving cup (60 g) chopped celery
- 1 teaspoon italian seasoning blend
- Protein content per serving teaspoon red pepper flakes, or to taste
- Protein content per serving teaspoon celery seed
- 4 cups water (940 ml), divided
- 1 can (14.5 ounces, or 410 g) crushed tomatoes or tomato puree
- 1 head roasted garlic
- 2 tablespoons (30 g) prepared vegan pesto, plus more for garnish
- 2 cans (each 15 ounces, or 425 g) different kinds of white beans, drained and rinsed
- Protein content per serving cup (50 g)
- 1-inch (2.5 cm) pieces green beans
- Salt and pepper

Directions

1. Heat the oil and salt in a large soup pot over medium heat. Add the onion, garlic, potatoes, carrots, and celery. Cook for 4 to 6 minutes, occasionally stirring, until the onions are translucent. Add the seasoning blend, red pepper flakes, and celery seed and stir for 2 minutes. Add 3 cups (705 ml) of the water and the crushed tomatoes.
2. Combine the remaining 1 cup (235 ml) water and the roasted garlic in a blender. Process until smooth. Add to the soup mixture and bring to a boil. Reduce the heat to simmer and cook for 30 minutes.
3. Stir in the pesto, beans, and green beans. Simmer for 15 minutes. Taste and adjust the seasonings. Serve each bowl with a dollop of pesto, if desired.

Nutritions: Protein content per serving: 21 g

Mean bean minestrone

Preparation:
45 Minutes

Serves:
6

Ingredients

- 1 tablespoon (15 ml) olive oil
- 1/3 cup (80 g) chopped red onion
- 4 cloves garlic, grated or pressed
- 1 leek, white and light green parts, trimmed and chopped (about 4 ounces, or 113 g)
- 2 carrots, peeled and minced (about 4 ounces, or 113 g)
- 2 ribs of celery, minced (about 2 ounces, or 57 g)
- 2 yellow squashes, trimmed and chopped (about 8 ounces, or 227 g)
- 1 green bell pepper, trimmed and chopped (about 8 ounces, or 227 g)
- 1 tablespoon (16 g) tomato paste
- 1 teaspoon dried oregano
- 1 teaspoon dried basil
- ⅓ teaspoon smoked paprika
- '¼ To ¼ teaspoon cayenne pepper, or to taste
- 2 cans (each 15 ounces, or 425 g) diced fire-roasted tomatoes
- 4 cups (940 ml) vegetable broth, more if needed
- 3 cups (532 g) cannellini beans, or other white beans
- 2 cups (330 g) cooked farro, or other whole grain or pasta
- Salt, to taste
- Nut and seed sprinkles, for garnish, optional and to taste

Directions

1. In a large pot, add the oil, onion, garlic, leek, carrots, celery, yellow squash, bell pepper, tomato paste, oregano, basil, paprika, and cayenne pepper. Cook on medium-high heat, stirring often until the vegetables start to get tender, about 6 minutes.
2. Add the tomatoes and broth. Bring to a boil, lower the heat, cover with a lid, and simmer 15 minutes.
3. Add the beans and simmer another 10 minutes. Add the farro and simmer 5 more minutes to heat the farro.
4. Note that this is a thick minestrone. If there are leftovers (which taste even better, by the way), the soup will thicken more once chilled.
5. Add extra broth if you prefer a thinner soup and adjust seasoning if needed. Add nut and seed sprinkles on each portion upon serving, if desired.
6. Store leftovers in an airtight container in the refrigerator for up to 5 days. The minestrone can also be frozen for up to 3 months.

Nutritions: Protein content per serving: 9 g

Sushi rice and bean stew

 Preparation:
45 Minutes

 Serves:
6

Ingredients

For the sushi rice:
- 1 cup (208 g) dry sushi rice, thoroughly rinsed until water runs clear and drained
- 1¾ cups (295 ml) water
- 1 tablespoon (15 ml) fresh lemon juice
- 1 teaspoon toasted sesame oil
- 1 teaspoon sriracha
- 1 teaspoon tamari
- 1 teaspoon agave nectar or brown rice syrup

For the stew:
- 1 tablespoon (15 ml) toasted sesame oil
- 9 ounces (255 g) minced carrot (about 4 medium carrots)
- 1/3 cup (80 g) chopped red onion or ¼ cup (40 g) minced shallot
- 2 teaspoons grated fresh ginger or ⅓ teaspoon ginger powder 4 cloves garlic, grated or pressed
- 1½ cups (246 g) cooked chickpeas
- 1 cup (155 g) frozen, shelled edamame
- 3 tablespoons (45 ml) seasoned rice vinegar
- 2 tablespoons (30 ml) tamari
- 2 teaspoons sriracha, or to taste
- 1 cup (235 ml) mushroom-soaking broth
- 2 cups (470 ml) vegetable broth
- 2 tablespoons (36 g) white miso
- 2 tablespoons (16 g) toasted white sesame seeds

Directions

1. To make the sushi rice: combine the rice and water in a rice cooker, cover with the lid, and cook until the water is absorbed without lifting the lid. (alternatively, cook the rice on the stove top, following the directions on the package.) While the rice is cooking, combine the remaining sushi rice ingredients in a large bowl.
2. Let the rice steam for 10 minutes in the rice cooker with the lid still on. Gently fold the cooked rice into the dressing. Set aside.
3. To make the stew: heat the oil in a large pot on medium-high heat. Add the carrots, onion, ginger, and garlic. Lower the temperature to medium and cook until the vegetables start to get tender, stirring often about 4 minutes.
4. Add the chickpeas, edamame, vinegar, tamari, and sriracha. Stir and cook for another 4 minutes. Add the broths, and bring back

to a slow boil. Cover with a lid, lower the heat, and simmer for 10 minutes.

5. Place the miso in a small bowl and remove 3 tablespoons (45 ml) of the broth from the pot. Stir into the miso to thoroughly combine. Stir the miso mixture back into the pan, and remove from the heat.

6. Divide the rice among 4 to 6 bowls, depending on your appetite. Add approximately 1 cup (235 ml) of the stew on top of each portion of rice. Add 1 teaspoon of sesame seeds on top of each serving, and serve immediately.

7. If you do not plan on eating this dish in one shot, keep the rice and stew separated and store in the refrigerator for up to 4 days.

8. When reheating the stew, do not bring to a boil. Slowly warm the rice with the stew on medium heat in a small saucepan until heated through.

Giardiniera chili

 Preparation:
35 Minutes

 Serves:
6

Ingredients

- 1 tablespoon (15 ml) neutral-flavored oil
- 1 medium red onion, chopped
- 4 carrots, peeled and minced (9 ounces, or 250 g)
- 2 zucchini, trimmed and minced (11 ounces, or 320 g)
- 4 roma tomatoes, diced (14 ounces, or 400 g)
- 4 cloves garlic, grated or pressed
- 1 tablespoon (8 g) mild to medium chili powder
- 1 teaspoon ground cumin
- ½ teaspoon smoked paprika
- ½ teaspoon liquid smoke
- ¼ teaspoon fine sea salt, or to taste
- ¼ teaspoon cayenne pepper, or to taste
- 2 tablespoons (32 g) tomato paste
- 1 can (15 ounces, or 425 g) diced fire-roasted tomatoes
- ½ cup (120 ml) vegetable broth
- ½ cup (120 ml) mushroom-soaking broth or extra vegetable broth
- 1 can (15 ounces, or 425 g) pinto beans, drained and rinsed
- 1 can (15 ounces, or 425 g) black beans, drained and rinsed
- ½ cup (60 g) nutritional yeast

Directions

1. Heat the oil on medium-high in a large pot and add the onion, carrots, zucchini, tomatoes, and garlic. Cook for 6 minutes, stirring occasionally until the carrots start to get tender. Add the chili powder, cumin, paprika, liquid smoke, salt, cayenne pepper, and tomato paste, stirring to combine. Cook another 2 minutes. Add the diced tomatoes, broths, beans, and nutritional yeast. Bring to a low boil. Lower the heat, cover with a lid, and simmer 15 minutes, stirring occasionally. Remove the lid and simmer for another 5 minutes.
2. Serve on top of a cooked whole grain of choice or with your favorite chili accompaniments.
3. Leftovers can be stored in an airtight container in the refrigerator for up to 4 days or frozen for up to 3 months.

Nutritions: Protein content per serving: 28 g

Shorba (lentil soup)

Preparation:
30 Minutes

Serves:
6

Ingredients

- 1 tablespoon (15 ml) olive oil
- 1 medium onion, minced
- 1 large carrot, peeled and chopped
- 1 fist-size russet potato, cut into small cubes (about 7 ounces, or 198 g)
- 4 large cloves garlic, minced
- 2 teaspoons grated fresh ginger root
- 1 to 2 teaspoons berbere, to taste
- 1/3 teaspoon turmeric
- 1 cup (192 g) brown lentils, picked over and rinsed
- 6 cups (1.4 l) water, more if desired
- 1 tablespoon (16 g) tomato paste
- 1 tablespoon (18 g) vegetable bouillon paste, or 2 bouillon cubes
- Salt and pepper

Directions

1. Heat the oil in a large soup pot over medium heat. Add the onion, carrot, and potato. Cook for 5 to 7 minutes, stirring occasionally until the onions are translucent. Stir in the garlic, ginger, berbere, turmeric, and lentils and cook and stir for 1 minute until fragrant. Add the water, tomato paste, and bouillon. Bring to a boil, and then reduce the heat to a simmer. Cook for 30 minutes, stirring occasionally until the lentils are tender. Taste and adjust the seasonings.

Nutritions: Protein content per serving: 10 g

The whole enchilada

Preparation:
20 Minutes

Serves:
6

Ingredients

For the sauce:
- 2 tablespoons (30 ml) olive oil 1/3 cup (80 g) chopped red onion 4 ounces (113 g) tomato paste
- 1 tablespoon (15 ml) adobo sauce
- 1 tablespoon (8 g) mild to medium chili powder
- 1 teaspoon ground cumin
- 3 cloves garlic, grated or pressed
- ⅓ teaspoon fine sea salt, or to taste
- 2 tablespoons (15 g) whole wheat pastry flour or (16 g) all-purpose flour
- 2 cups (470 ml) water

For the filling:
- 1 protein content per serving teaspoons olive oil
- ⅓ cup (53 g) chopped red onion
- 1 sweet potato, trimmed and peeled, chopped (about 8.8 ounces, or 250 g)
- 1 yellow squash, trimmed and chopped (about 5.3 ounces, or 150 g)
- 2 cloves garlic, grated or pressed
- 1 tablespoon (8 g) nutritional yeast
- 1 smoked paprika
- ¼ teaspoon liquid smoke
- Pinch of fine sea salt, or to taste
- 1 (258 g) cooked black beans
- 3 tablespoons (45 ml) enchilada sauce
- 12 to 14 corn tortillas
- 1 recipe creamy cashew sauce
- Chopped fresh cilantro, to taste hot sauce, to taste

Directions

1. To make the sauce: heat the oil on medium heat in a large skillet. Add the onion and cook until fragrant while occasionally stirring, about 2 minutes. Add the tomato paste, adobo sauce, chili powder, cumin, garlic, and salt. Saute for 2 minutes, stirring frequently. Sprinkle the flour on top and cook 2 minutes, stirring frequently. Slowly whisk in the water and cook until slightly thickened, about 6 minutes, frequently whisking to prevent clumps. Remove from the heat and set aside.

2. To make the filling: heat the oil in a large skillet on medium heat. Add the onion and sweet potato and cook 6 minutes or until the potato starts to get tender, stirring

650

occasionally. Add the squash and garlic and cook for 4 minutes, stirring occasionally. Add the nutritional yeast, paprika, liquid smoke, and salt, stir to combine, and cook for another minute. Add the beans and enchilada sauce and stir to combine. Cover the pan and simmer until the vegetables are completely tender about 4 minutes. Add a little water if the plants stick to the skillet. Adjust the seasonings if needed.

3. Preheat the oven to 350°f (180°c, or gas mark 4).

4. Place the sauce in a large shallow bowl. If you aren't using pre-shaped, uncooked tortillas, follow the direction in the recipe notes to soften the tortillas so that they are easier to work with. Ladle about 1/3 cup (80 ml) of enchilada sauce on the bottom of a 9 x 13-inch (23 x 33 cm) baking dish. Dip each tortilla in the sauce to coat only lightly. Don't be too generous and gently scrape off the excess sauce with a spatula; otherwise, you will run out of sauce. Add a scant ¼ cup (about 45 g) of the filling in each tortilla. Fold the tortilla over the filling, rolling like a cigar. Place the enchiladas in the pan, seam side down. Make sure to squeeze them in tight so that there's room in the dish for all of them. Top evenly with the remaining enchilada sauce. Add the creamy cashew sauce consistently on top.

5. Bake for 20 to 25 minutes or until the top is set, and the enchiladas are heated through. Garnish with cilantro and serve with hot sauce.

Nutritions: Protein content per serving: 6 g

Black bean and avocado salad

 Preparation:
45 Minutes

 Serves:
6

Ingredients

- 1 cup (172 g) cooked black beans
- ⅓ cup (82 g) frozen corn (run under hot water, drained)
- 3 tablespoons (15 g) minced scallion
- 2 cloves garlic, minced
- 6 cherry tomatoes, cut into quarters
- 1 teaspoon minced fresh cilantro, or to taste
- Pinch of dried oregano 1 chipotle in adobo
- 1 tablespoon (15 ml) fresh lemon juice
- 1 tablespoon (15 ml) apple cider vinegar 1 tablespoon (15 ml) vegetable broth
- 1 teaspoon nutritional yeast
- 2 tablespoons (15 g) roasted salted pepitas (hulled pumpkin seeds)
- 2 avocados, pitted, peeled, and chopped
- Salt and pepper

Directions

1. Combine the beans, corn, scallion, cherry tomatoes, garlic, cilantro, and oregano in a medium-size bowl. Using a small blender or a mortar and pestle, thoroughly combine the chipotle, lemon juice, vinegar, broth, and nutritional yeast to form a dressing. Pour over the bean mixture and stir in the pepitas. Gently stir in the avocados. Season to taste with salt and pepper. Serve promptly so that the avocado doesn't discolor.

Nutritions: Protein content per serving: 8 g

Mediterranean quinoa and bean salad

Preparation:
35 Minutes

Serves:
6

Ingredients

- 1¾ cups (213 g) dry ivory quinoa, rinsed
- 2 (590 ml) vegetable broth
- 2 tablespoons (30 ml) apple cider vinegar
- 2 tablespoons (30 ml) fresh lemon juice
- 3 tablespoons (45 ml) extra-virgin olive oil
- ⅔ cup (40 g) finely chopped red onion
- 2 to 3 cloves garlic, minced, or to taste
- Protein content per serving teaspoon red pepper flakes, or to taste
- Salt and pepper
- 1 (266 g) cooked cannellini beans
- 24 jumbo pitted kalamata olives, minced
- Half of red bell pepper, cored and diced
- Half of yellow bell pepper, cored and diced
- 8 ounces (227 g) mini heirloom tomatoes, halved or quartered depending on size
- 6 tablespoons (24 g) minced fresh parsley
- 15 leaves fresh basil, cut in chiffonade

Directions

1. Combine the quinoa with the broth in a medium saucepan. Bring to a boil and then reduce the heat to a simmer. Cover and cook until all liquid is absorbed, 12 to 15 minutes. The quinoa should be tender and translucent, and the germ ring should be visible along the outside edge of the grain. Set aside to cool completely.
2. In a large bowl, combine the vinegar, lemon juice, oil, onion, garlic, red pepper flakes, salt, and pepper. Stir the beans into the dressing. Add the cooled quinoa, olives, bell peppers, tomatoes, and parsley into the bowl with the beans. Fold with a rubber spatula to thoroughly yet gently combine.
3. Cover and chill for an hour to let the flavors meld. Garnish with basil upon serving. Leftovers can be stored in an airtight container in the refrigerator for up to 4 days.

Nutritions: Protein content per serving: 6 g

Chapter 6.
Dessert and Treats Recipes

Snickerdoodle Energy Balls

Preparation:
10 Minutes

Cooking:
0 Minutes

Serves:
20

Ingredients

- Medjool Dates (1 C.)
- Ground Cinnamon (2 t.)
- Cashews (1 C.)
- Vanilla Extract (1/4 t.)
- Almonds (1/2 C.)
- Salt (to Taste)

Directions

1. These little snacks are great op hand because they offer a boost of protein and are easy to grab on the go! To start out, you will want to place your Medjool dates into a food processor and blend until the Medjool dates become soft and sticky.
2. Next, you can add the nuts and seasoning along with the vanilla extract and blend until completely combined.
3. Now that you have your dough use your hand to create bite-sized balls and place onto a plate. You can enjoy them instantly or place them in the fridge for thirty minutes and wait for them to harden up a bit.

Nutritions: Calories: 100, Carbs: 15g, Fats: 5g, Proteins: 3g

Baked Carrot Chips

Preparation:
10 Minutes

Cooking:
30 Minutes

Serves:
8

Ingredients

- Olive Oil (1/4 C.)
- Ground Cinnamon (1 t.)
- Ground Cumin (1 t.)
- Salt (to Taste)
- Carrots (3 Pounds)

Directions

1. As you begin a plant-based diet, you may find yourself craving something crunchy. This recipe offers the best of both worlds by giving you a crunch and something nutritious to snack on. You can begin this recipe by heating your oven to 425 and setting up a baking sheet with some parchment paper.
2. Next, you will want to chop the top off each carrot and slice the carrot up paper-thin. You can complete this task by using a knife, but it typically is easier if you have a mandolin slicer.
3. With your carrot slices all prepared, next, you will want to toss them in a small bowl with the cinnamon, cumin, olive oil, and a touch of salt. When the carrot slices are well coated, go ahead and lay them across your baking sheet.
4. Finally, you are going to pop the carrots into the oven for fifteen minutes. After this time, you may notice that the edges are going to start to curl and get crispy. At this point, remove the dish from the oven and flip all of the chips over. Place the dish back into the oven for six or seven minutes, and then your chips will be set!

Nutritions: Calories: 100, Carbs: 12g, Fats: 8g, Proteins: 1g

Sweet Cinnamon Chips

Preparation:
5 Minutes

Cooking:
15 Minutes

Serves:
5

Ingredients

- Whole Wheat Tortillas (10)
- Ground Cinnamon (1 t.)
- Sugar (3 T.)
- Olive Oil (2 C.)

Directions

1. If you are looking for a snack that is sweet and simple, these chips should do the trick! You are going to want to start out by getting out a small bowl so you can mix the cinnamon and sugar together. When this is complete, set it to the side.
2. Next, you will want to get out your frying pan and bring the olive oil to a soft simmer. While the oil gets to a simmer, take some time to slice your tortillas up into wedges. When these are set, carefully place them into your simmering olive oil and cook for about two minutes on each side, or until golden.
3. Once the chips are all set, pat them down with a paper towel and then generously coat each chip with the cinnamon mixture you made earlier. After that, your chips will be set for your enjoyment.

Nutritions: Calories: 70, Carbs: 5g, Fats: 5g, Proteins: 1g

Creamy Avocado Hummus

 Preparation:
5 Minutes

 Cooking:
0 Minutes

 Serves:
4

Ingredients

- Olive Oil (1 T.)
- Avocado (1)
- White Beans (1 Can)
- Cayenne Pepper (1/4 t.)
- Lime Juice (2 t.)

Directions

1. When you are looking for something smooth and creamy to dip your vegetables or chips in, this is the perfect recipe to give a try! All you will have to do is place the ingredients from the list above into the food processor and process until smooth.
2. Place the avocado hummus into a serving bowl, and you are ready to dip.

Nutritions: Calories: 120, Carbs: 5g, Fats: 10g, Proteins: 1g

Cauliflower Popcorn

Preparation:
10 Minutes

Cooking:
0 Minutes

Serves:
4

Ingredients

- Olive Oil (2 T.)
- Chili Powder (2 t.)
- Cumin (2 t.)
- Nutritional Yeast (1 T.)
- Cauliflower (1 Head)
- Salt (to Taste)

Directions

1. Before you begin making this recipe, you will want to take a few moments to cut your cauliflower into bite-sized pieces, like popcorn!
2. Once your cauliflower is set, place it into a mixing bowl and coat with the olive oil. Once coated properly, add in the nutritional yeast, salt, and the rest of the spices.
3. You can enjoy your snack immediately or place into a dehydrator at 115 for 8 hours. By doing this, it will make the cauliflower crispy! You can really enjoy it either way.

Nutritions: Calories: 100, Carbs: 10g, Fats: 5g, Proteins: 5g

Banana and Strawberry Oat Bars

 Preparation:
10 Minutes

 Cooking:
1 h

 Serves:
5

Ingredients

- ▸ Rolled Oats (2 C.)
- ▸ Chia Seeds (2 T.)
- ▸ Maple Syrup (1/4 C.)
- ▸ Strawberries (2 C.)
- ▸ Vanilla Extract (2 t.)
- ▸ Bananas (2, Mashed)
- ▸ Maple Syrup (2 T.)
- ▸ Baking Powder (1 t.)

Nutritions:
Calories: 250,
Carbs: 50g, Fats: 5g,
Proteins: 5g

Directions

1. These oat bars take a few different steps, but they are a great snack to have when you are short on time! You are going to start off by making the strawberry jam for the bars. You can do this by placing the strawberries and two tablespoons of maple syrup into a pan and place it over medium heat. After about fifteen minutes, the strawberries should be releasing their liquid and will come to a boil. You will want to boil for an additional ten minutes.

2. As a final touch for the jam, gently stir in the one teaspoon of the vanilla extract and the chia seeds. Be sure that you continue stirring for an additional five minutes before removing from the heat and setting to the side.

3. Now, it is time to make the bars! You can start this part out by prepping the oven to 375 and getting together a baking dish and lining it with parchment paper.

4. Next, you are going to want to add one cup of your oats into a food processor and blend until they look like flour. At this point, you can pour the oats into a mixing bowl and place in the rest of the oats along with the baking powder.

5. Once these ingredients are blended well, throw in the other teaspoon of vanilla, maple syrup, and your mashed bananas. As you mix everything together, you will notice that you are now forming a dough.

6. When you are ready to assemble the bars, you will want to take half of the mixture and press it into the bottom of your baking dish and carefully spoon the jam over the surface. Once these are set, add the rest of the dough over the top and press down ever so slightly.

7. Finally, you are going to want to place the dish into the oven and cook for about thirty minutes. By the end of this time, the top of your bars should be golden, and you can remove the dish from the oven. Allow the bars to cool slightly before slicing and enjoying.

PB Cookie Dough Balls

Preparation:
10 Minutes

Cooking:
0 Minutes

Serves:
8

Ingredients

- Whole Wheat Flour (2 C.)
- Maple Syrup (1 C.)
- Peanuts (1/2 C.)
- Peanut Butter (1 C.)
- Rolled Oats (1/2 C.)

Directions

1. Is this recipe a snack or dessert? That is completely up to you! To start this recipe, you will want to get out a large mixing bowl and combine all of the ingredients from the list above.
2. Once they are well blended, take your hands and carefully roll the dough into bite-sized balls before you enjoy! For easier handling, you will want to place the balls into the fridge for about twenty minutes before enjoying.

Nutritions: Calories: 70, Carbs: 10g, Fats: 4g, Proteins: 4g

Almond Millet Chews

 Preparation:
15 Minutes

 Cooking:
0 Minutes

 Serves:
10

Ingredients

- Millet (1 C.)
- Almond Butter (1/2 C.)
- Raisins (1/4 C.)
- Brown Rice Syrup (1/4 C.)

Directions

1. This dessert is perfect for when you want something small after dinner. You will want to begin by melting the almond butter in the microwave for about twenty seconds. When this step is complete, place it into a mixing bowl with the brown rice syrup, raisins, and millets.
2. Once everything is blended well, use your hands to roll balls and place onto a plate. If needed, you can add a touch more syrup to keep everything together. Place into the fridge for twenty minutes and then enjoy your dessert.

Nutritions: Calories: 100, Carbs: 15g, Fats: 5g, Proteins: 2g

Simple Banana Cookies

Preparation:
5 Minutes

Cooking:
20 Minutes

Serves:
4

Ingredients

- Peanut Butter (3 T.)
- Banana (2)
- Walnuts (1/4 C.)
- Rolled Oats (1 C.)

Directions

1. For a simple but delicious cookie, start by prepping the oven to 35As the oven warms up, take out your mixing bowl and first mash the bananas before adding in the oats.
2. When you have folded the oats in, add in the walnuts and peanut butter before using your hands to layout small balls onto a baking sheet. Once this is set, pop the dish into the oven for fifteen minutes and bake your cookies.
3. By the end of fifteen minutes, remove the dish from the oven and allow them to cool for five minutes before enjoying.

Nutritions: Calories: 250, Carbs: 30g, Fats: 10g, Proteins: 5g

Basic Chocolate Cookies

 Preparation:
5 Minutes

 Cooking:
15 Minutes

 Serves:
10

Ingredients

- Cocoa Powder (1/2 C.)
- Almond Butter (1/2 C.)
- Bananas (2, Mashed)
- Salt (to Taste)

Directions

1. These chocolate cookies are a great way to get a touch of sweetness without overdoing the calories! To begin, prep the oven to 35
2. As that heats, take out a mixing bowl so you can completely mash your bananas. When this is complete, carefully stir in the almond butter and the cocoa powder.
3. Once your mixture is created, place tablespoons of the mix onto a lined cookie sheet and sprinkle a touch of salt over the top. When these are set, pop the dish into the oven for about fifteen minutes.
4. Finally, remove the dish from the oven and cool before enjoying.

Nutritions: Calories: 100, Carbs: 10g, Fats: 5g, Proteins: 5g

Quick Brownie Bites

Preparation:
10 Minutes

Cooking:
0 Minutes

Serves:
10

Ingredients

- Cocoa Powder (1/4 C.)
- Medjool Dates (10)
- Vanilla Extract (1 t.)
- Walnut Halves (1 ½ C.)
- Water (1 T.)

Directions

1. to be honest, who isn't guilty of eating cookie dough raw? Now, you can do it on purpose! To begin this recipe, you will first need to get out a food processor so you can break down the Medjool dates. Once these are broken down, add in the rest of the ingredients and blend until combined.
2. Now that you have your batter, roll it into small balls, and your dessert is ready in an instant!

Nutritions: Calories: 150, Carbs: 15g, Fats: 10g, Proteins: 5g

Peach Crisp

 Preparation:
5 Minutes

 Cooking:
15 Minutes

 Serves:
2

Ingredients

- Rolled Oats (2 T.)
- Flour (1 t.)
- Brown Sugar (2 T.)
- Peaches (2, Diced)
- Sugar (1 t.)
- Coconut Oil (3 t.)
- Flour (3 t.)

Directions

1. This recipe is built for two! You can begin by prepping the oven to 375 and getting out two small baking dishes.
2. As the oven begins to warm, take one of the mixing bowls and toss the peach pieces with the sugar, cinnamon, and a teaspoon of flour. When this is set, pour the peaches into a baking dish.
3. In the other bowl, mix together the three teaspoons of flour with the oats and the sugar. Once these are blended, pour in coconut oil and continue mixing. Now that you have your crumble, place it over the peaches in the baking dish.
4. Finally, you are going to pop the dish into the oven for fifteen minutes or until the top is a nice golden color. If it looks finished, remove and cool before slicing your dessert up.

Nutritions: Calories: 110, Carbs: 20g, Fats: 5g, Proteins: 2g

Chocolate Dessert Dip

 Preparation:
10 Minutes

 Cooking:
0 Minutes

 Serves:
6

Directions

1. Do you need to whip up dessert quickly? This is an excellent recipe to have on hand, especially if you want to impress your guests! All you have to do is place the three ingredients into a food processor and mix until blended.
2. Simply place the dip into a serving dish, and you are ready to go.

Ingredients

- Date Paste (1/2 C.)
- Cocoa (1/4 C.)
- Cashew Butter (1/2 C.)

Nutritions: Calories: 150, Carbs: 15g, Fats: 10g, Proteins: 5g

Lemon Coconut Cookies

Preparation:
15 Minutes

Cooking:
0 Minutes

Serves:
4

Ingredients

- Coconut Flour (1/3 C.)
- Shredded Coconut (1 ½ C.)
- Agave (6 T.)
- Almond Flour (1 ½ C.)
- Lemon Zest (1 T.)
- Lemon Juice (4 T.)
- Coconut Oil (1 T.)
- Vanilla Extract (2 t.)
- Salt (to Taste)

Directions

1. If you enjoy dessert but are looking for something that isn't chocolate, this recipe will be perfect for you! To make these incredible cookies, you will want to place all of the ingredients from the list, minus the shredded coconut, into the food processor, and blend until you have created a dough.
2. Once your dough is set, take your hands and roll the dough into small, bite-sized balls.
3. As a final touch, roll the balls in your shredded coconut and then place into the fridge for twenty minutes. After this time has passed, go ahead and enjoy your dessert!

Nutritions: Calories: 450, Carbs: 30g, Fats: 20g, Proteins: 10g

Watermelon Pizza

Preparation:
15 Minutes

Cooking:
0 Minutes

Serves:
4

Ingredients

- Watermelon (1, Sliced)
- Banana (1, Sliced)
- Blueberries (1 C.)
- Coconut Flakes (1/2 C.)
- Chopped Walnuts (1/4 C.)

Directions

1. This dessert is pretty simple, but it can be a lot of fun to make and eat if you have kids in the house! You will begin this recipe by taking the watermelon and chopping it up to look like pizza slices.
2. When the watermelon slices are set, you can then add the chopped fruit on top of the watermelon, followed by any chopped nuts and coconut flakes. For this recipe, we chose to use bananas and blueberries, but you can use any fruit that you like!
3. Just like that, you have watermelon pizza for dessert!

Nutritions: Calories: 50, Carbs: 10g, Fats: 3g, Proteins: 1g

Chapter 7.
Snacks and Salads Recipes

Cashew Siam Salad

 Preparation:
10 Minutes

 Cooking:
3 Minutes

 Serves:
4

Ingredients

Salad:
- 4 cups baby spinach, rinsed, drained
- ½ cup pickled red cabbage

Dressing:
- 1-inch piece ginger, finely chopped
- 1 tsp. chili garlic paste
- 1 tbsp. soy sauce
- ½ tbsp. rice vinegar
- 1 tbsp. sesame oil
- 3 tbsp. avocado oil

Toppings:
- ½ cup raw cashews, unsalted
- ¼ cup fresh cilantro, chopped

Directions

1. Put the spinach and red cabbage in a large bowl. Toss to combine and set the salad aside.
2. Toast the cashews in a frying pan over medium-high heat, stirring occasionally until the cashews are golden brown. This should take about 3 minutes. Turn off the heat and set the frying pan aside.
3. Mix all the dressing ingredients in medium-sized bowl and use a spoon to mix them into a smooth dressing.
4. Pour the dressing over the spinach salad and top with the toasted cashews.
5. Toss the salad to combine all ingredients and transfer the large bowl to the fridge. Allow the salad to chill for up to one hour – doing so will guarantee a better flavor. Alternatively, the salad can be served right away, topped with the optional cilantro. Enjoy!

Nutritions: Calories 160, Total Fat 12.9g, Saturated Fat 2.4g, Cholesterol 0mg, Sodium 265mg, Total Carbohydrate 9.1g, Dietary Fiber 2.1g, Total Sugars 1.4g, Protein 4.1g, Vitamin D 0mcg, Calcium 45mg, Iron 2mg, Potassium 344mg

Spinach and Mashed Tofu Salad

 Preparation:
20 Minutes

 Serves:
4

Ingredients

- 2 8-oz. blocks firm tofu, drained
- 4 cups baby spinach leaves
- 4 tbsp. cashew butter
- 1½ tbsp. soy sauce
- 1tbsp ginger, chopped
- 1 tsp. red miso paste
- 2 tbsp. sesame seeds
- 1 tsp. organic orange zest
- 1 tsp. nori flakes
- 2 tbsp. water

Directions

1. Use paper towels to absorb any excess water left in the tofu before crumbling both blocks into small pieces.
2. In a large bowl, combine the mashed tofu with the spinach leaves.
3. Mix the remaining ingredients in another small bowl and, if desired, add the optional water for a more smooth dressing.
4. Pour this dressing over the mashed tofu and spinach leaves.
5. Transfer the bowl to the fridge and allow the salad to chill for up to one hour. Doing so will guarantee a better flavor. Or, the salad can be served right away. Enjoy!

Nutritions: Calories 623, Total Fat 30.5g, Saturated Fat 5.8g, Cholesterol 0mg, Sodium 2810mg, Total Carbohydrate 48g, Dietary Fiber 5.9g, Total Sugars 3g, Protein 48.4g, Vitamin D 0mcg, Calcium 797mg, Iron 22mg, Potassium 2007mg

Super Summer Salad

 Preparation:
10 Minutes

 Cooking:
0 Minutes

 Serves:
2

Ingredients

Dressing:
- ► 1 tbsp. olive oil
- ► ¼ cup chopped basil
- ► 1 tsp. lemon juice
- ► ¼ tsp Salt
- ► 1 medium avocado, halved, diced
- ► ¼ cup water

Salad:
- ► ¼ cup dry chickpeas
- ► ¼ cup dry red kidney beans
- ► 4 cups raw kale, shredded
- ► 2 cups Brussel sprouts, shredded
- ► 2 radishes, thinly sliced
- ► 1 tbsp. walnuts, chopped
- ► 1 tsp. flax seeds
- ► Salt and pepper to taste

Directions

1. Prepare the chickpeas and kidney beans according to the method.
2. Soak the flax seeds according the method, and then drain excess water.
3. Prepare the dressing by adding the olive oil, basil, lemon juice, salt, and half of the avocado to a food processor or blender, and pulse on low speed.
4. Keep adding small amounts of water until the dressing is creamy and smooth.
5. Transfer the dressing to a small bowl and set it aside.
6. Combine the kale, Brussel sprouts, cooked chickpeas, kidney beans, radishes, walnuts, and remaining avocado in a large bowl and mix thoroughly.
7. Store the mixture, or, serve with the dressing and flax seeds, and enjoy!

Nutritions: Calories 266, Total Fat 26.6g, Saturated Fat 5.1g, Cholesterol 0mg, Sodium 298mg, Total Carbohydrate 8.8g, Dietary Fiber 6.8g, Total Sugars 0.6g, Protein 2g, Vitamin D 0mcg, Calcium 19mg, Iron 1mg, Potassium 500mg

Roasted Almond Protein Salad

 Preparation:
30 Minutes

 Cooking:
0 Minutes

 Serves:
4

Ingredients

- ½ cup dry quinoa
- ½ cup dry navy beans
- ½ cup dry chickpeas
- ½ cup raw whole almonds
- 1 tsp. extra virgin olive oil
- ½ tsp. salt
- ½ tsp. paprika
- ½ tsp. cayenne
- Dash of chili powder
- 4 cups spinach, fresh or frozen
- ¼ cup purple onion, chopped

Directions

1. Prepare the quinoa according to the recipe. Store in the fridge for now.
2. Prepare the beans according to the method. Store in the fridge for now.
3. Toss the almonds, olive oil, salt, and spices in a large bowl, and stir until the ingredients are evenly coated.
4. Put a skillet over medium-high heat, and transfer the almond mixture to the heated skillet.
5. Roast while stirring until the almonds are browned, around 5 minutes. You may hear the ingredients pop and crackle in the pan as they warm up. Stir frequently to prevent burning.
6. Turn off the heat and toss the cooked and chilled quinoa and beans, onions, and spinach or mixed greens in the skillet. Stir well before transferring the roasted almond salad to a bowl.
7. Enjoy the salad with a dressing of choice, or, store for later!

Nutritions: Calories 347, Total Fat 10.5g, Saturated Fat 1g, Cholesterol 0mg, Sodium 324mg, Total Carbohydrate 49.2g, Dietary Fiber 14.7g, Total Sugars 4.7g, Protein 17.2g, Vitamin D 0mcg, Calcium 139mg, Iron 5mg, Potassium 924mg

Lentil, Lemon & Mushroom Salad

 Preparation:
10 Minutes

 Cooking:
0 Minutes

 Serves:
2

Ingredients

- ½ cup dry lentils of choice
- 2 cups vegetable broth
- 3 cups mushrooms, thickly sliced
- 1 cup sweet or purple onion, chopped
- 4 tsp. extra virgin olive oil
- 2 tbsp. garlic powder
- ¼ tsp. chili flakes
- 1 tbsp. lemon juice
- 2 tbsp. cilantro, chopped
- ½ cup arugula
- ¼ tsp Salt
- ¼ tsp pepper

Directions

1. Sprout the lentils according the method. (Don't cook them).
2. Place the vegetable stock in a deep saucepan and bring it to a boil.
3. Add the lentils to the boiling broth, cover the pan, and cook for about 5 minutes over low heat until the lentils are a bit tender.
4. Remove the pan from heat and drain the excess water.
5. Put a frying pan over high heat and add 2 tablespoons of olive oil.
6. Add the onions, garlic, and chili flakes, and cook until the onions are almost translucent, around 5 to 10 minutes while stirring.
7. Add the mushrooms to the frying pan and mix in thoroughly. Continue cooking until the onions are completely translucent and the mushrooms have softened; remove the pan from the heat.
8. Mix the lentils, onions, mushrooms, and garlic in a large bowl.
9. Add the lemon juice and the remaining olive oil. Toss or stir to combine everything thoroughly.
10. Serve the mushroom/onion mixture over some arugala in bowl, adding salt and pepper to taste, or, store and enjoy later!

Nutritions: Calories 365, Total Fat 11.7g, Saturated Fat 1.9g, Cholesterol 0mg, Sodium 1071mg, Total Carbohydrate 45.2g, Dietary Fiber 18g, Total Sugars 8.2g, Protein 22.8g, Vitamin D 378mcg, Calcium 67mg, Iron 8mg, Potassium 1212mg

Sweet Potato & Black Bean Protein Salad

Preparation:
15 Minutes

Cooking:
0 Minutes

Serves:
2

Ingredients

- 1 cup dry black beans
- 4 cups of spinach
- 1 medium sweet potato
- 1 cup purple onion, chopped
- 2 tbsp. olive oil
- 2 tbsp. lime juice
- 1 tbsp. minced garlic
- ½ tbsp. chili powder
- ¼ tsp. cayenne
- ¼ cup parsley
- ¼ tsp Salt
- ¼ tsp pepper

Directions

1. Prepare the black beans according to the method.
2. Preheat the oven to 400°F.
3. Cut the sweet potato into ¼-inch cubes and put these in a medium-sized bowl. Add the onions, 1 tablespoon of olive oil, and salt to taste.
4. Toss the ingredients until the sweet potatoes and onions are completely coated.
5. Transfer the ingredients to a baking sheet lined with parchment paper and spread them out in a single layer.
6. Put the baking sheet in the oven and roast until the sweet potatoes are starting to turn brown and crispy, around 40 minutes.
7. Meanwhile, combine the remaining olive oil, lime juice, garlic, chili powder, and cayenne thoroughly in a large bowl, until no lumps remain.
8. Remove the sweet potatoes and onions from the oven and transfer them to the large bowl.
9. Add the cooked black beans, parsley, and a pinch of salt.
10. Toss everything until well combined.
11. Then mix in the spinach, and serve in desired portions with additional salt and pepper.
12. Store or enjoy!

Nutritions: Calories 558, Total Fat 16.2g, Saturated Fat 2.5g, Cholesterol 0mg, Sodium 390mg, Total Carbohydrate 84g, Dietary Fiber 20.4g, Total Sugars 8.9g, Protein 25.3g, Vitamin D 0mcg, Calcium 220mg, Iron 10mg, Potassium 2243mg

Lentil Radish Salad

Preparation:
15 Minutes

Cooking:
0 Minutes

Serves:
3

Ingredients

- 1 tbsp. extra virgin olive oil
- 1 tbsp. lemon juice
- 1 tbsp. maple syrup
- 1 tbsp. water
- ½ tbsp. sesame oil
- 1 tbsp. miso paste, yellow or white
- ¼ tsp. salt
- ¼ tsp Pepper

Salad:
- ½ cup dry chickpeas
- ¼ cup dry green or brown lentils
- 1 14-oz. pack of silken tofu
- 5 cups mixed greens, fresh or frozen
- 2 radishes, thinly sliced
- ½ cup cherry tomatoes, halved
- ¼ cup roasted sesame seeds

Directions

1. Prepare the chickpeas according to the method.
2. Prepare the lentils according to the method.
3. Put all the ingredients for the dressing in a blender or food processor. Mix on low until smooth, while adding water until it reaches the desired consistency.
4. Add salt, pepper (to taste), and optionally more water to the dressing; set aside.
5. Cut the tofu into bite-sized cubes.
6. Combine the mixed greens, tofu, lentils, chickpeas, radishes, and tomatoes in a large bowl.
7. Add the dressing and mix everything until it is coated evenly.
8. Top with the optional roasted sesame seeds, if desired.
9. Refrigerate before serving and enjoy, or, store for later!

Nutritions: Calories 621, Total Fat 19.6g, Saturated Fat 2.8g, Cholesterol 0mg, Sodium 996mg, Total Carbohydrate 82.7g, Dietary Fiber 26.1g, Total Sugars 20.7g, Protein 31.3g, Vitamin D 0mcg, Calcium 289mg, Iron 9mg, Potassium 1370mg

Shaved Brussel Sprout Salad

Preparation:
25 Minutes

Cooking:
0 Minutes

Serves:
4

Ingredients

Dressing:
▶ 1 tbsp. brown mustard
▶ 1 tbsp. maple syrup
▶ 2 tbsp. apple cider vinegar
▶ 2 tbsp. extra virgin olive oil
▶ ½ tbsp. garlic minced

Salad:
▶ ½ cup dry red kidney beans
▶ ¼ cup dry chickpeas
▶ 2 cups Brussel sprouts
▶ 1 cup purple onion
▶ 1 small sour apple
▶ ½ cup slivered almonds, crushed
▶ ½ cup walnuts, crushed
▶ ½ cup cranberries, dried
▶ ¼ tsp Salt
▶ ¼ tsp pepper

Directions

1. Prepare the beans according to the method.
2. Combine all dressing ingredients in a bowl and stir well until combined.
3. Refrigerate the dressing for up to one hour before serving.
4. Using a grater, mandolin, or knife to thinly slice each Brussel sprout. Repeat this with the apple and onion.
5. Take a large bowl to mix the chickpeas, beans, sprouts, apples, onions, cranberries, and nuts.
6. Drizzle the cold dressing over the salad to coat.
7. Serve with salt and pepper to taste, or, store for later!

Nutritions: Calories 432, Total Fat 23.5g, Saturated Fat 2.2g, Cholesterol 0mg, Sodium 197mg, Total Carbohydrate 45.3g, Dietary Fiber 12.4g, Total Sugars 14g, Protein 15.9g, Vitamin D 0mcg, Calcium 104mg, Iron 4mg, Potassium 908mg

Colorful Protein Power Salad

Preparation:
20 Minutes

Cooking:
0 Minutes

Serves:
2

Ingredients

- ½ cup dry quinoa
- 2 cups dry navy beans
- 1 green onion, chopped
- 2 tsp. garlic, minced
- 3 cups green or purple cabbage, chopped
- 4 cups kale, fresh or frozen, chopped
- 1 cup shredded carrot, chopped
- 2 tbsp. extra virgin olive oil
- 1 tsp. lemon juice
- ¼ tsp Salt
- ¼ tsp pepper

Directions

1. Prepare the quinoa according to the recipe.
2. Prepare the beans according to the method.
3. Heat up 1 tablespoon of the olive oil in a frying pan over medium heat.
4. Add the chopped green onion, garlic, and cabbage, and sauté for 2-3 minutes.
5. Add the kale, the remaining 1 tablespoon of olive oil, and salt. Lower the heat and cover until the greens have wilted, around 5 minutes. Remove the pan from the stove and set aside.
6. Take a large bowl and mix the remaining ingredients with the kale and cabbage mixture once it has cooled down. Add more salt and pepper to taste.
7. Mix until everything is distributed evenly.
8. Serve topped with a dressing, or, store for later!

Nutritions: Calories 1100, Total Fat 19.9g, Saturated Fat 2.7g, Cholesterol 0mg, Sodium 420mg, Total Carbohydrate 180.8g, Dietary Fiber 60.1g, Total Sugars 14.4g, Protein 58.6g, Vitamin D 0mcg, Calcium 578mg, Iron 16mg, Potassium 3755mg

Edamame & Ginger Citrus Salad

 Preparation:
15 Minutes

 Cooking:
0 Minutes

 Serves:
3

Ingredients

Dressing:
► ¼ cup orange juice
► 1 tsp. lime juice
► ½ tbsp. maple syrup
► ½ tsp. ginger, finely minced
► ½ tbsp. sesame oil

Salad:
► ½ cup dry green lentils
► 2 cups carrots, shredded
► 4 cups kale, fresh or frozen, chopped
► 1 cup edamame, shelled
► 1 tablespoon roasted sesame seeds
► 2 tsp. mint, chopped
► Salt and pepper to taste
► 1 small avocado, peeled, pitted, diced

Directions

1. Prepare the lentils according to the method.
2. Combine the orange and lime juices, maple syrup, and ginger in a small bowl. Mix with a whisk while slowly adding the sesame oil.
3. Add the cooked lentils, carrots, kale, edamame, sesame seeds, and mint to a large bowl.
4. Add the dressing and stir well until all the ingredients are coated evenly.
5. Store or serve topped with avocado and an additional sprinkle of mint.

Nutritions: Calories 507, Total Fat 23.1g, Saturated Fat 4g, Cholesterol 0mg, Sodium 303mg, Total Carbohydrate 56.8g, Dietary Fiber 21.6g, Total Sugars 8.4g, Protein 24.6g, Vitamin D 0mcg, Calcium 374mg, Iron 8mg, Potassium 1911mg

Taco Tempeh Salad

Preparation:
25 Minutes

Cooking:
0 Minutes

Serves:
3

Ingredients

- 1 cup dry black beans
- 1 8-oz. package tempeh
- 1 tbsp. lime or lemon juice
- 2 tbsp. extra virgin olive oil
- 1 tsp. maple syrup
- ½ tsp. chili powder
- ¼ tsp. cumin
- ¼ tsp. paprika
- 1 large bunch of kale, fresh or frozen, chopped
- 1 large avocado, peeled, pitted, diced
- ½ cup salsa
- ¼ tsp Salt
- ¼ tsp pepper

Directions

1. Prepare the beans according to the method.
2. Cut the tempeh into ¼-inch cubes, place in a bowl, and then add the lime or lemon juice, 1 tablespoon of olive oil, maple syrup, chili powder, cumin, and paprika.
3. Stir well and let the tempeh marinate in the fridge for at least 1 hour, up to 12 hours.
4. Heat the remaining 1 tablespoon of olive oil in a frying pan over medium heat.
5. Add the marinated tempeh mixture and cook until brown and crispy on both sides, around 10 minutes.
6. Put the chopped kale in a bowl with the cooked beans and prepared tempeh.
7. Store, or serve the salad immediately, topped with salsa, avocado, and salt and pepper to taste.

Nutritions: Calories 627, Total Fat 31.7g, Saturated Fat 6.1g, Cholesterol 0mg, Sodium 493mg, Total Carbohydrate 62.7g, Dietary Fiber 16g, Total Sugars 4.5g, Protein 31.4g, Vitamin D 0mcg, Calcium 249mg, Iron 7mg, Potassium 1972mg

Pear Lemonade

 Preparation:
5 Minutes

 Cooking:
30 Minutes

 Serves:
2

Ingredients

- ½ cup of pear, peeled and diced
- 1 cup of freshly squeezed lemon juice
- ½ cup of chilled water

Directions

1. Add all the ingredients into a blender and pulse until it has all been combined. The pear does make the lemonade frothy, but this will settle.
2. Place in the refrigerator to cool and then serve.

Tips:
Keep stored in a sealed container in the refrigerator for up to four days.
Pop the fresh lemon in the microwave for ten minutes before juicing, you can extract more juice if you do this.

Colorful Infused Water

 Preparation:
5 Minutes

 Cooking:
1 h

 Serves:
8

Ingredients

- 1 cup of strawberries, fresh or frozen
- 1 cup of blueberries, fresh or frozen
- 1 tablespoon of baobab powder
- 1 cup of ice cubes
- 4 cups of sparkling water

Directions

1. In a large water jug, add in the sparkling water, ice cubes, and baobab powder. Give it a good stir.
2. Add in the strawberries and blueberries and cover the infused water, store in the refrigerator for one hour before serving.

Tips:
Store for 12 hours for optimum taste and nutritional benefits.
Instead of using strawberries and blueberries, add slices of lemon and six mint leaves, one cup of mangoes or cherries, or half a cup of leafy greens such as kale and/or spinach.

Hibiscus Tea

Preparation:
1 Minutes

Cooking:
5 Minutes

Serves:
2

Ingredients

▸ 1 tablespoon of raisins, diced
▸ 6 Almonds, raw and unsalted
▸ ½ teaspoon of hibiscus powder
▸ 2 cups of water

Directions

1. Bring the water to a boil in a small saucepan, add in the hibiscus powder and raisins. Give it a good stir, cover and let simmer for a further two minutes.
2. Strain into a teapot and serve with a side helping of almonds.

Tips:
As an alternative to this tea, do not strain it and serve with the raisin pieces still swirling around in the teacup.
You could also serve this tea chilled for those hotter days.
Double or triple the recipe to provide you with iced-tea to enjoy during the week without having to make a fresh pot each time.

Lemon and Rosemary Iced Tea

Preparation:
5 Minutes

Cooking:
10 Minutes

Serves:
4

Ingredients

- 4 cups of water
- 4 earl grey tea bags
- ¼ cup of sugar
- 2 lemons
- 1 sprig of rosemary

Directions

1. Peel the two lemons and set the fruit aside.
2. In a medium saucepan, over medium heat combine the water, sugar, and lemon peels. Bring this to a boil.
3. Remove from the heat and place the rosemary and tea into the mixture. Cover the saucepan and steep for five minutes.
4. Add the juice of the two peeled lemons to the mixture, strain, chill, and serve.

Tips:
Skip the sugar and use honey to taste. Do not squeeze the tea bags as they can cause the tea to become bitter.

Lavender and Mint Iced Tea

Preparation:
5 Minutes

Cooking:
10 Minutes

Serves:
8

Ingredients

- 8 cups of water
- ⅓ cup of dried lavender buds
- ¼ cup of mint

Directions

1. Add the mint and lavender to a pot and set this aside.
2. Add in eight cups of boiling water to the pot. Sweeten to taste, cover and let steep for ten minutes. Strain, chill, and serve.

Tips:
Use a sweetener of your choice when making this iced tea.
Add spirits to turn this iced tea into a summer cocktail.

Thai Iced Tea

 Preparation:
5 Minutes

 Cooking:
10 Minutes

 Serves:
4

Ingredients

- 4 cups of water
- 1 can of light coconut milk (14 oz.)
- ¼ cup of maple syrup
- ¼ cup of muscovado sugar
- 1 teaspoon of vanilla extract
- 2 tablespoons of loose-leaf black tea

Directions

1. In a large saucepan, over medium heat bring the water to a boil.
2. Turn off the heat and add in the tea, cover and let steep for five minutes.
3. Strain the tea into a bowl or jug. Add the maple syrup, muscovado sugar, and vanilla extract. Give it a good whisk to blend all the ingredients together.
4. Set in the refrigerator to chill. Upon serving, pour ¾ of the tea into each glass, top with coconut milk and stir.

Tips:
Add a shot of dark rum to turn this iced tea into a cocktail.
You could substitute the coconut milk for almond or rice milk too.

Hot Chocolate

Preparation:
5 Minutes

Cooking:
15 Minutes

Serves:
2

Ingredients

- Pinch of brown sugar
- 2 cups of milk, soy or almond, unsweetened
- 2 tablespoons of cocoa powder
- ½ cup of vegan chocolate

Directions

1. In a medium saucepan, over medium heat gently bring the milk to a boil. Whisk in the cocoa powder.
2. Remove from the heat, add a pinch of sugar and chocolate. Give it a good stir until smooth, serve and enjoy.

Tips:
You may substitute the almond or soy milk for coconut milk too.

Chai and Chocolate Milkshake

 Preparation:
5 Minutes

 Cooking:
15 Minutes

 Serves:
2

Ingredients

- 1 and ½ cups of almond milk, sweetened or unsweetened
- 3 bananas, peeled and frozen 12 hours before use
- 4 dates, pitted
- 1 and ½ teaspoons of chocolate powder, sweetened or unsweetened
- ½ teaspoon of vanilla extract
- ½ teaspoon of cinnamon
- ¼ teaspoon of ground ginger
- Pinch of ground cardamom
- Pinch of ground cloves
- Pinch of ground nutmeg
- ½ cup of ice cubes

Directions

1. Add all the ingredients to a blender except for the ice-cubes. Pulse until smooth and creamy, add the ice-cubes, pulse a few more times and serve.

Tips:
The dates provide enough sweetness to the recipe, however, you are welcome to add maple syrup or honey for a sweeter drink.

Mango Lassi

 Preparation:
5 Minutes

 Cooking:
5 Minutes

 Serves:
2-4

Directions

1. Add all the ingredients into a blender, pulse until smooth, pour into glasses, top with mint and serve.

Tips:
As an alternative, you may use honey instead of maple syrup.

Ingredients

- Pinch of salt
- ½ teaspoon of turmeric, finely ground
- 1 cup of coconut milk
- 1 tablespoon of lemon juice
- 3 tablespoons of maple syrup
- 2 cups of mango, frozen
- ½ cup of ice

Health Boosting Juices

Preparation:
10 Minutes

Cooking:
15 Minutes

Serves:
2

Directions

1. Juice all ingredients in a juicer, chill and serve.

Ingredients

For a red juice:
- 4 beetroots, quartered
- 2 cups of strawberries
- 2 cups of blueberries
- Ingredients for an orange juice:
- 4 green or red apples, halved
- 10 carrots
- ½ lemon, peeled
- 1" of ginger

For a yellow juice:
- 2 green or red apples, quartered
- 4 oranges, peeled and halved
- ½ lemon, peeled
- 1" of ginger

For a lime juice:
- 6 stalks of celery
- 1 cucumber
- 2 green apples, quartered
- 2 pears, quartered
- Ingredients for a green juice:
- ½ a pineapple, peeled and sliced
- 8 leaves of kale
- 2 fresh bananas, peeled

Coffee Smoothie

Preparation:
5 Minutes

Cooking:
5 Minutes

Serves:
2

Ingredients

- 1 ½ cups of lite coconut milk
- 2 tablespoons of maple syrup
- 2 tablespoons of peanut butter or almond butter
- 2 teaspoons of instant coffee
- 3 frozen bananas, peeled and halved, freeze for 12 hours prior to use

Directions

1. Add all the ingredients into a blender, pulse until combined and smooth, serve in two tall glasses.

Tips:
You may use instant espresso powder for a stronger hint of coffee.

Mint Choc Chip Smoothie

 Preparation:
5 Minutes

 Cooking:
5 Minutes

 Serves:
2

Ingredients

- 1 and ½ cups of almond, soy or coconut milk, unsweetened
- 2 bananas, peeled and frozen 12 hours before use
- ½ teaspoon of vanilla essence
- ¼ cup of mint leaves
- 1 cup of spinach
- 1 tablespoon of vegan choc chips

Directions

1. Add all the ingredients into a blender, pulse until smooth and serve.

Tips:
If you want a more subtle mint smoothie opt for ⅛ cups of mint instead so it won't be as fragrant.

Peanut Butter Smoothie

Preparation:
5 Minutes

Cooking:
5 Minutes

Serves:
2

Directions

1. Add all the ingredients into a blender, pulse until smooth and serve.

Tips:
You may substitute the peanut butter for any other nut butter.

Ingredients

- 1 and ½ cups of almond, soy or coconut milk, unsweetened
- 2 bananas, peeled and frozen 12 hours before use
- ½ teaspoon of vanilla essence
- 1 tablespoon of cocoa powder
- 2 tablespoons of peanut butter

Cinnamon Smoothie

Preparation:
5 Minutes

Cooking:
5 Minutes

Serves:
2

Ingredients

- 1 and ½ cups of almond, soy or coconut milk, unsweetened
- 2 bananas, peeled and frozen 12 hours before use
- ½ teaspoon of vanilla essence
- ½ teaspoon of cinnamon
- ½ cup of oats, rolled
- 3 dated, pitted and halved

Directions

1. Add all the ingredients into a blender, pulse until smooth and serve.

Tips:
Feel free to add more cinnamon or oats for a more filling smoothie.

Green Smoothie

Preparation:
5 Minutes

Cooking:
5 Minutes

Serves:
2

Directions

1. Add all the ingredients into a blender, pulse until smooth and serve.

Tips:
You may substitute the almond milk for another milk of your choice.

Ingredients

- 2 cups of almond milk
- 1 banana, peeled and frozen 12 hours before use
- 1 cup of spinach
- ½ an avocado
- 2 tablespoons hemp hearts
- 2 tablespoons of chia seeds

Green Piña Colada Smoothie

Preparation:
5 Minutes

Cooking:
5 Minutes

Serves:
2

Ingredients

- 2 cups of light coconut milk
- 1 banana, peeled and frozen 12 hours before use
- 1 cup of pineapple, frozen
- 1 teaspoon of vanilla extract

Directions

1. Add all the ingredients into a blender, pulse until smooth and serve.

Tips:
For a creamier option, opt to use 1 cup of light coconut milk with 1 cup of full-fat coconut milk.

Ginger and Berry Smoothie

Preparation:
5 Minutes

Cooking:
5 Minutes

Serves:
2

Ingredients

- ▶ 2 cups of almond milk
- ▶ 1 knob of ginger
- ▶ 1 cup of strawberries, frozen
- ▶ 1 cup of raspberries, frozen
- ▶ 1 cup of cauliflower, steam before use in recipe

Directions

1. Add all the ingredients into a blender, pulse until smooth and serve.

Tips:
The reason the cauliflower is steamed before use is because it is easier on digestion.
Frozen fruits thicken a smoothie more than fresh fruits.

Lime and Raspberry Smoothie

 Preparation:
5 Minutes

 Cooking:
5 Minutes

 Serves:
2

Directions

1. Add all the ingredients into a blender, pulse until smooth and serve.

Tips:
Add blocks of ice to the blender for added texture.

Ingredients

- 1 cup of water
- 1 banana, peeled and frozen 12 hours before use
- 1 cup of raspberries, frozen
- 1 teaspoon of coconut oil
- 2 teaspoons of lime juice
- 1 teaspoon of sweetener of your choice

Avocado, Blueberry, and Chia Smoothie

Preparation:
5 Minutes

Cooking:
5 Minutes

Serves:
2

Ingredients

- 2 cups of almond milk
- 2 cups of blueberries, frozen
- 1 avocado, peeled and pitted
- 2 dates, pitted
- 2 tablespoons of flax or chia
- ½ teaspoon of vanilla extract

Directions

1. Add the blueberries, avocado, dates, chia or flax, and vanilla extract to a blender. Pulse until smooth.
2. Add in the almond milk and pulse until combined with the rest of the mixture, serve.

Tips:
Substitute the almond milk for coconut milk if you'd prefer.

Coconut, Raspberry, and Quinoa Smoothie

Preparation:
5 Minutes

Cooking:
5 Minutes

Serves:
2

Directions

1. Add all the ingredients into a blender, pulse until smooth and serve.

Tips:
Substitute the coconut milk for almond milk for a different taste.

Ingredients

- 2 cups of coconut milk
- 2 cups of raspberries, frozen
- 4 tablespoons of goji berries
- 2 dates, pitted
- 1 cup of quinoa, cooked
- 4 tablespoons of coconut, shredded

Chapter 9.
Plant Based Italian Style Special Recipes

Easy Mushroom Pasta

Preparation:
5 Minutes

Cooking:
10 Minutes

Serves:
4

Ingredients

- Chickpea Pasta (8 Oz.)
- Garlic Clove (2, Minced)
- Onion (1/4, Diced)
- Frozen Peas (1 C.)
- Vegan Butter (2 T.)
- Salt (to Taste)
- Bella Mushrooms (1 C., Sliced)
- Pepper (to taste)
- Italian Seasoning (1 t.)
- Optional: Fresh Parsley

Directions

1. The first step to making this quick and easy mushroom pasta will be cooking your pasta according to the directions in which are provided on the package.
2. As the pasta cooks, you can also get out a skillet and set it above a moderate heat. Once it is warm, insert the butter and cook the peas, garlic, onion, and mushrooms for roughly five minutes.
3. Once they are cooked through, you will want to plate your pasta and pour the mushroom mixture over the top.
4. For a final touch, add some fresh parsley, and your meal will be ready.

Nutritions: Calories: 260, Carbs: 50g, Fats: 3g, Proteins: 10g

Creamed Avocado Pasta

Preparation:
5 Minutes

Cooking:
15 Minutes

Serves:
4

Ingredients

- Whole-grain Pasta (3 C.)
- Olive Oil (1 T.)
- Spinach (1 C.)
- Garlic Cloves (2, Minced)
- Avocado (1)
- Pepper (1/4 t.)
- Lemon Juice (1 T.)
- Salt (to taste)
- Optional: Chili Flakes

Directions

1. First, cook your pasta according to the directions on the package.
2. As the pasta cooks, it is time to make the avocado sauce! You can do this by taking out your blender and adding in the avocado, spinach, garlic, olive oil, lemon juice, and seasonings. Go ahead and blend this all together until it is smooth. If needed, you can add some water to make the sauce thinner.
3. Next, you are going to want to plate your pasta and then serve the sauce over the top. For extra flavor, sprinkle some chili flakes before serving.

Nutritions: Calories: 300, Carbs: 50g, Fats: 9g, Proteins: 10g

Simple Hummus Pasta

Preparation:
5 Minutes

Cooking:
10 Minutes

Serves:
2

Ingredients

- Whole Grain Pasta (2 C.)
- Salt (to taste)
- Cherry Tomatoes (1/2 C.)
- Hummus (1/2 C.)
- Pepper (to Taste)

Directions

1. As usual, begin this recipe by cooking the pasta to your liking.
2. As the pasta cooks, prepare your tomatoes by chopping them in half.
3. Once the pasta is cooked through, add it to a pan on top of low temperature and add in the tomatoes and the hummus. With everything in place, stir together for two or three minutes, and then your meal is set to be served!

Nutritions: Calories: 350, Carbs: 50g, Fats: 3g, Proteins: 15g

Conclusion

To survive, we need to eat. As a result, food has turned into a symbol of loving, nurturing and sharing with one another. Recording, collecting, sharing and remembering the recipes that have been passed to you by your family is a great way to immortalize and honor your family. It is these traditions that carve out your individual personality. You will not just be honoring your family tradition by cooking these recipes, but they will also inspire you to create your own variations, which

By following the plant based diet, you are going to feel better. You are going to improve your mood and energy levels. If you have been battling mental health problems, then using the plant-based diet is going to help you work on those problems.

The recipes are just passed on to everyone, and nobody actually possesses them. I too love sharing recipes. The collection is vibrant and rich as a number of home cooks have offered their inputs to ensure that all of us can cook delicious meals at our home. I am thankful to each one of you who has contributed to this book and has allowed their traditions to pass on and grow with others. You guys are wonderful!

Printed in Great Britain
by Amazon